BRITISH IDEALISM
AND POLITICAL THEORY

BRITISH IDEALISM
AND POLITICAL THEORY

DAVID BOUCHER and ANDREW VINCENT

EDINBURGH UNIVERSITY PRESS

© David Boucher and Andrew Vincent, 2000
Transferred to Digital Print on Demand 2011

Edinburgh University Press Ltd
22 George Square, Edinburgh

Typeset in Bembo
by Norman Tilley Graphics, and
printed and bound by
CPI Group (UK) Ltd, Croydon, CR0 4YY

A CIP record for this book is available
from the British Library

ISBN 978 0 7486 1428 8 (paperback)

The right of David Boucher and Andrew Vincent
to be identified as authors of this work
has been asserted in accordance with the
Copyright, Designs and Patents Act 1988.

Contents

Acknowledgements   vi
Preface   vii

Introduction   1
1. T. H. Green: Citizenship as Political and Metaphysical   27
2. F. H. Bradley: Ethical Idealism and Hedonism   55
3. Bernard Bosanquet: The Sociology of Philosophy and the Philosophy of Sociology   87
4. David Ritchie: Evolution and the Limits of Rights   127
5. Henry Jones: Beyond Socialism and Liberalism   157
6. R. G. Collingwood: The Enemy Within and the Crisis of Civilisation   185
7. Michael Oakeshott: The Non-Economic Character of Civil Association   210

Biographical Materials   236
Index   243

Acknowledgements

Sources for cover images:

Henry Jones. Photograph by A. MacNab. From 'Old Memories' by Jones (London: Hodder and Stoughton, 1922)

Bernard Bosanquet. From 'Bernard Bosanquet and his Friends' edited by J. H. Muirhead (London: George Allen and Unwin, 1935)

T. H. Green. From 'The Works of Thomas Hill Green' Volume III (London: Longmans, Green & Co, 1888)

R. G. Collingwood. From 'Essays in Political Philosophy' edited by D. Boucher (Oxford: Clarendon Press, 1989)

F. H. Bradley. Portrait by R. G. Eves. Owned by the Warden and Fellows of Merton College, Oxford. By courtesy of the National Portrait Gallery, London

Michael Oakeshott. From 'On History' by M. Oakeshott (Oxford: Blackwell, 1983)

D. G. Ritchie. Photograph by E. Pannell. From 'Philosophical Studies' by D. G. Ritchie (London: Macmillan, 1905)

Preface

The scope of this book is deceptively broad in that it deals with seven British Idealist thinkers, all with their particular slant on Idealism, and all occupying their own distinctive places in the political and philosophical contexts of their day. In addition, each has affinities with and has something to contribute to later thought, including contemporary political polemics and political theory. In writing this book we are conscious of being enormously indebted to the painstaking work of our predecessors and contemporaries. Our personal associations with W. H. Greenleaf, Peter N. Nicholson, Raymond Plant and Rex Martin make it wholly appropriate that we should take this opportunity to thank them on behalf of ourselves and of others who have similarly been inspired by their example and academic integrity.

The breakdown of the writing of the present work has largely been based on our respective expertise and interests, accumulated over more years than we care to remember. Thus, Andrew Vincent wrote the essays on Green, Bosanquet and Bradley and David Boucher on Ritchie, Collingwood and Oakeshott. The Jones essay was a collaborative effort arising out of our first jointly authored book. However, this present book, *as a whole*, reflects the ideas and preoccupations of both authors and is the result of extensive intellectual collaboration over many years, beginning when we were colleagues in the Department of Politics at Cardiff in the early 1980s. At the turn of the millennium we are once again colleagues, this time in the Collingwood and British Idealism Centre in the School of European Studies at Cardiff University. This book is the first of what we hope will be many scholarly works to emanate from the Centre.

We were extremely fortunate in having two excellent reviewers of the original typescript. Both were fair and constructive in their criticisms, and we have benefited enormously from their expertise. We have endeavoured to improve the finished product along the lines they suggested, but are only too well aware that imperfections remain for which we are wholly responsible.

Finally, we would like to thank our long-suffering wives and families for their support and patience over these many years. Their contribution to this work is indefinable, but perhaps the most important of all.

David Boucher and Andrew Vincent
Collingwood and British Idealism Centre, Cardiff University

Introduction

This book is informed by three background assumptions: primarily, British Idealist arguments are well worth considering in their own right; further, the Idealists' writings, through their critical commentaries, throw considerable light on the work of many of their philosophical and political contemporaries; and, finally, their work is of relevance to contemporary philosophical and political discussion. The present book aims to justify these background assumptions through intensive studies of individual Idealist thinkers.

In the above context, therefore, T. H. Green is discussed with reference to deeper and longer-term philosophical debates between Kantianism and Hegelianism over metaphysics, in specific relation to late twentieth-century Rawlsian arguments about pluralism and citizenship. Bosanquet's practical involvement in, and ideas about, the development of early twentieth-century sociology are considered, with specific reference to his critical relation with Émile Durkheim's sociology. F. H. Bradley's work on ethics is examined in the context of his highly polemical confrontation with Henry Sidgwick's version of utilitarianism. Henry Jones's philosophy is focused on in the context of his cherished aim to overcome the tension – and forge some form of higher synthesis – between the ideologies of socialism and liberalism. David Ritchie's thought is looked at in the context of his vigorous philosophical confrontation with both evolutionary theory and natural rights argumentation. Collingwood's political philosophy is investigated in the context of his anxiety that civilisation (that is, civilisation as a thing of the mind and the self-understanding of the mind) is under continual threat. Collingwood's ideas are examined in relation to a number of contemporary political thinkers – Arendt, MacIntyre, Taylor and Rorty – who are also concerned with issues of both political fragmentation and the politics of recognition. Finally, Oakeshott's conception of civil association is examined in the context of contemporary theories of law and social justice. This selection of Idealist philosophers does *not* claim to be a definitive study of all the key British Idealists. Further, each study is a focused analysis of a particular issue or theme within that thinker's overall theoretical output. However, all the thinkers dealt with here are, none the less, profoundly significant contributors to British Idealist philosophy and may be taken as representative of its rich patterns of thought.

Most of the themes under discussion are common to all the Idealists. However, each is explored in the context of a particular thinker. Thus, for example, the most extensive discussion of evolution occurs in the chapter on Ritchie, but we should not forget that both Bernard Bosanquet and Henry Jones were tenacious contributors to evolutionary debates. Further, all of the British Idealists have distinctive views on the state, but, in this volume, the focus is on Michael Oakeshott's attempt to characterise the state as a civil association. Similarly, utilitarianism provides the focus for the chapter on Bradley, although it also surfaces, of necessity, in relation to Ritchie. Thus, our general approach is to focus selectively upon an aspect of the thought of a particular Idealist.

Having indicated the general theme of the book, we use the rest of this introduction to map out the common philosophical assumptions and differences within British Idealism.

British Idealism began to establish its roots in Scotland and Oxford during the middle of the nineteenth century and rapidly became the dominant philosophy, through the writings and personal influence of such exponents as Fraser Campbell, Edward Caird, T. H. Green, F. H. Bradley, Bernard Bosanquet, Henry Jones, Andrew Seth Pringle-Pattison, D. G. Ritchie, J. S. Mackenzie, William Wallace, W. R. Sorley, J. M. E. McTaggart and John Watson, until the turn of the century when its fundamental doctrines were challenged by philosophers such as John Cook Wilson, G. E. Moore and Bertrand Russell. From this time, the march of Idealism was hindered, and by the end of the First World War it was in partial retreat. However, the British Idealists managed through their teaching and personal influence to permeate the whole English-speaking world with their doctrines. Even after the death of its leading exponents in the mid 1920s – Bradley, Bosanquet, Jones and McTaggart – Idealism continued to dominate the professoriate and was able to count in its ranks able young converts such as R. G. Collingwood in Oxford, who published *Speculum Mentis* in 1924, and Michael Oakeshott in Cambridge, who published *Experience and Its Modes* in 1933.

In many ways, Oakeshott was the last well-known exponent of the Idealist tradition. Both Collingwood and Oakeshott are included to show the breadth and longer term impact of the movement. However, neither of the latter thinkers were part of the heyday of British Idealism. Both worked in a world which was largely antagonistic to Idealism and where the historical and cultural circumstances had changed. This marks out the character of their work. In this sense, many of the religious, moral, biological, ideological and economic themes which underpin thinkers like Green, Bosanquet, Bradley, Jones and Ritchie do not apply to the milieu of Collingwood and Oakeshott. Yet, it is worth noting that both the latter thinkers began their careers with forceful contributions to the philosophy of religion, a subject which was absolutely central to the concerns of their Idealist predecessors. Equally, both clearly rearticulated (in their own terms) the Idealist view of experience, in Collingwood's case viewing the 'totality' as a linked hierarchy of forms, and, in Oakeshott's, as co-ordinate modes, or arrests, with philosophy constituting the concrete totality of experience as a whole. Thus, despite their subtle differences from previous Idealism, it is important to bring both Collingwood and Oakeshott into this volume, because their impact has been considerable in keeping the spirit of Idealism alive, not only in social and political philosophy, but also in aesthetics, metaphysics, and the philosophy of history and the social sciences.

Despite internal differences of opinion, Idealism was a philosophy that was deeply responsive to many of the concerns of Victorian and Edwardian Britain. It directly addressed many of the religious anxieties of the time. It provided a coherent and attractive alternative to conventional utilitarian and naturalistic thought. It supplied a lucid discussion and, in many cases, justification for a changing conception of the state. In so doing, it engaged in a constructive dialogue with the more radical ideologies of the period. It was, in addition, closely linked with contemporaneous developments in the social and natural sciences. In this context, it has been little noticed the extent to which British Idealism, at its peak, rode the wave of enthusiasm for evolution. Essentially, it critically adapted evolution to its own ends by eschewing its naturalistic form and emphasising the developing spiritual unity of existence. Overall, at a time when religion was under attack from scientific orthodoxy, Idealism was able to provide a rational basis for belief, which together with its emphasis upon the unity and development of human potential, provided, at the same time, a philosophical basis for social and political reform. Idealists maintained that everything in experience is related to everything else. There could be no isolated individuals or facts. In the theory of knowledge this led to the coherence theory of truth, and in social philosophy it resulted in a liberal communitarianism which posited the mutual inclusion of society and the individual. Collingwood and Oakeshott, although more wary and sceptical, still became deeply engaged in the political, religious and moral controversies of their own times. Collingwood never tired of warning of the different threats to civilisation, including Nazism and Fascism. Oakeshott, affecting the philosophical guise of disinterestedness, none the less con-tinuously warned against the dangers of rationalist politics, manifestations of which he saw most pronounced in the drift towards socialism in Britain.

– THE IDEALIST WORLD-VIEW –

The world-view of British Idealism, at its inception, was something of an aberration in a philosophical culture characterised by the hard-nosed empiricism of Hobbes, Hume and the utilitarianism. The root of the Idealist view is well expressed by Andrew Seth Pringle-Pattison, who complained that thinking always involves a relation between the thinker and an objective world, but that it is a fallacy to begin by assuming that only one side of the dualism exists (the objective world or thought) independently of the other.[1] It was largely from Hegel that the British Idealists imported this idea of the complex unity of experience. From this starting point, the question of how the unity is differentiated into all its various modes becomes the central philosophical issue. This remained a central theme within Idealism up to Collingwood and Oakeshott. Ideas essentially unite the mind and its objects in mutual inclusion rather than antagonistically. This is not to deny the dis-tinction between thought and reality. As Henry Jones suggests, no Idealist denies this distinction. None asserts that knowledge of a fact *is* that fact. Objects do not disappear when we turn our backs.[2] Hastings Rashdall sums up the position when he says that Idealism assumes 'that there is no such thing as matter apart from mind, that what we commonly call *things* are not self-subsistent realities, but are only real when taken in their connection with mind – that they exist for mind, not for themselves'.[3]

Taking the isolated subject as the starting point in philosophy inevitably leads to a dilemma, since, in order to pronounce on the different forms of experience and their relation to reality genuine, a criterion of genuine knowledge has to be presupposed in advance of undertaking the investigation designed to establish it.[4] When thinking is taken to be the process by which Spirit or God realises itself, the subjective and objective are not separated by ideas, but instead are the differentiations of the one comprehensive unity.[5] Hegel's importance for the British Idealists here, then, is that he basically *dispenses* with the problem of epistemology and provides a metaphysic, which is also a logic of the process and development of mind.[6] Edward Caird sums up Hegel's position thus: the highest aim of philosophy

> is to reinterpret experience, in the light of a unity which is presupposed in it, but which cannot be made conscious or explicit until the relation of experience to the thinking self is seen, – the unity of all things with each other and with the mind

that knows them.[7]

For Green, Hegel's importance here was that he showed that the world is essentially an interrelated spiritual whole in which all that is real is the expression and activity of 'one spiritual self-conscious being'. We are related to this self-conscious being, not as parts to a whole,

> but as partakers in some inchoate measure of the self-consciousness through which it at once constitutes and distinguishes itself from the world; [and] that this participation is the source of morality and religion; this we take to be the vital truth which Hegel had to teach.[8]

It should be noted, however, that none of the major British Idealists accepted the stylised dialectic method which Hegel used to address the process of differentiation. Green, for one, complained that the method actually hindered Hegel in reaching his conclusions, and consequently accused Principal John Caird of too slavishly following Hegel's method.[9] Rather than the 'invariable self-repeating formula', it was the principle, rather than the method of dialectic, that attracted the Idealists, a principle that was to be even discerned in Plato.[10]

In summary, Idealists were dissatisfied with dualisms and sought to demonstrate that there could be no absolute ontological divisions, for example, between mind and nature, nature and environment, or individualism and collectivism. Each element includes something of the other. Their apparent opposition is overcome in a unity, not one which obliterates differences, but a genuine 'unity in diversity'.[11] This point is illustrated (on a political note) in Caird's and Jones's insistence that true Socialists and true Individualists have to acknowledge what is good in the views of their adversary. Both Jones and Oakeshott, for example, typically address theoretical problems by setting up opposing views, both sides of which are then convicted of being one-sided, that is, failing to take account of the other perspective. The dualism is invariably overcome in a synthesis that unites the element of truth expressed in both.[12]

There were though internal divisions among the Absolute Idealists. Jones, for example, accused both Bosanquet and Bradley of failing to overcome the dualism between appearance and reality, in positing an absolute that was ultimately *beyond* experience. For Bradley, our experience of the Absolute is most complete at the sentient level when it presents itself as an undifferentiated whole. Thought differentiates, or mutilates, the unity of experience. He therefore argues that, speaking properly, there is nothing which is perfect except the Absolute itself. Bradley did not, however, completely sever appearance from reality. He maintained their relation by means of two fundamental principles. First, the principle of non-contradiction. All reality must be consistent. If it is contradictory, it must be appearance. Appearance, nevertheless, in some way belongs to, or qualifies, reality. Secondly, consistency and non-contradiction is a matter of degree; therefore, there are degrees of reality, and not a yawning chasm between appearance and reality.[13] Collingwood takes Bradley's crucial argument here as a denial of the whole subjectivist or phenomenalist tradition associated with Locke, Hamilton, Mansel and Spencer.[14]

Absolute Idealists, such as Caird and Jones, while agreeing with the monistic unity of the whole, give much more emphasis than Bradley or Bosanquet to the reality of the appearances. For Caird and Jones, the unity embodies the principle of rationality which is expressed in and through all the differentiations of the whole. Jones argues that whilst Idealism repudiates the psychological introspective method of beginning a philosophical inquiry from the inner life of the subject, it does not attempt to do without that inner life altogether. Activity, emotions and purposes are all incorporated, but what is denied is any fundamental distinction between subject and object. These are distinctions made within an ontological unity. This ontological unity, Jones argues, is not incompatible with 'their equally real difference'.[15]

The above case is not so simple with regards to the contemporaneous Personal Idealist movement, which objected to the propensity of all Absolute Idealism to undervalue the individual, and to run the risk of allowing the individual to become absorbed into the Absolute. Personal Idealists none the less acknowledged that some monist exponents were closer to Personal Idealism than others.[16] Henry Sturt, for example, did not think that either Henry Jones or Josiah Royce were as philosophically suspect. Equally, Sturt believed that the movement to which he belonged was a development of, rather than a departure from, the Idealism of Green, Bosanquet and Bradley. Following Rudolph Eucken, another Personal Idealist, Boyce Gibson, contended that the central idea of Absolute Idealism – that the real is rational – was also upheld by Personal Idealism, but 'from the point of view of the personal experient'.[17] It is worth noting here that Absolute and Personal Idealism had a common philosophical enemy in naturalism. But, Absolute Idealism was still regarded as largely deficient in two important respects. First, it criticised human experience, not from the vantage point of human experience itself, 'but from the visionary and impractical standpoint of human nature'.[18] Secondly, it refused to give adequate recognition to volition in human nature. In Andrew Seth Pringle-Pattison's view, Absolute Idealism was always in imminent danger of consigning the individual to insignificance.[19] Yet, despite criticism, Absolute Idealism remained the most dominant element within the Idealist movement as a whole. All of the authors discussed in this book were committed to versions of Absolute Idealism, even the representatives of the new generation, Collingwood and Oakeshott.

– THE EVOLUTIONARY DYNAMIC –

When reading the Idealists one is often struck by the extent to which they alluded to and directly addressed issues in evolutionary theory. This is not surprising given the prevalence of this form of thinking during the latter part of the nineteenth century. Evolution was the first scientific theory to be more accessible to, and, to capture the imagination of, the educated public. The unity of Nature and Spirit in the theory of evolution held out the possibility of a common form of explanation in the natural and social sciences. The allure of such an all-encompassing way of understanding the whole of existence was almost irresistible. It found expression not only in biology, geology, palaeontology and anthropology but also in history, philosophy, poetry and even religion.[20] In poetry, for example, the works of Tennyson, Browning, Matthew Arnold, Edward Fitzgerald and Algernon Charles Swinburne dwell extensively upon the imagery and ideas of evolution.[21]

The extent to which Darwin influenced social evolutionists has been greatly exaggerated.[22] Long before Darwin, as he acknowledged, evolutionary ideas were being entertained and taken seriously by many eminent scholars.[23] Jean-Baptiste Lamarck argued in 1809 that species developed and transmuted. Idealist argument took on a veneer of evolutionary imagery to strengthen its conclusions. It was an immensely adaptable form of argument which could be invoked to support almost any conclusion, and which has endured to this day in the sociobiology popularised by Richard Dawkins and the social theory of W. G. Runciman. During the time that the first generation of British Idealists wrote, political debate was dominated by the vocabulary of evolution. It was used to support both socialist and extreme individualist positions. Herbert Spencer, Leslie Stephen and Benjamin Kidd were household names among the educated classes, and biologists such as Lamarck, Darwin, Wallace and Huxley were often drawn upon to support conclusions relating to issues of poverty, democracy, imperialism, social responsibility and education. Ideas relating to Lamarck's theory of inherited characters, espoused in conjunction with or opposed to Darwin's natural selection, permeated all serious discussion of social issues.

Further, Spencer's populist biology, philosophically conceived – which was quite clearly inadequately grounded in empirical research, and only analogously applied to society – was, none the less, received with immense enthusiasm by the reading public. Like Darwin, Spencer derived a good deal of impetus for his evolutionary theories from Malthus's theory of population.

As early as 1852 Spencer applied a novel interpretation of Malthus's theory to social development. Whereas Malthus had argued that population pressures placed limits on the development of society and tend towards equilibrium, Spencer adapted the theory to show that population pressures lead to a competition which eliminates the unfit and generates human progress.[24] Spencer, and Darwin for that matter, were thus frequently cited not as the originators of evolutionary theory, but as those most responsible for impressing it upon the popular consciousness.[25]

One of the crucial points of contention among evolutionists was the question of heredity. Did natural selection eliminate those least well-fitted to the environment, leaving those who survive to pass on their qualities through inheritance, or, could the environment modify organisms, by use or disuse, the modifications of which were then inheritable? Both forms of explanation are invoked, for example, in the political theories of Walter Bagehot and Herbert Spencer. Even though Spencer coined the term the 'survival of the fittest', and Darwin began to favour it in preference to his own 'struggle for existence', Spencer was far less convinced by the explanatory force of natural selection than by Lamarck's theory of 'use inheritance', or inherited character.

The British Idealists overall tended to reject the Lamarckian principle of inherited characters, or at least gave little significance to it, while at the same time stressing a strong environmental influence upon human personality. Natural selection, Ritchie argued, is an 'indisputable fact', and insofar as use inheritance, or inherited character, is still in doubt we should not revert to dubious or unknown causes when there are known causes that are sufficient. Natural selection was thus deemed to be at work in nature and society. Human beings inherit capacities which are capable of being developed or retarded by the social environment or civilisation which is inherited, but not biologically, by successive generations. Language, Ritchie argues, makes possible the transmission of experience which is not biologically inheritable. The possession of consciousness, the ability to reflect and the use of language give human beings a tremendous advantage in the struggle for existence. The origins of these human powers or capacities is best explained, however, by the hypothesis of natural selection.[26]

As we will see in the chapter on Ritchie, the British Idealists rejected naturalistic versions of evolution, but also rejected the disjunction between natural and ethical evolution posited by T. H. Huxley. On the Hegelian principle of unity (explored in the previous section) they could not accept the dualism of Nature and Spirit. In Hegel's perspective, we understand a part only by looking at it as part of a whole. The early stages of something are only properly understood when they are seen as the early stages of something more fully developed. This is the case in all specialist fields of knowledge.[27] In Ritchie's view, Spencer's evolutionary theory failed to acknowledge Aristotle's dictum that the true nature of a thing is to be found not in its origin, but in its end.[28] Edward Caird makes a similar point when he urges that: 'in the first instance at least, we must read development *backward* and not *forward*, we must find the key to the meaning of the first stage in the last.'[29] Elsewhere he argues that Spirit cannot be explained in terms of matter, and that matter itself is intelligible only in the context of the Spiritual World.[30] Similarly, Henry Jones argues that evolution is nothing other than another name for the development of Spirit. Evolution is the hypothesis which provides 'the methodizing conception which we employ to render intelligible to ourselves the process which spirit follows in becoming free'.[31]

By the time that Collingwood and Oakeshott wrote their seminal restatements of Idealism, the popularity of both Idealism itself and evolutionary theory had waned. We still, however, find in these latter-day exponents of Idealism the Hegelian principle of *emanation* at work – understanding what comes first in terms of what comes later – but the evolutionary vocabulary is largely jettisoned. In fact, both thinkers assert the autonomy and integrity of history as a form of knowledge, and resist any attempt to corrupt it with the import of natural scientific methods.[32]

– RELIGION AND PHILOSOPHY –

Religion was viewed by the Idealists, in general, as an inextricable part of the process of self-realisation. Again this was a view which was derived largely from Hegel. For many, God is immanent in the world – a view which can have many different theological ramifications. The divine and the human constitute the inseparable spiritual unity of the world. For Green and Ritchie, for example, Christ is incarnate in the world, reflecting the unity of God and man. For Ritchie, God is not merely the Creator, but reveals Himself in man.[33] Green further contended that the test of the morally worthwhile existence is the extent to which the individual attempts to do God's work in the world by achieving his or her own potential and contributing to the common good. Social reform and moral development were closely linked with religious self-realisation in what was essentially a civic conception of religion. This is explored in the chapter on Green. This is not to say that all the Idealists took the same view of religion. On the question of the relation of God to the Absolute, for example, there were serious disagreements. Thus, for Bradley, the meaning of God is tied to the religious consciousness. The Absolute, however, is complete experience. To worship it is to transform it into an object and therefore to make it into something less than infinite.

To attribute a personality to God is to posit a self and an 'other' that is not omnipotent. Religion, for Bradley, is contradictory experience because it at once demands and rejects the idea of a perfect God.[34] Jones, on the other hand, contends that the unity of the Absolute does not demand the absorption of personality, but, on the contrary, wills that are freely able to unite. The Absolute is realised in finite centres, and all the more so when they are spiritual. Man is what he is by virtue of God's presence in him.

Evolutionary theory tied into the religious beliefs of Idealism. For many Idealists, the idea of evolution enables us to comprehend religious experience and God all the better. Thus, evolution, for Edward Caird, bridges the divide between the present and the past, revealing the unity in the diversity of humanity by identifying 'the one spiritual principle which is continuously working in man's life from the changing forms through which it passes in the course of its history'.[35] For Jones: 'Evolution suggests a solution of the ultimate dualism of mind and its objects, and contains the promise of boundless help to religious faith'.[36]

– IDEALISM, MORALITY AND SOCIETY –

Although some critics have inveighed against Hegel for the practical implications of his political philosophy, Hegel himself was clear, in his own mind, that philosophy had little contribution to make to practical life. In *The Philosophy of Right*, for example, he maintains that philosophy always arrives too late to offer any practical advice.[37] However, for many British Idealists, with a few exceptions – notably Bradley, McTaggart and Oakeshott – philosophy *was* integrally related to practical life and should be directed to improve the condition of society.[38] Henry Jones, for example, thought that the most important work of the philosopher was to improve the condition of ordinary working people.[39] Further, in the development of social work theory and practice, the British Idealists have frequently been identified as probably the dominant influence. They showed the unity of theory and practice, and the relevance of philosophy to social problems.[40] Many Idealists were also directly engaged in extending university education to men and women throughout the community. Further, Idealist social and political thought became central to the development of public administration theory well into the interwar period.[41]

The religious backgrounds of many Idealists often predisposed them towards this idea of doing 'practical works' or performing the 'duties of citizenship'. Caird, Green, Muirhead, Jones, Watson and Mackenzie all had early aspirations to join the ministry before succumbing to the temptations of philosophy.[42] W. R. Boyce Gibson, the Personal Idealist, expressed the

Idealist sentiment well. He saw a clear practical value in the application of speculative thought to the spheres of education, sociology and economics. In addition, he emphasised the extent to which religion finds itself in need of philosophy, specifically in rationally trying to reconstruct the religious life via such concepts as love, communion and redemption. In this, he argued, the barrier between philosophy and theology can become permeable.[43]

Nineteenth-century individualists often viewed society either as an aggregate of separate atoms or an organism. The communitarian-inclined theories of the Idealists thus had to combat both utilitarianism individualism and the organic individualism of Herbert Spencer and Leslie Stephen. Utilitarianism was one of the more dominant vocabularies and Bradley and Green, amongst others, criticised it for failing to account for moral and political activity. Morality, for Idealism, was social in character. Acting morally entailed a reciprocal concern for others, and not merely a desire to achieve a private state of mind like happiness or utility. Green and Bradley both associated morality with self-realisation, which unlike pleasure, was the object of moral action. Bradley, for example, argued that self-realisation was a moral duty. We had a duty to realise our best self. Self-realisation was thus directly associated with the common good. The common good was inconceivable apart from membership in a society, and the self that was to be realised through moral activity was 'determined, characterised, made what it is by relation to others'.[44] These ethical themes are explored more fully in a number of the essays in this volume, most explicitly in the Green, Bradley and Ritchie chapters.

Individualist theory did not necessarily view society as a simple aggregate. Both Spencer and Stephen thought individualism deficient if it did not take account of the social factor and understand society as an organism. Both Spencer and Stephen, thus, simultaneously attempted to sustain the organic metaphor for society, but failed to liberate themselves from naturalism.[45] For Idealists, they therefore neglected the *spiritual* nature of the social organism, which is neither mechanical nor biological, but instead depends upon the *relation* in which each person stands with every other. The sinews and ligaments of society are the moral ideas and personal relations, without which a society would be a mere aggregation. For all Idealists, the state is comprised of numerous social organisms – the family, class, clan, church and city – and each individual inevitably belongs to multiple groupings and associations. Each social organism, Ritchie maintains, is thus engaged in a form of struggle for existence and competes for the allegiance of their members.[46] The state for the Idealists is therefore not only the apparatus of governance, but is also inclusive of the whole social organism. Furthermore, as Bosanquet suggests, it is important to distinguish the ideal character from the empirical fact of the state. By associating sovereignty with the state, Idealists posited a general will which was the 'real will' of the community and of which the real will of each individual was a manifestation. Organised society is seen to embody an ideal of life, along with the will to pursue more elevated and rewarding ends than any single individual can attain on his or her own.[47]

The state for the Idealists was therefore a moral agent, with ideals and purposes which it formulated and pursued for the betterment of society as a whole. Thus, Ritchie saw the state as the most adequate representative of the general will in the community.[48] For Bosanquet, it was the sustainer of the rights which underpinned any good life. Without the state the individual was nothing. This did not mean that the individual owed the state blind obedience. Contrary to the views of critics, such as Laski, Joad, Hobhouse and Hobson, the state for the Idealists was only a moral absolute when acting in conformity with its purpose of promoting and sustaining the common good. As Jones emphatically maintained, no individual can delegate responsibility for making judgements about what is right and wrong.[49] States which contravened their purpose and promoted factionalism had to be resisted on moral grounds. Green, for example, imposed no unconditional duty on the citizen to obey the law at all costs, 'since those laws may be inconsistent with the true end of the state, as the sustainer and harmoniser of social relations'.[50] It must be remembered that Green was a great admirer of the revolutionary impetus and achievements of the English civil war. He recognised that resistance, in certain circumstances, was absolutely necessary. Similarly, Ritchie argued that if a law was so at odds with a person's conscience, it must be disobeyed at any cost, otherwise one's self-respect and character would be degraded. The state had, however, no duty to find in favour of the individual, and an individual's resistance might, in fact, only be vindicated in the fullness of time.

Freedom and individuality were for most of the Idealists inextricably linked to citizenship, that is, to the idea of self-development within a civilised state. Freedom was not therefore associated with the absence of constraints, but, rather with acting in accordance with the higher good, or general will of the community. Freedom was associated with choice, yet to act rationally was to make choices in conformity with one's higher interests. The existence of poverty, social deprivation and appalling conditions of work were quite simply incompatible with these ideals. Economics had to be made subordinate to morality, and the state as the sustainer of the moral community had to take an active role providing the conditions in which this transformation could take place. Rights thus always belong to individuals as members of a community. They are justifiable claims recognised as rational and necessary for the common good.

In many respects, even though they were suspicious of the Idealists' emphasis upon the moral character and higher personality of the state, New Liberals, such as J. A. Hobson, L. T. Hobhouse, H. A. L. Fisher, C. F. G. Masterman, H. W. Massingham and to some extent Asquith, shared the same general moral and political ideals as Green, Caird, Ritchie, Bosanquet, Jones and Haldane.[51] It was widely recognised that liberalism had a duty to raise all members of society to a civilised condition of life. This necessarily entailed positive state intervention – although there were strong disagreements about the desirable level of intervention. Within the Idealist camp, Green and Bosanquet, for example, were much less overtly interventionist than Ritchie, Jones or Haldane. The disagreements always focused on the question of the right balance between individual and collective responsibility. Bosanquet thus endorsed the desirability of civilised society exercising its will through the state to encourage progress in the condition of its members, but not to the extent that it weakened the 'character' of the individual. As Muirhead remarked: 'What the State could do was to remove hindrances to the free action of what for lack of a better name moralists call "conscience" – a faculty that might be deadened rather than quickened by a hasty ill-considered collectivism.'[52] In one context, this view of the state invoked a particular liberal reading of socialism, which is explored in the chapter on Henry Jones.

Jones, like many of his fellow Idealists, including Caird, distinguished between true and false socialism. True socialism was ethical and communitarian in nature and provided conditions for individual moral development. False socialism allowed no scope for individual freedom. For many of the civic-minded Idealists, it was the large cities, faced with the consequences of rapid industrial growth, that had to confront the issue of the extent to which the community should 'interfere', in order to ameliorate the plight of the disadvantaged. The Idealists refused to accept that there was an absolute opposition between the individual and the state. True individualism, that is the self-realisation of one's capacities in the context of society, was enhanced by the true socialism, which used the state to advance freedom of choice by removing the obstacles. For the Idealists, morality presupposed freedom of choice. Necessity might produce results that could be condemned as wrong, but they could not be immoral if the actor was deprived of the element of choice. The liberal socialist state could not make men moral, but, it could remove the obstacles to self-realisation. For Green and Muirhead, social improvement was dependent upon the individual's power of seizing and making the most of external conditions. State action could not be ruled out or ruled in *a priori*, but instead had to be judged on its merits. Thus, the criterion of state action, for Henry Jones, was the contribution that legislation could make to moralising existing social relations, and in this respect Jones's views can be compared directly with R. H. Tawney's Christian Socialism.[53]

However, we still must not lose sight of the fact that there was considerable disagreement among the Idealists over the extent to which the state should intervene. Bosanquet and Green give a great deal of emphasis to self-reliance. Improved housing conditions, in themselves, do not improve moral character. People have to will self-improvement. Consequently, whereas Bosanquet took a harder minimalist line on poor relief, other Idealists, such as Jones and Muirhead, were much more sympathetic to its extension.[54] It is worth noting here that Collingwood also stood firmly in the social liberal tradition (qua Jones and Muirhead) and believed that blatant inequalities of wealth reflected unequal relations of force, which effectively undermined individual development and freedom of choice. The state, for Collingwood, thus had a positive role in eliminating force from relations among individuals in the same body politic, and between diverse bodies politic. Alternatively, Oakeshott (more in line with Bosanquet and Green) tended towards a more limited conception of state activity, in which its role was seen as upholding non-instrumental laws which provide conditions for individual initiative or choice.

– IDEALIST INFLUENCE –

In conclusion we would like to indicate something of the pervasiveness and influence of British Idealism in the early twentieth century.[55] Having been initially incubated in the Scottish universities and Oxford, and to a lesser extent at Cambridge, it was exported throughout the English-speaking world. In response to the growing demand for university teachers, following the founding of new universities throughout England and Wales, and in the British colonies and the USA, the pupils of many of the first generation Idealists were the vehicles through which Idealism colonised Australia, New Zealand, Canada, India, South Africa and the USA.

Even when newer philosophical movements arose, it was often the case that they grew out of an initial thorough grounding in Idealism. John Anderson, for example, whose name became synonymous with Australian Realism, was Scottish in origin. He was trained in philosophy by Henry Jones at Glasgow University and before moving to Australia he tutored for Jones at Glasgow. Anderson, who was the successor to the Absolute Idealist Francis Anderson, lectured extensively on T. H. Green's *Lectures on the Principles of Political Obligation* at Sydney University, as late as 1941, exerting a strong personal influence on a number of students, not least John Passmore and Eugene Kamenka. John Anderson personally spearheaded the often acrimonious conflict between Sydney and Melbourne philosophy departments. Melbourne's department, which had initially been under the sway of Henry Laurie's Absolute Idealism, moved, with the appointment of R. W.

Boyce Gibson in 1912, to the espousal of Personal Idealism. Boyce Gibson's son, Alexander Boyce Gibson, continued this Personal Idealist tradition and defended it vigorously against John Anderson's variant of Realism.

Anderson's elder brother William was also taught by Henry Jones at Glasgow and became Professor of Philosophy at Auckland University College in 1921. He expressed himself in the language and style of Green, Bradley, Bosanquet and Caird, although his basic sympathies owed more to Scottish common sense philosophy. In America, the pragmatism of James and Dewey grew out of an early fascination and absorption in British Idealism, and was, to some extent, a reaction against Josiah Royce's Absolute Idealism. There is a certain tenacity and longevity which characterised these Idealists. Brand Blanchard, who leaned more towards Personal Idealism, kept that tradition alive until relatively recent times. Blanchard died in 1987, at the age of ninety-five, some six years short of William Mitchell, an Edinburgh-educated Scot and Adelaide's Absolute Idealist, who died in 1962 at the age of 101. Blanchard, in fact, expressed a profound intellectual debt to Mitchell in his *Nature of Thought*. Another Glaswegian, John Watson, taught by Edward Caird, became Professor of Philosophy at the Queen's University, Kingston, Canada. When Watson arrived, John Clark Murray (1836–1917) had already established pre-Idealist Scottish philosophy. He had been particularly in-fluenced by William Hamilton. However, Watson introduced Absolute Idealism into Canada and became a formidable intellectual influence from the age of twenty-five until his death at the age of ninety-two in 1939. Another of Henry Jones's pupils, Hugh Reyburn, also became a professor of philosophy in Cape Town University, South Africa, in the early 1920s.

It was, nevertheless, a common complaint of those who worked in the colonial universities that the burden of teaching was so great it allowed very little leisure for research and writing. Bosanquet's student, R. F. Hoernlé, for example (who was a professor of philosophy in Witwatersrand University, Johannesburg, South Africa in the 1920s), wrote to W. R. Boyce Gibson in Melbourne complaining of the onerous teaching and administrative duties he carried in South Africa, expressing sympathy with what he assumed was Gibson's similar plight.[56] Mitchell, at Adelaide, described his professorial chair as more of a sofa, in terms of the breadth of subjects he was expected to teach. On the occasion of Francis Anderson's retirement, the author of an appre-ciation commented that Anderson had been 'bearing uncomplainingly the burden of several professors'.[57] When Henry Jones visited Australia he made a point, in his public lectures, of emphasising the research base, as well as the teaching function of a university, and the need to provide the leisure in which to carry out the former.

It would take too much space to explore in detail the whole expanse of

Idealism's impact, so we will focus on the Australian example, by way of illustration. Professional philosophy in Australia developed slowly during the nineteenth century and at first tended to be allied to literature, classics or theology. By the late nineteenth century, philosophy had largely established its autonomy, but nevertheless retained a significant religious and poetic element, which was typical of British Idealism. The chair at Adelaide, for example, had both literature and economics attached to it. The five most significant professors who contributed to the domination of Idealism in Australia were Francis Anderson at Sydney, Henry Laurie and his successor W. R. Boyce Gibson at Melbourne, and William Mitchell and Jethro Brown at Adelaide. Of these, Anderson, Laurie and Mitchell were born and educated in Scotland. Boyce Gibson was born in Paris, educated at Oxford, and was taught by Henry Jones in Glasgow, for a brief period. Brown was born in South Australia, but was educated in England, lived in a University Settlement in London, and taught Law at Aberystwyth University for six years before returning to Australia. In addition, there were numerous well-educated lay philosophers in politics, journalism and in other academic subjects who espoused Idealism.

Francis Anderson had graduated from Glasgow University and, like Henry Jones, had won the Clarke Fellowship which entailed assisting Edward Caird. Anderson was an Hegelian influenced directly by both Caird and Green. He was, like Jones and Caird, a 'preacher professor' who lectured with passion as he juxtaposed philosophy with great poetry to illustrate the spiritual nature of reality.[58] Mungo MacCallum was another influential exponent of Idealism, particularly through his literary criticism. His philosophical inclinations focused on Green and Caird, and it was MacCallum who was responsible for inviting Henry Jones to Australia to give an extensive series of lectures at Sydney, which were later published as *Idealism as a Practical Creed*. MacCallum and Jones had been fellow students at Glasgow, and later colleagues at the University College of Aberystwyth. MacCallum had initially been an assistant to John Nicol at Glasgow, who was one of Jones's Idealist teachers. So confident was Jones of the ascendancy of Idealism, and the receptiveness of Australians to it, that he opened his lecture in Sydney by announcing that he took philosophy simply to be that form of enquiry developed by Hegel, and with which the greatest modern minds were associated.[59]

An insight into how deeply rooted Idealism was in Sydney University remains in the unpublished autobiography of Mungo MacCallum, *Jottings Genealogical and Reminscential*, written in 1937.[60] MacCallum, who became Vice-Chancellor of Sydney University (1924–7), Deputy Chancellor (1928–34) and Chancellor (1934–6), records how Caird had imparted to him and his fellow students a sense of the unity and totality of the universe. It was not a naturalistic but a spiritual totality. Absolute Idealism was thus the foundation of MacCallum's constellation of ideas. In his early days at Sydney he records spending most Sundays reading T. H. Green's *Prolegomena to Ethics* with T. J. Wilson, later Professor of Anatomy at Sydney. Anderson, MacCallum and Wilson were three of the four most powerful men in the University in the early part of the century. They were also very friendly with Walter Scott, Professor of Classics and then of Greek. MacCallum describes him, in characteristic style, as 'a fine scholar, a man of integrity: a thorough and whole-hearted disciple of T. H. Green, with the requisite mixture of scepticism and Idealism that enabled him to treasure the kernel while rejecting the husk.'[61]

There were also a Dr Hunter, another ex-student of Henry Jones,[62] as well as Christopher Brennan, who by this time had rejected his earlier admiration for Spencer and begun to develop an interest in Idealism.[63] Sydney University was, in fact, dominated by Scottish graduates in the early part of the century, particularly those from Glasgow.[64] Glasgow graduates hosted a dinner in honour of Henry Jones when he visited Sydney to lecture, and resolved collectively to send a cable to Caird to convey their heartfelt greetings.[65] It is, therefore, ironic that Sydney, so thoroughly impregnated to its very core with the spirit of Scottish Idealism, should be at the centre of the later opposition to it. When John Anderson took up the chair at Sydney, both Francis Anderson and Mungo MacCallum were still immensely influential in the University. One of the reasons why MacCallum did not seek re-election to the chancellorship in 1936 was because he so disliked the totally negative style of teaching of John Anderson. He had no desire to silence him, but thought that a second philosophy chair ought to be appointed in order to counteract his insidious influence and to allow students to choose between alternative doctrines. What John Passmore found so exciting about John Anderson, despite his appalling delivery and impenetrable Lanarkshire accent, was that during a time when Idealists held Spirit to be ultimate, and Realists opposed them in holding sense-data to be ultimate, John Anderson contended that they were both wrong because there were no ultimates.[66]

Because of the size of Australia, its parochial transport system which required passengers to change trains at state borders, and the paucity of research and travel grants, there was very little personal contact among philosophers from the various universities. Participants in the Australasian Association of Psychology and Philosophy tended on the whole to be from Sydney or Melbourne. The Association was established by Sydney philosophers and the first editor of its journal was Francis Anderson. William Mitchell, for example, preferred to go to Britain for his philosophical company, and was the Gifford Lecturer in Aberdeen for 1925–6. If Samuel

Alexander, who was born in Australia, is excluded, Mitchell is the only Australian to have delivered the Gifford Lectures. Despite Mitchell's eminence, Passmore claims that he never set eyes on him. Mitchell was not particularly influential in Australia, due, in part, to the relative geographical isolation of Adelaide, but, further, to the obscurity of his writings. He was almost unintelligible to most readers, a condition which did not improve with age.

Of the three pioneer professors, Mitchell was by far the most able and the only one to establish for himself a significant international reputation. Like Laurie, Mitchell was taught by Campbell Fraser at Edinburgh. An early version of Mitchell's first book was submitted to Macmillan publishers for appraisal and Henry Jones acted as the reader. Mitchell, unlike Jones, was influenced by Bosanquet, but shared with Jones a commitment to Absolute Idealism. However, he placed a heavy emphasis upon psychology as the foundation of philosophy, instead of religion and poetry, despite his chair including both English language and literature. Jones was uncharacteristically positive about the book. He says of the book, that was subsequently published as *The Structure and Growth of the Mind*, that: 'It is not often that I have had the pleasure of approving a book so heartily. It is extraordinarily strong, and manifests throughout the most thorough philosophical grasp.'[67] Jones goes on to maintain that: 'I find it difficult to offer any criticism, or to qualify in any way, my admiration of this bit of work.'[68] While it is sometimes difficult to distinguish aspects of Mitchell's Absolute Idealism from materialism, in that he believed that thought should not be confounded with its object, he nevertheless denied the intelligibility of asking questions about things in themselves. Something that is isolated from other things and which is not perceived is beyond comprehension. In so far as Mitchell was sometimes accused of being too much of a realist and materialist, this actually allies him more closely to Bosanquet and Jones of whom similar criticisms were made. His *Structure and Growth of the Mind* was nevertheless highly acclaimed in the philosophical journals by such authorities as Kemp Smith in *The Philosophical Review* (1908) and Hoernlé in *Mind* (1908).

The Professor of Law at Adelaide, W. Jethro Brown, was another remarkable individual with wide-ranging interests. He was born in South Australia, educated in Oxford and Cambridge, and held academic posts in Tasmania, London and Aberystwyth, before taking up the chair in Adelaide. In 1916 he became President of the Industrial Court of South Australia.[69] Intellectually and politically one might say that Brown was a progressive. He was anti-positivist, as all of the Idealists were, and believed that the emergence of history in the nineteenth century provided the means by which we could enhance our understanding of constitutions and of law. Law, he believed, was an artefact, or historical construction, which could be understood properly only in relation to its context and development. Invoking the authority of Vico, he argued that we must immerse ourselves in the beliefs and ideas of the past in order to appreciate fully the nature and purpose of laws.[70] In addition, Brown argued for the extension of the role of the state to advance the condition of the populace as a whole, and increase the liberty of those who were enslaved under the system of *laissez-faire*. He wrote down his ideas upon the principles of government action in his *Underlying Principles of Modern Legislation,* extensively drawing upon the ideas of T. H. Green and Henry Jones.[71] Like them he rejected naturalistic organicism and perceived the state as a spiritual organism in which its members owed selfless devotion to their fellow citizens. In similar fashion to Ritchie, he rejected the individualism of social contract and natural rights theories and instead argued that: 'In the reconstructed doctrine of individual rights the common good takes the place of consent as the justification for the exercise of authority.'[72]

Henry Laurie of Melbourne was similarly well-disposed to Idealism, but while having affinities with Green and Caird, leaned more towards the Edinburgh Idealism of both S. S. Laurie and Campbell Fraser, and to the Personal Idealism of Pringle-Pattison. Henry Laurie is best known for having written one of the first histories of Scottish philosophy,[73] but his students were hard-pressed to detect where his philosophical sympathies lay. Laurie, like Henry Jones, was a passionate admirer of Browning, whose poetry is replete with Idealist and evolutionary imagery.[74] It was with Laurie that Jones stayed while in Melbourne, and both dined with Alfred Deakin, Australia's second Prime Minister, and with the State Governor of Victoria, Sir Thomas Gibson-Carmichael, who was also a friend of Jones.[75] Deakin was widely read in philosophy and was astute enough to discern that Jones's position was similar to that of Green, but nevertheless derived directly from Hegel.[76] The Prime Minister attended Jones's second lecture on 'The Individual and the State', on 11 August 1908. Deakin notes in his diary, for 12 August 1908, that he lunched with Jones, and after a Cabinet meeting in the evening walked home with Herbert Brookes, his son-in-law, and discussed the philosopher's ideas.[77] Furthermore, J. McKellar Stewart, one of Laurie's pupils, was an assistant minister at the Scots Church, Melbourne, at this time,[78] and Walter Murdoch, a lecturer in English, displayed, in his articles in the *Melbourne Argus*, a thorough knowledge of, and admiration for, the works of Green, Caird and Jones. Murdoch wrote excitedly of the immanent visit of Jones. He suggested that 'no philosopher that ever lived had been more keenly intent than Jones on applying philosophy to the problems of modern life'.[79]

William Ralph Boyce Gibson's appointment to the chair at Melbourne in 1912 owed much to the exponents of Absolute Idealism, although he himself was a Personal Idealist, sympathetic to some of the ideas of the pragmatists, particularly William James. He was also extremely important in introducing the ideas of the new generation of German philosophers into the English-speaking world, the most important of whom were Eucken and Husserl. Both Bernard Bosanquet and Henry Jones strongly supported Boyce Gibson's application, as did F. C. S. Schiller, a fellow contributor, with Boyce Gibson, to the *Personal Idealism* volume edited by Henry Sturt.[80]

From the early 1920s up to the late 1930s, after which former pupils of Wittgenstein emigrated to Australia and added a new dimension, philosophical disputes in Australia were largely between philosophical Idealists of different shades, and John Anderson, deeply intransigent in his unique brand of realism and materialism, and, at least at this time, in his Marxism.[81] The disputants all presupposed elements which, if not accepted at the outset, could not bear the weight of the argument. In other words, they tended to argue past each other. John Anderson, for example, complains that Alexander Boyce Gibson, the successor to his father's chair at Melbourne, refused to accept anything as proof that did not share his own premises, which is ironic, given that this was the chief complaint directed at Anderson by his critics. In a lecture on the dispute between Boyce Gibson and Anderson, in which the former asserts and the latter denies that 'the end sought is one of the factors contributing to the ethical character of the action that seeks it', Alan Ker Stout suggested that in the eyes of his critics, Anderson 'does not examine sufficiently his own fundamental premises. Instead of searching for possible ways in which he may be mistaken he seems to take for granted that he cannot be mistaken. To objections he opposes only emphatic reiterations which lead nowhere.'[82] Despite the fact that the character of philosophy changed considerably in Melbourne during the 1940s and 1950s, it was one of the few places that took R. G. Collingwood's philosophy of history seriously. It was taught to undergraduates in both philosophy and history, and it was in Melbourne that Alan Donagan became acquainted with Collingwood's work and subsequently went on to write *The Later Philosophy of R. G. Collingwood*, which was largely responsible for regenerating interest in him.[83]

Politically, Idealism in Australia was even more of a reaction against individualism in its utilitarian and organic forms than it was in Britain. There was a heated debate in Australia concerning the question of state intervention, and the issue of free trade versus protection. D. G. Ritchie's *The Principles of State Interference* was adopted as a significant contribution to this debate and its scathing attack on Spencer was widely read and appreciated in Australia.[84] Spencer had many followers in Australia, and the socially conscious Idealist reformers thought it imperative to counteract his influence. William Mitchell, in his 'Lectures on Ethics', convicted Spencer of positing an end towards which society is progressing, without providing the motivation for why one should 'be inspired by what is not his concern, i.e. an ideal society in which he shall not exist?'.[85] Henry Laurie vigorously attacked Spencer's doctrine of the Unknowable. 'It is strange,' Laurie told his students, 'that English-speaking people should have so readily accepted a philosophy which accuses human reason of endless absurdities.'[86] Francis Anderson criticised Spencer in his lectures for propounding a 'pseudo-religious agnosticism which worships it knows not what and finds peace in intellectual suicide'.[87] Such criticisms are in harmony with those of British Idealism. Jones, for example, complained that Spencer's attempt to 'base knowledge on the unknowable ... is about the maddest of all the projects propounded to suffering mankind'.[88]

Politically, Bosanquet, Caird, Jones, Ritchie, Anderson and Mitchell shared the same concerns. Following Green, they all wished to transcend what they believed to be the false opposition between individualism and collectivism, argued vociferously for educational reform at all levels, and believed that sociology had a significant contribution to make to the better understanding and organisation of society.[89] On the issue of individualism versus socialism, for example, Craig Campbell maintained that although most Australian people and politicians would not have read the works of British philosophers, such as Green on the role of the state, 'there were sufficient numbers acquainted with the debates to bring their terms of reference to Australia'.[90] Enlightened liberals had to acknowledge that the individualism of *laissez-faire* had been superseded by a move towards socialistic state intervention. Both Francis Anderson and William Mitchell envisaged overcoming the political dualism in a positive conception of the state, in which the criterion of intervention is the extent to which the individual spirit is empowered to act. Anderson argued that, 'Liberalism, as well as socialism, cannot do without Government intervention, whether we call such intervention grandmotherly legislation, or simply the necessary extension of the economic functions of the State.'[91] It was with extreme collectivism and not with the 'practical socialism' of the Labor Party that both disagreed. The state, Mitchell argued, in typical Idealist fashion, is best conceived as a person with the duty of eradicating poverty just as much as crime. There could be no limit on the state's right to taxation, he controversially proclaimed, as long as the revenue enhances individual freedom and contributes to a higher level of living.[92]

– CONCLUSION –

In summary, Idealism fulfilled a number of roles in societies that were experiencing the effects of rapid industrialisation, modernisation and secularisation.

It acted as a counterbalance to the individualism of the more brash variants of utilitarianism, offering a philosophy that gave a much needed emphasis to social cohesiveness and to the closeness of the relation between individual and collective responsibility. Its emphasis on the importance of active social, citizenship became an important theme in early twentieth-century politics and welfare theory. Against the conception of humanity in naturalistic theories of evolution, Idealists offered an elevated view of the relation between humanity and nature. For many of them, God (or the Absolute Spirit) was immanent in the development of freedom in the world and Spirit expressed itself through the finite centres of individual lives. This would be true of many Idealists.[93] Idealism was often an intensely moralistic philosophy, more than willing to condemn social evils. It emphasised both the responsibilities of individuals to seize the opportunities to make themselves more virtuous, and of the owners of capital to transform their workshops into schools of virtue. The role of the state in all this was to ensure that any impediments to self-realisation were removed.[94] Overall, the present volume of essays aims to provide more detailed examples of the manner in which certain Idealists responded to issues and problems both in their own terms and in relation to more recent discussions, thus revealing a coherent, rich and diverse pattern of thought on political and moral philosophy.

– NOTES –

1. Andrew Seth Pringle-Pattison, *Scottish Philosophy* (Edinburgh, Blackwood, 1890: 2nd edn), 11. Pringle-Pattison became one of the leading exponents of Personal Idealism which took its lead from Lotze and Rudolph Eucken.

2. Henry Jones, *A Critical Account of the Philosophy of Lotze* (Glasgow, Maclehose, 1895), 273. The idea that things exist only in being known is what J. S. Mackenzie calls 'False Idealism'. See 'Edward Caird as a philosophical teacher', *Mind*, n.s., 18 (1909), 519.

3. Hastings Rashdall, 'Personality: Human and Divine', in Henry Sturt (ed.), *Personal Idealism: Philosophical Essays* (London, Macmillan, 1902), 370. Rashdall as a Personal Idealist distinguished himself from Absolute Idealists. See below.

4. Richard Norman calls this the 'Dilemma of Epistemology' in his book *Hegel's Phenomenology: a Philosophical Introduction* (London, Chatto and Windus for Sussex University Press, 1976), Chapter 1.

5. Edward Caird, *Hegel* (Edinburgh, Blackwood, 1903), 55.

6. Henry Jones gives a detailed and critical account of the development of the epistemological dilemma through Hegelian eyes in his 'Idealism and Epistemology', *Mind*, n.s. II (1893), in two parts. See David Boucher and Andrew Vincent, *A Radical Hegelian: The Political and Social Philosophy of Henry Jones* (Cardiff and New York, University of Wales Press and St Martin's Press, 1993), ch. 2; and David Boucher, 'Practical Hegelianism: Henry Jones's Lecture Tour of Australia', *Journal of the History of Ideas*, 51 (1990), 429–32. See also the Jones chapter in this volume.

7. Edward Caird, 'Metaphysic', *Essays on Literature and Philosophy*, vol. 2 (Glasgow, Maclehose, 1892), 442.

8. T. H. Green, 'Review of J. Caird, *Introduction to the Philosophy of Religion*', in *Works*, III (London, Longman Green, 1883–6) 146.

9. Green, *Works*, III, 146.

10. Seth Pringle-Pattison, *Scottish Philosophy*, 198.

11. See Caird, 'The Problem of Philosophy at the Present Time', *Essays on Literature and Philosophy*, vol. 1 (Glasgow, Maclehose, 1892), 205–6.

12. Cf. John Watson, *The State in Peace and War* (Glasgow, Maclehose, 1919), 250.

13. F. H. Bradley, *Appearance and Reality* (Oxford, Clarendon Press, 1897: 2nd edn), 217. Also see Boucher and Vincent, *A Radical Hegelian*, 43–7.

14. R. G. Collingwood, 'The Metaphysics of F. H. Bradley: An Essay on *Appearance and Reality*'. Unpublished manuscript, Collingwood Papers, Bodleian Library, Oxford.

15. Henry Jones, *The Philosophy of Martineau* (London, Macmillan, 1905), 20–1. See Boucher and Vincent, *Radical Hegelian*, ch. 2, also Andrew Vincent, 'The Individual in Hegelian Thought', *Idealist Studies*, vol. XII, no. 2 (1982), 156–68.

16. Seth Pringle-Pattison, for example, objected to Absolute Idealism's 'unification of consciousness in a single Self'. Andrew Seth, *Hegelianism and Personality* (Edinburgh, Blackwood, 1888), 215. There was also a great deal more internal variety among Personal Idealists than among the Absolute Idealists. Among the more distinguished exponents of Personal or Subjective Idealism were Andrew Seth Pringle-Pattison, Hastings Rashdall, Henry Sturt, W. R. Boyce Gibson, the American Brand Blanchard, and the idiosyncratic James McTaggart Ellis McTaggart; see also Vincent, 'The Individual in Hegelian Thought'.

17. W. R. Boyce Gibson, 'A Peace Policy for Idealists', *The Hibbert Journal*, 5 (1906–7), 409.

18. Henry Sturt, ed., *Personal Idealism: Philosophical Essays* (London, Macmillan, 1902), p. x.

19. A. Seth Pringle-Pattison, *The Idea of God in the Light of Recent Philosophy* (Oxford, Clarendon Press, 1920), 266.

20. The success of Darwin's theory was, of course, possible because of the great strides made in geology and palaeontology in establishing that the Christian view that the earth was created a little over 4,000 years ago was a gross underestimation.

21. Lionel Stevenson, 'Darwin Among the Poets' (1932). Reprinted in *Darwin*, selected and edited by Philip Appleman (New York, Norton, 1979), 519.

22. J. W. Burrow, *Evolution and Society: A Study in Victorian Social Theory* (Cambridge, Cambridge University Press, 1966), 20 and 100.

23. Darwin added a historical sketch of his precursors to the third edition of *The Origin of Species* (1862). He expanded upon the sketch in subsequent editions.

24. Herbert Spencer, 'A Theory of Population Deduced from the General Law of Animal Fertility', *Westminster Review*, lvii (1852), and 'The Development Hypothesis' reprinted in Herbert Spencer, *Essays* (New York, Appleton, 1907).

25. David G. Ritchie, *Darwin and Hegel with other Philosophical Studies* (London, Swan Sonneschein, 1893), 42.

26. D. G. Ritchie, *Darwinism and Politics* (London, Swan Sonnenschein, 1901), 100–1. Also see pp. 131–2.

27. See Ritchie, *Darwin and Hegel*, 47.

28. D. G. Ritchie, *The Principles of State Interference* (London, Swan Sonnenschein, 1896: 2nd edn), 44.

29. Edward Caird, *The Evolution of Religion* (Glasgow, Maclehose, 1899), vol. I, 45.

30. Edward Caird, *The Critical Philosophy of Kant* (Glasgow, Maclehose, 1889), vol. I, 35.

31. Henry Jones, *Idealism as a Practical Creed* (Glasgow, Maclehose, 1909), 29. Elsewhere he argues that the power of the idea of evolution has 'transfigured the world'. Henry Jones,

The Working Faith of the Social Reformer (London, Macmillan, 1910), 36.

32. See David Boucher, 'Human Conduct, History and the Social Sciences in the philosophy of Michael Oakeshott and R. G. Collingwood', *New Literary History*, 24 (1993).

33. David G. Ritchie, *Philosophical Studies* (London, Macmillan, 1905), 241.

34. F. H. Bradley, *Essays on Truth and Reality* (Oxford, Clarendon Press, 1935), 428. For debates on this area see Boucher and Vincent, *Radical Hegelian*, ch. 3; also Alan P. F. Sell, *Philosophical Idealism and Christian Belief* (Cardiff, University of Wales Press, 1995).

35. Caird, *Evolution of Religion*, vol. 1, p. x. Cf. 24–5, and 27.

36. Henry Jones, *A Faith that Enquires* (London, Macmillan, 1910), 98.

37. G. W. F. Hegel, *The Philosophy of Right* (Oxford, O.U.P., 1967), p. 7.

38. Henry Jones, for example, believed that the practical purpose should be broad enough to make the universe an accomplice in the plot. Henry Jones, 'Francis Hutcheson', a discourse delivered in the University of Glasgow on Commemoration Day, 18 April 1906 (Glasgow, Maclehose, 1906), 20. The argument against the practical role of philosophy is covered in this volume in the Bradley and Oakeshott essays.

39. Henry Jones, *The Working Faith of the Social Reformer* (London, Macmillan, 1911), p. x.

40. Andrew Vincent and Raymond Plant, *Philosophy Politics and Citizenship* (Oxford, Blackwell, 1984), 116.

41. Jose Harris, 'Political Thought and the Welfare State 1870–1940', *Past and Present*, 135 (1992), 123.

42. Despite pressure from his father to enter the Anglican Priesthood, Green only gave a fleeting thought to becoming a Dissenting minister. Again the religious element is not to the fore in McTaggart and Bradley, nor in fact in Bosanquet who was one of the leading social reformers among the Idealists. Green's religious views, nevertheless, were broadly accepted by most of the Idealists. Vincent and Plant summarise the basic views in the following terms: 'The pursuit of a life greater than our own, to find the best that we know, to try to see the ideal in all our everyday activities, civic and personal, to unite the infinite with the finite, these were the basic views of religion shared by the Idealist philosophers.' *Philosophy Politics and Citizenship*, 16–17.

43. Boyce Gibson, 'A Peace Policy for Idealists', 407.

44. Bradley, *Ethical Studies* (Oxford, Clarendon Press, 1962: 2nd edn), 116. Cf. Green, *Prolegomena to Ethics* (Oxford, Clarendon Press, 1907), section 184.

45. Leslie Stephen, 'Ethics and The Struggles for Existence', *Contemporary Review*, 64 (1893), 165.

46. D. G. Ritchie, 'Social Evolution', *International Journal of Ethics*, vi (1896–6), 168.

47. The single best expression of this idea, J. H. Muirhead suggests, is Bosanquet's essay 'The Reality of the General Will'; see J. H. Muirhead, 'Recent Criticism of the Idealist Theory of the General Will', parts I, II and III, *Mind*, xxxiii (1924). For Bosanquet's essay see D. Boucher, ed., *The British Idealists* (Cambridge University Press, 1997), 130–41.

48. D. G. Ritchie, *The Principles of State Interference* (London, Swan Sonnenschein, 1891), 138.

49. Henry Jones, *The Principles of Citizenship* (London, Macmillan, 1919).

50. T. H. Green, *Lectures on the Principles of Political Obligation* (London, Longmans Green, 1917), 148.

51. See Vincent and Plant, *Philosophy Politics and Citizenship*, for full study of these themes. On the New Liberals see Chapter 5.

52. J. H. Muirhead, *Reflections by a Journeyman in Philosophy* (London, Allen and Unwin, 1942), 160.

53. These issues arise in a number of essays in this volume. The more explicit discussion of

socialism is in the Henry Jones piece.

54. On Bosanquet's work see Andrew Vincent, 'The Poor Law Reports of 1909 and the Social Theory of the Charity Organization Society', *Victorian Studies*, vol. 27, no. 3 (1984), reprinted in David Gladstone (ed.), *Before Beveridge: Welfare before the Welfare State* (London, Institute of Economic Affairs, 1999).

55. This section has been added at the request of the Editorial Board at Edinburgh University Press.

56. W. R. Boyce Gibson Papers, University of Melbourne, Correspondence, 1/15. Dates 14 January, 1914.

57. HTL (H. Tasman Lovell), 'Professor Anderson, M.A.', *The Arts Journal of the University of Sydney*, 4 (1921), 81.

58. S. A. Grave, *Philosophy in Australia* (Brisbane, University of Brisbane Press, 1978) 19.

59. 'Apostle of Ideas', *Sydney Morning Herald*, 11 July 1908; 'Philosophy and Modern Life', *Sydney Daily Telegraph*, 11 July 1908. Also see the published version in Jones, *Idealism as a Practical Creed*, 12.

60. Sir Mungo W. MacCallum Papers, Accession No. 1072 P9 Box 13, University of Sydney Library.

61. MacCallum, *Jottings*, 96.

62. 'True and False Socialism', *Illawarra Mercury*, 24 July 1908.

63. Grave, *Philosophy in Australia*, 27–8.

64. The Chancellor, for example, Sir Norman Maclaren, was a St Andrews man, where Jones had been Professor of Philosophy before taking up the Glasgow chair.

65. H. J. W. Hetherington, *Life and Letters* (London, Hodder and Stoughton, 1924), 209.

66. John Passmore, *Memoirs of a Semi-detached Australian* (Melbourne, Melbourne University Press, 1997), 93–4.

67. William Mitchell, *The Structure and Growth of Mind* (London, Macmillan, 1907).

68. Henry Jones's reader's report on *The Growth of Mind* being Part I of the *Principles of Education*. Macmillan Archives, series vol. MCC1, 1895–1904, pp. 103–4. British Museum MS 55988. The archives are published on microfilm by Chadwyck-Healy Ltd., Cambridge.

69. Michael Roe, *Nine Australian Progressives* (Brisbane, University of Brisbane Press, 1984), 22–56.

70. W. J. Brown, 'The Study of Law', an inaugural lecture delivered in the University College of Wales, Aberystwyth (London, 1902).

71. Jethro Brown, *Underlying Principles of Modern Legislation* (London, Macmillan, 1912: 3rd edn, 1914).

72. Cited by Michael Roe in *Australian Dictionary of National Biography*, vol. 10 (Melbourne, Melbourne University Press, 1986).

73. Henry Laurie, *Scottish Philosophy in Its National Development* (Glasgow, Maclehose, 1902).

74. For Laurie's interest in Browning see Morris Miller, 'Beginnings of Philosophy in Australia', Part II, p. 2.

75. See *Walter Murdoch and Alfred Deakin on Books and Men*, ed. J. A. La Nauze and Elizabeth Nurser (Melbourne, University of Melbourne Press, 1974), 37.

76. Letter from Alfred Deakin to Walter Murdoch, dated 1 August 1909. Reprinted in *Books and Men*, 43. Deakin is commenting upon Murdoch's review of J. H. Muirhead, a Scottish Idealist, *The Service of the State* (London, Macmillan, 1908), *Melbourne Argus*, 1 August 1909. Reprinted in Walter Murdoch, *Loose Leaves* (Melbourne, Melbourne University Press, 1910), 63–7. There is some correspondence between Deakin and Murdoch regarding arrangements for meeting Jones and having lunch. See *Books and Men*, 34–7.

77. Alfred Deakin Papers, National Library of Australia, Canberra. MS 1540 series 2, Diaries. Deakin was also a close friend of Josiah Royce, the American Idealist.

78. He published *Critical Exposition of Bergson's Philosophy* (London, Macmillan, 1911).

79. Elzevir, *Melbourne Argus*, 25 July 1908; and *Melbourne Argus*, 30 May 1908. Murdoch was a journalist; lecturer in English at Melbourne University; friend of Alfred Deakin the Liberal Prime Minister; and later Professor of English in the University of Western Australia, Perth. Also see the following: 'He is specially well known as an inspiring lecturer', *Adelaide Advertiser*, 12 August 1908; and 'He never fails to impress his hearers, whether he is addressing his class at the university, or a mixed audience that is numbered by thousands', 'The Visit of Professor Jones', *Adelaide Register*, 12 August 1908. All three citations were printed when Jones was in Sydney and Melbourne, that is, when Adelaide was awaiting his arrival. The last of the three was written by Mungo MacCallum, Jones's ex-colleague and friend, and had been published in the *Sydney Daily Telegraph* some weeks before. In his letter to Professor Henderson of the Extension Lectures Committee, University of Adelaide, MacCallum says of Jones; 'He is really an eloquent speaker; and also has something to say'. Letter dated 24 April 1908. University of Adelaide Archives, docket 372/08.

80. *Personal Idealism*, ed. by Sturt. W. R. Boyce Gibson Papers, University of Melbourne, Correspondence, 2/6/1; 2/28; 2/31/1.

81. Passmore, *Memoirs*, 123.

82. 'Anderson versus Boyce Gibson', Papers of Professor Alan Ker Stout, section 12/44, pp. 1 and 10, Sydney University Library.

83. Published by Clarendon Press at Oxford, 1962.

84. Ritchie, *Principles of State Interference*.

85 . William Mitchell papers, vol. 115, pp. 61–2, University of Adelaide.

86. Quotation from Laurie's lectures on Spencer cited by E. Morris Miller, 'The Beginnings of Philosophy in Australia and the Work of Henry Laurie', Part II, *Australasian Journal of Psychology and Philosophy*, VIII (1930), 7.

87. Cited by Alex Clark, *Christopher Brennan* (Melbourne, Melbourne University Press, 1980), 35.

88. Jones, *Working Faith of the Social Reformer*, 44.

89. See Francis Anderson, 'A Modern Philosopher – Green of Balliol', *University of Sydney Union Year Book 1902* (Sydney, Sydney University, 1902); Francis Anderson, 'Liberalism and Socialism', Presidential Address to Section G of the Australasian Association for the Advancement of Science, *Proceedings* (Adelaide, 1907). Also see the essay published after Jones's visit, Francis Anderson, *Sociology in Australia – A Plea for its Teaching* (Sydney, Angus and Robertson, 1912).

90. Craig Campbell, 'Liberalism in Australian History: 1880–1920', *Social Policy in Australia: some Perspectives 1901–1975*, ed. Jill Roe (Sydney, Allen and Unwin, 1976), 29.

91. Anderson, 'Liberalism and Socialism', 4.

92. William Mitchell, 'Christianity and the Industrial System', Adelaide, issued by the Methodist Social Services League, no date, 21–2.

93. Bradley (and to some extent Bosanquet) had his own more idiosyncratic views. Oakeshott is different again, although the recent volume of Oakeshott's writings, edited by Tim Fuller, *Religion, Politics and the Moral Life* (New Haven and London, Yale University Press, 1993), does something to change our perspective on Oakeshott, qua religion. For Collingwood's view on religion, see the chapter in this volume.

94. Again there are considerable variations here between Idealist thinkers.

CHAPTER 1

T. H. Green:
Citizenship as Political and Metaphysical

Citizenship has once again arisen as a motif in contemporary political thought. As is well known, citizenship was a particular and unique pre-occupation of the British Idealists. This essay concentrates on T. H. Green's notion of citizenship. However, to review Green's arguments in a broader context, the discussion is set up in a somewhat novel format. It utilises a current debate in political philosophy concerning the character of justice, namely, whether it is political or metaphysical. John Rawls's later writings are taken as the *locus classicus* reflection on this issue, putting the case for the *political* conception of justice. Rawls's work is but one example of a more general recent trend in political philosophy which is critical of metaphysics. This whole argument can, however, be turned with ease onto the question of citizenship. For Rawls, citizenship is also political not metaphysical. However, for Thomas Hill Green, citizenship is *both* political and metaphysical. Both philosophers claim to be liberal – in fact they might both be taken as arche-typal examples of 'social liberals'; both have communitarian aspects to their work; neither are unreceptive to the development of the welfare state.[1] Both see the origin of liberalism in similar terms, but they diverge wildly over the question of metaphysics. To analyse this issue in this manner reveals the major constituents of Green's political philosophy. In order to unravel this debate, this essay first analyses the concepts of liberalism and citizenship, on a general level; it then turns to the origins of liberal thought as understood by Green and Rawls. This entails, in turn, a more detailed and comparative analysis of Green's metaphysical and theological views. The essay finally focuses more sharply on the problematic relation of metaphysics and citizenship.[2]

– LIBERALISM AND CITIZENSHIP –

Although not an easy writer, Green had a significant and immensely positive effect on generations of students, including many future academics, churchmen, politicians and public servants, for example, men like Herbert Asquith, Edward Grey, Alfred Milner, Arthur Acland, A. C. Bradley, Arnold Toynbee, Bernard Bosanquet, R. L Nettleship, J. H. Muirhead, Charles Gore and Henry Scott Holland. As R. G. Collingwood noted in his *Autobiography*, Green's major effect was to send out into public life

> a stream of ex-pupils who carried with them the conviction that philosophy ... was an important thing, and their vocation was to put it into practice ... Through this effect on the minds of its pupils, the philosophy of Green's school might be found, from 1880 to about 1910, penetrating and fertilizing every part of the national life.[3]

After Green's death, in 1882, he also left a powerful legacy, and, in part, mythology, concerning his achievements, which carried through to the early twentieth century. His philosophy, which blended metaphysical, religious and epistemological concerns with a sophisticated theory of ethics and politics, set a standard of academic rigour which helped change the character of British philosophy from the early twentieth century.

Green's educational ideas on a 'ladder of learning' for all citizens directly influenced both R. B. Haldane and H. A. L. Fisher and, indirectly, early twentieth century education policy. The influence of Green's ideas was not only felt in spheres like education. Social work was another area of Green impact on early twentieth-century society, particularly through the burgeoning university settlements, such as Toynbee Hall (founded in 1884 in memory of T. H. Green's pupil and admirer Arnold Toynbee, or, 'apostle Arnold' as he was known to his friends) or the Passmore Edwards Settlement founded by Mrs Humphry Ward in 1896.[4] It is no exaggeration to say that the majority of those who worked on and supported the early twentieth-century welfare state reforms, for example, W. H. Beveridge, R. B. Morant, Llewellyn Smith, Ernest Aves, W. J. Braithwaite, J. A. Spender, R. H. Tawney and Clement Atlee, all had university settlement experience – many at Toynbee Hall – and were influenced by its culture of civic Idealism and social duty. Thus, if there is one important intellectual bequest from Green, it is an optimistic strongly liberal communitarian and ethical theory of citizenship and the state, devoted to the promotion of a worthwhile life for all citizens.

Green was an immensely important figure in a changing sense in the period 1870 to 1914. In politics, before 1914, Green's philosophy precipitated, in many minds, a reassessment of some of the key values of liberalism. He did not suggest a wholesale revision of liberalism, more a bringing to fruition of some of its latent tendencies for social reform. His ethical and political philosophy, which many contemporaries saw exemplified within Green's own life, provided a cogent rationale for a more statist and welfarist liberalism, enabling it to meet, more humanely, the problems of an increasingly complex industrial society. Green's lecture 'Liberal Legislation and Freedom of Contract' (1881) is important for understanding this changing conception of liberalism (*Works* III, 365ff.). The lecture was written to re-assure the Liberal party over the character of its legislative programme. Green constructed a historical picture of liberal concerns. First, liberalism had struggled for political freedoms against aristocratic privileges. Second, with figures like Cobden and Bright, it had struggled for economic freedoms against protectionism. However, liberalism was moving into a third phase, characterised by social freedoms. For liberals concerned about freedom of contract, Green asked, 'what is freedom?'. He answered that freedom was a 'positive power of doing or enjoying something worth doing or enjoying' (*Works* III, 371). Positive freedom was identified with rational and moral action, a reconciliation of the objects of will and the objects of reason, that is willing the common good. It was coincidental with self-realisation, character and genuine citizenship. The progress of society was measured by the growth of this freedom. Simply being left alone – negative freedom – was what Green called the primitive sense of the term and was of little or no assistance to a citizen's moral development. Thus, when liberals spoke of freedom of con-tract it was not just freedom from restraint, but the maximum power of all members of a community to make the best of themselves. State involvement in the regulation of drink, housing conditions, land ownership, employment conditions and education was justifiable on the above grounds. Interference should at all times be directed to removing barriers and providing the conditions for the realisation of citizens' powers.

The central category of Green's political philosophy was therefore citizenship, understood in a metaphysical framework. Citizenship implied a consciousness of the moral ends of human life as embodied within the institutional structures of the state; in other words, a consciousness of the common good. The state was the organised body within which this con-sciousness functioned. For Green, society and its institutional structures were therefore the means to individual self-realisation. Social institutions or legal practices were justified only to the extent that they furthered the self-realisation of individuals. The citizen, for Green, was not simply the passive recipient of rights, but rather an active self-realising being. Green viewed all political concepts from this standpoint. Rights, obligations, property or free-dom were devices to allow individuals to realise their powers and abilities. These, and other themes, are explored in his *Lectures on the Principles of Political Obligation*. The nub of Green's optimistic vision of liberal politics was that of providing an ethical 'enabling and educative state' for all its active citizens.

It is instructive to compare Green's perspective with that of a late twentieth-cntury liberal of equal intellectual stature. Focusing on the later work of John Rawls, it is noticeable that the whole tone is altogether more pessimistic and negative. Rawls's main problem is not morality or freedom, *per se*, but rather containment of the effects of pluralism.[5] Citizenship has little moral resonance. The pluralism which Rawls focuses on is one where *reasonable* citizens, accepting the basic structures of a liberal democratic constitutional state, none the less diverge on questions of the good. Rawls thinks this divergence inevitable. Reason does not unify. He succinctly states his problem: 'How is it possible that there may exist over time a stable and just society of free and equal citizens profoundly divided by reasonable though incompatible religious, philosophical and moral doctrines?'[6] Rawls's rough answer to the problem of reasonable pluralism is that in 'practical political matter no general moral conception can provide a publicly recognized basis for a conception of justice in a modern democratic state'.[7] Instead of a *metaphysical* liberalism and/or some notion of the an overarching moral good, Rawls suggests *political* liberalism.

Political liberalism – and thus political citizenship – takes reasonable pluralism for granted. Its task is to work out a conception of justice for a constitutional democratic regime embodying reasonable pluralism. Rawls does not seek a new metaphysical or true foundation. Rather, the 'aim of political liberalism is to uncover the conditions of the possibility of a reasonable public basis of justification on fundamental political questions'.[8] The argument is recognisably transcendental. The need is to set forth the content of these 'conditions of possibility'. This is a constrained view of theory which 'indicates that the principles and ideals of the political conception are based on principles of practical reason in union with conceptions of society and person, themselves conceptions of practical reason. These conceptions specify the framework within which principles of practical reason are applied.'[9] The principles of political justice are, thus, the result of political constructivism, in which rational persons, subject to reasonable conditions, adopt principles to regulate the basic structure of society. Thus, 'when citizens share a reasonable political conception of justice, they have a basis on which public discussion of fundamental political questions can proceed and be reasonably decided'.[10] Within liberal democratic societies we assume citizens are free and equal. We also assume that they have capacities for reason and morality. The idea of citizens, conceived in this way, is an intuitive idea embedded in liberal public culture.[11]

In summary, the problem of liberalism, for Rawls, is reasonable pluralism. Citizens will disagree about metaphysical and moral issues. However, we can draw upon the 'conditions of possibility' of interaction within liberal democratic culture. These provide a minimal structure of principles, of practical reason, which supply a regulative political groundwork for cooperation, in effect, an overlapping consensus. Rawls's vision of liberal citizenship is thus minimalist, constrained, protective and negative. Like Richard Rorty, he envisions his own version of liberalism as one arising out of 'fear', explicitly using Judith Shklar's thesis to characterise his position. The political citizen, for Rawls, is thus a fearful being, aware that any substantive moral beliefs he or she may have will not be carried into the public sphere and thus seeking minimal conditions for cooperation. Possibly this might be more a reflection on America in the 1990s than a permanent reflection on liberal thought. Equally, Green's reflections may well bear closely upon Britain in the 1870s and 1880s. For Green, the problem liberalism faces is an overly restrictive conception of negative freedom and a limited notion of public duty. Liberalism is viewed as a progressive force reflecting, more than other forms of thought, a historical teleology of freedom. Whereas in Rawls citizenship is largely a negative and protective idea, concerned with the regulative conditions of possibility for any cooperation, Green's citizenship is a historical, optimistic, promotional and ethical device, designed to enhance and develop positive freedom. It is viewed essentially as the moral achievement of a civilised community.

– Green, Rawls and Luther –

Why does Rawls adopt this more pessimistic fearful reading of liberalism and citizenship? The answer to this lies in his account of the origin of pluralism. Rawls offers a brief historical sketch map of the problem. Essentially, he thinks that ancient Greek societies did not have our problem of political philosophy – namely pluralism. Ancient Greek religions were civic and collective; there was no sense to individualised salvation or interests. Even within later Greek thought, when philosophy became the exercise of free disciplined reason, reasoning took place largely within the civic domain of the polis.[12] For Rawls, Christianity, on the other hand, unlike the older civic religion, tended to be authoritarian and politically absolutist. It was often focused, in a potentially uncivic manner, on personal or individual salvation. It was not directly concerned with social or moral unity in the community. It was doctrinal and premised on the idea that people must believe the creedal structure. Priests played a key role as authoritative mediators with God. Finally, Christianity was an expansionist religion, recognising no territorial limits.

For Rawls, this conception of Christianity might have remained unproblematic but for one event. The Reformation added a crucial dimension to the monistic vision of late medieval Christianity. The authoritarian, doctrinal, expansionist aspects of Christianity essentially fragmented. Each Reformation sect now *knew* the truth. Believers were not in any doubt about the highest good, but, they were divided. Persecution was one obvious path to pursue. However, in many situations this was not practical, especially for religious minorities. For Rawls, this basic pluralism of belief created the need for political liberalism. Although many Christians were in despair over such a idea, Rawls adds that,

> to see reasonable pluralism as a disaster is to see the exercise of reason under conditions of freedom itself as a disaster. Indeed, the sources of liberal constitutionalism came as a discovery of a new social possibility: the possibility of a reasonably harmonious and stable pluralist society.[13]

Thus, Rawls remarks unequivocally 'the historical origin of political liberalism ... is the Reformation and its aftermath'.[14] Political liberalism, qua Shklar, is a response to the fears generated by wars of religion, following the Reformation.[15] For Rawls, religious civil war

> profoundly affect[s] the requirements of a workable conception of political justice: such a conception must allow for a diversity of doctrines and the plurality of conflicting, and indeed incommensurable, conceptions of the good affirmed by members of existing democratic societies.[16]

Religious civil war thus created the need for tolerance and tolerance created the ground for political liberalism, where citizens are treated in abstraction from their substantive notions of the good. For Rawls, 'the public conception of justice should be so far as possible, independent of controversial philosophical and religious doctrines ... the public conception of justice is to be political, not metaphysical'.[17]

Green also had trenchant views on the Reformation, although, unlike Rawls, his reading is notably more confident. Historical events which interested Green, such as the temporary flowering of the English Commonwealth, were viewed through the lens of the Reformation. Green's general conception of history can be summarised in the title of his early essay 'The Force of Circumstance'. He commented that the poignancy of the English civil wars was the 'tragic conflict between the creative will of man and the hidden wisdom of the world, which seems to thwart it' (*Works* III, 278). Green indicates that this 'hidden wisdom' or 'force of circumstance' is part of an underlying teleology. Despite the individuals creatively seeking certain ends, their actions could be transformed beyond recognition by the 'force of circumstances'. This is not a blind force. It also bears more than a passing resemblance to Hegel's doctrines of *Geist* and of 'the cunning of reason'.[18] History is made sense of through an underlying teleology. This teleology is clearly not strongly present in Rawls, although at the same time it is not totally absent.

For Green, rare individuals can grasp something of this teleology before its full development. Such individuals provide insights which create the tensions through which societies change and develop. It is within this somewhat (for present readers) *speculative* context that Green reviews the significance of the Reformation. Such events are part of a historical teleology. Like Rawls, Green notes that the Reformation 'opened a breach in the substantial unity of Christendom' (*Works* III, 279). Yet, despite its conflictual character, Green sees this as a positive event. The perspective, enunciated by figures like Luther, was Reason, in a religious representational form, breaking out of its established mould. Luther (and certain English Republicans) had gained a rare insight into a fundamental shift in human consciousness. As Green commented:

> The opposition between the inward and outward, between reason and authority, between the spirit and the flesh, between the individual and the world of settled right, no longer a mere antithesis of the schools, was being wrought into the political life of Christendom. It gives the true formula for expressing the nature of the conflict which issued in the English commonwealth.   (*Works* III, 281)

The true significance, for Green, of these events is that they are indicative of a qualitative change and development in human consciousness.

Yet, for Green, one problem with such potent ideas is that they can, over time, become stultified and solidified into dogmas and institutions. Thus, an idea which was creative and liberating can become sublimated into dogmatic rules or ordinances. For Green, this solidification process provided the context for both the Reformation and the English civil war. He contended, for example, that the established Anglican church under Archbishop Laud had emulated the Catholic church, before the Reformation, and become fixed into abstract dogma and creedal adherence. It became typical of what Green referred to as a 'religion of ordinance'. In this setting, the individual's actions were not judged by God or some higher standard of Reason, but rather by the ordinances of the church. For Green, Catholicism and Laudian Anglicanism consequently encouraged an asocial, rule-governed and otherworldly stance. In Catholicism, particularly, for Green,

> the creature of the Jesuits is no longer spontaneously loyal to the institutions under which he is born, nor yet has he, like the Puritan, a new law written on his conscience which he is to enact in society, but he has a transaction of his own to negotiate with a power wielding spiritual terrors. He may be either rake or devotee, but never a citizen.   (*Works* III, 283)[19]

Citizenship implies, for Green, an active reflective moral engagement. It is not just a legal status or habitual rule following.

Green's negative appraisal of Catholicism permeated both his personal and academic life. Writing, with disapproval and some uncharacteristic peevishness, to his student Henry Scott Holland in 1869, on the issue of Holland's entry into the ministry of the Church of England, Green makes some acid comments about a former student of his at Balliol – Gerard Manley Hopkins. Hopkins not only converted to Catholicism but also joined the Jesuit order. Green interpreted Manley Hopkins's move as irresponsible behaviour which avoided the duties of citizenship. Such practices as Catholic monasticism, he commented, let 'the muddy tide have its way, and merely picks up a few stones thrown on the shore which will take the saintly polish – not without satisfaction the tide should be as muddy as it is by way of contrast'. Catholicism creates a false contrast between the church and the secular world, God and humanity. For Green, religion should neither try to place itself above secular authorities, nor fix God's presence into symbolic sacraments. The only hope, for Green, is a consciousness which moves beyond this dualism, one which is 'laboriously thoughtful' and apprehends (what we call) God in the rational educated conscience of humanity. The aim of such an essentially Protestant philosophy would be 'Christian citizenship' and 'because not claiming to be special or exceptional or miraculous, will do more for mankind than its "Catholic" form, hampered by false antagonisms'.[20]

The above remarks about Catholicism, despite their archaic sound, were exactly Hegel's views and, oddly, they do have some philosophical resonances. Hegel mentions the issue in many of his major writings. In the *Phenomenology of Spirit*, for example, Catholicism is dealt with characteristically in the section 'Unhappy Consciousness'.[21] From his earliest writings, Hegel had been deeply concerned about the relation of religion to social and political life and the integration of human personality within the community. Catholicism, in making religion superstitious, created division and fragmentation. As he stated, 'The Christian religion … is the religion of freedom, though it must be admitted that this religion may become changed in character and perverted from freedom to bondage when infected with superstition.'[22] Catholic monasticism is taken as the most extreme version of superstition and 'unhappy consciousness'. The discipline of the flesh and the opposition to the ordinary business of the world creates continual dissatisfaction, something which can only be symbolically overcome in 'absolution'. God always remains as outside the individual and is only mediated through, what Hegel calls, the 'mummeries' of the priest. Yet, for Hegel, the absolution of Catholicism symbolically anticipates the complete rational reconciliation of God and man (or the universal and particular). Lutheran Protestantism, for Hegel, appears in the next section of the *Phenomenology* argument as the 'revealed religion' most adequate to the rational realisation, that is, before philosophical knowledge.

Reformation Protestantism, in its initial stages, for both Green and Hegel, entailed overcoming a religion of ordinance. Religion is internalised and individuated. The individual exercises their individual judgement. Scripture is no longer a source of ordinances, but rather an inspiration to personal morality. For Green, whereas Archbishop Laud had tried to turn the clock back to a religion of ordinance, the diverse Puritan sects had struggled for private judgement and conscience. Green noted here, with approval, that the Puritan, Thomas Vane, was titled by his contemporaries 'the man above ordinances'. Thus, beneath the events of the English civil war, deeper ideas were at work, deriving from the Reformation. However, Green's conclusion is that the civil war moved events too fast. The English Commonwealth was a projection of freedom beyond its time. This was the tragedy of the English Republicans. Despite the fact that the civil war obstructed the transition from feudalism to absolute monarchy, prevented a Catholic reaction and facilitated sectarian growth, none the less, it was, as Green put it, 'a spirit without a body, a force with no lasting means of action on the world around it. Even at the present day its office is to work under and through established usage and interest' (*Works* III, 327). This last sentence indicates that Green (like Rawls) viewed his own time as still developing the seeds of the Reformation. For Green, though, the ideals of the Reformation and Commonwealth were still to be realised *within* modern liberalism.

In summary, Rawls's argument is that political liberalism came about as a result of religious and metaphysical conflict generated by the Reformation. The Reformation is thus, *prima facie*, viewed in a basically negative manner; by fragmenting Christendom, it fragmented truth, and created fear of religious civil war and thus the need for political liberalism. Political liberalism is addressed, almost as a council of despair, to the problems created by the Reformation. Green's (and Hegel's) argument, however, is that the Christian religion had introduced a principle of individualism and freedom, which fragmented, particularly, the unified civic world of the Greeks. This Greek civic world could never be fully recovered, although it could be integrated into something more developed. The recovery of an integrated community, which embodies all the key components of individual autonomy (introduced initially in the Christian perspective), is the central aim of both Green and Hegel. However, Christianity in one sense reached its apogee in the Reformation. The Reformation introduced a new positive form of autonomous consciousness, present in the liberal Protestant citizen, which is, in fact, at the very metaphysical heart of both liberalism and the Christian perspective. Yet, that new principle had, in turn, become stultified into dogmas and often into new superstitions. The Reason implicit in these ideas had to break out of such dogmatic structures. Liberalism is therefore not just

the condition of possibility of cooperation, it is rather the substantive fulfilment of metaphysical and teleological themes present in embryo in the
Reformation and the Christian religion.

– HOW DIALECTICAL IS THY DWELLING PLACE? –

It is worth dwelling for a moment on the more complete theoretical account
as to why the Reformation was so significant for Green. In sum, it introduced
the idea of a new conception of the individual – the Christian citizen. The
underpinning for this Christian citizen (and the interpretation of the English
Commonwealth) lay in certain theological and metaphysical perspectives. In
Green's case, these perspectives owe a great deal to his studies in German
theology, specifically of the Hegelian doyen of the Tübingen school of
theology, Friedrich Christian Baur.

It is well documented that Green started to translate Baur's magisterial
work, *Geschichte der Christlichen Kirche*. Christianity, to Baur, was not a finished
product but rather a developing process. The key to Baur's analysis lay in a
distinction between the Pauline and Petrine Christianity. The latter, for Baur,
lay in the soil of a more primitive Judaeo-Christianity, characteristic of Peter
and James. It was concerned with apocalyptic events and Messiahship. Baur
maintains that the Petrine Christians were in continual conflict with the
Pauline over practices like circumcision, Jewish festivals and the like. St Paul,
on the other hand, represented a new principle of life, a universalism, wherein
the individual re-enacts Christ's struggle within his personal life. New
Testament texts, like the Acts of the Apostles, Mark and Luke, were seen as
ravaged by attempts at conciliation between the two sides. Romans, Galatians
and Corinthians were, however, revered by Baur as authentically Christian. St
John's Gospel, fixed a century after the death of Christ, was viewed as the
metaphysical summation of Christian thought.

Baur's concerns, to subject the New Testament to a thoroughgoing historical analysis and his obvious favouritism for St Paul, were directly echoed in
Green's thought. Green's 'Essay on Christian Dogma' also complained about
the fatal habit of identifying Christianity with dogma (*Works* III, 161–85).
St Paul and Luther, he thinks, had gone beyond dogma. The original
Christianity of St Paul took the form of what Green calls an 'immediacy' or
intuitive certainty (*Works* III, 164). The intuitive certainty, however, became
gradually solidified into dogma and ordinance. The present concern, Green
argued, was to transform all Christian dogma through philosophy. As he
noted, on the question of Christianity, 'Its first characteristic, as an intuition
become abstract, must vanish, that it may be assimilated by the reason as an
idea' (*Works* III, 182). Green, therefore, resolves Christ into an 'idea of reason'

which can be intelligibly articulated. Christ, the historical figure, must become Christ the *idea of morality and reason*, or as Green put it 'The thing as sensible, i.e. as presented in an individual moment of time and space, must become the thing known, i.e. as constituted by general attributes' (*Works* III, 183). This is a direct echo of Hegel who remarked that religion

> is the consciousness of absolute truth in the way that it occurs for all human beings. Thus it is found in the form of representation. Philosophy has the same content, the truth; it is the spirit of the world generally and not the particular spirit. Philosophy does nothing but transform our representations into concepts. The content remains always the same.[23]

Christ was a visible saviour to the disciples, to St Paul he was the Christ of the Gentiles, to the modern philosopher 'the idea itself is the reality'. Christ became the 'necessary determination of the eternal subject, the objectification by this subject of himself in the world of nature and humanity' (*Works* III, 183). Critical philosophy, therefore, has no truck with either pure intuitions or abstracted historical figures. Its concern is to articulate the point that 'God has died and been buried, and risen again, and realised himself in all the particulars of a moral life' (*Works* III, 184).

Green's notion of moral agency, which underpins his concept of political citizenship, is also intrinsically a theological and metaphysical conception. Citizenship, correctly understood, is a form of divine service. The true citizen is the 'Christed personality'. This is the major theme of his lay sermons 'The Word is Nigh Thee', 'The Witness of God' and 'Faith' (*Works* III). J. H. Muirhead maintained that Green's lay sermons contained in fact the whole of his philosophy in 'condensed form', but expressed with 'singular clearness and with a telling application'.[24] It is in these writings, specifically the latter two, that we find the Baur emphasis on the universalism of St Paul. For Green, St Paul expressed clearly the war between the 'law of the members' and the 'life of the spirit'.[25] This distinction parallels that made in the *Four Lectures of the English Commonwealth* between the 'religion of ordinance' and 'inward light' of the new Protestant subject. Green essentially tries to spell out the philosophical import of St Paul's writings. One of the root questions is – is St Paul a Christian? Green distinguishes two views of Christianity, and considers that St Paul is more concerned with the second. The first view is that which focuses on the objective historical existence of Christ, the ordinances of the churches and the testimonies of the synoptic gospels. The second is that which is concerned with the death and resurrection of Christ perpetually re-enacted in the moral life of each human being. St Paul, as Green put it, 'seemed to himself to die daily and rise again with Christ, and it was this moral and personal experience that gave reality in his eyes to the supposed historical events' (*Works* III, 258).

This is the central theme which Green takes from St Paul, via Baur, that Christ is the eternal act of God, perpetually re-enacted in individual human lives. As Green puts it, 'If Christ dies for all, all died in him' (*Works* III, 233). Christ 'dying in us' is another way of saying that we have developed a new intellectual consciousness, which transforms the will and action of the agent and this is the basis of a new moral life. Christ is what all humans are in potentiality (*Works* III, 174). The Christ figure is thus part of the eternal objectification of God in the world. This, for Green, is the root Christian idea. Religion becomes active morality. This is the substance to the radically free subject, the Christian citizen. The movement toward this subject is the energy which underpinned the Reformation and its aftermath.

Green thinks of this process as a form of incarnation. The incarnation of Christ *is* a moral idea implanted in the consciousness of the radically free subject. Christ, as an idea, in structuring the new intellectual consciousness, is the 'true good' of Green's moral theory, i.e. the 'good' which provides abiding satisfaction. He is the ideal object or ideal self which is striven for in self-realisation. Thus, we see some of the context of Green's metaphysical doctrine of the reproduction of the eternal consciousness within the individual consciousness. The Reformation (and English Commonwealth) are taken by Green as exemplars of the effects of the eternal consciousness – the dynamic of the force of circumstances – being realised in the moral action of figures like Luther, Vane and Cromwell.

Green's reading of these questions is obviously reliant upon the background of an Hegelian theology – although there are problems here which will be returned to. It is worth noting, for a moment, that at the close of the nineteenth century there were heated metaphysical and theological debates between Kantians and Hegelians. For Hegelians, as noted above, religion did not entail the death of philosophical thought. Doubts could not be sidestepped through faith or authority. Green's judgement on religion and metaphysics here, although ambivalent, went against much of the prevailing ethos of Kantianism. Religion *was* concerned with reason and in the final analysis, it was identified with the everyday activities of human beings. There was no absolute separation of religious and secular concerns, value and science. The kingdom of God was manifestly upon earth.

One of the central implications of the Kantian position on knowledge was to distinguish the spheres of theoretical from practical reason. This distinction, in Kant's hands, became immensely influential. Theoretical pure reason was demonstrable. The categories of thought, space, time, quality, quantity and causality, referred to the interrelation between finite things and objects. Such categories were valid for the physical sciences; however, for Kant, they were *not* appropriate in the sphere of religion. Human beings were finite and their cognition and reason were linked to their finiteness. Infinite categories, like God, morality and freedom, could not be demonstrated in finite terms. Ultimate reality and metaphysical knowledge are impossible and fatally riven by unresolvable conflict. Propositions about the real nature of things are distinct from propositions about appearances. As Kant observed in the Preface to the first edition of his *Critique of Pure Reason*, human reason

> has this peculiar fate that in one species of its knowledge it is burdened by questions which, as prescribed by the very nature of reason itself, it is not able to ignore, but which, as transcending all its powers, it is also not able to answer.[26]

This point, as is well known, effectively undermined the claims for natural theology.

If natural theology was thwarted, what was the basis for religious or moral claims? Kant suggested that the only way out of the impasse was through the postulate of practical reason. Humans, unlike animals, can assign themselves an unconditional imperative of duty. In performing acts of self-legislated unconditional duty, humans raise themselves practically above their finiteness. Yet, they could never *know* anything above the finite. Thus, religion was not destroyed by Kant; conversely, it appeared as an appendix to both moral philosophy and practical reason – the more sceptical appraisal would say that religion and morality were an afterthought. We can know nothing of God, miracles or revelation. However, we can act 'as if' God existed and was linked to our moral conduct. For the neo-Kantians, particularly, if knowledge was removed it made room for the possibility of faith. Religion was, in essence, the recognition of moral duties as divine commands.

The late nineteenth-century German philosopher, Hermann Lotze, was deeply affected by Kant's discussion of religion. Lotze was probably, at the time, the most revered and respected of the neo-Kantian writers, in both Britain and Germany. Green, Bradley and Bosanquet were all immensely impressed with his work. While at the University of Göttingen, from the mid-1860s onwards, Lotze had a profound influence on the young theologian Albrecht Ritschl. Significantly, Ritschl had originally been a disciple of Friedrich Christian Baur – Green's theological mentor. Ritschl subsequently transferred his allegiance from Hegelianism to a Lotzian-inspired neo-Kantianism. Kant's distinction between theoretical and practical reason became a central motif in Ritschl's theology and latterly that of his neo-Kantian disciples, Wilhelm Herrman, Theodor Haering and Adolf von Harnack. Ritschl thought that Christian theology and philosophy had to be purified from its metaphysical Hegelian accretions. His views subsequently became one of the more dominant theological preoccupations in Germany, and later the USA, till after the First World War.

For Ritschl, theology could not articulate the infinite or divine. Religion, as in Kant, was an appendix to the ethical personality. Ontology gave precedence to morality. Christianity could not therefore make any rational ontological statements concerning religion, but only comment upon practical value judgements. Christianity liberated human beings, through practical reason, from their passions and the determinacy of the natural world. In other words, we judged Christ by his ethical personality, as historically revealed. Christianity was thus intimately tied into ethical philosophy and value judgement. The philosophy of religion became an adjunct to moral philosophy.

The fact that Rawls work is so deeply rooted in neo-Kantian thought is certainly not unrelated to his judgement about the nature and role of metaphysics and theology and thus the problem of pluralism. Rawls is, in his own terms, a Kantian constructivist, although it is a much transformed Kantianism. It embodies a political constructivism rather than a moral constructivism.[27] Rawls's Kantianism is one without any sense of God, even as an afterthought; it has given up the supremely regulative role and overtly transcendental significance of autonomy; it has no interest in Kant's trans-cendental Idealism (there is also an absence of any overarching substantive values that can be constituted through autonomy); Rawls works with a considerably chastened, thinned down, view of reason, which has little or nothing of the optimism of the Enlightenment. Rawls's Kantian construc-tivism therefore lacks the will or ability to defend the overarching substantive significance and coherence of reason. Yet, despite Rawls's difference from Kant, he still none the less works in the same generic Kantian philosophical framework. He largely accepts the background Kantian assumptions con-cerning the limits to reason. Kantians, in effect, have all tended to be deeply uneasy with metaphysics. Rawls is one in a long philosophical tradition. Faith and reason are always rigorously separated. Metaphysical conflict is not some-thing to be resolved. It is always caught in antinomies. Forms of scientific reason come to the fore as the epitome of knowledge. Kantianism has thus become, for many, phenomenalism – a doctrine about the critical limitations of knowledge to sense perception and the natural sciences.

For Hegelian writers, however, these dualisms of reason and emotion, reason and value, fact and value, have always been regarded with deep suspicion. Such dualisms tried to salvage religion from the encroachments of natural science, but they did so at a cost – namely, relegating reason from the religious sphere. In this context, Rawls's judgements about metaphysical, theological, moral or comprehensive doctrines become more understandable. He is even that bit more pessimistic and sceptical about metaphysics than Kantians earlier this century. Further, his response to the Reformation (like

Green's own judgements) fits into a broader philosophical and metaphysical debate. Thus, the judgements that both thinkers made about the Reformation need to be placed into a much broader philosophical framework, and a deeper-rooted philosophical debate from the nineteenth century, to make complete sense. We should not be misled by the idea that Rawls's response to metaphysics is simply a way of coping with modern pluralism and multiculturalism. Rawls views multiculturalism and the like in the same manner as he views Reformation sectarianism; both exhibit a diversity of metaphysical positions which are unresolvable by Kantian reason.

– Metaphysics and Citizenship –

The argument now turns to a sharper analysis of metaphysics. It will be instructive to shift focus to the better known metaphysically orientated statements on moral theory in Green's *Prolegomena to Ethics* and then to compare these with the arguments in the lay sermons and Rawls's own views on metaphysics. This will demonstrate the point that moral action, for Green, can be fully articulated from both a theological and metaphysical standpoint. It will also reveal more clearly the depth of Rawls's ambivalence on metaphysical issues.

Green's argument begins with the fact that action originates in desire. This is not, however, merely 'felt desire'. The human being is distinct from animals on the basis of having 'conceived desires', i.e. they are grasped and understood self-consciously by the agent. The conceived desire is what Green calls a motive for action. Since the desire is conceived, it implies a something which does the conceiving, or something which, in Green's language, distinguishes itself from the desire. Presupposed within action, therefore, is the concept of the subject or agent, namely, that which distinguishes itself from the desire.

Green uses a similar transcendental argument in his discussions of knowledge and experience. In human action the subject places before itself objects which will satisfy the 'conceived desire'. The capacity to conceive desires and objects of satisfaction is, for Green, the will. The will is, thus, what Green calls (following Kant) 'free cause' or 'self-cause', namely, it is the capacity to choose to determine actions. Free will is, in this sense, a pleonasm. Human action is the result of will, will implies a motive and a motive implies a conceived desire. This conceived desire implies, in turn, a self-distinguishing subject – namely that which distinguishes itself from the desire. That which provides the satisfaction is a good. However, 'the good' is distinguished by Green from 'true good'. A true good is that which gives abiding or more complete satisfaction, which is, in effect, the more complete realisation of the capacities and potentialities of the self. Since the good is located in the realisation of the potentialities of the self any action to realise a good is a form of self-realisation, however incomplete that good may be. It follows, for Green, that the true good can be described as the most complete form of self-realisation.

For Green, therefore, human will, intellect, desire and moral agency imply, transcendentally, a unifying subject; however, they also imply an eternal subject. This is also the subject implied in the Greenian metaphysics of knowledge and nature.[28] This is the self-distinguishing eternal subject implied in human knowing and nature, which Green deals with in the first books of the *Prolegomena to Ethics*. Green's method, crudely stated, is to argue that knowledge of the world and nature does not explain the nature of knowledge. The producer precedes the product. Knowledge of the world, including time and space, exist for the self-conscious subject, since the concepts of space and time presuppose this subject. Psychological introspection will not tell us about the nature of knowledge, because it also presupposes the conscious subject. There can be no experience of the world antecedent to consciousness. Thus, Green maintains that pure sensationalism would be speechless. There may well be an external world, but it could not be external to the conscious subject. Paralleling Kant's transcendental unity of apperception, Green argues that the self, the subject, relates the phenomena of perception. The unity to this system of relations that we grasp in the world, and the fact that we communicate in detail about the world, implies, for Green, that over and above individuals as separate particulars – rather like discrete sensations for individual minds – there is logically implied a unifying eternal subject. The eternal consciousness, in Green, is analogous to an expanded individual mind. Knowledge of relations implies a combining agency. The eternal consciousness is the final transcendental unity of apperception.

Green is, however, frustratingly vague about this latter issue. It is also an issue which generated heated philosophical debates into the early part of the twentieth century. Many philosophers, initially the personal Idealists, objected to the unexplained move from individual subject to eternal subject. They claimed that there was a notable difference between the proposition that an external world could not exist without a cognising subject and the proposition that matter and mind are inseparable. The former is a kind of personal or subjective Idealism based ultimately upon Kantian epistemology, the latter is a form of inclusive Absolute Idealism. The latter entails the kind of move that Andrew Seth Pringle-Pattison criticised as the unwarranted jump from epistemology to metaphysics.[29] Whereas, the major problem for subjective Idealism is solipsism, the difficulties of 'spiritualism' or Absolute Idealism are legion. Absolute Idealism was accused of pantheism, the negation of the individual, avoiding the problem of evil and making nonsense of any distinctions between God and man, mind and nature, and God and nature. Green never really addressed these difficulties and elided the problems.

Thus, in summary, Green maintains that each individual subject ultimately implies an eternal subject or consciousness. Nature, as the object of possible experience, a connected order of knowable facts, also implies something which stretches before and after the individual. Individuals, as finite centres, do not hold together this total system of relations. Nature implies something other than itself, as the condition of its being what it is. Nature and knowledge thus imply, through their uniform system of relations, an eternal consciousness, a non-natural principle independent and not reducible to the relations for which it is a precondition. This is not a causal proof of God's existence but rather one based on sufficient reason, in the sense that a knowable world necessarily implies an eternal consciousness. This eternal consciousness, which underpins knowledge and nature, is the same as that which underpins history or the force of circumstances, also morality and social life. Even the quality of human character is underpinned by this same theme. Thus, moral action is 'the expression of man's character' (*PE*, 120). Character is a quality of the self which is implied in action, in that the self presents to itself objects which provide satisfaction. Abiding or more complete satisfaction is found in the true good of the possible self, which is the Christed self. True ethical character is therefore the ideal Christed self incarnated in the everyday moral life of the citizen. Citizenship is thus at the same moment *both* political and metaphysical. The two terms are inseparable.

Given Rawls's neo-Kantianism (as discussed earlier) it is not surprising that he should express disquiet with the metaphysical conception of justice and citizenship. For Rawls, Green would be part of a metaphysical tradition, including Plato, Aristotle, Augustine, Aquinas and, more recently, embracing J. S. Mill, and even Ronald Dworkin and Joseph Raz. This tradition is committed to a rational monistic good. Such theories also tend to be teleological. Institutions are thus just in so far as they promote this good. Rawls sees this as the dominant tradition in moral philosophy. In response, he adopts a form of modified Kantian constructivism, trying to avoid the question of metaphysical truth in order to accommodate pluralism. Political citizenship is thus premised upon 'intuitive ideas that are embedded in the political institutions of a constitutional democratic regime'. The religious or metaphysical loyalties which citizens regard as central to their identity, are part of what Rawls calls our 'non-public identity'. They may shape our lives, but humans can convert. The non-public identity then changes, but the public (or political) identity remains. Citizens in democratic societies think of themselves in a particular way, they do not have to invent it. It is a *condition* of their activity. They regard themselves as being able to take responsibility for their lives. These ideas are all embedded in political liberalism. One can accept these notions without necessarily being committed to any comprehensive metaphysical liberalism. Thus, the core of Rawls's argument is that metaphysics is not a good ground for unifying society – 'philosophy as the search for truth about an independent metaphysical and moral order cannot, I believe, provide a workable and shared basis for a political conception of justice'. Unless one accepts political citizenship and justice, the only alternative is the coercive state power – a rather far-fetched notion, given that political liberalism has never been realised.[30]

Rawls does though have a problem here. The distinction between politics and metaphysics is central. Yet, he openly admits that there is no commonly accepted understanding of metaphysics. He also agrees that one could unwittingly presuppose a metaphysics. He comments that 'it is not enough simply to disavow reliance upon metaphysical doctrines, for despite one's intent they may still be involved'. He continues that, 'To rebut claims of this nature requires discussing them in detail and showing that they have no foothold.' This is a fairly significant charge, but Rawls concludes, 'I cannot do that here.'[31]

Despite the above avowal, Rawls does attempt an answer of sorts in a footnote. He is prepared to admit that there may be a deep-rooted latent metaphysical belief in his view of liberalism and citizenship. For example, to try to categorically do without a metaphysical doctrine may be to presuppose one. Rawls also suggests that the conception of persons, as the basic units of deliberation and responsibility, may presuppose certain metaphysical ideas about persons. Rawls remarks, 'I should not want to deny these claims.' None the less, he still insists that, as regards political liberalism, 'no particular metaphysical doctrines about the nature of persons, distinctive and opposed to other metaphysical doctrines, appears among its premises or seems required by its argument'. He continues,

> If metaphysical presuppositions are involved, perhaps they are so general that they would not distinguish between the metaphysical views – Cartesian, Leibnizian, or Kantian; realist, idealist or materialist – with which philosophy has traditionally been concerned. In this case they would not appear to be relevant for the structure and content of a political conception of justice one way or the other.[32]

This is a fairly tangled series of claims and there is something rather disingenuous in Rawls's statements. First, Rawls admits that there is no common understanding of metaphysics. It is also not at all clear what Rawls himself means by it, although it looks like a more generic Kantian mistrust. The term metaphysics seems, in fact, gradually less in evidence as Rawls has developed his ideas on political liberalism; maybe this is not wholly fortuitous. The sheer vagary of Rawls's remarks here is potentially damaging, given the centrality of the metaphysics/politics distinction. Second, Rawls does hint at some meanings to the term. It can imply any fundamental assumption we make, almost in the Collingwoodian sense of an absolute presupposition. Absolute presuppositions arise where no conception of truth or falsity is involved, rather, they are absolutely presupposed and no prior questions arise concerning them. Thus, to deny metaphysics absolutely is, paradoxically, to affirm metaphysics. Third, Rawls suggests that conceptions of the 'rational person' might be considered metaphysical in character. This is a more substantive absolute presupposition. Rawls oddly does not deny the possibility of the second and third ideas. Yet, he also contends that his theory does not consciously pursue any metaphysical thesis. Further, if there are metaphysical themes in his work (which he admits is possible), they are so general as to be irrelevant to his theory. How one reconciles these points is left in the air.

Rawls's answers here are clearly unsatisfactory. Because metaphysical ideas are not articulated by a thinker does not lessen the significant point that there are metaphysical premises. This 'inner citadel' of the argument is often its most significant aspect. In fact, Rawls, unexpectedly, admits that there *is* such a metaphysical premise to his political liberalism, but, it remains unarticulated. Rawls, thus, says it is irrelevant. This is surely a *non sequitur*? Why does deeprooted and unarticulated entail irrelevance? Rawls assures his readers that the political notion of the rational person (and citizen), and the assumptions we make about the moral powers of that person, are already deeply embedded in the public reason and public culture of liberal democratic societies. This might be seen as the lurking communitarian thesis in Rawls's argument. Yet, the fact that he assumes persons are like this *and* that he assumes such ideas are embedded, we are to believe, has nothing to do with metaphysics. His contention appears to be that he is offering an empirical account of what is the case. Yet, clearly, there is nothing remotely empirical about such claims about persons. As T. H. Green put it, with tongue in cheek, 'It is not those … who cry "Lord, Lord!" the loudest, that enter the kingdom of heaven, nor does the strongest assertion of our dependence on experience imply a true insight into its nature' (*Works* I, 291). Rather, we might redescribe Rawls's ideas as plausible metaphysical assumptions about human beings and their relation to society. Metaphysics is not about blind prejudice, it rather refers to the most deep-rooted, yet often quite reasonable presuppositions we make about the character of our reality.

Rawls's difficulties with metaphysics (particularly any notion that a liberal society or liberal citizenship could be based upon metaphysics) are not only due to his incipient Kantianism. As part of a powerful generation of post-1945 American intellectuals, Rawls would have been subject, directly and indirectly, to a range of intellectual pressures. In political science the hegemonic theories during this period were neo-behaviourism, elite theories, pluralism and neo-pluralism, forms of Marxism, rational choice and economistic accounts; all tended to treat politics in an instrumental empirical manner. Metaphysics and moral argument were viewed with deep scepticism, if not outright hostility. David Easton, the doyen of political scientists during the 1950s, tended to view traditional metaphysical political theory as simply parasitic, feeding on past ideas and retailing antiquarian information about past values. In fact, such metaphysical theory was of little use at all. Herbert Simon, in the same period, bewailed that

> there will be no progress in political philosophy if we continue to think and write in the loose, literary, metaphysical style ... The standard of rigour that is tolerated in political theory would not receive a passing grade in an elementary course in logic.[33]

This perspective was still prevalent in the 1960s judgement of David Easton, that in political science

> The factual aspect of a proposition refers to a part of reality; hence it can be tested by reference to the facts. In this way we check its truth. The moral aspect of a proposition, however, expresses only the emotional response of an individual ... Although we can say that the aspect of a proposition referring to a fact can be true or false, it is meaningless to characterize the value aspect of a proposition in this way.[34]

Empirical facts had to be kept rigidly apart from 'woolly metaphysical values'. It is no surprise therefore that voting behaviour, economic rational choice theory, the exercise of power and the like, took on the alluring shape of the natural world – empirical facts to be described and studied.

In mainstream philosophy, also, the incipient Kantian mistrust of metaphysics was unwittingly supported, not only by the early twentieth-century waves of denunciation in empiricism, naturalism and realism, but closer to the 1950s and 1960s, in the strictures of logical positivism, linguistic philosophy and analytic philosophy in general. Ordinary language philosophy and Wittgensteinianism were as suspicious of metaphysics as logical positivism. As G. J. Warnock commented in 1969 'there are no doubt in "our climate of thought" many factors ... that are in some way unfriendly to the metaphysical temperament'. For Warnock, one key reason for this unfriendliness is that 'metaphysical speculation has often arisen from, and often too been a substitute for, religious or theological doctrine'.[35] Some philosophers, like Strawson, in the 1970s, did try to modify the understanding of metaphysics, but the basic enmity has remained an undercurrent, even to the present day in some quarters.[36] Rawls, coming from the hybrid stable of politics and philosophy, could not help but have reflected this general intellectual disquiet with metaphysics. Perhaps the fact that he assumes that many of his readership will share that same disquiet, that he, almost symbolically, distances 'political' from 'metaphysical' liberalism and also believes that he does not really have to explain what he means by metaphysics. Metaphysics is simply wrong-headed. Yet, viewing metaphysics in a longer-term philosophical framework, it is clear that there is nothing intrinsically that rules it out of court, except an overzealous and uncritical adherence to a particular, if dominant, intellectual and philosophical tradition, in Rawls's case neo-Kantianism.

_ THE PROTESTANT STATE AND AUTONOMOUS _ CITIZENS

Any notion that we have of the citizen inevitably develops against the background of notions of human nature, the community, priority of values, and the conceptions of human powers and capacities. If we backtrack for a moment here and recall that, for Green, the 'ideals of the possible self' are derived from or communicated to the individual from the earliest age through the complex institutions of social life, we touch upon the heart of Green's political philosophy. The 'Witness of God' sermon demonstrates this view. When Green asks how the Christed life may be attained, his answer is deceptively simple. It is attained within the limitations of our everyday life in the community, if we, with honesty and sincerity try to follow certain very familiar communal moral ideals; as he puts it: 'in the self-denying love which we have known from the cradle, in the moralising influences of civil life ... here God's sunshine is shed abroad' (*Works* III, 248). Green in both the sermon of 'Faith' and the 'Witness of God' sums this up as Christian citizenship. Society is part of an unfolding of Reason in the world. We thus come into a world embodying Reason. To Green, the individual must overcome the pure familiarity of the ordinary institutions in order to apprehend the indwelling Reason of the world.

When the individual consciously internalises the communal norms, from the family, neighbourhood and state, in his or her willing, he or she adopts an ideal self as his or her own. The norms, as the constituents of his or her will, structure his or her action. This is the citizen for Green, namely, one who acts autonomously and rationally, who perceives the common good and who has internalised the fundamental communal norms. This is the citizen possessing character and a qualitatively developed consciousness. Since these norms relate to the incarnated Christ the citizen is better described as a Christian citizen. The political citizen is intrinsically a metaphysical category.

Yet, it is important to note that Green's metaphysics claims, at root, to be an understanding of our everyday consciousness – where we are in the world. It is not an abstracted invention or some perfected ideal to aspire to. It claims to be rather a systematic unpacking of what we already know. Metaphysical analysis makes explicit what is implicit in our conduct. The ideas embedded within our conduct are the result of long-standing traditions. Green's view that ideas of individualism, personal ethical development and human freedom, bear a strong conceptual relation to embryonic themes in the Reformation, is thus not as far-fetched as it might initially sound. Indeed, Rawls also, oddly, uses a similar claim for different purposes.

The problem for the Idealist argument here is that 'what we know' or 'where we are' in contemporary liberal societies is now extremely diverse – multicultural. Does the Idealist metaphysical account match what we know in present-day societies (as opposed to late Victorian and Edwardian society)? There are late twentieth-century problems which Green did not really anticipate and Rawls feels he has to deal with. The divisiveness of class, cultural and gendered politics, the increasing impersonality and power of the state, the growing power and influence of the natural sciences, the detailed observations on human irrationality, the complex and unpredictable character of market capitalism and the decline of religion. Green touches upon the margins of many of these issues. However, as a historical thinker we could hardly expect him to be *fully* aware of such issues. If Green were alive today and believed in the same basic philosophy he would presumably try to account for the present developments within his historical teleology. How he would do that remains unknown. However, if we just focus on citizenship and the state, Green's conception of the state as committed to providing the conditions for the best life for its citizens – even if that 'best life' looks more complex and problematic – is still a relevant metaphysical commitment. Further, the tremendous potency of the idea of individual freedom within modernity (which Green saw as a key metaphysical theme arising from the Reformation period) is certainly not absent from contemporary politics. If anything it has become even more potent, global and unpredictable. The paradox of the relation between Green and Rawls lies in this theme. Both thinkers see the notion of individual autonomy, manifest in the Reformation, giving rise to the problem of modernity and liberalism. But, whereas Rawls focuses on the problematic consequence of this autonomy – substantive metaphysical pluralism – Green (like Hegel) sees the autonomy *itself* as a metaphysical idea with an unpredictable teleology, but, none the less an idea which provides a singular metaphysical ground to pluralism.

Another criticism which could be offered here against Green, is that either his theory of citizenship has become so metaphysical that it loses all track of ordinary notions of political life, or, on the other count, that these metaphysical ideas have become so secularised that we might as well ignore the religious dimension, since it is simply a window dressing to a secularist philosophy. It was often a puzzle to Green's contemporaries whether or not he could really be classed as a genuinely religious. The same issue arises with Hegel. Although this essay may seem to have emphasised the religious and metaphysical aspect, there is a good reason for this. The religious conscience and the Christed self, correctly understood, are neither wholly separate from the political realm, nor from the philosophical grasp of the world. It might be thought, from what has been argued, that the religious and metaphysical side of Green's thought is uppermost. Far from it; rather the correct articulation of religion necessarily expresses the sense of politics and philosophy. As Hegel put it, 'the new religion expresses itself precisely as a new consciousness, the consciousness of a reconciliation of humanity with God ... The souls and heart [of individuals] are reconciled with God, and thus it is God who rules in their hearts.'[37] The unifying theme can be articulated through Hegel's notion of the 'Protestant State'. Hegel's idea of the Protestant state embodies the free subject, which provides the unifying theme for religion, morality, politics and philosophy. They all have the same metaphysical substance. It is quite clear, from Green's historical and theological writings, that he believed the Protestant principle of freedom is a qualitative advance on Catholicism. Green may well have been partly reflecting a wider cultural perception of Catholicism in nineteenth-century Britain.[38] It is also clear that, for him, the ideas implicit in the Reformation have not finished. The 'Christian citizen' is essentially Hegel's free subject in the Protestant state and (for Green) the citizen of progressive liberalism in the 1880s.

One of the better expositions of Hegel's argument is section 552 in the *Philosophy of Mind*.[39] He argues that the division between church and state is an unacceptable abstraction. Rather, he maintains that the 'moral life is the state retracted into its inner heart ... while the state is the organisation and actualisation of moral life; ... religion is the very substance of the moral life and of the state.' He continues that

> if the truly moral life is to be a sequel of religion then perforce religion must have the genuine content ... The ethical life is the divine spirit as indwelling in self-consciousness, as it is actually present in a nation and its individual members.[40]

The separation between religion and morality, morality and politics, and hence religion and politics is overcome in the free subject, the 'thinking ethical life'. Hegel, as mentioned earlier, is equally critical of Catholicism which separates religion and politics and externalises God, as well as an ignorant Protestantism which is not prepared to think deeply through its own faith. Philosophy, this laborious thinking process, embodies the truth of religion. The holiness of an external God becomes rationalised into an actual moral life of duty, essentially into *Sittlichkeit* (ethical life). The divine inter-penetrates the secular. The individual citizen is no longer opposed to God or the state as object (subject to object), rather the citizen recognises that God is his or her freedom, and in Green's terms, ideal or possible self, a freedom and ideal embodied in the integuments of communal life. The personality and freedom of the individual become concretised. Hegel saw previous cultures, like the Greek and Roman worlds, in a teleological framework, embodying filaments of the free subject. But, it is only in the gradual and tortured development of Christianity that the free subject becomes fully manifest. For Hegel, the synthesis which Christianity presents is that man's 'truth and reality is free-mind itself, and it comes into existence in his self-consciousness'.[41] Hegel was deeply suspicious of any attempt to found religion outside the communal ethical order. Only the Christian order, which sees the person as the embodiment of Absolute being, could, in its political realm, give actuality to the free subject. As Hegel put it:

> Self-realising subjectivity is in this case absolutely identical with substantial uni-versality. Hence, religion as such, and the state as such – both as forms in which the principle exists – each contain the absolute truth; so that the truth, in its philosophic phase, is after all only in one of its forms.[42]

The religious and secular worlds do not lose their independent identities, but rather they are the same, as seen from different perspectives in a scale of comprehensiveness. To put this in Green's terminology: the Christed self and metaphysical eternal subject are, at the same moment, the true common good of the citizen and the principle of individual moral agency. Green's Christian citizen is Hegel's free subject. Green thus wholeheartedly agreed with Hegel's view that 'In the Protestant state, the constitution and the code ... embody the principle and the development of the moral life, which proceeds from the truth of religion.'[43] Hegel was more confident than Green that the Protestant state had become actualised in the world. Green showed considerably more reticence on this latter point, nevertheless, he still held to the same essential view that a new notion of freedom or autonomy had arisen from Reform-ation Christianity. It was still very much part of our culture and it had unpredictable consequences for humanity. Pluralism, for example, is ironically a consequence of that autonomy. This is the central metaphysical dilemma for humanity.

– CONCLUSION –

The problem for the contemporary reader of Green is that the language of the 'protestant state' and 'Christian citizen' appears remote and anachronistic.

There is some truth to this point, although it is important to realise that this is not an argument against a metaphysical reading of citizenship or liberalism. In fact, what has been revealed, in the comparisons between Rawls and Green, is that there are much deeper intellectual, philosophical and cultural roots to each thinker than normally appreciated. In another 100 years, Rawls's language may well appear as anachronistic as Green's, although many of the problems he addressed will still be relevant. We need a little more historical humility here. One can, therefore, read the comparison between Green and Rawls as an aspect of a broader and long-running metaphysical debate between Kantianism and Hegelianism.

For Rawls, the central problem for political philosophy is a pluralism of unresolvable metaphysical beliefs, thus 'we turn to political philosophy when our shared understandings ... break down'. The task of political philosophy is Kantian, namely, to 'examine whether some underlying basis of agreement can be uncovered and a mutually acceptable way of resolving these questions publicly established'.[44] This argument occasionally drifts into something that looks like communitarianism. For Green, the central problem of political and moral philosophy is to analyse human conduct, expose human motives 'the spiritual endowments implied in it, the history of thought, habits and institutions through which it has come to be what it is' (PE, 394). The function of the philosopher is to understand the historical development of the ideas.

Green does offer a notion of comprehensive unity premised upon a historical development of ideas, although it is an equivocal unity. Despite appearances, it is not a comforting unity. In our present world, affected by claims of postmodern fragmentation, distinct forms of life, strong ethnic or national difference and multicultural theory, and the like, Green's vision could look remote on one level. But, on the one hand, it is important to realise that Green's vision does not ignore group difference or individual autonomy. Yet, on the other hand, neither does it celebrate difference in itself. It rather argues that this fragmentation is the *result* of modernity, but modernity also embodies historical and metaphysical teleological themes. The task of the philosopher is not so much to recommend where we might go, as to show us how we arrived at where we are and what is implicit in our present. This might also provide some pointers to where we go next. Green's arguments on citizenship show the deep-rooted metaphysical themes implicit within our political understanding and the practices of citizenship. He tries to show us the forms of thought which accompany such practices as citizenship. In this sense citizenship is unavoidably both political and metaphysical.

– Notes –

The following abbreviations are used in the text for Green's writings:

Works I   *Works of T. H. Green Volume I*, ed., R. L. Nettleship (London, Longmans, Green, and Co., 1885)

Works II   *Works of T. H. Green Volume II*, ed., R. L. Nettleship (London, Longmans, Green, and Co., 1886)

Works III *Works of T. H. Green Volume III*, ed., R. L. Nettleship (London, Longmans, Green, and Co., 1888)

PE   *Prologomena to Ethics* (Oxford, Clarendon Press, 1907)

1. In the case of Green this might be seen as contentious. However, I would suggest that Green, minimally, was concerned that the state should take a more active, interventionary role in providing the conditions for the 'best life' for its citizens. This entails that he was minimally concerned with the state as a welfare institution of a certain type. The extent of his welfare interest is a matter of scholarly debate.

2. Green's collected works have been recently republished, with some additional scholarly materials, by Thoemmes Press in five volumes (1997), edited by Peter Nicholson. My own work over the last two decades references the older Nettleship edition. The new reprint does not alter the texts of the earlier edition, but rather adds materials.

3. Collingwood, *Autobiography* (Oxford, Clarendon Press, 1970), 15–17.

4. Toynbee died in 1883. Mrs Humphry Ward was also an intense admirer of T. H. Green and founded the settlement in the context of Green's thought; see Mrs H. Ward, *A Writers Recollections 1856–1900* (London, Collins, 1918). Her novel *Robert Elsemere* (1888) exemplified the same concerns and focus. T. H. Green appears, thinly disguised, as the fictional Professor Grey in the novel; see Andrew Vincent and Raymond Plant, *Philosophy Politics and Citizenship: the Life and Thought of the British Idealists* (Oxford, Blackwell, 1984), ch. 7.

5. There are two stark dimensions to this problem of pluralism, which might be called radical and reasonable pluralism. The first concerns extremes of difference. The second concerns reasonable difference which can be negotiated through reason. Some postmodern writers are exercised by the first form of difference. For W. E. Connolly, for example, a postmodern position rejects *all* closure. Connolly celebrates strong identities and difference. Where liberals try to shield society from strong identities, Connolly wants a future society to encompass them; see W. E. Connolly, *Identity/Difference: Democratic Negotiations of Political Paradox* (Cornell University Press, 1991), 29. Rawls is only concerned with the reasonable pluralism.

6. John Rawls, *Political Liberalism* (New York, Columbia University Press, 1993), xviii.

7. John Rawls, 'Justice as Fairness: Political not Metaphysical', in Tracy B. Strong (ed.), *The Self and the Political Order* (Oxford, Blackwell, 1992), 96.

8. Rawls, *Political Liberalism*, xix.

9. Rawls, *Political Liberalism*, xx.

10. Rawls, *Political Liberalism*, xxi.

11. Rawls, 'Political not Metaphysical', 104.

12. Rawls, *Political Liberalism*, xxi–xxii.

13. Rawls, *Political Liberalism*, xxiv–xxv.

14. Rawls, *Political Liberalism*, xxiv. Charles Larmore also, for example, comments on political liberalism in similar terms on the origins of liberalism. 'Political Liberalism', *Political Theory*, vol. 18, no. 3 (1990), 339.

15. See Judith Shklar, *Ordinary Vices* (Cambridge, MA, and London, Belknap Press of the Harvard University Press, 1984).
16. Rawls, 'Political not Metaphysical', 96. The historical origins of this in liberal theory 'is the Reformation and its consequences. Until the Wars of Religion in the sixteenth and seventeenth centuries, the fair terms of social cooperation were narrowly drawn ... one of the historical roots of liberalism was the development of various doctrines urging religious toleration.' Rawls, 'Political not Metaphysical', 115.
17. Rawls, 'Political not Metaphysical', 95.
18. See G. W. F. Hegel, *Logic: Part One of the Encyclopaedia of the Philosophical Science*, translated by William Wallace (Oxford, Clarendon Press, 1975), section 209, 272–3.
19. Green continues that the Romance nations of Southern Europe have been particularly subject to this kind of caprice since they lack 'the spiritual completeness of the Teutonic' (*Works* III, 283).
20. S. Paget (ed.), *Henry Scott Holland: Memoir and Letters* (London, John Murray, 1921), 30–2. This latter work now appears in volume 5 of the Nicholson edition of the *Collected Works of T. H. Green* (1998), 426ff.
21. G. W. F. Hegel, *Phenomenology of Spirit*, translated by A. V. Miller (Oxford, Clarendon Press, 1979), 136–8.
22. G. W. F. Hegel, *The Philosophy of Right*, translated by T. M. Knox (Oxford, Clarendon Press, 1971), para. 269, addition 161, 284.
23. G. W. F. Hegel, *Lectures on the Philosophy of Religion*, in one volume (Berkeley and London, University of California Press, 1988), 78.
24. J. H. Muirhead, *Reflections by a Journeyman in Philosophy*, ed., J. W. Harvey (London, George Allen and Unwin, 1942), 42.
25. For Green, however, even St Paul had also become dogmatised.
26. I. Kant, *Critique of Pure Reason*, trans. N. Kemp Smith (London, Macmillan, 1933), A vii.
27. Rawls, *Political Liberalism*, 99ff.
28. It is quite obvious to the close reader of Green that he is essentially a religious philosopher. As he confessed to Scott Holland in a personal letter, his philosophical conclusions overall were 'the inevitable result of thinking together God, the world, and the history of man', Green quoted in Paget (ed.), *Scott Holland*, 65–6; see also the Nicholson edition of the *Collected Works*, vol. 5, 441–3.
29. Andrew Seth Pringle-Pattison, *Hegelianism and Personality* (Edinburgh and London, William Blackwood, 1887).
30. Rawls, 'Political not Metaphysical', 109–12 and 101.
31. Rawls, *Political Liberalism*, 29.
32. Rawls, *Political Liberalism*, 29, n. 31.
33. Herbert Simon, 'The Development of the Theory of Democratic Administration: Replies and Comments', *American Political Science Review*, 46 (1952), 494–6.
34. David Easton, *The Political System* (New York, Alfred Knopf, 1967), 221.
35. G. J. Warnock, *English Philosophy Since 1900* (Oxford, Oxford University Press, 1969), 96.
36. See P. F. Strawson, *Individuals: An Essay in Descriptive Metaphysics* (London, Methuen, 1974). As one commentator sensibly noted the 'contrast between speculative and critical philosophy, or if we prefer between metaphysics and analysis, is overdrawn. One can perhaps occupy oneself with problems of analysis without beating a metaphysical drum, or at least without beating one very loudly; but there is no clear dividing line between the two activities, for metaphysicians necessarily engage in analysis, whilst analytic philosophers tend to make covert metaphysical assumptions. Things might be different if metaphysical

neutralism were really defensible, but despite the fact that it had the support of Austin as well as Wittgenstein I cannot see that it is. The principle that if you once scratch an analyst you find a metaphysician underneath has been proved true many times in the past … and I see no reason why it should not apply to the present and the future too.' W. H. Walsh, *Metaphysics* (London, Hutchinson, 1966), 194–5.

37. Hegel, *Lectures on the Philosophy of Religion*, 459.

38. Anti-Catholic sentiment is something that Linda Colley, for example, sees as a defining aspect of British nationalism in the eighteenth and nineteenth centuries. See Colley, 'Britishness and Otherness: An Argument', in *Journal of British Studies* 31 (1992), 316, 319, 321.

39. Hegel, *Philosophy of Mind: Part Three of the Encyclopaedia of the Philosophical Sciences*, translated by William Wallace and A. V. Miller (Oxford, Clarendon Press, 1971), section 552, 282–91.

40. Hegel, *Philosophy of Mind*, 283.

41. Hegel, *Philosophy of Mind*, 289.

42. Hegel, *Philosophy of Mind*, 290–1.

43. Hegel, *Philosophy of Mind*, 291.

44. Rawls, 'Political not Metaphysical', 97.

CHAPTER 2

F. H. Bradley:
Ethical Idealism and Hedonism

In the 1870s there was an episode in British philosophy which still has underlying substantive resonances for contemporary moral and political philosophy – particularly to current debates between universalism and particularism in morals. Two philosophers were working simultaneously on treatises on ethics. Both treatises were influential on twentieth-century moral philosophy. The first of these to be published was Henry Sidgwick's *Methods of Ethics*, in December 1874 (the same year as the publication of T. H. Green's famous introduction to Hume and also William Wallace's edition of Hegel's *Encyclopaedic Logic*). The second was F. H. Bradley's *Ethical Studies*, published in 1876.[1]

Sidgwick's book went initially from strength to strength, up to the new century, selling well over a thousand copies for each edition. It reached its seventh edition in 1907, after Sidgwick's death. Bradley's book, however, after a limited run, went out of print soon after its first publication in 1876. This, in itself, was strange, since for a generation of British Idealist philosophers up to the early 1900s, it remained a locus classicus text of Idealist moral philosophy. *Ethical Studies* stayed out of print until the 1920s. Bradley began to make notes in early 1924 (which he did not complete) towards a second edition. He died in September 1924. The second edition of *Ethical Studies* appeared posthumously in 1927.[2] After the late 1920s, Bradley's work again fell into relative obscurity. By the time of the 1962 reprint of *ES*, he was probably better known as a dated metaphysician, and, in ethics, through the encrusted conservative caricature of 'My Station and its Duties'. Sidgwick's *ME* also fell into relative obscurity, although in the 1960s and 1970s, his reputation, as a sophisticated analytically-minded, utilitarian-inclined, moral philosopher, picked up again, specifically for the Rawlsian generation.[3] Since the 1970s, there has been a rediscovery of Sidgwick in certain contemporary utilitarians. Robert Goodin, for example, in recently formulating his own conception of utilitarianism as a public philosophy (rather than a doctrine of private conduct or private ideals), explicitly cites Sidgwick's 'public' approach as one which was unfortunately occluded in much twentieth-century utilitarian thought.[4]

Since the late 1980s Bradley studies have also gone though a slow renaissance – although mainly focusing on the metaphysical and logical writings. This renewed interest has been due to a combination of factors. The focus on Bradley's ethical philosophy has developed in the context of a more general revival of interest in British Idealist thought and its subtle and complex relation to contemporary movements in communitarian moral and political philosophy. To some extent, it is helpful for the new reader of Bradley's ethical writings to view his thought, initially, in a similar context to recent communitarian writing, although there are subtle and unmistakable differences. Further, Bradley's logical and metaphysical work has continued to be seen as a positive challenge by certain analytically-inclined philosophers.

From Bradley's own comments, it appears that *ES* was well on the way to being finished when Sidgwick's *ME* was published. Bradley's aim in *ES* was to criticise determinism, hedonism, Kantianism, egoism, utilitarianism and the foundational empiricism at the root of these. According to Bradley, one of the more famous essays within *ES* – 'Pleasure for Pleasure's Sake' – was already completed when Sidgwick's *ME* appeared in print. Bradley, however, added a note to the end of the above essay, remarking that it was the immediate philosophical reputation of *ME* which called forth some response. Bradley's note, though fairly cursory, contended that Sidgwick 'had left the question [of Hedonism] exactly where he had found it', although as one recent commentator remarks on this, Bradley's note 'suggests that [he] had not had time to study his opponent's book very carefully' (*SE*, 392). The target for Bradley's original critique, in the above essay, was Mill's utilitarianism, although the 'generic empiricist mentality' was also under close scrutiny.[5]

Sidgwick does not refer to Bradley in his letters or *Memoir* – although there are illuminating asides on both Hegelianism and Green. Bradley, also, does not mention the debate much in any biographical sense.[6] The apparent silence obscures the ascerbic relation between the two thinkers. Although never reaching anywhere near the heights of invective of the Ruskin/Whistler interchange, Bradley's and Sidgwick's Victorian disputation has all the qualities of finely honed academic viciousness. Schneewind remarks – in what many appear to agree is the most comprehensive text on Sidgwick's moral philosophy – that Bradley's work (particularly his pamphlet) on Sidgwick 'is the major effort of the Idealist school to come to grips with hedonism and consequentialism in their recent form … it is the only sustained criticism of the *Methods* by a thoroughly unsympathetic opponent in Sidgwick's lifetime'

(*SE*, 392).

– REVIEWS AND RESPONSES –

Sidgwick reviewed Bradley's *ES* in *Mind* in 1876, noting the comments written on him in the appendix to Essay III in *ES*. Bradley was stung enough to immediately respond, in the same year in *Mind*, to Sidgwick's critical notice. Sidgwick, not to be outdone, immediately replied to Bradley's response. Bradley then followed this with a pamphlet critique in 1877. Sidgwick, in redrafting his 2nd edition of *ME*, changed some passages, presumably in response to Bradley's objections, although it is not explicit. He waited, it appears, until the pamphlet appeared before completing his alterations. Sidgwick did not, however, actually respond to the pamphlet. Schneewind comments here that 'perhaps he [Sidgwick] felt he would not maintain a proper tranquillity of temper himself if he tried a direct reply' (*SE*, 400). When Sidgwick later examined Idealist thought (which he carried on doing on and off up to his death), he focused on T. H. Green, whom he considered to be the more significant thinker. One of Sidgwick's last publications in 1901 was another critique of Green.[7] Schneewind suggests that we can ascertain how he would have responded to Bradley by scrutinising the Green critique (*SE*, 393).[8] However, it is apparent to most scholars of British Idealism that there are significant differences between Bradley's and Green's ethical and metaphysical *oeuvres*. In this context, Schneewind's comment sounds more than slightly skewed.

Bradley clearly viewed himself as a 'tough-minded' sceptical philosopher. Out of all the British Idealists, he has been the one most attractive to twentieth-century analytically-inclined philosophers, beginning with Bertrand Russell.[9] Sidgwick, however, in his initial critical notice of *ES*, brushes aside this self-image, describing Bradley as 'an uncritically dogmatic Hegelian', 'propagandist' and 'rhetorician'. Sidgwick is prepared to admit that there are suggestive elements to his attack on Hedonism, but Bradley is seen to descend most of the time into 'debating club rhetoric'. His understanding of the views he attacks is 'superficial' and 'unintelligent'. Bradley is also accused of complete ignorance of English ethical philosophy and lacking 'intellectual sympathy' and 'tranquillity of temper' – a department that Sidgwick himself seems somewhat deficient in as one reads on. Ending his notice, Sidgwick concludes that Bradley 'has a considerable gift for smart and epigrammatic writing', but he 'hardly possesses the gift of lucid exposition … on the whole, his book [is] crude and immature'. Such was the review from the newly elected Cambridge College Praelector of Moral and Political

Philosophy, at the mature age of thirty-seven years (quotations from *CN*, 545–9).

Bradley's response was swift. He noted, with some rancour, Sidgwick's remark about his inability to engage in 'patient effort of intellectual sympathy', and suggests that he could go through Sidgwick's piece point by point, but does not wish to, since many of the remarks have a 'personal and generally deprecatory nature', which seems a fair response on Bradley's part. Sidgwick, on occasions, does note his own irascible style. As he morbidly remarked 'it is poor stuff, this sterile criticism, and I am rather ashamed of it'. Excusing himself, however, he continues, it is only that 'the pretensions of these people irritate me into the belief that it is a public duty to repress them'.[10] Bradley, however, does think that misunderstandings need correcting and he goes on to complain that 'the reviewer ignores my interpretation of self-realisation' (quotations from *SES*, 122–5).

Sidgwick immediately responded to the above response, noting that he was not out to defend his own view in reviewing Bradley's *ES* – it not being part of a reviewer's 'station and duties' [sic]. Rather, he passed judgement on the basis of views that he 'expects his readers to share with me'. Bradley's *ES* Essay III, 'Pleasure for Pleasure's Sake', is passed over without comment, since for Sidgwick 'I thought it less interesting and important'. Much of it 'either has no bearing on Hedonism as I conceive it, or emphasises defects which I have myself pointed out'. The freshest argument on hedonism he sees as Green's (recently published) critical presentation of Hume. Bradley's extra note to Essay III is thus seen as 'uninstructive' and 'too full of misunderstandings to be profitable for discussion'. Sidgwick remarks that Bradley's note requires 'explanation rather than defence'. He concludes that he has nothing therefore to retract from his review, except 'a pair of inverted commas which were accidentally attached to a phrase of my own'. In parting company with Bradley he remarks that he is glad to concede the inverted commas and that he was probably wrong to describe Bradley's style as 'over-rhetorical'. It was not over-rhetorical, although it was 'pathetic' and 'declamatory' (*R*, 125–6).[11]

It has been suggested that Bradley wrote a pamphlet, *Mr Sidgwick's Hedonism* (1877), simply because he felt that he needed to do more justice to Sidgwick's *ME*. Peter Nicholson, for example, remarks that Bradley's pamphlet can be read as 'an appendix to Essay III [of *ES*]'.[12] Given the interchange, there is something rather disingenuous about Bradley's comment, in his next riposte to Sidgwick, that his reflections were stimulated by the genteel impulse that 'the remarks which I found space to make in my *Ethical Studies* [about *ME*] were, I fear, too brief and condensed' (*SH*, 71), and that he just wished to expand some points. Given the heat of the interchange, both thinkers had some deeper scores to settle than 'an expansion of points'.

In summary, for Bradley, in assessing Sidgwick's *ME*, he comments that he 'can find no unity of principle which holds its part together'. Bradley sees 'hedonism and Individualism on the one side, and abstract rationalism on the other' and they do not come together in Sidgwick. We only have mere 'syncretism' a 'mechanical mixture' (*SH*, 124). Sidgwick also fails to take account of opposing ideas from the non-English traditions. More recently, however, Schneewind, taking on Sidgwick's terminology and virtual persona, notes that Bradley, despite 'rhetorical vigour', shows 'no serious deficiencies in Sidgwick's ethics'. Thus, he comments that Sidgwick's foremost critic 'failed to force him to undertake a major re-examination of his views' (*SE*, 393). Whereas Bradley thinks there is no unifying principle to *ME*, Schneewind comments that 'since [Bradley] has failed to find the total argument it is no surprise'. Sidgwick's review of *ES* had noted that Bradley 'lacked maturity'. Schneewind passively concurs, noting that 'though Bradley's attack on Sidgwick makes a few telling points, it largely illustrates the truth of [Sidgwick's] comment' (*SE*, 400).

Schneewind's deeply partisan assessment does not really explain the character of this interchange. The speed and heat of the debate requires further reflection. It cannot really be explained away by fatuous comments about immaturity and the like. My argument would be that there are some deep-rooted philosophical points at issue, which are not and have not been fully or systematically articulated. Rather than follow the minutiae of the debate, I will discuss it through the following themes: the nature of philosophy, ethics, common sense and the ordinary, the social organism, reason and pleasure. These do not encompass the totality of the debate, but they provide a gloss on the underlying depth of the conflict.

– PHILOSOPHY –

One foundational element of the debate between the two thinkers focuses on the character of philosophy itself. The matter, however, is not as simple as an analytical utilitarian and Idealist in contest. Neither thinker can be so easily categorised. There are some definite similarities between the two philosophers. Both clearly prided themselves on their analytical rigour. In many ways, Bradley was the most sceptical and analytical of all the British Idealists. As such, he stands out from writers like Green and Bosanquet and remained an enigma to many of his Idealist contemporaries. Equally, Sidgwick was so concerned to maintain a self-critical analytical stance that he tended, at times, to undermine his own work. This invokes a ghost which, as Alisdair MacIntyre commented (in the 1970s), 'haunts much recent writing' on analytic philosophy. The careful, inconclusive, hedging ending to *ME* highlights this style. As F. W. Maitland remarked, 'I sometimes think that the one and only prejudice that Sidgwick had was a prejudice against his own results.' Because of its minute attention to detail, C. D. Broad described Sidgwick's philosophical approach as 'heavy and involved', as any reader of Sidgwick could no doubt concur.[13]

One dimension of a neutral critical exposition and analysis of what 'is', rather than what 'ought' to be, is a stock accusation of philosophical conservatism. Strangely, both thinkers can qualify for this judgement on both a philosophical and practical level. It is a hackneyed criticism of Hegelianism (and some manifestations of twentieth-century analytic philosophy, particularly late Wittgensteinian thought) that they both tend towards a philosophically conservative imprimatur on what is – the Owl of Minerva usually 'hoots' at this point, for Hegelians at least. Bradley thus remarks in *ES*:

> All philosophy has to do is 'to understand what is', and moral philosophy has to understand morals which exist, not to make them or give directions for making them. Philosophy in general has not to anticipate the discoveries of the particular sciences nor the evolution of history; the philosophy of religion has not to make a new religion … political philosophy has not to play tricks with the state, but to understand it; and ethics has not to make the world moral.   (*ES*, 193)

Philosophy looks back at the world cut and dried and reflects critically upon what is.[14] In one sense this position is still being articulated, in a slightly less obvious way, by contemporary moral philosophers, like Bernard Williams, when he observes that 'morality is not an invention of philosophers. It is an outlook, or, incoherently, part of the outlook, of almost all of us.' For Williams, we live morally before, during and after reflection and the important business is living, not so much the reflection.[15] Moral practice is not something which flows from a philosopher's premises. Much moral philosophy, for Williams, therefore does not really grasp the complex relation between reflective philosophical thought and moral practice – a view that Bradley would have fully concurred with.

Philosophy, also, to Sidgwick, did not provide prescriptive answers to moral or epistemological issues; conversely, it introduced clarity into a reasoning with which we are already familiar.[16] With Bradley, Sidgwick also rejected any genetic reduction of philosophy to psychology, biology or religion. Sidgwick's vigorous assaults on nascent sociology and evolutionary theory would have derived some sympathy from Bradley.[17] Philosophy, however, could not be itself edifying or productive. It could only neutrally make explicit the rational foundation of what is the case. Philosophy was thus different from ordinary opinion, although its ideal should be a more precise, rigorous and rational formulation of the ordinary (to which we will return).

In fact, the notions of 'ordinary language' and 'common sense' (and thus G. E. Moore's philosophy) were but a short step from Sidgwick's basic philosophical reflections. This is essentially a form of 'underlabourer' conception of philosophy, a point which was not lost on Sidgwick's admirers within analytic philosophy during the twentieth century. However, Sidgwick was also quite depressed by this limitation, at one level, given his nascent religious yearnings. This was not a conception of philosophy which necessarily inspired schools, although this may have been partly due to the style in which it was written.[18] Bradley's style, although arriving at comparable conclusions, is much more approachable, playful and ironic, as well as immensely rigorous.

Yet, there is something puzzling in Sidgwick's conception of philosophy. His assumption of the common-sense character to utilitarian thought, its embodiment within Victorian culture, was also a quasi-Hegelian judgement of sorts.[19] Ironically, Sidgwick's 'Owl on Minerva' also sensed the moral *Sitten* of Britain at the time as utilitarian. Sidgwick thus assumed that utilitarianism (more than anything) marked out his own time and culture. Both his *ME*, and his later *Elements of Politics*, were painting grey on grey. This was Benthamism, as has been remarked, 'grown sleek and tame'.[20] Collini thus sees Sidgwick using Bentham (in his *Elements of Politics*) to justify Burke.[21] The upshot of this position, in Sidgwick, was, as many have noted, both theoretically and practically conservative. Sidgwick, in the late 1880s, had moved on a practical level from Millean radicalism to quite explicit Burkean conservatism. In the 1886 election, he returned early from a holiday in Europe specifically to vote conservative in a notably safe conservative parliamentary seat. Bradley, also, less publicly, was giving his philosophical benediction to Victorian culture, although it was not utilitarian. His caricatured reputation for conservatism also has roots in an 'underlabourer' Hegelianism; it also reflects, to some degree, Bradley's own sentiments. Both men clearly shared a mutual detestation of Gladstone and Gladstonian liberalism, although Bradley's own practical political sentiments remained, in the final analysis, slightly more elusive.

Another implication of this analytical expository style is a logical unease in both thinkers with normative moral philosophy and the role of theory qua practice. In fact, one might have expected utilitarianism, *prima facie*, to have subscribed to the normative dimension. Sidgwick is ambivalent here and clearly smarts when Bradley suggests he is fostering hedonistic utilitarianism. Yet, one can almost see a contest between the two as to who could be the most distanced from the path of moral edification. The stakes are high, since both sense in the other an underlying normative proposal. Neither quite believed each other's scepticism.

Overall, one might describe both philosophers as engaging in a form of underlabourer, hermeneutic, expository (almost phenomenological) and critical approach. One crucial difference here though is that Bradley's approach is dialectical. There is thus an underlying sequential development to the exposition. This allows a more positive fluid critical relation *between* ideas to develop – a form of continual higher order commentary within a structure of ideas. Sidgwick, although aware of the Hegelian approach (including dialectics), seems, in his interchange with Bradley, to have quite intentionally ignored the dialectical aspect to *ES* (see *CN*, 457).[22] It is clear that Sidgwick, early on, had made up his mind on post-Kantian Idealism, well before reading Bradley.[23] Writing to a friend in 1866 from Germany, he confessed that 'I am coming more and more to the opinion that the whole '*Identitäts-philosophie*' (Fichte, Schelling and Hegel) is a monstrous mistake' (*M*, 151). In 1870, he noted in his journal that 'The post-Kantian philosophy is a tower of Babel', and

> before I left Halle I had made up my mind about Hegel … No, I shall read no more of it … But if Hegelianism shows itself in England I feel equal to dealing with it. The method seems to me a mistake, and therefore the system ruin. (*M*, 238)

Yet, whereas Bradley's conception of philosophy at this stage is identifiably Hegelian in texture, Sidgwick's conception is more problematic (this will be taken up again). Sidgwick's conception hovered somewhere between a deep escoriating analytical scepticism, Millean positivism and an unexpected touching faith in Kantian practical reason.

– ETHICS –

It is no surprise that there appears to be distinct views of Sidgwick's ethics. In one reading, Sidgwick's ethics is an *ex post facto* philosophical reflection upon 'methods'. In the second interpretation, ethics is a normative universalist utilitarianism which can provide clear ethical guidance (the moral almanac view). In a third view, utilitarianism is embedded in common sense, which, if criticised, clarified and highly refined provides some limited ethical guidance. The third view is the most persuasive interpretation, but it is not clear that it can be completely reconciled with the first account, which also undoubtedly figures in *ME*. The terminology surrounding this debate is not helped by the fact that Bradley suggests at times separating out utilitarianism and hedonism. He has no objection to utilitarianism, qua happiness, being subsumed under the Aristotelian or Greek notion of happiness. He does, however, object to its reduction to pleasure. He suggests that the hedonistic view is the more pervasive reading and thus, at other times, dismisses both hedonism and utilitarianism. Terminology aside, we might call these three perspectives on ethics, the hermeneutic, normativist and integral readings.

In the hermeneutic view, ethical science is an abstract discipline focusing on the ends or dictates of practical reason. It is free from metaphysics, psychology, religion and any practical edification. Sidgwick thus claims fiercely not to have been promoting *any* one particular position in ethics. The ethical thinker empathetically enters into and expounds the varying methods used in daily practice and criticises them from an 'impartialist perspective'. A method is a 'rational procedure by which we determine what individual human beings "ought" to do' (*ME*, 1). Methods vary with ends. Sidgwick saw two ends – happiness and perfection; the latter is rejected. Happiness (and pleasure) is the only thing that is desirable. Happiness has two forms: 'one's own' or 'others'. Ethical methods are divided, however, by Sidgwick into three types: egoistic hedonism (every man ought to seek his own pleasure/happiness in any volition), universalistic hedonism or utilitarianism (every man ought seek the general happiness/pleasure) and intuitionism (which largely premises itself on self-evidence). All three methods to Sidgwick are 'more or less vaguely combined in the practical reasoning of ordinary men' (*ME*, 496). No complete synthesis is attempted in *ME*.

Sidgwick virtually summarised his own contribution to ethics, in typically mordant style, in a letter in 1873, *before* the publication of *ME*:

> Ethics is losing its interest for me rather, as the insolubility of its fundamental problems is impressed on me. I think the contribution to the *formal* clearness and coherence of our ethical thought which I have to offer is just worth giving.
>
> (*M*, 277)

Ideal utilitarianism – to guide the enlightened agent through moral issues – was something he found unacceptable. He is also clear that those who attribute to him an 'ideal' utilitarianism, hedonism, or in fact any position, were mistaken. For example, he noted in the preface to the 2nd edition of *ME* that many critics have assumed that he is an 'assailant of two of the methods ... and a defender of the third' (*ME*, x). He continues, pretty certainly against Bradley, that one writer 'has gone to the length of a pamphlet under the [wrong] impression ... that the "main argument of my treatise is a demonstration of Universalistic hedonism"' (*ME*, x). There is a strong sense of sceptical modernity in Sidgwick's presentation, particularly in terms of twentieth century moral philosophy. Basically, he serves up a limited smorgasbord of conflicting ethical positions – flavoured with microscopic critical analysis – and then appears powerless to recommend any. As MacIntyre comments, 'Sidgwick painstakingly examined all the possible ways of assimilating intuitionism and utilitarianism, or in bridging the gap between the goals of private and public happiness. But in the end there remain three distinct sources of morality.'[24] He assumes, in fact, in the final chapter of *ME* that no method or approach can be proved or shown without some metaphysical or theological notion and that none are at least philosophically available. His lifelong quasi-scientific interest in psychical research, automatic writing and paranormal phenomena are related to this latter point. Namely, Sidgwick clearly harboured the hope that these empirical studies of the paranormal might provide the scientific evidence of spiritual phenomena that metaphysics and theology had manifestly failed to produce.[25]

There is another dimension to this repudiation of edification and prescription, focused on Sidgwick's occasional remarks on history. He developed a conception of ethics which, although progressive, was also historically sensitive (an uncharacteristic move in the utilitarian tradition), suggesting that one could not attain any 'ethics' outside a particular community and moral tradition, although the roots are still loosely utilitarian.[26] Philosophical ethics is rooted in an existing moral order and community and comes on the scene to reflect on what is the case. Sidgwick commented that 'the variation of the moral codes of different societies at different stages corresponds in a great measure to differences in the actual or believed tendencies of certain kinds of conduct to promote the general happiness of different portions of the human race' (*ME*, 497). There is a marked intellectual parallel here not only to Bradley and Hegel (and sociological relativism), but also to more recent communitarian thinkers such as Michael Sandel, Michael Walzer, Alisdair MacIntyre and Charles Taylor (also see *ES*, 196–7).

However, a strong normativist perspective has also been identified, even by Sidgwick's sympathetic interpreter Schneewind, who remarks that

> there are places where Sidgwick seems to be saying quite plainly that utilitarianism is the best available ethical theory. From his other writings we know that he thinks of himself as committed to utilitarianism, and that he assumes it in analysing specific moral and political issues. (*SE*, 192)

This is a subtle, but slightly confusing, detail that arises at various points in *ME*. A pure unqualified normativist conception would be a misreading of Sidgwick's ethics. Yet, at the same time, Sidgwick's ethics are still, in the final analysis, a form of demure Benthamism. His ethics lack the brash confidence of Bentham or the positivistic yearnings of J. S. Mill. They are more eclectic, sceptical and wavering, yet, still committed, in the end, to utilitarian calculation, consequentialism and recommendation. His 'empirical-reflective-method' was essentially a more tempered form of Bentham's felicific calculus. The theorist consults and reflects on the common sense of the normal 'Benthamite Mensch'. This leads to the 'integral perspective'.

In the integral perspective, common sense embodies utilitarianism. Yet, it does not just embody it. It also reveals important moral beliefs – providing 'axiomata media' for potential prescription. The axioms provide practical aid for ethical dilemmas. As one recent writer comments,

> In Sidgwick's hands, the status of Utilitarian axioms is revised: no longer presented as the lemmas of a science of man, they figure more modestly as principles implicit in the common political [and moral] reasoning which it is the task of reflective analysis to systematise.[27]

These moral beliefs, if refined and reflected upon, do provide some modest utilitarian norms – probably understood more precisely as a public philosophy, rather than a guide for private conduct.

Bradley's critique of Sidgwick inevitably gets strung out between these perspectives – perspectives which are not reconciled by Sidgwick. It is not surprising that Bradley complains that, on one reading of *ME*, he 'can find no unity of principle which holds its part together' (*SH*, 124). In concurrence with the hermeneutic Sidgwick, Bradley consistently holds that ethics, like philosophy, is not concerned with practical edification. Ethics is simply about *understanding*, with clarity, the day to day communal practices of morality. Truth or falsehood in ethics are not decided by an appeal to something else, some exterior standard. Yet, Bradley also notes: 'Theory stands and falls by the theoretical text alone.' Practice is different. There is one niggling element, though, even within this hermeneutic parity between Sidgwick and Bradley. For Bradley, theory starts from and is verified in experience, yet, as Bradley remarks 'it is *not* mere experience. It is reflection and interpretation; and when mere experience pronounces on the abstract conclusions of science, then it ceases to be experience and, becoming theory, must itself stand and fall by the theoretical test' (quotations from *SH*, 114–15). The epistemology embodied in these points is suspicious of unalloyed empiricism and the confusion of modes of understanding. This is an argument which reappears, somewhat modified, in the writings of Michael Oakeshott in the later twentieth century. Sidgwick's position on this issue is far less clear.

Bradley, however, does not really pick up on the hermeneutic Sidgwick (although he is aware of it). He focuses instead on the normativist Sidgwick. In other words, he usually takes Sidgwick to be a normative hedonistic utilitarian. Sidgwick complains bitterly here against Bradley's misinterpretation, and he has a point, but, it is not Bradley's fault. At root, for Bradley, a normative 'ethical science does not exist yet'. He raises a number of objections to this conception of ethics, but most congregate around his contention that Sidgwick's conception of ethics is 'jural' or rule-governed. For Bradley, whereas law has to regulate a diversity of situations with one rule, morality does not. In morality, we take a particular case and ask is it right or wrong.

(see *SH*, 104–7) It is tempting to suggest, against Bradley, that surely morality can also have this abstracted jural quality. Yet, his argument gains more clarity and bite as he continues, and, it is important to grasp that Bradley is presuming a difference between reflective judgement in ethics, as against the practice of morality. Bradley finds, in the 'normative utilitarian Sidgwick', a strong suggestion of a 'moral nautical almanac' (as in Mill), namely, an abstract reflective code, which tells us what we ought to do on a practical level. We are back again to the complex relation between moral and political philosophy and moral and political practice.

First, for Bradley, such a code would have to cover all possible moral and political contingencies to be viable. Yet, to have such complete knowledge is impossible. He comments,

> Even if the world never altered, to have a complete knowledge of the laws of life, and to be able to judge correctly the enormous complication of detail so as to say, This act will increase the surplus and that act will not – goes beyond the human knowledge that we find in experience. And if the world alters, then the idea of knowing beforehand the laws of that alternation and of calculating existing data … is the mere dream of a doctrinaire.

Second, the underlying assumption in Sidgwick is that it is the individual that makes moral judgements about objective rightness. The modality of the argument, for Bradley, inevitably remains *with* the individual (whether individual citizen or policy maker). He remarks,

> When we look things in the face, is it not moral for any one, who likes to call himself a moralist, to use and act on his private judgement as to the means which will produce the maximum pleasure in any and every case in which he choose to do so? And has not so far the result proved mere individualism, and the objective criterion turned out 'subjective'?

One way out of this subjectivity problem is to appeal to an ideal enlightened objective utility. For Sidgwick, many of the puzzles he deals with would disappear in an 'Ideal' enlightened utilitarianism. Bradley, again, finds this puzzling; namely, does Sidgwick want to maintain a distinction between the 'enlightened' and 'vulgar' interests – which would not, in fact, be far from J. S. Mill's position? (all quotations *SH*, 111–13).[28] In fact, Sidgwick clearly rejects enlightened 'Ideal utilitarianism' in many parts of *ME*. The Ideal may solve problems, but once the 'enlightened' Ideal perspective is rejected one is left with the isolated individual. In addition, to even suggest something is objectively right is to imply no other course is possible, which, for Bradley, is plainly ridiculous. As mentioned above, for Bradley no one has this kind of knowledge. Objective rightness in morality (or public policy for that matter) thus remains a chimera.[29]

Finally, there is a dilemma on the question of moral theory and practice (which relates to the conception of philosophy). For Bradley, in Sidgwick's ethics, '*any* act, no matter how seemingly immoral, is moral for you if you have a sincere opinion that it will increase the surplus [of happiness]' (*SH*, 107). An act therefore becomes moral by simply adding a formulaic rule.[30] This is the result of utilitarianism, in general, being a second order theory. Yet, for Bradley, when ethical science then ceases to understand and proposes to alter the facts, then something has gone sadly wrong. Sidgwick is thus seen to mix up reflective judgements with everyday intuitive moral judgements. A rule held in the 'reflective mind' allows interpretations to be made. But this 'rule reflection' does not exist in everyday moral practice. Sidgwick's utilitarianism does not want, in the end, to *understand*, rather to *alter* ordinary moral facts, and this is casuistry. Utilitarian ethical ideas thus invade 'non-theoretical morality' confusing and distorting it. Of course, this whole critique may be nugatory if the hermeneutic Sidgwick is a more accurate assessment. Yet, Sidgwick's ethics continually hovers between the hermeneutic and integral perspectives, with some occasional forays into a fulsome normativist view. If Bradley appears to misread Sidgwick it is definitely not his fault.

– THE STRUGGLE OVER THE ORDINARY –

There is clearly a crucial issue in Bradley's and Sidgwick's conceptions of the relation between moral theory and practice, or, on another level, between reflective philosophical ethics and practical ethical activity, and, in another format, between common sense moral judgement and reflective morality. Both thinkers focus on the 'ordinary' or 'common sense' as a touchstone for morality. Bradley, in fact, admits that he and Sidgwick appear to *agree* on what ordinary morality contains; however, he adds

> The difference [between them] is one of principle, not detail. I object not to the
> things he teaches us to do, but to the spirit and the way in which he teaches us to
> do them. It is not the particular conclusions of his Casuistry, but the whole
> principle of it, that seems to me both false in theory and corrupt in practice.
>
> (*SH*, 116)

Many philosophers have felt uncomfortable with the use of common sense. A recent moral philosopher, R. M. Hare, for example, suggested that common sense has no 'probative force' whatsoever in moral theory. It cannot tell us 'about what we ought to do'.[31] A twentieth-century Marxist, like Gramsci, saw common sense embodying the hegemonic ideas of a dominant regime and consequently requiring serious criticism. For Sidgwick, however, common sense embodied neutral standards. It needed to be continually referred to and cast in scientific format. All the practical common sense virtues we use in everyday practice are, in essence, utilitarian. Ordinary practice provides the 'middle axioms' for utilitarianism. When carefully criticised and refined these axioms give ethical guidance. Utilitarianism is *the* 'adult' morality. Sidgwick claims that the decisive influence in formulating this perspective was Aristotle. He comments that Aristotle's *Ethics* provides 'the common sense Morality of Greece, reduced to consistency by careful comparison: given not as something external to him but as what "we" … think, ascertained by reflection'. Sidgwick continues, 'Might I not imitate this: do the same for our morality here and now [in Victorian England] in the same manner of impartial reflection on current opinion' (*ME*, 6th edition, Preface, xix–xx). Utility is thus embodied in the ethos of certain historical communities.

Despite the fact that utilitarianism is embedded in the 'ethos' of England (no doubt determining the station and duties of citizens), the focus for Sidgwick's critique of Bradley, in *CN*, is still the 'station and duties' mentality. Sidgwick's argument makes some telling hits in a short compass, although his purposeful avoidance of certain key assumptions in Bradley's approach inevitably weakens his case. First, he totally ignores the dialectical sequence of *ES*. This allows him to express surprise at Bradley's own self-critique in later essays of *ES*. He, thus, simply notes Bradley's critique in the 'Ideal Morality' essay, where beauty and truth transcend the 'station and duties' scenario, and interprets this as self-contradiction. Secondly, he continues, on this same assumption, that Bradley's 'Ideal morality' will conflict with the ordinary morality of a community. Thus, what has happened to Bradley's much vaunted 'ordinary' use of common sense? He thus ironically turns the tables on Bradley's comments on Ideal utilitarianism, suggesting Bradley himself wants to refine ordinary morals. Further, what is the authoritative relation between ordinary common sense and ideal morality? Sidgwick argues that Bradley himself acknowledges the authority of 'cosmopolitan morality' (as well as truth, religion and beauty), which transcends country or state. The 'Station and Duties' theme thus loses all its distinctiveness within *ES* and is 'reduced to little more than a vague and barren ethical common-place, dressed in a new metaphysical formula' (*CN*, 549).

Thirdly, given the perception that morals can be refined and improved upon, Sidgwick suggests that even Bradley's ordinary unreflective man of *ES*, would be surprised by the ethical standards he is supposed to agree with. In fact, such surprise is almost inevitable (from point two). Sidgwick then twists the knife, suggesting, in effect, that Bradley is surreptitiously fostering his own normative morality. He comments, 'I doubt whether he [the ordinary un-reflective agent] will be quite consoled by learning that [Bradley's] justi-fication is not "meant to influence practice": though I admit that [Bradley's] consolation is well adapted to the average philosophical capacity of the non theoretical person' (R, 126). It is highly characteristic of Sidgwick not to be able to resist this final unnecessary carping comment.

Bradley's response to this is fairly weak. He does not complain about the misreading of the 'dialectical sequence'. Bradley's sensitivity to Hegel's influence (which gets more pronounced in later years) may well have been in the background. This unwillingness to comment hamstrings his response. He simply asks where Sidgwick gets the quotation on 'unsophisticated common sense' (SES, 124). Sidgwick admits in his next response to Bradley that he invented the phrase (and thus is prepared to give up the inverted commas), but still thinks it appropriate for Bradley's argument (R, 126). Bradley further asserts that there is no conflict with ordinary morality. His assertion is, in fact, rooted in a deep philosophical premise, which has already been discussed.

In summary, Bradley has little complaint about the content of common sense in Sidgwick, but, like Hare or Gramsci, he has worries as to exactly what Sidgwick is doing with this neutral common sense. He suspects him of wanting to modify it in line with abstract reflective jural utilitarian rules. For Bradley, moral philosophers are not the best or most authoritative guides to what 'ought' to be done in moral practice – a truism which remains to the present day. He was also concerned about the philosophy which allows Sidgwick leeway to 'modify' ordinary morals. Given Bradley's conception of the nature of philosophical ethics (premised on a distinction between reflective judgement and intuitive judgement), this view is hardly surprising. Sidgwick, on the other hand, conscious of the close parallels between his and Bradley's approach, is determined to damn Bradley for remaining with and proclaiming the importance of the unrefined 'ordinary' morals. He thinks that Bradley also signals his own unease with unreflective common sense and is determined to push the contradiction. Sidgwick does put his finger here unerringly on a problem of Hegelian ethics which is better dealt with under the rubric of the social organism.

– THE SOCIAL ORGANISM –

There is a rolling sequence of complex related arguments focusing on the relation of 'ordinary morality' and 'philosophically refined morality', practice and theory, individuality and community and later, public and private reason. The central problem remains elusive and can be viewed from different angles. In this section it is the community/individuality angle which will be focused on. The gist of the debate between Sidgwick and Bradley relates to distinct ontologies, each with their own characteristic problems. Bradley's ontology was particularistic, communitarian and Hegelian; Sidgwick's ontological roots lay in a Millean and Benthamite universalistic empirical individualism. It is this latter ontology which underpins his critical response to Bradley's *ES*.

First, Sidgwick notes that self-realisation is a central theme of *ES*, yet, Bradley [for Sidgwick] appears to admit that he does not know what 'self' means; an admission which Sidgwick says, 'disarms satire'. For Sidgwick, there is, in fact, little coherence in the idea of the self throughout *ES*. There is some sense to it in Essay 1, yet, Sidgwick complains that Essay II 'starts afresh, and offers us various new meanings of his cardinal term' (*CN*, 545–6). It is worth immediately noting here that Sidgwick's criticisms rely, once again, on a now repetitious avoidance of the dialectic sequence of *ES*. Bradley responds by claiming that he has not attempted to solve the problem of the origin of the self, but, he suggests that his view 'is not incoherent' (*SES*, 123). Whereas Sidgwick's Millean self is a fairly static sentient being with identifiable interests, Bradley's self is an 'evolving process'. This difference would account for Sidgwick's impatience with Bradley's mutations.

The root of Bradley's 'process self' lies in conceptions of self-realisation, action and will. For Bradley, action is thought translating itself into external existence. Action is the self positing an end. An end implies something to be reached (otherwise it is not an end). Any action 'I' perform must be something that I posit as an end. The only end 'I' can posit is my self in another state. Thus, any action is self-realisation, since it is an end posited by me. In making something real, my will is realised. Nothing can be foreign to me since 'what we desire must be in our minds' (*ES*, 82). Therefore, to will is to self-realise, to will is to realise a self-posited desired object. In effect, the will is the self. The self as a whole is the content of the will. As Bradley put it, 'The will must be in the act, and the act in the will' (*ES*, 34). Bradley's self changes with each object and end it places before itself. When we *will* we have a sense of our incompleteness. Morality is addressed to this sense of incompleteness.

Second, Sidgwick takes issue with Bradley's idea of the 'self as a whole' (an inclusive end which embraces other ends). Sidgwick comments, 'I hardly think that the lives of ordinary men are actually as much systematised as Mr. Bradley supposes.' As reasoning creatures, humans try to systematise, but Sidgwick comments, do we gain 'anything by calling the object of our search "the true whole which is to realise the true self"?' (*CN*, 546–7). Bradley views this point differently. The self is envisaged as an 'incompleteness' with an underlying sense that there may well be a systematic completeness. What the self desires is systematic non-contradictory wholeness. The premise behind this is that human beings cannot logically abide contradiction. The human self develops by positing greater and more systematically inclusive ends. Bradley admits that this thesis requires metaphysics (qua the individuality of the absolute), which he does not pursue in *ES* (*ES*, 65). The metaphysical premise underpinning this is that the higher sense of reality overcomes and incorporates contradiction. Lower ends subsist in contradiction. Given that morality is always premised on imperfection and contradiction, although it implied completeness and wholeness, it can never provide wholeness or non-contradiction. The whole argument of *ES* is the gradual development of more systematic and inclusive 'wholes'. In sum, it charts in outline the process of the self seeking non-contradiction. This is though not an abstracted sense of the self. Bradley claims to be basing his reflective observations here on the 'ordinary' common sense moral activity of the world, almost in the sense of a phenomenological description.

Third, Sidgwick pursues the above point further, asking what Bradley's idea of a systematic whole means? Taking the argument directly to the 'Station and Duties' essay again, Sidgwick remarks,

> Mr. Bradley has no difficulty in showing that we cannot logically pass from the mere notion of a self-consistent universal will to the determination of a particular concrete good act: but when, in order to supply the deficient particularity and concreteness, he accepts a merely relative universality as a sufficient criterion of goodness, his reasoning seems dangerously loose and rash.　　　(*CN*, 547)

Bradley, quite legitimately, responds to this, noting, 'that this is what I do *not* say' (*SES*, 123). For Bradley, it is both relative and absolute. Sidgwick once again ignores the dialectic sequence. In responding to Bradley, Sidgwick comments that the social organism is neither a relative nor an absolute whole, that is, 'it is not the universe: and we have no reason to identify its will – granting this to be real and cognisable – with the universal or Divine Will to which our wills should conform' (*R*, 126). There is, however, no sense in Bradley of a static divine will within the station and duties setting. If any reader of *ES* ignores the sequential dialectical setting, they will derive a skewed view of its argument.

Fourth, Sidgwick's central criticism is focused on Bradley's 'concrete universal'. He sees it as nothing but the 'old doctrine – to which modern sociology has given a new form and new emphasis – that the individual man is essentially a social being' (*CN*, 547–8). He thinks that Bradley does not really advance beyond this crude sociological level, noting that he 'attributes to the social organism not merely a common life which the individual shares, but a rational will, expressed in the laws, customs and common moral judgements of his society'. The good life is one 'lived according to the moral spirit of my community' (*CN*, 548). This is Bradley's 'systematic whole'.[32] For Sidgwick, this creates a scenario of both sociological crudity and profound social relativity – although there are arguments in Sidgwick's own *ME* which drift in the same direction. Bradley, in reply, notes that if his view is *like* another, is that an objection to it? If there is a confusion in the argument it should be pointed out. There is a sense that Sidgwick does not offer an argument here, but 'sloganises'. Sidgwick refines the point in replying, complaining this time that Bradley does not distinguish the cruder view of society, simply being a natural organism, from society as organism possessing a rational will. Thus, he concludes,

> The result of the non-distinction is that much of this polemical argument – as far as I can trace it through the fold of rhetoric – is directed against an individualism which will find no defenders: the individualism, namely, to which the 'Social Compact,' belongs, and to which Utilitarianism long since gave the *coup de grâce*.
>
> (R, 126)

In effect, Sidgwick claims he has a more sophisticated conception of moral and social theory, although what it is is never made clear. It is apparent that Sidgwick's theory is neither Spencerian nor straightforwardly Millean, Comtean or Burkean, but what it is remains slightly mysterious.[33]

If one reconstructed Sidgwick's moral theory here (and by inference his political theory), it is clear that he plays between two methods, both of which attracted him – egoism and universalistic utilitarianism. The third method, intuition, appears largely as a cheering chorus for utilitarianism. Sidgwick's egoist is one who produces the maximum amount of his own pleasure. Universalistic hedonism or utilitarianism suggests that the egoistic individual can rationally inculcate self-sacrifice and look to the general happiness. It was obviously deeply irritating to Sidgwick, in this context, that Bradley insisted that any consistent hedonism must remain egoistic and egoism is irreconcilable with morality. This undermined his whole strategy. Possibly, Bradley suggests, Sidgwick could also have drawn attention to the immorality and irrationality of egoism (*SH*, 99). Instead, he tries, for Bradley, to use egoism up to a certain point, then suppresses it surreptitiously to get to the next step – universalistic hedonism.

For Bradley, Sidgwick's argument with the egoist is fallacious. The egoistic hedonist could never *logically* assert something as objectively desirable without refuting himself. Pushing this point home, Bradley comments that Sidgwick 'dares not break entirely with this view [egoistic hedonism] for fear his own ground should give way beneath him' (*SH*, 102). Sidgwick is thus hoisted by his own philosophical petard. In sum, egoism is both ontologically crucial and at the same time fatal to Sidgwick's theory. Despite Sidgwick's remarks to the contrary, the lonely single sentient individual hovers at the ontological roots of *ME*. For Bradley, Sidgwick tries to universalise egoistic hedonism into utilitarianism. Thus, in '*my pleasure* he [Sidgwick] wants to keep one part (pleasure) and drop only the *my*. And to do this the Egoist must be won over' (*ES*, 128). Yet, he cannot win him over without making him a non-egoist. For Bradley, Sidgwick's 'ontological alternative' is obvious, if veiled. Sidgwick sees the 'social being' argument as 'a vague and barren ethical commonplace'. Bradley continues, 'his book [*ME*] … must be taken to deny it, for he finds the end, and, I suppose, the essence of man by examining a "single sentient being"' (*SES*, 124). The root therefore to Sidgwick's whole perspective is a metaphysical individualism/egoism which remains largely unexamined.

For Bradley, there are ways around egoism. One path is for Sidgwick to give up all claims to 'my' or 'yours', thus egoism goes out of the frame altogether. For Bradley, this would be a position close to Schopenhauer. He thinks, correctly, that Sidgwick would not be comforted by such an idea. Another alternative for Sidgwick would be to appeal to intuitions. Sidgwick in fact does this. In this case, every 'single sentient' must have an intuition 'of my pleasure as pleasure in general'. Yet, intuition is, at the best of times, a tricky philosophical device. Bradley thinks the idea of such mass coincidence of egoistic intuitions plainly ridiculous. Sidgwick, who, earlier in life, had rejected forcefully Whewell's use of intuition, came to rely on something like it as a device to move beyond egoism. It was thus intuitively true, for Sidgwick, that individuals would will the general happiness. Intuitionism and utilitarianism were not at loggerheads. Both were rooted in ordinary 'common sense' – which was the nearest thing to being uncontested. In response, Bradley simply asks 'whose intuitions?' (*ES*, 128). He obviously did not share Sidgwick's. It is difficult to know what answer Sidgwick could give to this, although there is one which we will turn to under the use of reason.

Bradley's own answer to the above conundrum (concerning individuality and universality) is embedded in the whole dialectical sequence of *ES*. This is a subtle mediation between the individual and universal. Within the moment of the 'social organism', there is quite definitely a different ontology at work, which could hardly be called crude sociological determinism. Basically, the self-realising individual is not asked to personally invent a moral content, conversely, the content comes to the individual in a pre-existing form of life. It is already present. It arises in the form of social habits, conventions and traditions, which we assimilate, at first by rote and play and then through self-conscious reflection. This is a view which would not be unfamiliar to most current virtue ethicists and communitarians. A moral vocabulary, *per se*, makes sense in the context of existing forms of life, containing well-defined roles, which agents progressively place before themselves. It is difficult to see how it could exist outside of this. In the language of modern communitarianism, the moral self is constituted through a community. There are no 'unencumbered selves' (to use Michael Sandel's term) standing outside a community frame. There is thus no sense that moral issues or moral vocabularies can be addressed independently of a community. Morality and politics are not invented, but interpreted from within a particular community. We therefore read off an existing tradition of moral discourse. The community is constituted by such internal pre-understandings.[34] As Bradley concurs, in a somewhat purple passage, the child is not born

> into a desert, but into a living world, a whole which has a true individuality of its own, and into a system and order which it is difficult to look at as anything else than an organism … the tender care that receives and guides him is impressing on him habits, habits, alas not particular to himself, and the 'icy chains' of universal custom are hardening themselves round his cradled life. (*ES*, 171)

The community thus represents what Hegel called 'objective mind'. Agents place the rules of the communal ethos before themselves. The community is quite simply a larger and more systematic whole, containing sedimented rules and social functions, which most humans assimilate and posit to themselves. All morality is, though, an imperfect realisation of human wholeness. This implies some degree of relativity of morality to historical communities, a point at times recognised by the hermeneutic historical Sidgwick.

Many of Sidgwick's criticisms do however make palpable hits on Bradley. A characteristic difficulty with the Hegelian argument (indicated at the close of the previous section) is the manner in which morality comes to the individual. Morals appear from the 'relative' historical community and from 'outside' the autonomous will of the individual. Yet, Bradley's thesis did not deny the independence of the individual. It did not imply, as Sidgwick suggests, that others can therefore determine my actions (a critical point, on positive liberty and common will arguments, raised by Sidgwick, which has been constantly repeated thereafter by liberal critics up to Isaiah Berlin). Bradley repudiates the idea that 'the doctrine that the mere bringing about by some one else of anything desired by me is my self-realisation', arguing, in effect, that Sidgwick did not take full cognisance of his argument (*SES*, 123). It is true that morality has no place or situation outside of a community. It is also clear that no social function, state or community is perfect. An ethos may be corrupt and all communities are limited by other communities. A bad self, with bad habits, can remain in a particular station. The human self is also subject to many psychological unpredictabilities. What, for example, should one make of Bradley's remark:

> Many of us show selves to ourselves and the world, which are not the realisation of another element which we take about with us, and which quietly, or it may be longingly, remains below the 'floor of consciousness', and perhaps never to appear, perhaps to burst out in we know not what, in light and love, or in 'dirt and fire'.

(*ES*, 54–5)

'Ideal Morality', and later essays, in *ES* address some of these problems and move the argument beyond the station and duties thesis. In addition, overall, for Bradley, morality always implies imperfection. It tries to gain an end which makes it (morality) impossible. Morality is, thus, an effort after non-morality. Morality is always trying to cease to exist. Unless the agent divined him- or herself to be a whole he or she could not feel the sense of his or her own imperfection and try to pass beyond it. This is one reason why religion figures at the end of *ES*. Religion, in effect, gives us what morality cannot.

– THE DUALISM OF REASON –

There is an elusive problem in Sidgwick which we have already encountered in the contrast between egoism and universalistic utilitarianism. The problem appears again in the contrariety between duty and self-interest and reappears in two notions of rationality. Sidgwick calls the latter issue the 'dualism of reason'. The central question behind this is: what does reason require of us in an ordinary [moral] life? There appear to be two answers in Sidgwick's *ME*, one optimistic and integrative, the other pessimistic and pluralistic. Bishop Butler and Kant jostle for attention here.

The focus for this tangled debate is, first, on reason understood as a generic tool of logic (as well as being central to formal understandings of justice and equality). In effect, Sidgwick takes up the 'universalisability rule', via Kant's categorical imperative.[35] For a utilitarian, this introduction of Kantian practical reason is novel.[36] Sidgwick formulates it thus: 'That whatever is right for me must be right for all persons in similar circumstances' (*ME*, xvii). In other words, in moral terms, reason directs that we should treat others equally unless relevant reasons can be shown why someone should be treated differently. The second use of reason is calculative. It directs us from maxims to actions. This is more instrumental and prudential in character. Bradley, focusing immediately on the two senses of reason, remarks that 'we have to deal with a strict and a loose use of reason'. Bradley senses – as one would expect – conceptual confusion (*SH*, 74–5).

Sidgwick's optimistic integral reading sees no problem with reason.[37] There is, often, a confident rationalism present in his writings. In fact, one central thought of *ME* 'is that morality is the embodiment of the demands reason makes on practice under the condition of human life' (see *SE*, 303–4).[38] The optimistic argument develops as follows: reason provides self-evidence through direct intuitive insights. It directs us initially to seek our own good. But, it also implies, self-evidently, that one should prefer, prudentially, a greater future good to a present lesser one. It is reasonable to seek self-interest, but reason also directs us to treat like cases alike, namely, to consider the good of others as equal to my own and to consider others' happiness with my own.

How does the reasonable egoist arrive at the above conclusions? In effect, it is an intuition derived from reason itself. Sidgwick was particularly impressed by Kant's rule of practical reason. As Sidgwick noted,

> I certainly could will it to be a universal law that men should act in such a way as to promote universal happiness: in fact it was the only law that it was perfectly clear to me that I could decisively will from a universal point of view.   (ME, xx)

Even outside the frame of both Kantian reason and Bishop Butler's reasonable self-love, Sidgwick suggests other contributory factors weakening pure egoism in practice. Excessive concentration on one's own interest is not seen by most human beings as quite sane or rational. Further, to focus so much on one's self produces rapid satiety and ennui (ME, 501–2). Yet, for Sidgwick, even linking Kant and Butler could not fully explain matters. He suggests that it was rereading Aristotle's Ethics that set his argument on track. His ME was uncovering, hermeneutically, the existing rational structures of moral experience within common sense and the ordinary. Intuitively, therefore, we feel that it is reasonable to move beyond our immediate self-interest. As a rational being I ought therefore to aim at the general good, since every one's good is the same as any other's. Benevolence means that each one of us is bound to regard the good of each individual as much as our own, unless (under the same impartialist rule) I judge differently. One seeks the good of all, including one's own good. Self-love and benevolence are not therefore automatically in contention. The compatibility of practical reason and utility also provided a ground for the normative 'calculative' side of Sidgwick to come forward.

Bradley concentrates his fire on what 'reasonable' intuition leads to in Sidgwick, in terms of the 'Rule of Equity' and 'Rule of Benevolence'. The first refers to the universalisability rule, namely, like cases should be treated alike. For Bradley, this is simply tautologous. Thus, 'the right, the objective, the reasonable, is, by definition, what holds in abstraction from the "mere fact that I and he are different individuals" ... [thus] the meaning of "reasonable" is what holds in abstraction from the individual'. The idea of any 'me' or 'her' (Harry or Sasha) refers to particulars and therefore is unreasonable. The Reasonable is the universal. It has no *particular* content. The 'Rule of Benevolence' (the good of any one individual cannot be any more desirable than the equal good of any other individuals), invokes another tautology, namely, that 'X cannot regard his own happiness as more desirable than the equal happiness of Y'. For Bradley, this is either another 'tautology' or 'nonsense'. In these 'rules', Sidgwick has reiterated 'the postulates which he [the egoist] denies'. The rational egoist could not logically universalise or make objective his particular position. The rational egoist is one who rationally asserts that nothing is objective or universal (all quotes *SH*, 99–101).[39]

When we come to Sidgwick's notion of practical reason, as Bradley remarks, the light grows 'dimmer and dimmer' (*SH*, 76). What does 'reason' direct the individual to do? Sidgwick's argument gives different answers. It appears practically reasonable to both seek one's own maximum pleasure and that of the whole creation. The arguments of *ME* rests, therefore, on 'a thesis the contradictory of which is no less true'. It appears to be a matter of life and death to Sidgwick's whole enterprise to show that the only true selfishness is morality. The solution here, for Sidgwick, is that 'certain quantities of pleasure and pain should be attached to individuals, that they should be adequately rewarded for obeying the rule of duty and punished for violating it' (quotes from *SH*, 117). Yet, Bradley continues, how is this attachment of pleasure and pain to be achieved? Humans cannot carry it out. Average individuals appear in Sidgwick to be often stupid, impulsive and egoistic. It surely needs, Bradley suggests, a *deus ex machina*, but, unfortunately 'the days of Paley are long gone' when a god guaranteed the utilitarian calculus, something that Sidgwick was, at times, painfully aware of.

Bradley's critique of Sidgwick here underscores Sidgwick's own latent pessimism and *Weltschmerz*. This is the 'other Sidgwick', in despair of ethics, and consequently flailing about in 'psychical research', automatic writing, and the like. In this 'despair mode', the conflict of 'rationalities' literally explains the whole character and layout of *ME*. Sidgwick raises the questions himself. How can the egoist look to the general happiness? How can duty appeal to the self-interested? Reason appears to be linked to both methods. In effect, the rationality of self-regard and the rationality of self-sacrifice were both 'undeniable'. Sidgwick commented, 'I could not give up this conviction, though neither of my masters, neither Kant nor Mill, seemed willing to admit it' (*ME*, xviii). In other passages of *ME* an even more despondent Sidgwick acknowledges a resilient and 'fundamental contradiction in our apparent intuition of what is Reasonable' (*ME*, 508). Further, no religious grounds or sanctions can link rational egoism and utilitarianism. All the gods are *in absentia*. There is also no possibility of demonstrating any linkage empirically. The problem of reason, in the final analysis, for Sidgwick, is that if we admit that we cannot demonstrate the connection between duty and self-interest and that the notion we have of what is reasonable is not ultimately demonstrable, then we must realise that although we do not abandon morality, we *cannot* completely rationalise it. We see this especially in the 'hard cases' or 'rarer cases' where we clearly identify 'a recognised conflict between self-interest and duty, practical reason, being divided against itself, would cease to be the motive on either side; the conflict would have to be decided by the comparative preponderance of one or the other of two groups of non-rational impulses' (*ME*, 508). In effect, this is a *fin de siècle* conception of ethics, which looks towards twentieth-century analytic liberal moral philosophy and points to some postmodern nostrums on contingency, difference and incommensurability.[40]

– PLEASURE –

On one level it may seem strange to have arrived at the final section of the essay and to only now be focusing on pleasure. My argument would be that the confrontation between Sidgwick and Bradley has much deeper roots than a conflict between utilitarianism and Idealist ethics. There is an altogether more complex and nuanced relationship. The confrontation over pleasure and the ends of morality is part of a much larger package which has been gradually unpicked during the course of this essay. It would take too much time to unravel all the arguments on the issue of pleasure, thus only the highlights will be examined. The debate can be subdivided between, first, the metaphysics of utilitarianism, second, terminological issues, and third, utilitarianism's ability to guide practice and its relation to ordinary morality (a point glossed earlier). Each of these arguments is nested within the previous sections of this essay.

First, the metaphysical argument that Bradley directs against Sidgwick refers back to the earlier ontological issues. Pleasure-based arguments all tend to rely on the 'single sentient individual' to make morality possible. For Bradley, the whole of *ME* is premised upon this unexplained metaphysical dogma of individualism. It is no wonder that Sidgwick says that he wants nothing to do with metaphysics. For Bradley, utilitarianism and hedonism, basically, have not articulated the nature of the individual self, a point that is as true today of utilitarian thought as it was of Sidgwick's work.[41] There is no way that any of us could really imagine (except in our wildest flights of fantasy) being utterly alone (atomised) and still thinking morally – especially in abstract utilitarian terms. Bradley ironically comments, *ad hominem*,

> Figure yourself then, reader – your imagination, not like mine, may keep pace with the author's – figure yourself as a single sentient being in a non-sentient universe, and tell us, would you not believe in 'a real end of Reason, the absolutely Good of Desirable'? (*SH*, 95)

Individuality to Bradley is not a metaphysical abstraction, but a concrete existence.

Furthermore, this abstract 'sentient individual' in Sidgwick is too conveniently rolled back into the universal (see *ES*, 127). In Sidgwick, pleasure for each becomes, by magic sleight of hand, pleasure for all. This is an issue which has figured importantly in previous sections. For Bradley, Sidgwick has no reason for this move except intuition.[42] Where precisely the limitations on the egoist comes from remains a mystery. Consequently, the utilitarian argument always has the tendency to collapse back into egoism, unless some other factor is injected, like intuition or 'higher and lower' pleasures. Sidgwick rejected the latter. The 'greatest happiness' therefore always has a fictional status for Bradley. As a particular individual, my pleasures remain mine. On the individualist premise, I can only desire things which relate to *my* feelings. Even desiring a general pleasure is still irrevocably *mine*. Other's pleasure, logically cannot be *my* pleasure. As Bradley comments, 'pleasure of others is neither a feeling in me, nor an idea of a feeling in me' (*ES*, 129). Bradley continues 'if I desire my pleasure as mine in particular, is it not a flat contradiction to say I desire it as *not* mine in particular?' Further, '*can* I desire *my* pleasure as pleasure in general?' In other words, is *my* feeling pleased anything other than *my* feeling pleased? Can one separate out the 'my' and 'feeling pleased'? (*ES*, 128). Bradley thus claims that the notion of disinterested action in Sidgwick is meaningless. Individual pleasure is either the end or it is not. Interestingly, Bradley suggests that the more honest statement of metaphysical egoism can be found in Max Stirner's writings, which he recommends to Sidgwick! (*ES*, 128).

The second issue concerns the vagueness of Sidgwick's key terminology. Pleasure is seen as too abstract and contentless to be of much use. Pleasure and pain are transient feelings. The concepts are abstractions of these feelings – feelings which are infinitely coming into being and perishing. They are, in fact, abstractions from a 'whole psychical state' (*ES*, 116). A number of points arise from this. First, Bradley complains that Sidgwick initially separates pleasurable feelings from the conscious self which feels them. This enables Sidgwick to make an abstract case for pleasurable feeling in the first place. Yet, at the same time, in making a case for pleasure, he tries to make it synonymous with the conscious self. However, for Bradley, the conscious self is broader than feelings. Feeling is one dimension of the conscious self, thus, he comments that, 'while [in Sidgwick] on the one hand feeling and consciousness seem convertible, on the other hand consciousness is by far the wider term, and covers the whole self' (*SH*, 81). Sidgwick slides together 'conscious life' and 'pleasurable feeling'. Consciousness, in Sidgwick, is thus 'the same as feeling and yet includes [unaccountably] thought and action' (*SH*, 82). This bears again upon the debates about the nature of reason.

Similarly, Bradley accuses Sidgwick of sliding together (definitionally) 'I desire' with 'what I ought to desire', and, 'I like' with 'what I ought to like', 'preference' with what 'I ought to prefer'. He notes that the overall thesis to be proved in *ME* is 'that mere pleasure is the end', yet adds, 'Mr Sidgwick writes conscious life for pleasure and adds desirable (which *means* end) to the definition' (*SH*, 93). The basic point which Bradley drives home repeatedly is that Sidgwick continually imports his conclusions into his premises – classic *petitio principii*. Sidgwick's defender, Schneewind, comments here that Bradley 'is led to this charge, despite his having noticed that Sidgwick formally treats "desirable" as meaning "what should be desired", by a misstatement of Sidgwick's account of pleasure'. Bradley takes Sidgwick to define pleasure as 'desirable feeling', while Sidgwick, for Schneewind, actually defines it as 'the kind of feeling that we judge to be preferable'. He continues that 'since Sidgwick makes it clear … that he thinks no kind of judgement is immune from error, his position, … requires rational assessment of the judgement involved in the feeling of pleasure, and so does not leave him guilty of Bradley's charge' (*SE*, 394). I fail to see the logic of Schneewind's response. Bradley's point is that Sidgwick never gives an account as to how (genealogically) pleasure, feeling and desire incorporate reason and thought (other than by stipulative assertion). Before we can 'rationally assess' the judgement, we need to know how it got there within pleasure and feeling.

Second, for Bradley a 'series' of transient feelings is impossible to configure. The idea of a 'sum' of such feeling is conceptually meaningless. How could I have a sum of infinitely passing moments which are still proceeding? In a similar way it is difficult with regard to preference or even welfare utilitarianism to see how one could gain clear interpersonal comparisons of utilities (whether it is preferences, pleasures or welfare). The greatest sum of utility, in any of these formats, is thus the wildest of fictions. A number of questions are raised here for Bradley concerning Sidgwick's arguments. Can one compare the pleasantness of diverse transient pleasures? Can one identify a sum of pleasures? Can there be quantitative pleasures, for example, a science of quantity? These questions contain their own substantive debates which will not be pursued.

Third, Bradley suggests that Sidgwick's theory is no guide to conduct. Following on from the above idea, a series of pleasures, in diverse sentient individuals, cannot function as a guide to conduct. The idea of 'greatest possible' is a pure fiction – an infinite quantity of pleasures is utterly incoherent, if postulated as an end. A realisable end should be minimally realisable (*SH*, 85). Consequently, the idea of any calculus of pleasures or interests (or preferences) strikes Bradley as meaningless. This is the point Bradley developed under the rubric of a 'moral almanac'. Schneewind, in replying to this point for Sidgwick, comments that these objections depend on certain doctrines, concerning either the internality of relations, which makes certain types of abstraction illegitimate, or the concrete universal as the necessary structure of the moral end, which makes it impossible that the end should be a 'mere aggregate'. Yet, as neither Bradley nor Green, in presenting the objections, explains their conceptual bases, it is easy to feel sympathy with Sidgwick when he allows that he finds it hard to state the point of Green's version of them in a convincing manner. (*SE*, 395)

Again, Schneewind appears to be engaging in empty philosophical posturing. Is it surely nothing much to do with 'conceptual bases' to ask how something so weird and inchoate as an unrealisable infinite series of transient contingent changing pleasures (or interests for that matter) could serve as a guide to moral conduct? Bradley's notion that such calculative utilitarianism is just extremely strange seems quite sensible – whether or not he is an Hegelian.

For Bradley, pleasures may not always be good and pain not always bad. Some pleasures and pains may, in fact, be neither good nor bad. Pleasure, in other words, is not coterminous with morality. If pleasure is the end, it would appear to be more significant than virtue. Virtue becomes merely a means. In addition, virtuous acts, as we commonly recognise them, do not always conduce to happiness.[43] The greatest good and most virtuous acts do not necessarily lead to the greatest pleasure. This would appear to be a mundane observation on moral experience. Thus, hedonism and utilitarianism clash with ordinary morality. Morality may include pleasure, but it is not the end of moral action. Pleasure may supervene on morality, but is not coincidental with it. Further, utility does not tell us how to act. To think of pleasure as a motive is to confuse a 'motive' (the object before the mind) with a 'psychical stimulus' (which is not an object before the mind).

– CONCLUSION –

Sidgwick saw the task of moral theory to make moral methods clear and explicit. Theory can also take the extra hesitant step and prescribe actions. In some ways, Sidgwick hovers in between these tasks – the 'hermeneutic underlabourer' and 'normative'. Bradley, on the other hand, represents a more distinct anti-theoretical strand in moral philosophy, also identifiable in current writers like Bernard Williams or Alisdair MacIntyre, and from a different angle in Michael Oakeshott, which suggests that rationalist moral philosophy is part of the problem, rather than the solution. In fact, much moral philosophy presents a rather poverty-stricken straitjacket of what actually constitutes moral discourse – if it is not about clear obligations and consequences it is seen as not counting. This is though not an anti-morality position. For Bradley, everyday morality is just not philosophically discursive.

The agent knows what is right or wrong in moral conduct 'by an intuitive subsumption, which does not know that it is a subsumption' (*ES*, 196). To deliberate in moral conduct is to be lost. The Hegelian and communitarian perspective underpinning Bradley's argument is very much to the fore here. If morality becomes reflective and tells us what we ought to do, then we move, wittingly or unwittingly, into the realm of casuistry. This is Bradley's reading of Sidgwick, although, as argued, whether it is *totally* accurate is open to question.

In terms of the relative merits of the above debate, Bradley's critique anticipates many of the late twentieth-century criticisms of utilitarianism, although the maximand 'pleasure' has now been replaced by 'preferences', 'interests' and 'welfare', partly because of the kind of criticism that Bradley (and others) offered of hedonism. Utilitarianism is now no longer 'hedonic'; although it is far from clear the modern utilitarians can avoid the general critical thrust of Bradley's position in *ES*. Sidgwick, however, also offered a more morally eclectic and analytical argument, which not only looks to later utilitarian thought, but also to many of the developments in twentieth-century analytic moral philosophy and postmodern theory which reconciles itself to the contingency in morality. Bradley's arguments, as suggested earlier, also relate closely to late twentieth-century arguments for communitarianism, although his thought is more subtle, dialectical and nuanced. However, it is also important to see that both Bradley and Sidgwick reveal, in the course of the debate, the strengths and weaknesses of nineteenth-century utilitarian and communitarian perspectives. Since both Bradley and Sidgwick were such powerful polemical thinkers, capable of detailed clear-headed analysis, the confrontation between them reveals a philosophical fragility (of sorts). Both cut through each other's arguments so quickly, that it is almost alarming to find the frail-looking metaphysical roots so completely exposed. In this sense, their confrontation is immensely revealing.

– NOTES –

The following abbreviations will be used in the text for commonly cited works:

ME   *Methods of Ethics*, by Henry Sidgwick (London, Macmillan 1907: 7th edn)

M   *Henry Sidgwick: A Memoir*, by A. S. and E. M. S. Sidgwick (London, Macmillan, 1906)

CN   'Critical Notice of *Ethical Studies*', by Henry Sidgwick, *Mind*, vol. 1 (1876)

R   'Response' [Note on Bradley's note], by Henry Sidgwick, Notes and Discussions, *Mind*, vol. 2 (1877)

SE   *Sidgwick's Ethics and Victorian Moral Philosophy*, by J. B. Schneewind (Oxford, Clarendon Press, 1977)

ES   *Ethical Studies*, by F. H. Bradley (Oxford, Clarendon Press, 1962: 2nd edn)

SES   'Mr. Sidgwick on "Ethical Studies"', by F. H. Bradley, Notes and Discussions, *Mind*, vol. 2 (1877)

SH   *Mr. Sidgwick's Hedonism*, in F. H. Bradley, *Collected Essays*, vol. 1 (Oxford, Clarendon Press, 1935)

1. T. H. Green's own much more fulsome and, at the time, better known Idealist ethical treatise, the *Prolegomena to Ethics*, was published posthumously in 1883.

2. As to why Bradley did not revise *ES* sooner remains an open question. It has been suggested that he had developed increasingly a 'distaste' for ethics and that he had become that much more sceptical about moral judgement, see Carol A. Keene introduction, *Collected Works of F. H. Bradley, Refinement and Revision 1903–1924*, vol. 3 (Bristol, Thoemmes, 1999), xx; see also Keene's Introduction to *Collected Works of F. H. Bradley, Selected Correspondence 1872–1904*, vol. 4 (Bristol, Thoemmes, 1999), xxiii–xxiv. Bradley obviously was very much in and out of love with his own book (*ES*). Keene comments in the Introduction to the above volume that 'In 1886, responding to a suggestion about an American reprint, he ... speaks of the need to rewrite the book, though he doesn't object to such a reprint nor does he repudiate the work. Then, in *Appearance and Reality* he notes that *Ethical Studies* in the main continues to represent his views, but in 1901, he says to Stout that he declined a request from his publisher to reissue *Ethical Studies* whether revised or not, and felt like asking them: "Am I a dog to return to my vomit?" ... In 1906, however, while in one instance stating that his work includes certain opinions no longer held by him, in another instance ... he confides to Stout that he doesn't mind ... [it] being reprinted.' By 1914, Bradley signalled that the idea of a reissue in the Preface to his *Essays on Truth and Reality* would be acceptable. By the 1920s, however, he regretted that the work had been so long out of print, xxiii–xxiv.

3. It was probably C. D. Broad (in his *Five Types of Ethical Theory*, published originally in 1930, and reaching its eight impression in 1962) who kept alive much of the interest in Sidgwick in university moral philosophy courses. Broad's book was a convenient text for ethics courses. The 1962 impression of *Five Types* coincided with the 1962 reprint of Sidgwick's (1907) 7th edition of *ME*. Oddly, Sidgwick's 1907 *ME* had also been republished in 1922, and then 1962; also Bradley's *ES* (2nd edition) was published in 1927 (ed. Marian de Glehn and H. H. Joachim) and then (with Richard Wollheim's Introduction) in 1962. This may all be purely coincidental.

4. See R. E. Goodin, 'Utilitarianism as a Public Philosophy' in Andrew Vincent (ed.), *Political Theory: Tradition and Diversity* (Cambridge, Cambridge University Press, 1997), 70.

5. At the time, we must recall, Mill's *Utilitarianism* was an immensely well-known and popular text, which had been written only fifteen years before *ES*. For Bradley's preparatory notes to *ES* see *Collected Works of F. H. Bradley: A Pluralistic Approach to Philosophy 1865–1882*, ed. Carol Keene (Bristol, Theommes, 1999), 199–232.

6. Sidgwick was obviously still occasionally in Bradley's mind in later years, and the irritability is still very much present. In a letter to A. C. Bradley, in November 1883, he notes that the 3rd edition of Sidgwick's *ME* is published, remarking 'Sidgwick is going into a third edition and anything more lamentable than the confusion "reason" brings in with him I can hardly conceive'. *Collected Works: Selected Correspondence 1872–1904*, 15.

7. Henry Sidgwick, 'The Philosophy of T. H. Green', *Mind*, vol. 10, N. S. (1901).

8. Sidgwick had been a school friend of Green's at Rugby and had travelled with him in Europe, although their relationship was somewhat tense. As the years went by it became more strained.

9. See, for example, Nicholas Griffin, *Russell's Idealist Apprenticeship* (Oxford, Clarendon

Press, 1991) and Peter Hylton, *Russell, Idealism and the Emergence of Analytical Philosophy* (Oxford, Clarendon Press, 1990).

10. Sidgwick quoted in S. Collini, 'The Ordinary Experience of Civilised Life: Sidgwick and the Method of Reflective Analysis', in S. Collini, D. Winch and J. Burrows (eds), *That Noble Science of Politics* (Cambridge, Cambridge University Press, 1983), 299. Bradley also came to regret some of his harsh critical style in works like *ES*, although there appeared to be no overt regret with regards to Sidgwick's thought; see Keene's Introduction to *Collected Works, Selected Correspondence 1872–1904*, xxv.

11. 'Pathetic' here is more than likely indicating strong emotion or passions, or, overly earnest, rather than 'feeble' or 'contemptuous' (a more modern usage). My thanks to Peter Nicholson for pointing this out to me.

12. Peter Nicholson, *The Political Philosophy of the British Idealists* (Cambridge, Cambridge University Press, 1990), 234, n. 2.

13. A. MacIntyre, *A Short History of Ethics* (London, Macmillan, 1974), 244. The Frederick Maitland quote is from Sidgwick, *M*, 306. On Sidgwick's writing style, C. D. Broad remarked '[Sidgwick] incessantly refines, qualifies, raises objections, answers them and then finds further objections to the answers ... the reader is apt to become impatient; to lose the thread of the argument; and to rise from his desk finding that he has read a great deal with constant admiration and now remembers little or nothing'; quoted in D. G. James, *Henry Sidgwick: Science Faith and Society in Victorian England* (London, Oxford University Press, 1970), 29–30. Sidgwick's reviewing and oral styles were clearly a lot livelier and more incisive.

14. Bradley's view here reflects closely Hegel's own conception of philosophy; see, for example, G. W. F. Hegel, *The Philosophy of Right*, trans. T. M. Knox (Oxford, Oxford University Press, 1971), Preface, 10–11. The next clear and forceful statement of this position, in the British Idealist tradition, can be found in Michael Oakeshott (no doubt influenced by Bradley, as much as Hegel), who also declared unequivocally that philosophy, or any theoretical mode such as history or science, was incapable of offering injunctions for practical conduct; see the Oakeshott essay in this volume and Oakeshott, *Experience and Its Modes* (Cambridge, Cambridge University Press, 1933).

15. See Bernard Williams, *Ethics and the Limits of Philosophy* (London, Harper Collins, 1993), 174. This argument forms an important theme of his whole book.

16. The first preface to *ME* notes that the book 'claims to be an examination, at once expository and critical, of the different methods of obtaining convictions as to what ought to be done which are found ... in the moral consciousness of mankind' (*ME*, 1st edition, Preface, v)

17. This became a standard criticism of all forms of positivism. For the various debates around this point at the turn of the twentieth century see the essays in this volume on Bosanquet and Ritchie.

18. As he noted in a letter (with an obvious niggling image of T. H. Green in mind), 'I naturally shrink from exercising on others the personal influence which would make men [resemble] me ... I would not if I could, and I could not if I would, say anything which would make philosophy – my philosophy – popular' (*M*, from Journal 1884, 396).

19. D. G. Ritchie commented in his review of Sidgwick's *Elements of Politics* (although it applies equally to the *ME*) that it was 'much that we might expect from the end of the century Blackstone, or from an English Hegel, showing the rationality of the existing order of things with only a few modest proposals for reform'. D. G. Ritchie, 'A Review of *The Elements of Politics*', *International Journal of Ethics*, 2 (1892), 255.

20. The term was D. G. Ritchie's from the above review in n. 19.

21. See Collini, *Noble Science*, 294. Sidgwick would, in fact, probably still be partly right today about utilitarianism. As Iris Murdoch has remarked, 'Some form of utilitarianism is probably now the most widely and instinctively accepted philosophy of the western world.' Iris Murdoch, *Metaphysics as Guide to Morals* (Middlesex, Penguin Books, 1993), 47.

22. This is partly explained by Schneewind, who comments that 'Bradley's view rests on the unstated Hegelian idea that the world spirit, operating through us, moves ever onward to new stages of development ... philosophy can no more anticipate its evolution in morality than it can in science'. Apart from the addition of 'unstated Hegelian idea that the world spirit', the position attributed to Bradley is not unlike Sidgwick's. It is also not clear what 'world spirit' means here (in Schneewind's comment) and whether Bradley is concerned by such an idea. Schneewind continues that Bradley's 'position is thus at odds with Sidgwick's belief that the same principle which provides an adequate explication of the "morality current in the world" must also provide the basis for a method of rectifying morality' (*SE*, 399). It is not clear what Schneewind is suggesting here. Bradley certainly does not say that anything 'outside the world' can be used to resolve issues; like Sidgwick he appears to think that all that we have is to hand. One difference to Sidgwick is that Bradley considers that one can identify a critical sequence within the moral forms and arguments and that we can also gain a critical insight into where we stand. Bradley is also more secure in the belief that moral philosophy cannot *prescribe* a future course of action. Sidgwick wavers on this issue.

23. There was also a strong sense of long-standing personal rivalry and impatience with his old school friend, T. H. Green (and Green's public reputation), which adds something piquant to his criticisms of Idealism.

24. MacIntyre, *A Short History of Ethics*, 243–4.

25. Bradley's own deeply sceptical views on spiritualism (which might not be unrelated to Sidgwick's more positive interest) can be found in 'The Evidences of Spiritualism' in the *Fortnightly Review* in 1885, republished in his *Collected Essays* (Oxford, Clarendon Press, 1968), vol. II, 595–617. For additional notes and materials on spiritualism see *Collected Works of F. H. Bradley: Refinement and Revision*, ed. Carol Keene, 297–307.

26. Utilitarians have often claimed, to the present day, that utilitarianism is a second order moral doctrine which universally, impersonally and neutrally provides a way of solving and reconciling first order particular moral preferences. In this sense, the historically and communally focused notion of utility in Sidgwick is unusual and problematic.

27. Collini, *Noble Science*, 291.

28. In fact, the 'enlightened' and 'vulgar' distinction, which in J. S. Mill appears as 'higher' and 'lower' pleasures, reappears in twentieth-century utilitarianism. Harsanyi, for example, in order to make his case, tries to distinguish 'manifest' and 'true' preferences, which unwittingly echoes the same theme of 'real or enlightened interests' as against 'false or vulgar interest'; see J. C. Haransyi, 'Morality and the Theory of Rational Behaviour', in *Utilitarianism and Beyond*, ed. A. K. Sen and B. Williams (Cambridge, Cambridge University Press, 1982), 55.

29. Thus, 'the attempt to make right "objective" in abstraction from the individual, has issued in the confession that right is "subjective", and individual judgement the practical criterion' (*SH*, 114).

30. Yet, 'just as in metaphysic we see abstract individualism and abstract universalism turn round the one into the other, just as in Kant's Practical Philosophy the categorical imperative covered in the end anything or nothing, so in our author's Hedonistic casuistry

we shall find that "objective rightness", just because he has made it objective, becomes in fact merely subjective' (*SH*, 107).

31. R. M. Hare, 'The Argument from Received Opinion' in Hare, *Essays on Philosophical Method* (London, Macmillan, 1971), 122.

32. 'In order to will we must will something; the universal side by itself is not will at all. To will we must identify ourselves with this, that, or the other; and here we have the particular side, and the second factor in volition. Thirdly, the volition as a whole … is the identity of both these factors, and the projection or carrying of it out into external existence … The unity of the two factors we may call the individual whole, or again the concrete universal' (*ES*, 72).

33. As one contemporary of Sidgwick remarked: Sidgwick had a clear recognition of the 'inseparable connection of Ethics and Sociology. Yet I doubt whether he has done everything that this connection would impose upon him', A. Bain, 'Mr Sidgwick's Methods of Ethics', *Mind*, vol. 1 (1876), 196.

34. Michael Sandel, *Liberalism and the Limits of Justice* (Cambridge, Cambridge University Press, 1982). See also S. Mulhall, and Adam Swift, 2nd edition, *Liberals and Communitarians* (Oxford, Blackwell, 1996); also E. F. Paul, F. D. Miller and J. Paul (eds), *The Communitarian Challenge to Liberalism* (Cambridge, Cambridge University Press, 1996).

35. The universalisability rule implies 'the formal property of holding for all rather than only for some cases within a specified domain'; see Onora O'Neill, *Towards Justice and Virtue* (Cambridge, Cambridge University Press, 1996), 4.

36. Not totally novel, for example, if one looks at the writings of R. M. Hare.

37. As Schneewind remarks, 'Sidgwick has little to say about reason as such, and what little he says he puts in commonplace terms' (*SE*, 229–30).

38. For Schneewind, 'Sidgwick's [moral] axioms … have their source in our reason. They are obtained not by mental inspection of esoteric entities or qualities, but by considering what reason requires of action under the conditions set by the most basic facts of human life. They function by requiring us to generalise whenever we assign a reason for an act or a desire' (*SE*, 303–4).

39. For Schneewind, the unstated point behind Bradley's comments is the Hegelian one 'true rationality cannot be found either in abstract universals or in bare particulars but only in the concrete universal' (*SE*, 393). There is something in his point, but it is certainly not the whole case, as Sidgwick himself admits.

40. In the manner that Richard Rorty develops in *Contingency Irony and Solidarity* (Cambridge, Cambridge University Press, 1989).

41. Bernard Williams comments on this that utilitarianism assumes 'the mind, before any experience is empty … it involves elaborate and implausible explanations about evolution and human learning', Williams, *Ethics and the Limits of Philosophy*, 106.

42. Bradley notes that Sidgwick appears to be saying that 'I intuitively think that Utilitarianism is right'. Bradley comments, 'I do not' (*ES*, 128).

43. Bradley obviously enjoyed this quote from Sir James Fitzjames Stephens, 'If I wanted to make you happy, which I do not, I should do so by pampering to your vices, which I will not' (*ES*, 105).

CHAPTER 3

Bernard Bosanquet:
The Sociology of Philosophy
and the Philosophy of Sociology

In terms of the philosophical traditions of the nineteenth and twentieth centuries, it is notable that the Idealists, *par excellence*, can be described as being both *political* and *social* philosophers.[1] The concepts of *society* and *state* form crucial motifs, both being fully integrated into the larger systematic structures of Idealist thought. However, the subtle and insistent emphasis laid on the concept on society – as none the less subtly and structurally related to the state and prefaced in Hegel's rich distinctions between civil society (and the system of needs) and the state – is relatively unique in political philosophy, even to the present day. One noteworthy point here on the Idealists – particularly the generation of British Idealists who were writing at the turn of this century – is that their conception of society and social philosophy interacted in complex ways, not only with the social policy, but also with burgeoning ideas of the new discipline of sociology. This latter point has been explored very fruitfully in some recent work; however, I wish to concentrate particularly on Bernard Bosanquet's responses to this issue to reveal important aspects of his thought.[2] The crucial question behind Bosanquet's discussion was: was sociology a discrete discipline which had, by cultivating itself as a 'science', transcended philosophy. In other words, could sociology ultimately explain (in a Comtean manner) even the philosophical impulse; or, conversely, did philosophy still have a pre-eminent place in reflective study, such that it was able to incorporate sociological findings, no matter how empirical, within a broader interpretative philosophical framework?

The primary focus of this essay will thus be on the nascent discipline of sociology, as perceived through the writings of Bernard Bosanquet. The discussion will initially examine the general contours of sociology at the turn of the century and Bosanquet's general involvement. The discussion will then turn to Auguste Comte and the perception of positivist science within sociology. Three substantive areas will then be examined – biology, political economy and psychology – which, in Bosanquet's view, colour the whole debate about sociology. Each of these will be discussed in the context of Bosanquet's critical reflections. Finally, the discussion will focus on a comparison between Émile Durkheim's and Bosanquet's understanding of sociology. Bosanquet regarded Durkheim as one of the most original and forceful of all sociological thinkers at the time.[3] There are a number of significant areas of agreement, as well as major differences, between the two thinkers. This comparison reveals significant dimensions, not only of Bosanquet's general theory of society, but also of the general parameters of the debate about sociology in the twentieth century.

– CONTOURS OF SOCIOLOGY IN BRITAIN –

It is important to realise that, in the 1890s and 1900s, what we now think of as relatively discrete disciplines were much less well-defined. There was also a considerable practical and theoretical overlap of concerns. This would particularly be the case with subjects like politics, history, law, anthropology, philosophy and sociology. Sociology was a neologism from the nineteenth century – invented by the French theorist Auguste Comte. The first British interests in sociology arose in the 1830s, in the context of statistical empirical concerns about levels of poverty.[4] This would include debates from 1834 up to 1909 – and continuing in some cases into the 1950s and 1960s. The quantitative statistical approach gradually took hold over the nineteenth century, on both governments and social investigators. The later nineteenth century studies of Booth and the early twentieth-century work of Rowntree, and the Webbs, were still rooted strongly in this quantitative tradition. British sociology, thus, from its inception, always had a strong empirical positivist bent. It is thus not surprising that the earliest society, showing sociological interests, was the Statistical Society of London founded in 1834. A comparable statistical organisation was founded in the USA at the same time. The British society was minimally united by a common belief in the utility of quantitative information. Early sociology – notably within the Statistical Society – also had strong links with political economy and individual philanthropy. Philip Abrams sees this latter dimension connected to a form of 'social ameliorism', which was eventually given institutional shape in the National Association for the Promotion of the Social Sciences, founded in 1856. The ameliorist thrust continued into the twentieth century in the Webbs, T. H. Marshall and later R. M. Titmus. For Abrams, the outstanding and dominant representative of this ameliorist impulse was the Charity Organization Society.

The first university chair in sociology was established in 1907, from a private trust in the University of London. Its first occupant was L. T.

Hobhouse, who would now probably hardly be recognised as a sociologist. This was the only chair in sociology in Britain until after 1945, which tells us a lot about the way the discipline has been viewed academically. After 1900, particularly, the key reason for the slow growth of sociology was the refusal of the older universities to endorse it. It was often seen as a form of 'undisciplined eclecticism'.[5] A number of notable academic writers – including Henry Sidgwick, T. H. Huxley and Leslie Stephen – had expressed deep suspicions of the new discipline and its knowledge claims from the 1880s. Alternatively, figures like Patrick Geddes, who acclaimed sociology, upbraided the ineffectual role of universities. However, by and large, the philanthropic, empirical and ameliorist aspect of the discipline carried it forward. The Sociological Society was founded in June 1903. The idea for such a society had originally been discussed in the Royal Statistical Society. As most commentators have noted, the Sociological Society was a mixed bag.[6] It embodied a wide cross-section, representing virtually all shades of social and political opinion – evolutionary/biological theory, eugenics, civics (the study of urban environments), Idealism, positivism, statistical concerns, socialism and new liberal ideas. Émile Durkheim, Ferdinand Tönnies and E. Westermarck were corresponding members by 1904. Some saw it inheriting the role of the National Association for the Promotion of the Social Sciences, in providing proposals and empirical data for government departments, although the picture had become more cloudy in the 1900s. Between 1905 and 1907 the Society published annually a series of *Sociological Papers*. These three volumes of papers, according to Abrams, contain sixty-one distinct definitions of the new discipline. The only partial consensus in the society was that the sociology was some kind of science. There was less agreement about the contents or nature of that science. Abrams noted, 'It is in this chaos that the origins of British sociology are to be found.'[7]

Bosanquet's own involvement in sociology and social philosophy began in the late 1880s, in the context of a number of voluntaristic London-based groups. The most significant of these was the very practically minded Charity Organization Society. However, Bosanquet was also involved in the London Ethical Movement, where his sociological interest was also pursued. Initially, he lectured for the London Ethical Society, founded in September 1886. However, in 1897, he shifted with others, like J. H. Muirhead, to a newly constituted body, the 'School of Ethics and Social Philosophy'. His move was due to some philosophical unease about the London Ethical Society's Comtean direction. Under the Chairmanship of E. J. Urwick, the new School of Ethics and Social Philosophy had strong aspirations for university teaching status within the University of London.[8] With Bosanquet's assistance, they tried to seek recognition for their teachers under the 1899 University of

London Act. The application was refused and the school was ultimately taken over by the London School of Economics.[9]

With Bosanquet's enthusiastic support, the Charity Organization Society also set up its own school of sociology, in 1896, premised on a training programme for their social workers.[10] Sociology figured prominently in this programme, although it was a rather particular conception of the discipline. The training programme eventually assumed the title 'School of Sociology and Social Economics' in 1903, although its primary task was still seen as the provision of proper training in social work – something dear to the heart of Charity Organization leaders. Bosanquet was the leading light in the new school, although E. J. Urwick, a former sub-warden at Toynbee Hall and director of the School of Ethics and Social Philosophy, was the main organiser. The teaching of the school focused on sociology, social theory and practical instruction in charitable and poor law administration. It became independent of the Charity Organization Society within a year, although it was unofficially still propounding the Charity Organization Society position on social work training and sociology. Bosanquet chaired its executive from 1908–12. However, the school was closed in 1912, due to financial difficulties. It was then quickly amalgamated into the London School of Economics, much to Bosanquet's deep annoyance. Despite his wide-ranging philosophical interests, Bosanquet retained a keen interest in developments in sociology up to and beyond the First World War.

Bosanquet's fuller discussion of sociology and philosophy appeared in chapter two of his *Philosophical Theory of the State* (1899), where he noted that his use of 'social philosophy' was very close to the term 'sociology', although there were also significant differences.[11] At the turn of the nineteenth century there was little agreement, as mentioned, on the terminology of sociology – let alone its subject matter. Other terms were in use at the time as equivalents for sociology, for example, 'social physics' (originating with Auguste Comte), 'science of man', 'social theory', 'social ethics' and 'social philosophy'. In some readings, because of the particular etymological root *socio*, sociology was also seen as equivalent to socialism. This idea would have been further unwittingly facilitated by claims in the 1890s, qua German Marxism, for 'scientific socialism'.

The term sociology, in 1900, suggested a number of possible substantive meanings. First, at the most general level, sociology could be equivalent to the reflective study of society or humans in society. In this context, any more profound reflection on social life by biologists, political economists, philosophers or statisticians could be regarded as sociological, at the most general level. Sociology thus acted as a refractor for a number of intellectual tendencies. The development of sociology in Britain, in the nineteenth century and early twentieth century, focused these various tendencies increasingly into a singular, if internally complex, discipline. Second, at the time of the publication of Bosanquet's *Philosophical Theory of the State*, it would be a rough and ready truism to say that the specifically 'natural science' sense of sociology was becoming more prominent in Anglo-French perceptions. Some German critics were more suspicious of this move.[12] The most inclusive term to cover this 'natural science' movement is 'positivism', although this also covers a multitude of ideas. As one contemporary Idealist thinker put it in 1895: 'It is the sense in which the now familiar term Sociology is commonly accepted, which may be described as the study of society as the object of an empirical science. It is evident that human society may be made the object of such a study, just as any other collection of facts may.'[13]

This positivistic tendency often focused on the biological sciences. Evolutionary theory was particularly significant here, as well as the multiple offshoots from evolution, like eugenics. This focus on the more positivistic sense of sociology also coincided with the long-standing empirical interests in statistical explanation and liberal political economy. The problem for this reading of sociology, for certain commentators in the 1900s, was that themes which often animate social life could not be directly observed in the same way as other 'natural' phenomena. In addition, it is 'we who observe ... are ourselves a portion of it, and ... our observation of it may become a factor in the modification of its course'.[14] These philosophical issues, which are central to Bosanquet's response to sociology, still resonate within contemporary philosophy of social science.

A third sense of the term sociology was concerned with 'the systematic effort to deduce the laws of social life from certain primary principles, which are ascertained by philosophical analysis'.[15] In this more *a priori* context, sociology *could* even be synonymous with, or be included within, political philosophy. Political philosophy would therefore be seen to have a socio-logical moment.[16] Thus, one of Bosanquet's Idealist contemporaries sug-gested that 'The beginnings of [sociology] are seen in the *Politics* of Aristotle. In more modern times it owes much to Hobbes, Spinoza, Shaftesbury, Hutchenson, Rousseau, Montesquieu'.[17] Thus, even now, if we look back at L. T. Hobhouse's (in his own view) 'sociological writings', for example, *The Metaphysical Theory of the State*, *The Rational Good*, *Mind in Evolution*, we would be hard put not conceive of them as political philosophy, rather than sociology. Apart from recent social and critical theory, this may be a sense of the term that we have partially lost in the late twentieth century. The more inclusive strategy, incorporating sociology as a moment of philosophy, charac-terised many of the British Idealists of this period, including Bosanquet.

– COMTE AND SCIENCE –

Positivism is conceptually linked to a number of cognates like empiricism and naturalism.[18] However, the term can broadly denote two related things. First, it indicates those who accept the designation positivist, as in the followers of Auguste Comte, or the twentieth-century Viennese logical positivism movement, although the latter are occasionally cited as neo-positivist. Comte's legacy – especially via 'positivist sociology' – formed a backcloth of beliefs which resonate with other positivist sympathisers in the twentieth century. Comte's ideas, developed in the *Cours de philosophie positive*, maintained that positive science would triumph ultimately over metaphysics and religion, both of the latter being viewed as prior stages of human development. As Comte noted,

> now that the human mind has founded astronomy, and terrestrial physics – both mechanical and chemical – and organic physics – both botanical and biological – it remains to finalise the system of the sciences by founding *social physics*, such is, in several capital respects, the greatest and most pressing intellectual need today.[19]

Comte also insisted on a clear boundary between tested facts and imaginary theoretical constructions; he had a strong belief in progress through science; and asserted a linkage between moral and material progress, namely, that the knowledge that science provides would allow all manner of technological control in both natural and the social and political fields. All these themes impacted on early twentieth-century positivist theory, particularly in the social sciences. Comtism entered British intellectual life between the 1850s and 1870s with the publication of a translation of Comte's *Cours*. There was a small and active positivist group who participated in associations, like the London Ethical Society and Sociological Society. In many ways, Comtists fitted well into the scientific and ameliorist tradition of British social science. Many, like Sidney Webb, however, admired Comte's 'scientific method' rather than his vision of a 'positive polity' or 'positive church of humanity'. However, as one commentator noted, on the broader level of method 'all the pioneers of British sociology were positivists however much they might dissociate themselves from Comte'.[20]

The second sense of positivism – which reasserts many of the Comtean ideas – embodies a more general adherence to certain epistemological theses. For example: the unity of the sciences, the belief that the only valid standard of knowledge we have lies either in the empirical sciences or logic and mathematics, the assumption of the reality of sense impressions, the conception of a scientific theorist as a dispassionate observer who never asserts anything which has not been empirically proved, an intense dislike and mistrust of metaphysical thought, adherence to a notion of philosophy as impartial second-order analysis, and its being parasitic upon first-order science, the acceptance of the clear distinction between fact and value, more specifically, the belief that the natural and social sciences share a certain common methodology, also the belief in a growing body of empirically tested positive knowledge.[21]

Bosanquet was very much preoccupied with the 'natural science' and positivist reading of sociology. He gave an interested, if wary, response to Comte. He noted, for example, that, as far back as Vico, there had been attempts to found a 'science of society'. In the nineteenth century, this tendency found its most distinctive utterance in Comte's work. For Bosanquet, the essence of this 'positivist' approach was 'the inclusion of human society among the objects of natural science'. It thus, characteristically, functioned in terms of the terminology of 'law' and 'causation', although Bosanquet saw some parallels between Comte's view of unity of man and nature and the interdependence of phenomena and the general thrust of Ancient Greek philosophy. However, there were differences between Comte and Greek thought. For the 'modern' Comtean enquirer, interested in this tendency in social study, the central question is 'what are the laws and causes operative among aggregations of human beings, and what are their predictable effects?' (*PTS*, 17). The social philosophy (and Idealist-based) approach – which resonates with the Greeks – asks a different question, namely, 'what is the completest and most real life of the human soul?' As Bosanquet stated, in another essay, social philosophy can in fact be defined as concerned with the 'art of living together'.[22] He added here, in a slightly more captious tone, that we often become so habituated to this 'art' that we often mistakenly perceive it as 'solid fact'.

The latter comment is the clue to Bosanquet's whole perspective on positivist sociology. The above two questions underpin Bosanquet's thoughts on this issue. The central concern, for Bosanquet, is the relation between these two questions. It is clear from his writings that he was not rejecting outright the empirical or natural science approach, rather, it had to be blended within a broader interpretative framework. It is characteristic, in fact, of Bosanquet's overall approach, in many of his areas of study, to look for lines of convergence and synthesis rather than antagonism. Sociology is but one example of this idea of potential convergence.

Bosanquet noted that certain modes of experience 'colour the mind' and have consequent deep effects on other modes of theory. The precision which Newtonian science, astronomy and mathematics require had also been demanded in social study. Bosanquet did not deny the possible merits of this precision, but noted that, first, we must initially be careful in the use of the terms science itself. Science does not always mean 'natural science' (see *PTS*,

19ff.). Bosanquet was keying into an intellectual truism here. Science could mean – certainly in the Germanic tradition – either 'systematic study' (*Wissenschaft*) or 'natural science method' (*Naturwissenschaft*). One can thus be systematic (qua scientific) in social theory without being 'naturally' scientific.

Second, he expressed some unease with the idea of mathematical precision, as the model for social study. Sidney and Beatrice Webb, for example, amongst many others at the time, were keen proponents of precise scientific observation and quantitative method in sociology – a theme that continued in British sociology (and social science) throughout the twentieth century. The Webbs were positively antagonistic to philosophy and saw no place for it in sociology.[23] This thesis contained direct echoes of Comte, who saw philosophy as a stage of development prior to genuine positive science. Positive science could thus explain even the philosophical impulse. This point also has some direct echoes with the 'underlabourer' conception of philosophy, logical positivism and various forms of empiricist philosophies of the sciences developed in the twentieth century. For example, the writers of the Vienna circle (focused on logical positivism), in the 1920s and 1930s, moved in this general direction; although philosophy still had a role, it was none the less only as a handmaid to genuine scientific knowledge. Bosanquet's response to positivist theories was to float the syncretic idea of a possible systematic reconciliation between philosophy and empirical science. This was part of the root of his interest in Durkheim. Some of his contemporaries shared this belief that a rapprochement of sorts was possible. L. T. Hobhouse, for example, saw a symbiotic relation between social philosophy and natural science. In 1907, in his inaugural lecture for the first Sociology Chair in Britain, Hobhouse noted that 'The ideal sociologist will be both a social philosopher and a social scientist, continuously testing his science against his philosophy and his philosophy against his science.'[24] In many ways, Hobhouse empiricises or naturalises Green's Idealism, which again has some parallels with both Bosanquet's and Durkheim's aims.[25]

Third, however, the specific 'mode' of natural science – particularly as found in positivism – was regarded with scepticism by Bosanquet. This natural science perspective in 1900 was strongly equated with Baconian method and direct observation of facts. Comte, and to some extent Durkheim, were both Baconians. In fact, the Baconian method was very much present in the inductivism of social investigators like the Webbs. Sidney Webb, particularly, was a devout early admirer of Comtean method.[26] For Bosanquet, the basic fallacy of this position, and something that Baconians thereafter have fallen into, was 'to suppose that facts can be collected first and theorising put off till afterwards'.[27] If one wishes to examine empirical detail, then theory is required. Without theory we examine unrelated facts. Facts alone tell us nothing in themselves. For Bosanquet, it is 'philosophically important, to claim that the serious survey of human conduct in the concrete has always ... been the special tendency of Idealist philosophy'.[28] Natural science may provide insights, but 'the essence of philosophy lies in the connected vision of the totality of things'.[29] Bosanquet was affirming a basic philosophical point, which resonates within the whole Idealist school, namely, that

> if you ask what reality is, you can in the end say nothing but that it is the whole which thought is always endeavouring to affirm. And if you ask what thought is, you can in the end say nothing but that it is the central function of mind.[30]

Bosanquet's arguments here are not without contemporary resonance. One aspect of the philosophy of social science, even in the last forty years, has been a deepening suspicion about the whole Comtean ideal of science, or, more generally, the suspicion of natural science method qua social theory. One path of doubt was originally articulated by Max Weber (via Nietzsche), namely, that the reason of positive sciences was an 'iron cage', although Weber himself still held to a fairly rigid distinction between facts and values. Weber's view of reason was taken up by many of the key early members of the Frankfurt school, who saw scientific reason (or scientism) and 'technical reason' as a form of repression – whether it appeared in the more orthodox liberal enlightenment thinkers or in 'positivistic Marxism'.[31] In fact, the critique of positivism has been one of the central preoccupations of over two generations of critical theorists from Adorno, Horkheimer and Marcuse up to Habermas. Reason, in these theorists, should not be seen as a technical or instrumental idea. More than anything, genuine reason should be viewed as a transforming faculty tied to human freedom. In many ways, this represents an older theme in political philosophy, which positivists had tried to undermine, namely the recovery of 'mind', the emancipatory role of practical reason and the relevance of some notion of metaphysics – if only, in the case of Adorno, through negative dialectics and a more tempered view of the cunning of reason.

Bosanquet would have accepted the emancipatory conception of reason (and some elements of the critique of technical reason) as it developed in certain philosophies in the mid to late twentieth century. Yet, in many ways, Bosanquet is more optimistic in his conception of reason than the Frankfurt school. His ideas on the philosophy of the social sciences bear closer comparison with the hermeneutic conceptions of reason, rather than critical theory. Certain modern philosophers of hermeneutic interpretation, in the words of a recent text, 'have continued the Aristotelian notion of reason as a vital aspect of human existence, a means toward awareness and self-reflection, yet thoroughly embedded in the practices of everyday life'.[32] The world of social and political events is seen as a preinterpreted cultural world saturated with ideas (and mind). Meaningful conduct in the social world is pre-constituted through a social and cultural background. Social laws, in this context, cannot be the primary task of social understanding. Such laws introduce causal principles and technical reasoning into a sphere which is not wholly amenable to such ideas. Similarly, the separation, in positivist philosophy, between facts and value often tends to relegate culture, mind, value and human practice to the irrational sphere, and thus fails to grasp social reality.

It would not be too strong a claim to make here that the opposition that one sees developing to positivist thinking in the twentieth century, in hermeneutic writers like Gadamer, and post-Wittgensteinian writers like Winch, owes a great deal to the background of philosophical Idealism. Kuhnian 'paradigms' and Wittgensteinian 'language games', in their diverse ways, are all seen to have a constitutive character, functioning in a similar 'quasi-Idealist' manner to Bosanquet's deployment of mind and ideas. Philosophies of social or natural science which emphasise the 'theory-impregnated' character of observation are, however indirectly, keying into this Idealist theme. The distinction between explanation and understanding reiterates a similar point. Dilthey, a contemporary of Bosanquet's, also contrasted his hermeneutic views to the empiricism and social science perspective of both J. S. Mill and Comte. However, like Bosanquet, Dilthey also tries to blend empiricism with a more Idealistic 'understanding'. Hermeneutic philosophy is subject to the same form of criticism as Bosanquet's philosophy of mind, namely, that entering empathetically into the mind, character or 'life-world' of an agent, does not reveal any observable, measurable, testable or verifiable behaviour. This is not just the response of empiricist or realist philosophers to continental hermeneutics and *verstehen* theories, it is also the gist of the Webbs' critical response to Bosanquet's conception of sociology, social investigation social casework theory in the Charity Organization Society. In many ways, though, Bosanquet is closer to some later developments in hermeneutics, namely, that the understanding is not just a 'method' of cultural investigation, as in Dilthey, it is rather an implicit ontological assumption about social reality itself. This is a view he shares with Gadamer – in the latter's critique of 'method'. Gadamer however develops this ontological dimension of hermeneutics in the context of intersubjective 'language', something that remains undeveloped in Bosanquet.[33]

For many contemporary social philosophers, the human sciences cannot follow precisely the same path as the natural sciences. For the human sciences, the observer and the observed, the language we use to describe social events and the event so described, are implicated with one another. The rational agent capable of using knowledge, intending and acting is also central to social investigation in hermeneutic and Idealist writing. This is something that is implicitly or explicitly denied in most positivist writings from Comte and Durkheim through to Talcott Parsons. Individuals, political events and political behaviour, from voting to revolutions, are social objects which have to be explained without reference to intentionality. However, for hermeneuticists (and Bosanquet), we are, as Charles Taylor put it, 'self-interpreting creatures'. In politics and sociology, we have to deal with actions by interpretative agents. Politics is not an instrumental activity. No categories that we use in social study are free of deliberation and interpretation.[34] Where Bosanquet differs from most modern exponents of the interpretivism in social study (apart from the dimension of 'language'), is that, first, he thinks that the 'empirical' can be integrated within philosophical study as a *moment* of understanding. The empirical fact may be transcended by reason, but it integrates the rich detail of empirical science within itself. Second, Bosanquet has a strong teleological theory of mind and social study. Thus, reason and mind have a telos. The bulk of modern interpretivists (and hermeneuticists) are Idealists without any explicit teleology. Thus, Bosanquet would not have accepted the postmodern-inclined view that we simply make or constitute our truths. He is adamant that '*You* do not make the world; *it* communicates your nature to you.'[35] This is the mark of his Absolute Idealism.

In summary, as one of Bosanquet's Idealist contemporaries put it, metaphysics (qua Comte) is not referring to some abstruse body of abstractions, predating positive science, but rather, it is 'simply the attempt to think things out – to exhibit the relation of the facts to one another and thereby to reduce them finally to a coherent system. To do this is to disclose the informing principle of the whole.'[36] Science (and social science) therefore logically embodies its own metaphysical components. Thus, Edward Caird's assessment of Comte, on the question of the priority of positivist Baconian science over metaphysics, was that: '[Comte's] defect lies in his unconsciousness of his metaphysics, i.e. of the categories which rule his thought, and which enable him to interpret the facts of experience, and especially the facts of man's social life, so differently from his predecessors.' For Caird, as for Bosanquet, if Comte had asked himself the basic Kantian question – what is experience? – he might have discovered, 'that his own so-called positive thought was … metaphysical'.[37] Thus, metaphysics is not something to be separated from science or social existence. It is rather integral to it. Positivism and natural science are intrinsically interpretative and metaphysical and the idea that they transcend philosophy is simply mistaken. This view reconfigures the relation between sociology, philosophy and positivism and forms an important foundation to Bosanquet's position.

– BIOLOGY –

Darwin's impact, from the mid nineteenth century, on the general perception of sociology was profound. It is difficult now to appreciate the level of interest in evolutionary theory at the time. Biological and evolutionary theory permeated intellectual life, enthralling the intellectual public imagination. As J. H. Muirhead commented, 'The rise of biology into prominence in the middle of the nineteenth century ... at once began to revolutionise thought in every department'.[38] In the sphere of social science, evolutionary biology maintained, at root, that the relation between animals and humans was only one of degree and not kind. Natural evolution thus posited an elusive identity between social and biological evolution. By 1900, there were many who saw sociology as almost equivalent to biology. Works like *Social Evolution*, by the sociologist Benjamin Kidd, achieved enormous attention and wide circulation. Many of the key theoretical works of sociology at the time, for example, Herbert Spencer's *The Study of Sociology* and *The Principles of Sociology*, Gabriel Tarde's *Les lois de l'imitation*, Albert Schäffle's *Bau und Leben des socialien Korpers* and Georg Simmel's *Ueber sociale Differenzierung* and *Einleitung in die Moralwissenschaft* and, in America, Franklin H. Gidding's *The Principles of Sociology*, all converged on organic and biological themes – although often interpreting evolution in markedly different ways.

Herbert Spencer, at the time, was probably the dominant figure on the sociological scene dwarfing Comte's reputation. From his early work *Social Statics* (1851), Spencer was insistent that society was directly analogous to a natural organism. He suggested, for example, that the circulation of the blood and the distribution of nutrients around the body were equivalents to the distribution of goods around the body politic; blood corpuscles were analogous to the circulation of money in the economy; nerves in the body were comparable to telegraph wires alongside railway lines. Although distinguishing between natural and super-organic evolution both were still ultimately premised on biological naturalism. Spencer represents a strong variant of this naturalistic evolution. Naturalistic evolution emphasised that the mechanisms, through which organic species develop and emerge, are subject to continual variation and extinction in a competitive struggle premised on the survival of the fittest. Social life thus appeared largely in the form of struggle and competition. Most of the eugenicists, like Karl Pearson and Francis Galton, as well as certain Fabian contemporaries, fell within this general perspective.

For Spencer, social and organic development were subject to the same biological laws. These ideas were developed in works like the *Principles of Sociology*. For Spencer, everything from cells up to higher organisms were subject to an endless process of competition, adaptation through integration, differentiation and the seeking after higher unities. Life might thus be described as the progressive adaptation of organisms to the environment. In any such situation of adaptation the unfit and dysfunctional perish as part of the process of differentiation and integration. In fact, for evolutionary survival of a species, it is crucial that they do. Out of the 'life force' (the unknowable), cells develop, fragment and seek higher unities, more sophisticated organisms develop, in trying to adapt to the environment. At a certain point, consciousness (and mind) develops as part of this same process. Out of mind, societies develop and from societies whole civilisations. All can be accounted for in this evolutionary development of adaptation. Thus, from the above first principles of evolutionary development, Spencer tried to deduce the constituents of the major sciences – psychology, physiology and sociology and so forth.

In terms of social evolution, Spencer saw two main stages – militant and industrial societies. Militant society had adapted to a particular environment. It was essentially despotic and militarised, ruling from the top down. As societies evolved, became more complex and civilised, these despotic units fragmented and evolved into the higher more complex unity of the industrial society. Industrial society was contractual and individualised.[39] The perfectly industrialised and most evolved and civilised society, for Spencer, was equivalent to the most perfect liberalism and market-based society. The militant society was, conversely, an imperfect, less evolved society and equivalent, in Spencer's mind, to socialism and/or collectivism.

Bosanquet observed that the analogy between biological organisms and society had an ancient genealogy.[40] However, with the advent of evolution, the analogy had taken on enormous significance. For one thing, it enhanced the scientific status of disciplines like sociology and anthropology. Yet, for Bosanquet, the biological analogy often tended to explain the higher by the lower – the social by the biological. Biology, also, appeared as a form of philosophical materialism, explaining human action by lower levels of development. The higher degree of reality was, therefore, often equated with that which comes earlier in the temporal chain. For Bosanquet, this logic was a simple unexplained prejudice. It assumed that what comes first in a temporal succession must be of a higher order of reality, in terms of explanatory force. It becomes, in other words, a 'cause'. Bosanquet remarked that, 'so strong has been this bias among sociologists, that the student, primarily interested in the features and achievements of civilised society is tempted to say in his haste that the sociologist as such seldom deals seriously with true social phenomena at all' (*PTS*, 20). The focus was thus on the more primitive social or organic phenomena.

The problems Bosanquet had in mind here were threefold. First, the higher stage of human evolution, which has produced unparalleled levels of scientific development and cultural sophistication, was not something that could be evaluated by earlier stages of human development. Secondly, Bosanquet questioned the precision of the analogy between an organism and a complex industrial society constituted by human action. Within the organism, there is a single dominant nervous system with controlling powers. In the complex society, there are immensely complex and diverse organisations of individuals. Thirdly, biology might have some direct application vis-à-vis elementary instincts. Yet, natural selection and organic analogies did not really explain the way society functioned. The state, for example, in helping the weak or protecting the vulnerable, appeared to stand for none of the things which evolution indicated as crucial.[41] Thus, the idea of natural selection and the 'struggle for existence' were not necessarily adequate to explain advanced social life.[42]

For Bosanquet, biological ideas had a double effect on sociology. One whole aspect of sociological theory – which Bosanquet associated with Spencer – converged on the application of biological notions, like the survival of the fittest thesis, to human society. The central issue was that 'life can be maintained only in virtue of definite qualities adapted to that position'. It was the species rather than the individual which was at issue. Another school, however, not only insisted on the comparison of society with an individual organism, but, also maintained that the view of continual conflict was too superficial in grasping society. As Bosanquet commented, competition and cooperation were the negative and positive aspects of the division of labour (*PTS*, 23). Spencer did, in fact, have a particular intellectual problem with the notion of mind and state institutions taking any control and it was here that Spencer introduced the idea of the 'super organism'. For Bosanquet, however, Spencer's super-organic category 'brings us perhaps to the limit of what biological sociology is able to suggest with regard to the unity of the commonwealth' (*PTS*, 24). There is more than an element of truth to this point, even to the present day with sociobiology. Contemporary sociobiology in many ways continues the Spencerian conception of evolution. It also embodies the same difficulties as Spencer with explanations of advanced human societies.[43]

Another response, at the time, to the question of the relation of the biological to social realms, was to separate out the ethical process from nature. Bosanquet saw this idea developed in Huxley's famous essay on 'Evolution and Ethics'. This could be a path for sociology to cut itself free from natural science. Bosanquet however suggested that a careful study would recognise 'competition and cooperation as ineradicable and inseparable moments in human society'. A Charity Organization doctrine appeared here, namely, that competition was needed, it 'being the rejection and suppression of members who are unable to meet the ever advancing demand for co-operative character and capacity'. The social residuum idea is a lurking theme – referring to those who showed no capacity or will for self-maintenance. Stern conditions were thus needed, for Bosanquet, to deal with the problems of social parasitism (PTS, 25). For Bosanquet, the survival of the fittest doctrine 'reveals the full unity and significance of organism and environment' (PTS, 25). He contended that 'biological categories do not ... appear [in Huxley or Spencer] to have afforded any suggestion for the treatment of the social self as more and greater, in a positive sense, than the self which is less bound up with social obligations' (PTS, 25). Society always appears as a limitation and nature as self-assertion. The idea of society seems always to be explained by the nature.[44] Bosanquet was not discounting biology; he was, conversely, placing a much more radical emphasis on human will and action (and thus social existence). Human action and social life were not simply explicable from a biological perspective. As he argued in another essay, 'mind is nearer to mind than to matter, and in copying the methods of science we are abandoning the advantage of our object of study being not matter but humanity'.[45] Again Bosanquet shows the strong tendency to try syncretically to link advances in empirical sciences with philosophy.

– POLITICAL ECONOMY –

For Bosanquet, political economy predated sociology. It was also, in his view, one of the more successful forms of social explanation, from the late eighteenth century. Writers like Malthus, J. S. Mill, Ricardo and Torrens were central to many social debates, specifically in the nineteenth century. Political economy thus had had a wide-ranging impact on public policy. Bosanquet also saw important resonant aspects of the discipline embedded in Hegel's distinction between 'bourgeois society' and the 'State'. Whereas Bosanquet was wary of the rationalistic conception of social order embedded in political economy – in particular its social atomism as basis for analysis – he was sympathetic to its aims of attaining consensus and a community of interests among classes and individuals. However, the substance of that consensus, for Bosanquet, was markedly different in kind from that of orthodox political economy. Sociology was viewed by many in the nineteenth century – as others viewed biology – as an extension of political economy. Bosanquet read the impact of political economy in a more philosophical light. It embodied a thesis that humans were determined by certain basic impulses and interests.

This was yet another root to a materialist view of sociology. Karl Marx, Buckle and LePlay are *specifically* mentioned by Bosanquet as key representatives of this philosophical materialism combined with political economy. Bosanquet saw the basic argument of the materialist school as the claim that structures of society and civilisation have been 'determined by the primary necessities of human existence, and the conditions of climate and nutrition under which these necessities are met. Economic facts alone ... are real and causal; everything else is an appearance' (*PTS*, 26). To consider this thesis in more depth Bosanquet suggested that we have to examine materialism as a broader philosophical thesis.

The generic sense of materialism, to Bosanquet, meant, 'that nothing is real but that which is solid, or, ... which gravitates' (*PTS*, 26–7). This thesis was then extended, without explanation, by analogy, to the body, mind and society. The economic view therefore suggests that 'pretty much what is expressed in saying that while statesmen are arguing, love and hunger are governing mankind' (*PTS*, 28). Political economy therefore tied itself to the commonplace idea that 'certain passions and necessities, which it takes to be fundamental, are apt to be called material as opposed to ethical'. For Bosanquet, there appeared to be no satisfactory philosophical justification for this. Bodily needs and appetites were an 'element' of mind. Appetites did not explain mind, since mind *was* the medium of appetites. The idea of basic material necessities being opposed to or accounting for the ethical was therefore not logically correct. Against the Marxist view, which Bosanquet suggested might be 'an echo of true materialism', he notes that 'bodily passions' are no more 'material' than a moral doctrine like the 'categorical imperative'. Bosanquet also objected to the idea that such bodily or material passions should be considered causal (*PS*, n. 1, 27). Climate, occupation, agriculture, industry all make a difference, but they were not 'antecedent' to human life or human consciousness. Economics should not therefore be considered a science of simple material causation. There was no absolutely prior determining framework, but, 'simply certain important aspects of te operation of the human mind, rather narrowly regarded' (*PTS*, 28). For Bosanquet, if we placed too much emphasis on political economy, then we receive a false overemphasis on the mechanical pressure of facts and a consequent downplaying of the role of ideas in influencing human conduct. Economics can *only* develop through the medium of human beings in relation to their judgements and evaluations.

Thus, both evolutionary theory and political economy, together, asserted that human beings lived in the context of certain determining conditions. If those conditions came to be treated as *alien* influences, where persons became products of such forces, then serious interpretative problems arose. Consequently, Bosanquet asked rhetorically – can we explain the totality of, say, Homer's work through material conditions in Greece? Did Homer's work mean anything outside the material conditions? The crux of the matter, for Bosanquet, was that 'the world in which man lives *is* himself, but is constituted, of course, by presentation to a mind and not by strictly physical causation'. All physical conditions must pass into a world 'which a human being presents to himself' (*PTS*, 29). He thus lamented that, if only modern sociologists and economists paid more attention to Plato and Aristotle, they would not make such basic epistemological mistakes. For the Greek, 'form' was the life or organising element in 'matter'. As Bosanquet noted, 'the relation of "matter" or "conditions" to "form" or "purpose" is not, for the Greek thinker, the pressure of an alien necessity, of a hostile environment, but the upspringing of a life continuous in principle through all its phases' (*PTS*, 30). Material conditions are mediated through human judgement.

For Bosanquet, the modern sociologists, through their emphasis on a weak-minded materialism, did not appear to grasp the above points. In sum, on the one hand, society was not a sphere of simple biological or economic causation, although, on the other hand, neither could such empirical observations be ignored. 'Empiricism' and 'interpretation' had to be blended as parts of the large whole. Biology and political economy provided *conditions* with and through which human beings act in the social world. These conditions interacted in complex ways with the psychical life of human beings – a psychical life 'corresponding to external facts which admit of more or less precise statement' (*PTS*, 31). The latter clause allowed considerable space (for Bosanquet) for empirical study. However, to neglect this psychical life and the role of ideas and interpretation of events is to neglect a crucial facet of social existence.

– PSYCHOLOGY –

If Bosanquet was asking for evolutionary biologists and political economists to acknowledge the role of the human psyche and the role of human cognition, one might have expected him to take a sympathetic view of developments in psychology. Bosanquet did examine the current psychology of his day in his *Philosophical Theory of the State*. He also gave a series of lectures on psychology, a few years before the publication of the latter book, to the School of Ethics and Social Philosophy, later published as *Psychology of the Moral Self* (1897). Some sociologists, such as Tarde, at that time, were definitely attracted to a form of psychological sociology and Bosanquet was appreciative of such developments, although uneasy with some variants. He defined the subject matter of psychology as 'psychical events … or the facts experienced within a soul; together with their laws or ways of happening'

(*PMS*, 4). It is an *observation* of the machinery of mind, considered as an object. It deals with the *how* rather than the *why* or justification of psychical events, a phrase which again reiterates the distinction between explanation and understanding.

As a discipline, psychology had moved on from the earlier association-ist and atomistic variants, which T. H. Green had criticised in the 1870s. Bosanquet noted this in his psychology lectures, commenting that psychology had begun with the associationism of Hobbes, Locke, Hume and Hartley where mind was conceived (in Hume particularly) as analogous to 'a string of beads without a string' (*PMS*, 21). The gist of his response to associationism was the Kantian query, namely that something needs to be doing the associating. In fact, Bosanquet's rejection of associationism in psychology is precisely equivalent to his rejection of social atomism in Spencer's biological sociology. His remark about Hume's notion of mind as a 'string of beads without a string' is also directly analogous to his assessment of Spencer's notion of community as a 'joint-stock company *minus* a written instrument of association' (*PTS*, 71–2). Something needs to unify both mind and community.

From the 1890s, under the influence more particularly of French writers, psychology became more receptive to 'social logic' and 'social psychology'. Bosanquet found this attention to 'society' immediately appealing, as one might expect from a sophisticated Hegelian communitarian. Important writers at the time who addressed these issues were Gustav Le Bon, Gabriel Tarde and William McDougall. Tarde's *Les lois de l'imitation* (1890) and Le Bon's *Psychologie des Foules* (1893), particularly the latter, used pathological data on suggestibility taken from psychiatrists like Charcot and Janet. In Le Bon's case, he applied it to crowds. As Le Bon noted,

> Thousands of isolated individuals may acquire at certain moments, and under the influence of certain violent emotions – such, for example, as a great national event – the characteristics of a psychological crowd ... Whatever be the individuals who compose it, however like or unlike ... the fact that they have been transformed into a crowd puts them in possession of a sort of collective mind which makes them feel, think and act in a manner quite different from that in which each among then would feel, think and act were he in a state of isolation.[46]

Such group behaviour was often shown to be blind, irrational and instinctive. Following the Darwinian emphasis on unknown mechanistic factors con-trolling adaptation, this was one powerful contribution to the thesis that individual humans were socially conditioned in social masses and crowds. Graham Wallas deployed this argument in relation to democratic voting behaviour, to great effect, in his *Human Nature in Politics* (1908).

Whereas Le Bon developed a crowd psychology, Tarde's approach was more individualistic. In the 1890s, Tarde was deeply critical of the use of biology in social study in Herbert Spencer and based his own system of sociology on an individualistic psychology (what he later called 'inter-psychology'). For Tarde, 'everything in the social world is explained in terms of beliefs and desires that are imitated, spread and susceptible of increasing and diminishing, and these rises and falls are measured by statistics'.[47] Society is a union of sorts, but that unity derives from individual minds subconsciously imitating practices within groups. All social phenomena were therefore reduced to the elementary fact of imitation. Tarde did not attempt a fully developed psychology of imitation, but rather assumed it to be true. He was also deeply critical of Durkheim 'methodological collectivism'. He was, in effect, a psychologically based methodological individualist. Society, to Tarde, did not rest on any civic sense or mutual concern. Societies were rather based upon contractual agreements. But the rights implicit in such agreements were not adopted consciously, they were simply the products of imitation. Society itself was thus defined by Tarde as 'an organization of imitations'. As his English admirer William McDougall put it,

> Imitation is the prime condition of all collective mental life … when men think, feel, and act as members of a group of any kind – whether a mere mob, a committee, a political or religious association, a city, a nation, or any other social aggregate – their collective actions show that the mental processes of each man have been profoundly modified in virtue of the fact that he thought, felt, and acted as one of a group and in reciprocal mental action with other members of the group and with the group as a whole.[48]

With the emphasis on the non-rational in behaviour, social psychology developed, at this point, into a theory about mass subconscious instinct. The crowd, imitation and so forth, stressed this instinctive quality. The individual had no insight therefore into the fact that his or her actions might be explained outside the context of his or her beliefs or intentions. McDougall developed this concept of both imitation and instinct in his *Introduction to Social Psychology* (1908). This thesis was also explored before 1914 by diverse writers like George Sorel, Lévy-Bruhl and Graham Wallas.[49] Wilfred Trotter's *The Instincts of the Herd in Peace and War* (1917) carried the instinct thesis one logical step further, seeing whole nations as expressing instincts. The 'instinctive' and 'unconscious' arguments became an immensely popular part of both social and individual psychology in the 1920s in the writings of social psychologists such as Knight Dunlap and L. L. Bernard. Sigmund Freud and Carl Jung were better-known investigators of the 'instincts and unconscious thesis' from an individualist perspective.[50]

Whereas Bosanquet rejects (with Green) the earlier associationist psychology as atomistic, he is also uneasy with aspects of social psychology.

Notions like the 'mind of the crowd' and 'imitation' strengthen the role of society in relation to mind. It therefore reinforces Idealist theses about collectivities. For Bosanquet, such social psychology is clearly on the right lines. However, a crowd is not quite the same as a society *per se* and mass instinct is not the same as the general will. Thus, Bosanquet makes a distinction between an *association* and an *organisation*. A crowd (qua Le Bon) is an association of sorts, but it is markedly distinct from, say, an army, which is organised and purposive. For Bosanquet the mind of the crowd is a superficial connection between unit and unit. The crowd may act as a single being, but its level of responsibility will be insignificant and meagre. Mere linkage of units does not determine an organisation like an army. An army embodies 'operative ideas' which make sense of its actions. The army moves through operative ideas.[51] Bosanquet links the idea of a crowd, qua association, with association in psychology. *Association* in psychology is again parallel to the Humean conception of mind, whereas, *organisation* parallels the Idealist theory of the mind. This did not mean that association (qua psychology and mind) had no role to play; however, it needed supplementation by the organisation of operative ideas, that is, 'systematic connection or association between whole and part, as opposed to the same principle operating casually and superficially between unit and unit' (*PTS*, 155). One can see here the enormous philosophical, psychological and ontological resonance that the mere *title* 'Charity *Organization*' had for Bosanquet.

For Tarde, imitation and repetition were crucial for social life. These were the means (or contagion) by which ideas spread through groups. Bosanquet suggested that each man, in Tarde's reading, became a 'hypnotical creature' – 'a somnambulist acting under suggestions' (*PTS*, 42). This appeared to deny agency and rationality. Yet Bosanquet also noted that suggestion or imitation were not harmful, as long as they contributed to the best life, or provided the conditions for the development of a more rational nature. Through imitation and suggestion a society can become 'habitually recognised as a unit lawfully exercising force', and thus becomes a fully-fledged state (*PTS*, 182ff.). If the habit has the end result of establishing a secure rule of law and liberating worthwhile aspects of human character and opening up new possibilities of self-conscious development, then it is justified.

Imitation and automatism therefore are useful within limits. Mental development and cognition develop in the formation of groups through blending (assimilation) and reproduction. Humans can develop at one level through association and imitation. Bosanquet is not suggesting here that all humans are rational or could act rationally or that this is the only factor to be considered. For Bosanquet the average mind is far from being a rational system. But imitation and association, as psychological processes, are seen as subordinate to apperception. The human mind develops by transcending blind association or imitation through apperception. Apperception is the 'process by which a mental system appropriates a new element, or otherwise receives a fresh determination' (*PMS*, 40). Apperception implies some control of interests and circumstances (even to the most mundane level as to how one spends money). Each human mind is characterised by a dominant idea or ideas. The level and nature of the control is determined by the substantive nature of the ideas. Each system or grouping of ideas Bosanquet called an 'appercipient mass' – 'a set of ideas, bound together by a common rule' (*PTS*, 154). Apperception enables new ideas of experiences to be assimilated and systematically classed. It also determines the circumstances of an individual's existence – 'the eye only sees what it brings with it' (*PTS*, 155). Some ideas control us without our being fully aware of them. Some systems, while active, suppress others. But, importantly, Bosanquet believed that it is the essential nature of mind 'to be a unity of organised ideas answering to the actual set of parts which the individual plays in the world of space and time' (*PTS*, 162).

Bosanquet, thus, did not deny that ideas of association, imitation and automatism had a role. Where they fell short was in the emphasis on the 'non-rational' and instinctive to the exclusion of rationality, and in assuming that the totality of human action and thought could be explained in this way. He commented that '[Social psychology] aims at referring things to a whole; and there is no true whole but mind. Necessarily, therefore, with widening experience and deepening criticism, mind has become the centre of the experience focused by sociology' (*PTS*, 40). The neglected factor in social psychology was reflective rational mind. The notion of mind was at the heart of social life and was the key to Bosanquet's (and his wife Helen's) understanding of 'social economics' – an idea which was central to the Charity Organization Society's (COS) understanding of social work training in the School of Sociology and Social Economics.

For Bosanquet, the way humans organise elements in their own minds is analogous to the way social groups are organised. The associated crowd is often unaware of the ideas which motivate it. The organisation, however, is aware of the dominant operative ideas. Society is considered by Bosanquet as a vast conglomerate of such systems of ideas, some more conscious than others. Each group, trade or profession has its own dominant themes. Thus, as Bosanquet comments,

> To say that certain persons have common interests means that in this or that respect their minds are similarly or correlatively organised that they will react in the same or correlative ways upon given presentations. It is this identity of mental organisation which is the psychological justification for the doctrine of the General will. (*PMS*, 43)

Social psychology, if understood correctly, can thus provide important insights into the background of the social philosophy of the general will. In addition, using the insights provided by the psychology of 'will formation' – qua organisation over association – the subtle interrelation of sociology, psychology and the philosophy of mind can be firmly established. As Bosanquet noted, 'mind, and society or the State, are identical in the characteristic of being organisations, each composed of a system of organisations, every superior and subordinate grouping having its own nature and principle' (*PTS*, 158).

However, the relation between mind and society remains immensely complex. To be understood, even at the micro level, needs careful and sensitive study – which was, again, the core to Bosanquet conception of social casework and the sociology curriculum in the COS training college – vis-à-vis 'social economics'. Although human beings are subject to imitation, non-rational impulses and internal contradictions between apperceipient systems, none the less, the contradictions are lessened by the fact that the substantive content of many ideas are derived from social groups. These can exercise a unifying and rational effect, that is, through the ideas themselves and their effect on the will. Each individual, therefore, in his or her own disposition to the world, 'is an expression or reflection of society'. Individuals reflect, internally, the organised external disposition embodied in social groups. At best, the ideas of such groups reflect the integuments of the 'best life' for human beings. As Bosanquet put it, 'All the great contents of developed human self – truth, beauty, religion, and social morality – are all of them but modes of expression of the Ideal self' (*PMS*, 95).[52] At worst, individuals can reflect attitudes of irresponsibility and egoism. An individual is, in day-to-day activity, what he has habitually absorbed. If individuals have absorbed irresponsibility and self-interest, they will act it out until they are persuaded (or coerced) to do otherwise.

One final argument, in Bosanquet, stresses the Idealist doctrine of 'identity and difference'. He suggests that sociology, in all its facets, circles around this fundamental issue. Thus, the crowd in Le Bon is seen as a collective entity, but it is a collectivity which excludes individuals. Social psychologists, like Le Bon, are unable to conceive a collectivity which embodies individuality, or, an identity which embodies difference. For sociology, in general, identity and difference are regarded as separate. For Bosanquet, the 'separation of Imitation and Invention is simply the popular exclusion of Difference from Identity'. The logic, for Bosanquet, is that identity implies difference. The individual cannot do without society since the very nature of individuality implies society. Yet, this does not entail that individuality is lost, rather, both are preserved in a deeper and richer unity. Society and the individual have the same substance and both 'ideally' can strengthen each other.

The basic thesis underlying Bosanquet's argument here is that the philosophy of mind is premised on the idea that, in reviewing nature and the social world, mind is revealing its own structures. The ability to grasp the interconnections of the whole is what Hegel termed Reason (*Vernunft*). Reason apprehends the unity of mind in the vast array of its different manifestations in the world. Thus, truly cooperative structures are not premised on simple repetition, but 'identity in difference' (*PTS*, 43–4). For Bosanquet, social psychology, even in Tarde, Le Bon and McDougall remained still essentially atomistic. Identity is not necessarily incompatible with difference. Imitation does not necessarily exclude difference. Sociologists and psychologists thus neglect the question as to how a social whole can remain internally different and yet whole. Bosanquet's reading of psychology here is idiosyncratic. In one sense, it was a philosophical psychology which envisages psychology as part of a larger more inclusive philosophical whole. In another sense, it views psychology as something which needed to be supplemented by a sensitive philosophical anthropology and sociology. It is also interesting that when Bosanquet delivered his psychology lectures in London he was amused (but obviously not surprised) to have one of the students ask 'whether he would not give one on "real psychology"'.[53]

– DURKHEIM AND SOCIOLOGY –

The discussion now refocuses on the intellectual relation between Bosanquet and Durkheim over the issue of sociology and philosophy. This enriches and focuses the discussion more precisely on the relation between sociology and political economy, biology and psychology discussed in the previous sections. On 20 June 1904, the Sociological Society met at London School of Economics for a paper by Émile Durkheim dealing with the relation between sociology and philosophy. As one scholar has commented 'Durkheim interpreted this controversy as evidence of a still prevalent and unfortunate confusion between sociology and philosophy'.[54] The meeting included figures like Hobhouse and J. A. Hobson and written responses came from Bertrand Russell, Ferdinand Tönnies, Lévy-Bruhl and others. Durkheim could not get to the meeting and his paper was read for him (with Durkheim's approval) by Bosanquet. Bosanquet had already commented on Durkheim's writings some years earlier as 'among the most original and suggestive works of modern sociology' (*PTS*, 35). His responses to Durkheim are thus instructive on his general view of the nature of sociology.

There are a number of parallels between the work of Bosanquet and Durkheim. Both had a strong sense of the importance of societies as collective wholes embodying collective values. Both were deeply suspicious of the exclusive use of either psychology or evolutionary biology in sociology.[55] In an essay written in 1898, 'Individual and Collective Representations', Durkheim, echoing these sentiments in a more strident manner than Bosanquet, argued that biological sociology, qua Spencer, was 'worthless'. He noted that, 'Instead of trying to control their studies of society by their knowledge of biology, they tried to infer the laws of the first from the law of the second' (ICR, 1). Others, like Tarde, focused on individual psychology. Durkheim, again, was far tougher in his criticism than Bosanquet. Individual psychology was viewed, by Durkheim, as a fundamental mistake. To reduce social life to individual psychology was analogous to reducing mind to cells in the organism, which would, he claimed, deny 'all specificity' to mental life. Similarly 'life' itself could be reduced to oxygen, hydrogen, carbon and so forth. It would be lost in the particulars to which it was reduced. Yet, as Durkheim adds, 'life cannot be thus divided; it is one' (ICR, 29). The reason Durkheim was more stringent in his criticism here than Bosanquet was that he was more intrinsically mistrustful of mental introspection – which he regarded as mere dilettantism. Social investigation could not rely on subjective reports of mental life. Minds simply reflect social facts. As Durkheim put it, social facts are 'ways of acting, thinking and feeling, external to the individual and endowed with a power of coercion, by reason of which they control him'.[56] Such social facts needed presuppositionless scientific assessment, and sociology provided this science.

For Durkheim, individualist psychology was premised on an old idea dressed up in new 'scientific' clothes. It applied traditional 'principles of materialist metaphysics to social life'. It explained the complex by the simple, the whole by the part. Bosanquet would have accepted the logic of Durkheim's argument against atomistic and associationist psychology. However, he would have denied its application to a more collective and philosophically orientated psychology, which integrated part and whole within an identity in difference argument. Durkheim's response to this was that the science of collective ideation was probably a necessary future development within sociology (ICR, 32), but that, in sum, 'collective psychology is sociology, quite simply' (ICR, 34 n. 1). This was a direct, if slightly elusive, response.

Durkheim also expressed deep suspicion of all metaphysics.[57] He rejected Idealist metaphysics, in particular, which derived the part from the whole – 'since the whole is nothing without the parts which form it and cannot draw its vital necessities from the void' (ICR, 29). Interestingly, he interpreted Idealist metaphysics as propounding an undifferentiated and abstract holism. This was the same critique (discussed above) that Bosanquet offered against Le Bon's understanding of the 'associated crowd', thus, Durkheim's analysis fails to hit the mark on Bosanquet's Idealism. In fact, Bosanquet, remarked that Durkheim's social holism did not adequately meet the point that Durkheim himself laid at the door of Idealism. Bosanquet commented that

> The conception of a whole held together by its differences, its identity consisting in and being measured by their ... individuality is not at the command of [most sociological] writers, although the greater part of M. Durkheim's theory seems imperatively to demand such a conception. (*PTS*, 44)

Durkheim's theoretical stress did appear to fall on the ontology of the organic whole. In fact one might say that Durkheim was intoxicated with the idea of the group. The reality of the individual thus became a moment of the organic whole. As Durkheim commented, 'The group thinks, feels, and acts quite differently from the way in which its members would were they isolated. If, then, we begin with the individual, we shall be able to understand nothing of what takes place in the group.'[58]

Durkheim classifies himself in a midway position between individualist psychology and Idealism, namely, as a 'sociological naturalist', although 'sociological holist' would now be more common. As Durkheim remarked, 'We must ... explain phenomena that are the product of the whole, since the whole is nothing without the parts which form it' (*ICR*, 29). He concludes that we should explain the parts by the properties of the whole. This sounds, again, similar to Bosanquet's conception of an identity in difference argument, with the proviso that the ontological stress falls on the social whole. Thus, Durkheim comments that 'social facts are in a sense independent of individuals and exterior to individual minds'. This is an affirmation of the autonomy of the social world (and the science of sociology).[59] For Durkheim, society does not depend upon the nature of the individual person. One needs only to take the totality of society into consideration to grasp the individual sentiment. It is worth noting here that he does not deny the notional importance given to individuals. He only contends that individualism, as we see it, is the product of a particular society. He thus notes that 'moral individualism ... is in fact the product of society itself. It is society that instituted it and made of man the god whose servant it is' (*DMF*, 59).

For Bosanquet, Durkheim did not envisage society as a sphere of *natural* causation, rather *social* causation. Society provided a set of conditions 'in psychical life, corresponding to external facts which may have some uniformity' (*PTS*, 31). Crime, for example, is not something that could be biologically or economically explained. An act is a crime, in Durkheim, when it 'offends the strong and definite collective sentiments of society' (*PTS*, 35). Bosanquet (summarising his reading of Durkheim here) saw this as still aiming at a social cause – 'The act is a crime because it offends; it does not offend because it is a crime' (*PTS*, 35). There is a broader logic at stake here. For Durkheim, space, time, logic, rationality, morality, religion, aesthetics, as well as crime, are all effects, and the social whole is the cause. This is the reason why Durkheim regarded sociology as the most fundamental of all the sciences, more fundamental than natural science. For Bosanquet, however, crime is found offensive. It is a mental reaction and judgement. In this interpretation, 'we see at once the unity of aspects which the forms of law, and legal or philosophical theory, tend later to dissociate in a fictitious degree'. A law, for Bosanquet, 'must have something behind it'; it embodies an idea or conviction (*PTS*, 35–6).

But, Bosanquet asks, can law be reduced to a 'collective sentiment'? Crime offends the collective conscience – the collective conscience refers to the collective psychic symbols which have a common meaning for all the members of a society. Crime, like suicide, is rooted in social causation. It is not a matter of individual judgement. Yet, for Bosanquet a penal law is different from the anger of a mob. Law has some degree of 'permanence'. It is embodied in codes. There is also a right and wrong distinction implicit within it. Law implies something is worthwhile and is widely recognised as such. Thus, Bosanquet notes that 'the relation of pure "sociological" causation to juristic facts is the well-known relation of the more abstract to the more concrete science' (*PTS*, 36). To approach law as a 'collective social sentiment' which can be objectively and causally studied is equivalent to the physicist's analysis of musical sound. It is the same, for Bosanquet, with regard to the relation of 'strong collective sentiment' and a 'true law'. A strong sentiment is a factual force. A law, however, involves will, ideas, a sense of justice and rational judgement. It has to be apprehended, understood and judged by the rational agent. It is, thus, far more than just a collective sentiment to be scientifically studied. Law points to a good; mere force alone 'cannot by its reaction constitute a crime' (*PTS*, 37).

In summary, for Bosanquet, jurisprudence – the science of right – shows us 'a formal act of mind and will, aimed at maintaining some relative right or hindering some relative wrong' (*PTS*, 32). Right is embedded in the *facts* of jurisprudence. Such social phenomena are ideal at heart. They involve conscious recognition by intelligent beings. Society and its laws are thus the product of will, rational design and agreement between conscious beings. In society, we are always dealing with self-conscious purposive intelligence. Law has been interpreted by political economy, evolutionary biology and naturalistic sociology. Bosanquet acknowledges that statutes do indeed have an economic and social context, but 'this focusing of social influences makes the laws not less acts of social will, but more. To suppose to the contrary would be like supposing that nothing is a true act of will which embodies an individual's distinctive purposes in life' (*PS*, 34). In this context, Bosanquet uses the discussion of law and crime as a marker for a larger question about sociology, namely, how useful scientific sociology is in really understanding legal phenomena. His conclusion is that scientific sociology provides rich empirical detail, but to grasp legal phenomena, sociology needs to be supplemented by a psychologically sensitive social philosophy. For Bosanquet, 'the generalities of Jurisprudence are vitalised and completed by the work of the sciences of culture' (*PTS*, 38–9). Mind must take its central place in social theory.[60] The role of mind and judgement in social logic is therefore central to the difference between Bosanquet and Durkheim.

– FACTS AND VALUES –

In a paper in 1911, Durkheim made a conventional positivist distinction between facts and values. Scientific statements about the volume of gas were distinct from statements about human 'preferences'. The former statements did not attach value to an object. This definition would be recognised by most positivist writers to the present day. However, value judgements, at the same time (and here Durkheim adds his own unique perspective), 'have the objectivity of things'. This view carried Durkheim beyond more orthodox 'fact value' definitions. Values were objective social facts, which, although qualitatively distinct from facts in nature, were nonetheless 'social objects' which could be scientifically studied and measured. Thus, a state of feeling could be 'independent of the subject that feels it' (*VJJR*, 81–2). This might be explained through intrinsic value theory. Yet, for Durkheim, intrinsic value theory simply could not account for value pluralism. Private judgement was not the same as objective value judgements. In objective social morality the scale of values is 'released from the … subjective evaluations of individuals' (*VJJR*, 84). All of us are bound by the objective social morality – collective conscience. This was the nub of his sociological treatment of values.

Neo-Kantians have often argued (again, to the present day) that 'value' and the 'empirically real' are distinct. It is in this context that metaphysical and ethical statements have been regarded as either subject to different criteria, or, as, alternatively, cognitively suspect. Moral *knowledge*, in this reading, is not strictly possible. Knowledge is concerned with what is verifiable, testable or falsifiable. As one 'social science' exponent, George Homans, noted: 'As we have come to accept … the standards of natural science for testing the truth of propositions, so we should take more seriously [in the social sciences] the standards of natural science in explanation. In that we have been laggard.'[61] The general conception of the social theorist is that of a neutral scientific observer who carefully describes and explains the objective world. The function of the theorist is not to interpret or change the world, but rather to explain it through rigorously verifiable categories. The mirror image of this analytic/synthetic distinction reappears in the noncognitive moral doctrines of emotivism, voluntarism and prescriptivism. This older variant of the distinction between facts and values continues to have considerable appeal to neo-classical economists and indeed to lay persons, if no longer for most analytic philosophers. For philosophers now, as Quine put it (with regard to the analytic/synthetic distinction in Carnap), 'the lore of our fathers is black with fact and white with convention, but there are no *completely* white threads and no black ones'.[62]

However, the fact/value distinction has not disappeared from contemporary discussion. It has moved into a more relativistic *modus operandi*, and, as opposed to totally repudiating metaphysics, it more or less accepts its own metaphysical status. The major difference between contemporary philosophy usage and the older logical positivist sense, is that moral notions can now *be* true or false (which the older logical positivism denied), but the truth or falsity is now seen more perspectivally. Truth or falsity relate to particular 'perspectives' and are true or false in the context of those perspectives – which is another form of relativism.[63]

In one sense, Durkheim blends aspects of both logical positivism and perspectivism. He does see a distinction between facts and values, but, he then interprets facts and values as different 'objects' to be scientifically studied. Durkheim also anticipates the argument that 'moral truths' can actually exist within communal perspectives. This latter point also links Durkheim with many modern communitarian writers. However, unlike communitarians and perspectivists, he also insists that moral truth can itself be studied objectively through positive sociology. His theory thus contains something of both the relativism of ethics (implicit in logical positivism, perspectivism and communitarianism) combined with the objectivism of positivist natural science. As Durkheim comments, 'If the Ideal does not depend on the real it would be impossible to find in the real conditions and causes which would make it intelligible' (*VJJR*, 88). If we desire an ideal, it must be something more than empty speculation or emotional posturing. It must be part of the furniture of our universe.[64] Thus, we should be able to analyse it. Value systems do change in distinct groups; however, respect for human persons in groups is, for Durkheim, 'at the root of the moral ideal of contemporary societies' (*VJJR*, 89).[65] In many societies, however, this common ideal is poorly rooted. Yet, society is still the centre of the moral life. Groups have a unique psychic life, which is distinct from the individual *per se*. Group thoughts and group moralities are distinct from the private experiences of the individual. Yet, the individual 'forgets himself for the common end and his conduct is orientated in terms of a standard outside himself' (*VJJR*, 91). This is often mistaken for the 'ideal' and 'real' distinction, in fact, 'society moves ... the individual to rise above himself' (*VJJR*, 92). Society embodies collective ideals. Such ideals are not abstractions, but conversely constitute the very dynamism of society. Ideals are both natural and moral at the same time. An ideal is both immanent and transcendent.

Thus, for Durkheim, value judgements are not separate from nature. Value is '*of* and *in* nature' (*VJJR*, 94). It can be examined like any other 'physical universe'. Collective thought, qua morality, is something that can be studied by positive sociology. There is therefore no fundamental ontological difference here between value judgements and judgements of fact. A value judgement 'expresses the relation of a thing to an Ideal'. All judgements are based on fact. All judgements bring some concept or ideal into play. There is only one *undivided* faculty of judgement. However, there are different types of ideal. Some ideals are concepts which try to 'express the reality to which they adhere' – the ideal is a symbol of a thing; others try to 'transfigure the realities to which they relate' – the thing here symbolises the ideal and acts 'as a medium through which the ideal becomes capable of being understood' (*VJJR*, 95–6). These are often mistakenly divided up on the basis of ideal and real.

Durkheim viewed morality through the same sociological lens. Society 'constitutes a moral authority which, by manifesting itself in certain precepts ... confers upon them an obligatory character' (*DMF*, 38). Each individual thus expresses the social morality. Individuals articulate an objective morality. As Durkheim argues:

> If we cannot be bound by duty except to conscious beings and we have eliminated the individual, there remains as the only other possible object of moral activity the *sui generis* collective being formed by the plurality of individuals associated to form a group. Further, collective personality must be thought of as something other than the totality of individuals that compose it ... We [therefore] arrive then at the conclusion that if a morality, or system of obligations and duties, exists, society is a moral being qualitatively different from the individuals it comprises.

He continues that the

> similarity between this argument and that of Kant in favour of the existence of God will be noted. Kant postulates God, since without this hypothesis morality is unintelligible. We postulate society specifically distinct from individuals, since otherwise morality has no object and duty no roots.　　　　(*DMF*, 51–2)

Thus, the real choice facing us is between God and Society! Therefore, 'to love society is to love both something beyond us and something in ourselves' (*DMF*, 55).

In summary, Durkheim contended that positive sociology does not make a fetish of facts. Religion, morality and aesthetics all embodied ideal values. Sociology moved in this field of values, dealing with them as a science. It was not *constructing* ideals *per se*, conversely it treated such entities as objects for study. In fact, for Durkheim, sociology *per se* contained a complete epistemology, which provided clear answers to all the older philosophical problems of knowledge. Sociology even explained the philosophical impulse. Humans (and their cognitive existence) had no distinctive attributes outside of society. As indicated in the above reference to Kant, Durkheim offers a form of 'sociological Kantianism'. Society is the transcendental subject – and unity of apperception – which is the logical precondition to individuals and their activity. Society makes experience possible. Thus, sociology provides answers to all the Kantian problems of knowledge. Durkheim, in fact, always retained, from his student studies with the neo-Kantian philosopher M. Renouvier, a deep admiration for Kant. However, it was a transformed empiricised Kantianism which had become, in effect, a realistic sociological epistemology.[66] In many ways, Durkheim also absorbed Comte's impatience with metaphysics, reinforced by an empiricised Kantianism. It is little wonder, in this scenario, that Durkheim should have felt a disquiet with the metaphysics of Hegelian Idealism.

In considering Bosanquet's response, it is important to bear in mind certain aspects about Idealism here. First, thought, ideas or concepts enter in subtle ways into the constitution of our experience, although it is worth noting that this is not something that the Kantian Durkheim wholly denies. Secondly, all objects and facts are also linked subtly to the constituting activity of self-consciousness. Self-conscious thought, articulated in a communal and historical setting, is the uniting principle of all the spheres of knowing. The separation between facts and values exists – but for self-conscious minds. Thus, Bosanquet comments:

> My individual consciousness does not make or create the differences between the species … although it does create my knowledge of them … The actual facts of this world do directly arise out of and are usually sustained by conscious intelligence; and these facts form the world above sense.[67]

In discussing Durkheim's position of sociology, Bosanquet notes that every student of social affairs will have noted that social facts are not physical things. There is some qualified agreement here again between Bosanquet and Durkheim. Both recognise the ideality at the heart of facts. Social facts are facts but they are still intangibles. No statistical datum can be handled. All such facts attach themselves, as Bosanquet put it, to 'an underlying relation of mind as the only unity which will make it intelligible' (*PTS*, 39). Statistics sees a moving social creature, as if through a wall of holes. He thus remarks that 'to see the creature as he is ... you must get him into the open' (*PTS*, 40).[68] To do so is 'hermeneutically' to *reconstruct the mind* – although Bosanquet does not use the term hermeneutics. Without interpretation and reconstruction all we have are mere fragments of reality. Thus, 'with widening experience and deepening criticism, mind has become the centre of the experiences focused by sociology' (*PTS*, 40). In Durkheim, we reconstruct the social whole to understand the particular event. Intentional agency therefore drifts into the background of sociology.

It is worth pausing for a moment on the above ideas, in the light of arguments which have developed later in this century. Thus, Peter Winch notes, in his classic 1958 text on the philosophy of social science, that 'a man's social relations with his fellows are permeated with his ideas about reality. Indeed, "permeated" is hardly a strong enough word: social relations are expressions of ideas about reality.' If the listener did not know the context of the above comment, the passage could almost be read as pure Bosanquet from his philosophical theory of the state. The major differences between Bosanquet and Winch here is that the latter focuses (like Gadamer) on the ontological significance, qua Wittgenstein, of language. He also has little interest in teleology. Interestingly, though, on the same page, above, the theorist to whom Winch directly contrasts his own views is Durkheim.[69] It is also hardly surprising in this context to find that Winch, later, in the same text, utilises, with some Wittgensteinian qualifications, the ideas of both Collingwood and Oakeshott (and Idealism in general) to articulate his own understanding of sociological investigation.[70] Nearer the end of his book, he remarks that his theory may 'make possible a new appreciation of Collingwood's conception of all human history as the history of human thought'. Winch suggests here that 'Collingwood is right if he is taken to mean that the way to understand events in human history [or society] ... is more closely analogous to the way in which we understand expressions of ideas than it is the way we understand physical process'.[71] The view that Winch expresses here is, in one sense, a commonplace of Idealist, hermeneutic and *verstehen* writing this century.

What did Bosanquet mean by getting a social entity into the open? The answer is a form of hermeneutic reconstruction of the mind, idea or purpose embedded within the social action. This again parallels Winch's reading. Sociology should focus on what Winch calls 'meaningful behaviour'. Understanding actions means 'grasping the *point* or *meaning* of what was being done or said'.[72] This, for Winch, does not involve causal or statistical regularities. He thus notes that 'people do not first make generalisations and then embody them in concepts: it is only by virtue of their possession of concepts that they are able to make generalisations at all'.[73] Actions embody concepts. To grasp the action is to understand the concept. For Durkheim, however, the whole process is less straightforward. Although he used empirical statistics in works like *On Suicide*, the empirical detail only made sense in terms of the ontology of the whole understood as an object. Interestingly, Winch, in criticising attempts to 'eliminate ideas … from the sociologist's account of social life', explicitly cites Durkheim's work *On Suicide* as an archetypal offender.

Thus, whereas, Bosanquet and Winch stressed mind (public rules and concepts) within the facts, Durkheim stressed (qua his empirical Kantianism) the collective whole, presupposed within the facts, and this 'whole' could be treated as an object. This strategy led Durkheim, in one direction, to positivism and empirical social science – the whole is thus an 'object' distinct from the subject that cognises it. In another direction, it also led Durkheim to almost absurd extremes of sociological relativism – in fact, a highly self-referential and reflexive relativism. Even the reasoning and structure of Durkheim's own sociology had to be subject, by its own logic, to the structural determinism of a particular social whole. This highly self-referential structural determinism is not that distant from later complex developments in French structuralist-inclined sociology and philosophy, in theorists like Althusser, Foucault, Derrida or Bourdieu, where ideology, philosophy or academic disciplines themselves become 'social objects' to be explained.

In another direction, Durkheim stressed the 'ideality' of *all* social facts. This gives his theory a distinctly philosophical, in fact, Idealist feel. It is not surprising, in this context, that many deeply sympathetic commentators, like Talcott Parsons, saw Durkheim shifting and hesitant between positivism and philosophical Idealism. It is also not surprising to find Durkheim, nearer the end of his life in 1914, giving an enthusiastic reception to the philosophical pragmatism of William James and John Dewey. His enthusiasm is for aspects of the pragmatic 'action-based' conception of truth. Truth is that which can be used or 'cashed out' within a particular 'social whole'. This view ties in with his sociological relativism. However one impact of this – as in the writings of Dewey – is a blurring of the lines between social science and literary humanistic study. Thus, Durkheim's critical anxiety about pragmatism is over the manner in which it potentially undermines the objectivity of scientific rationalism. Understandably – given Durkheim's ontological schizophrenia – he did not wish the positivistic rationalism of scientific sociology to be weakened by pragmatism.[74]

For Bosanquet and Winch, Durkheim's insistence upon social facts illustrates something worrying in the character of twentieth-century sociology. Empirical facts and statistics alone tell us little, but, 'to focus a number of groups of fact, and coordinate the points of view which they substantiate, into the conception of a living being, with its individual character and spiritual utterance, needs more than a merely literary or statistical study' (*PTS*, 45). This does not mean that the empirical social world is dependent for its existence on cognition. As Bosanquet commented, in one of his last works, the philosopher does not deny or alter 'our world of fact and externality, but accepting for it all its claims of existence and reality, then passes on to interpret its conditions, and assigns its significance more profoundly'.[75] Empirical description has a positive role to play. However, this should not lead the social investigator to forget that 'no fact has a true social bearing except in as far as, sooner or later, it comes to form part of the world which a being capable of sociality and therefore intelligent, presents to himself and his theatre of action' (*PTS*, 45). This connects up with Bosanquet's earlier point about appercipience.

The error of much sociology this century, including to some degree Durkheim's, is 'not in identifying the mind and the environment, but in first uncritically separating them, and then substituting not merely the one for the other, but wretched fragments of the one for the whole in which alone either can be complete' (*PTS*, 48). When philosophy deals with society it has to deal with the problems which arise 'out of the nature of a whole and its parts, the relation of the individual to the universal' (*PTS*, 48). Durkheim has a partial answer to this through his emphasis on social wholes. However, for Bosanquet and Winch, Durkheim's collapse of individuality and rationality into a social holism which could be rendered scientifically, not only relied upon a thin faulty empiricism (with a questionable distinction between observer and observed), but also, as Bosanquet noted, appeared to reflexively refute itself through its own social logic. It is thus worth noting here that the substantive contents of the debate in which Bosanquet engages with Durkheim is far from defunct in the social sciences. In many ways, Idealist arguments like those of Bosanquet anticipate many of the critical in-terpretivist, *verstehen* and hermeneutic points made later this century by those, like Winch, who have been uneasy with positivist-inspired social science.[76]

– PHILOSOPHY OR SOCIOLOGY? –

Gabriel Tarde and Durkheim had a number of heated public disputations in Paris. In the final debate, in 1903–4, they contested over the status of sociology vis-à-vis philosophy. Lukes comments that

> Durkheim's lecture argued that sociology was the daughter of philosophy ('born in the womb of the Comtist philosophy, of which it is the logical completion') but now it must specialize in studies of complex, concrete phenomena, rather than seeking abstract, general laws. Special disciplines must become truly sociological

sciences, becoming infused with the ideas evolved originally by social philosophy.[77]

Sociology, in Durkheim's estimation, had thus gone beyond philosophy. It had matured intellectually as a discipline. Sociology, also in Comtean mode, had transcended and could even *account* for the philosophical approach, as a stage of scientific immaturity. There was, in other words, a sociology of philosophy. For Durkheim, as also for Comte and Bosanquet, psychology was also inadequate. To study society, one had to have some grasp of collective ideation, collective morality, collective representations, and so forth. Such collective entities were discrete and unique and needed their own distinctive form of analysis – scientific sociology.

Idealism, on the other hand, had a basic problem with accepting the methods of positive natural science. For many commentators, the particular sciences – physics, biology, psychology, mathematics, economics, history alike – all assume that the object studied is distinct from and independent of our cognitions of it. This might not be so strongly the case with contemporary physics, but in Bosanquet's time, this assumption was widespread. The idea that sociology was a science of society which stood apart from, for example, moral beliefs and studied them as objects, was something Idealists found philosophically problematic. First, the observer was actually involved in the process of observation and might modify the actual nature of the observed. The Idealists were thus more directly sympathetic here to (what might now be known as) an interpretivist or hermeneutic approach. Idealism thus saw sociological theory as not so much discovering some 'inner empirical secret', as making or constituting the world through complex cultural vocabularies. Second, social facts or statistics do not 'speak for themselves'. As Thoreau once said, it is not worth it, to go round the world to count the cats in Zanzibar. Facts are not tangible entities in themselves. Rather, to gain any sense of meaning one has to grasp the fact in terms of what it embodies. Facts (especially social facts) embody ideas, values and interpretative judgements. Third, for the Idealist, it was a very basic detail of philosophical argument that in order to determine what something is we must think it. Cognition is always involved in the nature of the world. This did not mean that the objective world was dependent on our cognition. We do not *think* the weather. Rather, what we call knowledge involves a knower. The subject/object relation is viable as long as we realise that it is premised on the prior unity of thought.

For Bosanquet, social phenomena all embody ideals or dominant ideas which make sense of our experience and order our activities. Social reality can only really be explained via these dominant ideas. Society, *per se*, is seen as an organisation of such ordered experiences. Idealists thus called society a concrete, as opposed to an abstract, universal. This did not deny the significance of the findings of empirical sociology, political economy, biology or psychology.[78] But these sciences, for Bosanquet, had to be considered in the completer context of the rational agent, cognition and evaluative judgement. Mind was crucial to the understanding of social existence. Empirical sociology or psychology were not therefore regarded as alien. They were complementary and contributed rich details to a larger picture; but they did *not* provide the larger picture. To grasp this larger picture one needed to be acquainted with the mind and/or dominant ideas of participants. To grasp the character of mind, in this larger context, requires philosophy. Social study therefore needs philosophy and this, for Bosanquet, is what is fundamentally missing in Durkheim. There was, therefore, a need for a philosophy of sociology. Thus, for Bosanquet, 'philosophy gives significance to sociology; sociology vitalises philosophy. The idea of mind is deepened and extended by the unity and continuity which sociological analysis ... vindicates' (*PTS*, 48). Although the particular vocabulary and manner in which Bosanquet expresses his idea may sound slightly unusual to the contemporary ear, his problems, and the manner in which he criticises positivist sociology and positivist social science, are not strange; in fact, they are profoundly familiar and still as pertinent in the year 2000 as they were in 1900.

– NOTES –

The following abbreviations will be used in the text for Bosanquet's and Durkheim's frequently cited writings:

PTS   Bernard Bosanquet, *The Philosophical Theory of the State* (London, Macmillan, 1923), reprinted in *Collected Works of Bernard Bosanquet* [in twenty volumes edited by William Sweet] (Bristol, Thoemmes Press, 1999)

PMS   Bernard Bosanquet, *Psychology of the Moral Self* (London, Macmillan, 1897)

DMF   Émile Durkheim, 'The Determination of Moral Facts' (1906), in Durkheim, *Sociology and Philosophy* (New York, Free Press, 1974)

ICR   Émile Durkheim, 'Individual and Collective Representations' (1898), in Durkheim, *Sociology and Philosophy*

VJJR   Émile Durkheim, 'Value Judgements and Judgements of Reality', in Durkheim, *Sociology and Philosophy*

1. See, Andrew Vincent and Raymond Plant, *Philosophy Politics and Citizenship: The Life and Thought of the British Idealists* (Oxford, Blackwell, 1984), ch. 6; also Andrew Vincent, 'The Poor Law Reports of 1909 and the Social Theory of the Charity Organization Society', *Victorian Studies*, vol. 27, no. 3, (1984); and Andrew Vincent, 'Citizenship, Poverty and the Real Will', *The Sociological Review*, 40, 3 (1992).

2. See particularly Sandra Den Otter's, *Idealism and Social Explanation: A Study in Late Victorian Thought* (Oxford, Clarendon Press, 1996) and Stefan Collini, *Liberalism and Sociology: L. T. Hobhouse and Political Argument in England 1880–1914* (Cambridge, Cambridge University

Press, 1983).

3. As Bosanquet put it in one essay, 'I have a high esteem for M. Durkheim, and I believe myself to have learned a great deal from him.' Bosanquet, 'Atomism in History', in Bernard Bosanquet, *Social and International Ideals: Being Studies in Patriotism* (London, Macmillan, 1917), 30.

4. As Philip Abrams noted, poverty debates 'had powerful effect on the development of British sociology', P. Abrams, *The Origins of British Sociology* (Chicago, Chicago University Press, 1968), 24–5. In poverty studies it was often difficult to separate fact and opinion. But, as Abrams notes, 'the great debates on the meaning of statistics of poverty and economic progress of the 1880s and 1890s were still to come, and beyond them lay the Majority and Minority Reports ... in 1909. But even such extreme evidence of the ambiguity of facts would not shake the distaste of a critical group of social investigators for controversies of principle, or their faith that facts properly gathered would eventually speak for themselves. The strength of the tradition was such that even twenty years later the Webbs made it the basis of the true method of social science', 23.

5. Abrams, *The Origins*, 65.

6. Abrams, *The Origins*, 3.

7. Abrams, *The Origins*, 3.

8. See J. H. Muirhead (ed.), *Bernard Bosanquet and his Friends* (London, Allen and Unwin, 1935), 92ff.

9. Interestingly, one of the early enthusiasts and lecturers for this School – J. H. Muirhead – later helped found and was the first president of the 'British Institute for Philosophy', which was inaugurated in University Hall, Gordon Square, in the University of London, the earlier birthplace of the Ethical Society. The coincidence was not lost on Muirhead, although it is doubtful that many shared Muirhead's ethico-philosophical concerns at the time; see J. H. Muirhead, *Reflections by a Journeyman in Philosophy* (London, George Allen and Unwin, 1942), 89.

10. See E. J. Urwick, 'A School of Sociology', in C. S. Loch (ed.), *Methods of Social Advance* (London, Macmillan, 1904), and Helen Bosanquet, 'Methods of Training', in *The Charity Organization Review*, no. 44, 1904.

11. See also Bosanquet, 'The Relation of Sociology to Philosophy', *Mind*, n.s. VI (1897). The chapter in the *Philosophical Theory of the State* was a revision of this earlier piece.

12. See W. Dilthey, *Introduction to the Human Sciences* (London, Harvester Wheatsheaf, 1988), 126ff.

13. J. S. Mackenzie, *An Introduction to Social Philosophy* (Glasgow, James Maclehose, 1895), 12–13.

14. Mackenzie, *An Introduction*, 13.

15. Mackenzie, *An Introduction*, 13.

16. William Wallace, 'Ethics and Sociology', *Mind*, VIII, 1883.

17. Mackenzie, *Manual of Ethics* (London, Clive, 1897), 113.

18. I am not suggesting that positivism, naturalism and empiricism are automatically equivalent, however, suffice to say that many writers appear to wish to use these as equivalents in speaking about political and social science. I have followed this usage.

19. Auguste Comte, *Cours de philosophie positive*, vol. 1 (Paris, 1975), 29.

20. Abrams, *The Origins*, 57.

21. There have been two broad manifestations of this positivist tendency in the early stages of the twentieth century. One relates to the neo-Kantian distinction between theoretical and practical reason, a distinction which was supposed to make room for autonomy and moral

judgement. Increasingly neo-Kantianism became sceptical of the moral autonomy that Kant had postulated. Values, *per se*, became increasingly suspect. This distinction became a central plank in the neo-Kantian background to Max Weber's work and in his distinctions between value-free social science and moral discourse. Weber was no simple-minded positivist, but he did adhere to the idea that there was a heterogeneity between facts and values and that science provided no means to answer the question 'how ought we to live and act'. Under Nietzschean tutelage, Weber certainly faced the 'disenchanting' issue that there might not be any rational foundation for our basic values. The other, more familiar, manifestation of positivism is Anglo-American 'liberal social science', which largely adopts the positivist position on consequentialist grounds (as in many eighteenth-century conceptions of social science). Many disciplines, like politics, sociology and anthropology, became enthralled with the prospect of attaining positivistic scientific rigour. The overt aim was to emulate the natural sciences, namely, to collect empirical data, discover empirical correlations, draw up generalisations and formulate testable theories which allowed prediction. The general conception of the theorist was that of a neutral scientific observer who carefully describes and explains the objective world. Categorical distinctions were thus observed between the nature of theory and the character of political action. The function of the theorist was not to interpret or change the world, but rather to explain it through rigorously tested categories.

22. Bosanquet, 'Life and Philosophy', in J. H. Muirhead (ed.), *Contemporary British Philosophy* (London, Allen and Unwin, 1924), 52.

23. See Beatrice Webb's attack on Haldane's interest in philosophy in her *Our Partnership* (London, Longmans, 1948), 99.

24. Quoted in Abrams, *The Origins,* 95.

25. See L. T. Hobhouse, 'The Philosophy of Development', in Muirhead (ed.), *Contemporary British Philosophy* (London, George Allen and Unwin, 1924).

26. See A. M. McBriar, *An Edwardian Mixed Doubles* (Oxford, Clarendon Press, 1984), 18 and 147.

27. Bernard Bosanquet, *Science and Philosophy and other essays* (London, Allen and Unwin, 1927), 169.

28. Bosanquet, *Science and Philosophy*, 168.

29. Bosanquet, *Science and Philosophy*, 25–6.

30. Bosanquet, 'Life and Philosophy', in Muirhead (ed.), *Contemporary British Philosophy*, 60.

31. Theodore Adorno and Max Horkheimer, *The Dialectics of the Enlightenment* (London, Verso, 1973).

32. Paul Rabinow and William M. Sullivan (eds), *Interpretive Social Science* (Los Angeles, University of California Press), 10.

33. As Gadamer comments, 'There is no societal reality, with all its concrete forces that does not bring itself to representation in a consciousness that is linguistically articulated. Reality does not happen "behind the back" of language'. H. G. Gadamer, *Philosophical Hermeneutics* (Berkeley, University of California Press, 1977), 35.

34. As Taylor argues, 'mainstream social science is kept within certain limits by its categorical principles which are rooted in the traditional epistemology of empiricism; and secondly, that these restrictions are a severe handicap and prevent us from coming to grips with the important problems of our day, which should be the object of political science. We need to go beyond the bounds of a science based on verification to one which would study the intersubjective and common meanings embedded in social reality ... But this science would be hermeneutical ... It would not be founded on brute data; its most primitive data

would be readings of meanings.' Taylor, 'Interpretation and the Sciences of Man', in Rabinow and Sullivan (eds), *Interpretive Social Science*, 74–5.

35. Bosanquet, *The Meeting of Extremes in Contemporary Philosophy* (London, Macmillan, 1924), 3.

36. A. Seth Pringle-Pattison, *The Idea of God* (Oxford University Press, 1920), 136.

37. Edward Caird, *The Social Philosophy and Religion of Comte* (Glasgow, James Maclehose and Sons, 1885), 79–80.

38. J. H. Muirhead and H. J. W. Hetherington, *Social Purpose: A Contribution to a Philosophy of Civic Society* (London, George Allen and Unwin, 1922), 34.

39. Spencer compared these types of society, in one slightly bizarre analogy, to the alimentary system as against the nervous system of the body, the former being a symbiotic co-ordination of parts without central control.

40. For a fuller exposition of Idealist understandings of evolution see David Boucher and Andrew Vincent, *A Radical Hegelian: The Political and Social Philosophy of Henry Jones* (Cardiff, University of Wales Press, 1993), ch. 4; also David Boucher, 'Evolution and Politics: The Naturalistic, Ethical and Spiritual Bases of Evolutionary Arguments', *Australian Journal of Political Science*, vol. 27 (1992).

41. The notion of natural selection does not adequately account for 'the growth of sympathy together with the whole system of laws and institutions which have for their object the preservation of the weak', Muirhead and Hetherington, *Social Purpose*, 41.

42. Bosanquet admitted that there were sociologists who dealt with developed societies. Interestingly, however, Bosanquet remarked that he did not consider the Webbs' activity as strictly sociological at all. He noted that they did not 'attach themselves to the peculiar method and language of sociology' (*PTS*, n. 1, 22). This judgement would be partially true, at the time, of some French and German sociology, which did have a distinct vocabulary and theoretical bent. However, the comment would be less accurate of British sociology which was less self-consciously theoretical. However, Bosanquet considered that when dealing with contemporary problems in pauperism, charity, sanitation, education and the like, sociologists had generally had little success. In fact, he considered that all sociologists had much to learn from those on the ground dealing with such practical problems – the Charity Organization Society was obviously his reference point here.

43. For a critical analysis of present-day sociobiology on these grounds, see Mary Midgely, *Beast and Man: The Roots of Human Nature* (London, Methuen, 1978), xviiiff., and *Evolution as Religion* (London, Methuen, 1985), 121ff. Midgley remarks, for example, that 'The idea of a vast escalator, proceeding steadily upwards from lifeless matter through plants and animals to man, and inevitably on to higher things was coined by Lamarck and given currency by Herbert Spencer under his chosen name "evolution". Darwin utterly distrusted the idea, which seemed to him a baseless piece of theorising, and avoided the name … From that time to this, Spencer's bold, colourful and flattering picture of evolution has constantly prevailed over the more sober, difficult one of Darwin, not only in the public mind, but also surprisingly often in the mind of scientists.' Midgley (in line with Bosanquet's judgement on Spencer) goes on to remark on the disastrous and misplaced attempts to apply it to politics into the twentieth century; see Midgley, *Evolution as Religion*, 35–6.

44. There are two ways to view this evolutionary process; one is to explain humanity through the lower material forms seen as a competitive struggle for existence, the other is to humanise nature. Not only can altruistic tendencies in humans be seen in a similar evolutionary light, but mind itself can be seen in its controlling and organising function as

a fact of evolution.

45. Bosanquet, 'Atomism in History', 40.

46. Le Bon, *Psychology of the Crowd*, in A. Widener (ed.), *Gustav Le Bon: The Man and his Work* (Indianapolis, Liberty Press, 1979), 59.

47. Tarde, quoted in Steven Lukes, *Émile Durkheim: His Life and Work* (Middlesex, Penguin Books, 1973), 302.

48. William McDougall, *Introduction to Social Psychology* (London, Methuen, 1913: 7th edn), 326.

49. Even Durkheim's thought, which looked like a rationalist and enlightenment attempt to study society, none the less incorporated the quasi-structuralist thesis that the social whole *is* the premise to even our ordinary notion of rationality. This provided, unwittingly, the groundwork for the idea that mass social determinism or mass instinct is almost inevitable. Mass actions could hardly be evaluated by an independent standard of rationality.

50. Bosanquet did not incorporate any of the new Freudian psychology; see Den Otter, *British Idealism*, 148. Whether he was aware of Freud is open to question. However, how he would have reacted to Freud (and Jung for that matter) is probably not in dispute.

51. Haldane was later to utilise these ideas. As Minister of War in the pre-1914 Liberal government and involved in the organisation of the British Expeditionary Force he was asked by the General Staff what kind of army he wanted; Haldane replied that he wanted an 'Hegelian army'. The operative leading idea was the key. It is interesting to speculate on the reaction to his answer.

52. Bosanquet is basically using here Hegel's idea of the transition from consciousness to self-consciousness, as equivalent to a form of social evolution of the person. The individual and the social world are looked at as two sides of the same coin. The self is envisaged as 'the organised fabric, or organism, of which the material is ideas taken in the widest sense and carrying with them the accompaniment of feeling' (*PMS*, 89). The complete science of the realised moral self is developed in what Hegel called 'Objective Mind'.

53. Muirhead (ed.), *Bosanquet and his Friends*, 86, n. 1.

54. Den Otter, *British Idealism and Social Explanation: A Study in Late Victorian Thought* (Oxford, Clarendon Press, 1996), 133.

55. For example, Durkheim engaged in heated critical exchanges with Tarde. For Tarde, social reality was composed of psychological states of individuals.

56. E. Durkheim, *Rules of Sociological Method* (1895), ed. George E. G. Catlin (Illinois, Free Press, 1938: 8th edn), 3.

57. He contended that 'sociology does not have to choose between hypotheses which divide metaphysicians. It needs to affirm free will no more than determinism. All that it asks is that the principle of causality be applied to social phenomena'; quoted from Durkheim's *Rules of Sociological Method*, in H. Stuart Hughes, *Consciousness and Society* (Sussex, Harvester Press, 1979), 281–2.

58. Durkheim, *Rules*, 103–4.

59. Durkheim comments, 'Society has for its substratum the mass of associated individuals. The systems which they form by uniting together, and which varies according to their geographical disposition and the nature and number of their channels of communication, is the base from which social life is raised. The representations which form the network of social life arise from the relations between individuals thus combined ... If there is nothing extraordinary in the fact that individual representations, produced by the action and reaction between neural elements, are not inherent in these elements, there is nothing surprising in the fact that collective representations, produced by the action and reaction

between individual minds that form society do not derive directly from the latter' (*ICR*, 24–5).

60. Bosanquet also raises the issues of comparative politics, which he thinks brings out the 'conscious character of society' and corrects the view that government is a natural phenomena.

61. G. Homans, *The Nature of Social Science* (New York, Harcourt Brace and World Inc., 1967), 28.

62. W. V. Quine, 'Carnap on Logical Truth', in P. A. Schilpp (ed.), *The Philosophy of Rudolf Carnap* (LaSalle, IL, Open Court, 1963).

63. Bernard Williams's work articulates this conception in *Ethics and the Limits of Philosophy* (London, Collins Fontana, 1993); also David Wiggins, *Needs, Values and Truth* (Oxford, Oxford University Press, 1987).

64. Lukes remarks here that Durkheim's neo-Kantian teacher, M. Renouvier, had already prepared the ground for this interpretation. Renouvier contended that Kant's theoretical reason was subject to practical reason – namely, will and choice. The basic categories of our thought are thus more contingent than other Kantians had suggested. Lukes remarks 'One can see that it is a relatively easy step from this to the sociological epistemology which Durkheim began to elaborate', Lukes, *Émile Durkheim*, 56–7.

65. In many ways this is a strangely cosmopolitan remark from a sociological relativist.

66. On the powerful impact of Renouvier's Kantianism on Durkheim, see Lukes, *Émile Durkheim*, 54ff.

67. Bosanquet, *Science and Philosophy*, 324.

68. Bosanquet commenting on the general positivist perspective remarks 'this accumulation and copying of minute facts and references is really an indolent and depressing occupation; and being made a substitute for the reading and interpretation, the translation or criticism of great authors in literature, for the exercise of judgement and insight into history, for thought and appreciation in philosophy, is really a substitution of deadening mechanical labour for the true toil and expression of intelligence'; Bosanquet, 'Atomism in History', 32.

69. Peter Winch, *The Idea of a Social Science and its Relation to Philosophy* (London, Routledge and Kegan Paul, 1973), 23.

70. See, for example, Winch, *Idea of a Social Science*, 54–5, 90–1, 131–3.

71. Winch, *Idea of a Social Science*, 132.

72. Winch, *Idea of a Social Science*, 115.

73. Winch, *Idea of a Social Science*, 44.

74. On Durkheim's reception of pragmatism see Lukes, *Émile Durkheim*, 486ff.

75. Bosanquet, *Meeting of Extremes*, 2.

76. Idealists 'defined social philosophy in terms of problems which were endemic in the varieties of nineteenth century positivism and which remain at the heart of the philosophy of the social sciences – tensions between causal and interpretative explanations and between facts and values'. Den Otter, *British Idealism*, 55.

77. Lukes, *Émile Durkheim*, 312.

78. 'The origin of forms of consciousness is one thing, their status and value in the life of the mind as a whole is another,' Muirhead and Hetherington, *Social Purpose*, 44.

CHAPTER 4

David Ritchie:
Evolution and the Limits of Rights

'"Natural rights" – that once useful fiction, of which American citizens find it particularly hard to clear their minds.' (*MW*, Review of Burgess, 440)

One of David Ritchie's contemporaries described him as a 'socialist' and 'zealous' democrat whose way of thinking seemed to have little in common with ordinary people. He was indeed an early member of the Fabian Society, but left in 1893. He was never as committed a Fabian as is often implied by commentators. He was less than enthusiastic about being associated with its ideas, and asserted his freedom to express his own, many of which were out of sympathy with Fabian Webbite orthodoxy. He did not, for instance, subscribe to the Fabian position on taxation and socialism, advocating instead the unpopular idea of a poll tax. He also was not at all as politically active as T. H. Green and almost never got involved in public political controversies. He took a firm stand on Gladstone's side over the issue of Home Rule for Ireland, and was elected to the Committee of the Home Rule League at Oxford University.[1] He resigned over the issue of Fabianism abandoning the idea of permeating the Liberals and setting up a new party instead. He claimed that he had not been consulted on being elected to the Fabian Society, and had never been faithful to its fundamental precepts.[2] *The Principles of State Interference* was, nevertheless, one of the most widely read political tracts in the English speaking world.

In this chapter David Ritchie's relation with and contribution to the evolutionary theories of his day is explored. He was at the forefront in criticising the application of naturalistic theories of evolution to society and in this respect we examine W. G. Runciman's comparatively recent attempt to revive social evolutionary theory in order to draw parallels. Modern genetics, in isolating the selfish gene as the unit of selection, has superseded some of the biological detail of Ritchie's theory, but the idea of institutional evolution and its contribution to socially desirable practices foreshadows theorists like Runciman. The essay then goes on to show how Ritchie's discussion of natural rights transcends the shortcomings of intuitionism and Benthamite utilitarianism in a synthesis described as 'evolutionary ethics'. This concept of ethics posits social recognition of both legal and moral rights as part of what the concept of right means, and advocates the criterion of the common good as the justification of rights. We then go on to draw the political implications of his conclusions when applied to specific problems such as animal rights, the limits of state interference, civil disobedience and humanitarian intervention.

– EVOLUTION AND SOCIETY –

Towards the end of the nineteenth century most of the significant forms of social understanding were converging upon the view that the idea of evolution provided the key to unlock the secrets of natural and human experience. Sociology, no less than poetry, political science, philosophy and the natural sciences, was enticed by the allure of the explanatory potential of the idea of evolution. Very soon, however, especially in respect of the sociological variants, it was discredited and even held up to ridicule. Talcott Parsons, towards the end of his life, was perhaps the last significant sociologist to attempt the formulation of a systematic theory of the evolution of societies. W. G. Runciman, in the second volume of his proposed trilogy, resurrected the idea of social evolution in a more theoretically rigorous manner than did John Hall in his recent philosophically and sociologically inspired account of the historical development of the West.[3] Runciman attempts to divest the theory of social evolution of those elements which had previously undermined it. In his view, past unsuccessful attempts at theories of social evolution shared two assumptions. First, that evolutionary change was equivalent to progress, and second, that this progress was unilinear following a path towards a predetermined goal. Runciman rejects these assumptions but still wishes to maintain that social evolution, although not reducible, is properly analogous 'to the theory of the evolution of species by natural selection'.[4] The evolution of societies proceeds by means of social selection, but the unit of selection, and herein lies Runciman's originality, is not the whole society, or class, but specific functionally defined practices comprised of particular distributions of power which confer upon groups or categories of persons competitive advantages in the evolutionary process. One of the purposes of social theory is to explain the survival, modification, eradication or other changes in such functionally defined practices. Society, Runciman claims, has to be conceptualised in terms of the allocation of power among its members and is therefore as crucial to social science as energy is to physical science. The competition inherent in the relations among individuals, and various collections of individuals, is directed towards the attainment of power in the form of enacting, or occupying roles, which have the capacity to influence other people's behaviour. Power, however, has a number of distinct, but overlapping, dimensions which distinguish the competition for control and access to the means of production, persuasion and coercion: economic, ideological and political power respectively. In other words, power is the generic essence manifest in different degrees and combinations in the various species of society. The evolution from one combination, or distribution of power to another, depends upon the process of the social selection of practices and the functions they are selected for.[5]

This theory is articulated, exemplified and refined in the course of answering two questions concerning, first, the distinctive types and sub-types of society possible at a given point on the scale of evolution, and second, the reasons why particular societies evolve into the types they do, rather than into any of the other possibilities. Although the possible far exceeds the actual modes and sub-modes, one cannot help but be impressed by the breadth and depth of scholarship which Runciman draws upon to construct his Darwinian/Linnaean classification of social evolution.

For the purposes of the classifying and explanatory exercise, however, a great many complex developments are treated at such a high level of generality that one cannot help but be disturbed by the simplifications entailed. Such a schematic treatment of the evidence is necessary, Runciman contends, if he is to do for the social sciences what Darwin did for the natural sciences. If such sacrifices have to be made in the name of science, one wonders whether knowing that, on a very general level, similar modes of society have existed at different times and developed through social competition, actually tells us less, rather than more, about what we already have achieved through detailed historical enquiries. Indeed, the whole exercise entails accepting historical 'facts' as they are given in history books, without entering into the attendant controversies.

Like Runciman, Ritchie sees considerable merit in applying the categories of evolution to social development, and similarly suggests that we should not equate the natural selection of institutions with progress. His theory is functional in that it focuses on the adequacy of institutions to contribute to socially useful practices, and the propensity for those which fail to do so to become less favoured in the struggle for existence. Like Henry Jones, Ritchie finds considerable merit in Burke's claim that there is reason in tradition. Any institution that has endured, he argues, must have served some useful purpose and evolved to meet the needs of the people it serves. If it had not been advantageous to society then on the principle of natural selection it would not have survived. The conservatism of Burke, however, was replaced by radicalism in both Ritchie and Jones. The assumption that long-established institutions must have had a value and served a purpose, does not preclude asking the question whether they continue to retain their value for our own generation (NR, 17). The reformer of current institutions is in fact faithful to the principles of evolutionary science by attempting to mitigate unnecessary suffering resulting from natural selection (NR, 18).

In an allusion to Spencer and other popular evolutionary theorists, Ritchie maintains: 'The phrases "social organism" and "evolution" are on everybody's lips, but those who use them most frequently have often grasped their significance the least' (NR, 277). Ritchie, like Henry Jones, was quick to acknowledge the profound significance of evolutionary theory, but thought that its overnaturalistic tendencies needed to be tempered. Evolution was indeed completely compatible with Idealism, partly because Idealism was itself intrinsically an evolutionary philosophy. The starting point of Hegelian Idealism is the unity of experience, and in Ritchie's view scientific thinking, particularly evolutionary thinking, assumes a similar premise, a monistic metaphysics, the fundamental unity of phenomena (PS, Memoir, 22).

Social theory was, by implication, normative because Idealist metaphysics characterised reality with reference to immanent ideals and ends. The self always projects a conception of a better self, which in principle it attempts to realise. Self-realisation is the attaining of a good that is common to individuals who comprise the same moral organism.[6] Many Idealists were convinced, particularly Ritchie, Bosanquet and Jones, that evolution was the key to understanding the ultimate character of the universe, and testimony to this belief was to be found in the fact that all of the separate forms of knowledge or experience, such as poetry, history, philosophy and natural science were converging on the universal form of explanation. All three thinkers, but none more explicitly and forcefully than Ritchie – who overtly saw his task as applying Darwin's concepts to human society – believed that the categories of biological evolution, heredity, inheritance, natural selection and the struggle for existence, had to be accommodated in Idealist social explanation. Like Jones, he denied T. H. Huxley's disjunction of cosmic evolution – nature red it tooth and claw – and ethical evolution, the mitigation of the naturalistic struggle for existence. Ethical evolution opens up a division between Nature and Spirit, contending that organic evolution and moral evolution are the result of different causes. This position is argued in different ways by Wallace and Huxley. Alfred Russel Wallace while not wanting to deny 'the law of continuity in physical or mental evolution', nevertheless attributes to Nature and Spirit different generative capacities. He rejects, for example, natural selection as the mechanism by which morality and the higher intellectual capacities develop. Organic evolution, including the development of the human organism, is subject to different laws from the development of the civilised mind. He argues that the spiritual world supervenes on the natural and generates in humans ethical, mathematical, metaphysical and aesthetic qualities. He also attributes to this 'unseen universe of Spirit' gravity, electricity, cohesion, chemical force and radiant force, without which the natural world is almost inconceivable.[7] By including such forces in the realm of Spirit, Wallace hardly left any grounds for the distinction between Nature and Spirit that he had posited. Ritchie contends that the possession of consciousness, language and reflection is an obvious advantage in the struggle for existence, but their development need not be attributed to a mysterious supervening force. The hypothesis of natural selection is perfectly adequate to account for their development (DP, 102).

Huxley, a friend and admirer of Darwin, on the other hand, takes a much bolder step towards the divorce of Nature and Spirit. Huxley was a distinguished natural scientist who thought humans suitable subjects for zoological investigation. On scientific criteria, he classified humans with the apes. Both humans and apes were identified as having a common origin and as having undergone evolutionary processes. Darwin's Descent of Man, published in 1871, relied heavily upon Huxley's findings to substantiate Darwin's own arguments.[8] Huxley believed, however, that zoological categories and explanations could not exhaust all that is to be comprehended in human existence. Social existence required the amelioration of the struggle for existence, rather than its encouragement. The pursuit of natural rights, which he understood in naturalistic terms, benefited only the individual at the expense of society. Moral rights, on the other hand, have correlative obligations and are conducive to social progress.[9] The survival of the fittest could not, in Huxley's view, constitute an ethical standard because fitness is circumstantially related to the variability of nature. Ethics are not 'applied Natural History'.[10] The evolution of Nature and moral evolution are for him two different and discontinuous processes. The idea of the survival of the fittest belongs to the cosmic process which governs the evolution of nature and the human organism. But the capacities which lead to success in this process are a disaster for social existence. Morality emerges when the cosmic process is checked first by fear of the opinions of others, and then by shame and sympathy. Moral rules arise as a result of our feelings of approbation and disapprobation. These rules are acquired and we gradually become used to thinking about conduct in terms of them. This is what Huxley calls the artificial personality, or conscience, which counters the natural character of man. Huxley gave ammunition to his critics, however, by introducing an ambiguity. In a famous qualifying note, in 'Evolution and Ethics', he says that 'strictly speaking, social life, and the ethical process in virtue of which it advances towards perfection, are part and parcel of the general process of evolution'. Furthermore, Huxley contends, that the 'general cosmic process begins to be checked by a rudimentary ethical process, which is strictly speaking, part of the former …'.[11]

Spiritual evolution is the self-conscious synthesis of the naturalistic and ethical theories. The unity of nature and spirit is reasserted, but instead of the former accounting for the latter, the explanatory power is reversed. It is reference to the higher that accounts for the lower. Nature is infused with spirit, not because it is intelligent, but because it is intelligible. Ritchie wants to maintain the unity of nature and spirit by suggesting that natural selection can just as easily account for both moral progress and organic development. The recognition of the spiritual principle at work in the universe is the condition of our understanding nature (DP, 115).

On the principle of unity, there could, for the Idealists, be no discontinuity between nature and spirit, the natural and ethical realms. Like the Darwinists, they asserted an essential continuity between the two. Where they differed from Darwinian evolutionists was in refusing to denigrate spirit by giving priority to nature. Human beings, then, were not to be understood with reference to their origins, but instead in relation to their ultimate end or purpose which is immanent in those origins.[12] Bernard Bosanquet, Henry Jones and Andrew Seth Pringle-Pattison directly address Huxley's arguments. Whereas Bosanquet believes that Huxley's distinction is a 'fatal misconception' (BI, 57), Jones and Pringle-Pattison maintain that Huxley has provided an invaluable corrective to those theories which associate ethical life too closely with organic and physical processes. Jones argues that however committed we may be to the unity of existence it would be folly to ignore or understate the difference between naturalistic processes and rational moral activity. By suggesting that nature and spirit were continuous, they were not suggesting that nature was intelligent. Nature contains immanent within it spirit, and while not being intelligent, it is intelligible. In other words, nature is inconceivable and unintelligible without mind, and mind has no existence without nature. They are mutually inclusive. Nature, on Huxley's terms, can neither know, nor think, and therefore it is not moral. On the other hand, Jones argues, knowing and thinking presupposes nature. Nature furnishes the data which intelligence interprets, an intelligence that nature herself has evolved. The product of intelligence, namely knowledge, belongs just as much to nature as to man. Intelligence is the instrument through which nature is expressed, and although it is not itself intelligent, it is intelligible only to mind. Mind and nature are interdependent, neither can exist without the other. Far from being opposed to morality, nature is a willing partner in its development.[13]

Pringle-Pattison argues that the strength of the naturalistic theories of evolutionary ethics is their explicit recognition of the unity of the cosmos. Unity is not a proposition to be proved, but instead an inescapable assumption (*BI*, 38), what Jones calls a colligating hypothesis or absolute assumption.[14] Both Pringle-Pattison and Jones, having re-established the unity of Nature and Spirit, immediately differentiate themselves from the naturalistic evolutionists. Pringle-Pattison, although critical of Hegel on many points, agrees with him that: 'Nothing can be more certain than that all philosophical explanation must be explanation of the lower by the higher.'[15] And Jones contends in his Gifford Lectures that modern Idealism refutes all theories that attribute explanatory power to origins. The last cannot be explained by reference to the first.

Modern evolutionary theory tends to favour the unity of nature and spirit, rejecting the idea that there is a fundamental break in naturalistic and ethical evolution. What is fundamentally different, however, is what they identify as the unit of selection. At the time that Ritchie wrote, genetics were barely understood. Weissman's germ-plasm theory postulated the basic theory of heredity which undermined Lamarck's ideas on inherited character through use and disuse. Herbert Spencer favoured the Lamarckian idea because its concept of use inheritance provided the link between biological and social evolution.[16] Weismann's theory was speculative and posited the constancy of germ plasm, which he claimed could be the component which transmitted inherited traits. This was elaborated by Hugo de Vries who contended that characters were inherited by means of units he called pangenes in the nucleus of cells. Subsequently research led to speculation about a connection between the morphological structures of the nucleus, that is chromosomes, and heredity which was confirmed by the use of Mendel's theory in 1903. Although Gregor Mendel first published the results of his experiments on plant hybridisation in 1865, and although his work was not completely neglected, his ideas were not well known until after 1900.[17] It was not until the 1930s and 1940s that the concept of a unit of selection captured the imagination of biologists. The idea of a unit of selection was not systematically articulated, however, until the 1960s. Matt Ridley maintains that:

> There was a revolution in biology in the mid 1960s, pioneered especially by two men, George Williams and William Hamilton. This revolution is best known by Richard Dawkins' phrase 'the selfish gene', and at its core lies the idea that individuals do not consistently do things for the good of their group, or families, or even themselves. They consistently do things that benefit their genes, because they are all inevitably descended from those that did the same. None of your ancestors died celibate.[18]

The British Idealists look to Hegel, and not to the naturalistic theories of Spencer and Darwin, for their inspiration. Hegel himself lived during a time when biological theories of evolution were beginning to emerge. He favoured the idea of emanation over that of evolution. In Hegel's mind, we understand a part only by looking at the whole. The early stages of something are only properly understood when they are seen as the stages of something more fully developed. This is the case in all specialist fields of knowledge.[19] In Ritchie's view, Spencer's evolutionary theory failed to acknowledge Aristotle's dictum – that the true nature of a thing is to be found not in its origin but in its end (PSI, 44; MW, 'Rationality of History', 131). Edward Caird makes a similar point when he urges that: 'in the first instance at least, we must read development *backward* and not *forward*, we must find the key to the meaning of the first stage in the last.'[20] Elsewhere he argues that spirit cannot be explained in terms of matter, and that matter itself is intelligible only in the context of the spiritual world.[21] Jones also argues, for example, that evolution is nothing other than another name for the development of spirit. Evolution is the hypothesis which provides 'the methodizing conception which we employ to render intelligible to ourselves the process which spirit follows in becoming free'.[22] Even though L. T. Hobhouse was a severe critic of what he took to be the absolutist and invidious implications of the Idealist metaphysical theory of the state, he acknowledged the importance of such thinkers as Ritchie in reformulating the theory of evolution. Consciousness distinguished the social from the natural organism, and was an undeniable factor in progress.[23] 'The study of mind,' Hobhouse argued, '… takes us at once to the highest thing that evolution has produced, and when we compare the different phases of mental growth, we get into the way of judging the lower by the higher.'[24] Hobhouse, however, went further than most Idealists could allow in separating mind from nature,[25] although he did not go as far as Huxley. Hobhouse, while agreeing with Huxley that evolution was not co-existensive with progress, nevertheless sought to discover 'at least one upward line in the evolutionary tree'.[26] Ritchie criticised both Herbert Spencer and Sir Henry Maine for reducing evolutionary history to one schematic and simple formula. They both contended that history progresses from status to contract, stabilises at that position, or regresses. Ritchie contends that beyond these two extremes there is a third conception, which is a synthesis of the two, which retains what is most valuable in individualism, in conjunction with the conditions of social stability which individuals undermined (DP, 69–71).

NATURAL RIGHTS AND EVOLUTIONARY UTILITARIANISM

Ritchie, like many of the Idealists, thought that ideas had to be understood in their historical contexts. This did not preclude criticism, but it could never be sufficient in itself to declare an opinion erroneous without trying to discover why it was widely believed (*NR*, ix). Its full meaning remains concealed unless it is understood in relation to the circumstances in which it was espoused. The doctrine of natural rights must first of all be seen in its negative aspect. The appeal to nature was an appeal against authorities whose sacredness had become diminished; against obsolete institutions; against contrived artificiality in art, literature, manners and dress. It was also an appeal to nature against wigs and hair powder (*NR*, 13)! For Ritchie, the doctrine of natural rights derives from Protestantism, applying its principles to earthly affairs, and whose political descendants are Rousseau, who hailed from Calvin's Geneva, and the American Declaration of Independence, the manifestation on American soil of English Puritanism.

Ritchie, like Bosanquet and most of the British Idealists, was concerned to advance our understanding of rights beyond the negative conception of liberty. Even though Spencer advanced a form of natural rights theory, he nevertheless adhered to the negative conception of liberty, held by Jeremy Bentham and J. S. Mill.[27] Contemporary western society, and particularly the United States, has sought to define itself, and the person, in terms of rights. There has been a proliferation of legal rights in both domestic and international law, and a considerable extension of the province of moral rights claimed in the spheres of women's rights, animal rights, gay rights, medical rights and human rights.[28] Richard Rorty has suggested, for example, that we live in a human rights culture.[29] It is not surprising, then, that this obsession with rights should lead to a revival of interest in the natural rights tradition. One leading rights theorist, Jeremy Waldron, has developed his own theory through a compilation of the criticisms made of natural rights by Burke, Bentham and Marx. Waldron's ultimate purpose is to defend a limited conception of human rights which emphasises the necessity of relating them to the broader context of the moral, cultural and institutional practices of a community. This line of argument is insinuated by the editor in the course of a volume principally dedicated to the case against natural rights, presented in the words of Bentham, Burke and Marx, whose actual contribution constitutes less than half of the text, with the rest devoted to the development of human rights, explanatory remarks on the principal theorists, and a long reply relating the objections against natural rights to contemporary discussions.

Underlying these differences, there is, nevertheless, a unifying theme, and that is the attempt to identify, in the works of different theorists, a criterion of moral and political action in terms of which choices can be made about what to do, justifications can be given of what has been done, and appraisals can be made of the actual and potential actions of others. Burke was an unequivocal opponent of natural rights, pouring scorn upon generalised abstract principles, except when it suited him to employ them himself. Burke explicitly invokes universal abstract principles, in his almost obsessive desire to bring Warren Hastings to justice for his corrupt conduct as the Governor of Bengal and officer of the East India Company. Burke's reputation was at stake, and he was determined to indict Hastings on whatever grounds he could. Hastings's use of arbitrary power, Burke claimed, transgressed both British and Indian principles of government and justice, and the plea that different standards of morality are applicable to different geographical areas was ridiculed on the ground that there are 'eternal laws of justice', that is, the 'law which governs all law, the law of our Creator'.[30] Whilst Burke rejects natural rights, especially in the secularised form claimed in his own day, he did not subscribe to orthodox theories of natural law, as a standard of political conduct. Was Burke, then, putting forward a pragmatic or utilitarian principle, as was so often claimed at the end of the nineteenth and beginning of the twentieth centuries? While acknowledging that aspects of this criterion emerge in a modified form, from time to time, in Burke's writings, they can never be appealed to as the foundation to his political theory. Bentham, for example, when he rejected natural rights, sought to substitute an alternative set of enduring and universal innate natural human characteristics, as the criteria of political action. The ineradicable disposition to pursue pleasure and avoid pain provided a firm empirical foundation for ethics, based upon real desires and wants, rather than upon imaginary rights. But Burke, and Marx for that matter, makes no such appeal to an enduring human nature, from which ethical principles can be deduced. Human nature, for both Burke and Marx, is historically constituted, and the 'civil social' person is a product of circumstances. In this respect, we can concur with Waldron's view that 'Burke writes often as though the entry into society produces a different new man for each society'.[31]

If Burke rejects natural rights and is unwilling to present either natural law, or utilitarianism, as the foundation of ethics, then what does he offer as a criterion of conduct? Waldron is sensitive to the fact that Burke's denial of natural rights, his equivocations regarding natural law, and his modified utilitarianism, point to the presentation of different principles of action and appraisal, which actually emerge within the context of human practices and the circumstances of their association. It is the relations among individuals which give rise to the conventions, by which they are governed.[32] This is not to suggest that Burke offers a pragmatic, or capricious, standard. His scepticism about the powers of human reason, and faith in the efficacy of prejudice, made the criterion of action not so arbitrary as to be based upon passing notions of pleasure and pain, nor so abstract that it stands outside and independent of the circumstances in which we find ourselves. He is not suggesting that we can dispense with abstract principles, only that those principles have little significance or meaning divorced from the circumstances to which they are applicable. Nothing of a moral or political nature can be universally affirmed, and hence no form of government can be pronounced best in the abstract, because it is 'the circumstances and habits of every country' which give rise to the type of government which best suits it.[33]

Natural rights theories had been severely undermined by Burke's charge of metaphysical abstractness, Bentham's contention that they were merely nonsense upon stilts, and Marx's indictment of the whole bourgeois individualist basis of rights talk and its bolstering of capitalist interests.[34] So why did Ritchie feel it necessary to lay the ghost to rest once again, given that he himself said 'It becomes tiresome to kill the dead too often' (MW, review of Veitch, *Knowing and Being*, 575). Ritchie, along with many of his fellow British Idealists, was motivated more by practical than philosophical concerns when political issues were on the agenda. Basically, the idea of natural rights was being co-opted by opponents of any increase in the sphere of state activity. Ritchie wryly comments that Tom Paine would get perverse pleasure out of hearing that natural rights had been commandeered by the Knights and Dames of the Primrose League and were espoused by a Tory Lord Chancellor.[35] This was because the abstractness of natural rights made them particularly amenable to diverse and conflicting applications from the anarchist's use to condemn current inequalities in society, to the Conservative attempts to maintain the status quo by opposing state interference (NR, 14–15). This, in Ritchie's view, is a fault of abstract theorising in general. In discussing Mill's famous example of preventing a man crossing a bridge which you know to be unsafe, Ritchie argues that the principle which Mill puts forward admits of diverse and opposite applications. Mill contends that restraint in this instance would not constitute an infringement of liberty, because no one could be construed as desiring inadvertently to fall into the river. The desire to cross the bridge is trumped by the more general desire to stay alive and dry. A heretic, however, may be construed as not desiring to be condemned to eternal damnation, and the inquisitor who wants to save that person is therefore justified in torturing him or her, equally convinced of the unsoundness of the heretic's beliefs as any one else could be of the unsoundness of the rotten planks on the bridge. Mill's defence of liberty is just as much an apology for despotism because 'it is the characteristic of an abstract theory to admit of quite opposite applications' (*PSI*, 87).

Ritchie's approach to natural rights follows a well-established Idealist path. He identifies two antithetical and one-sided views of the idea and arrives at a synthesis by acknowledging what is best in each theory and transforming those elements. What was valuable and 'true' about the theory of natural rights, what gave it its practical import, was the belief in nature as an ideal embodying a divine purpose, which was discoverable through the exercise of reason, and which human beings should attempt to emulate. Its defect was that the ideals were conceived in abstract terms, antithetical to the actual historical circumstances to which they were meant to be a guide. He abhorred intuitionism which proclaimed *a priori* natural rights in the name of liberalism.

With advances of our understanding of society in terms of evolutionary theory, and by use of the historical method in exploring institutions and problems, it was now possible to think of the ideal associated with natural rights theories, not as something fully formed and definitive, but as something whose revelation is gradual in the education of the human race. Following Hegel, Ritchie maintains that any satisfactory theory of rights or of the state must rest upon a philosophy of history (*NR*, 286). For him, philosophical reasoning went hand in hand with historical studies.

Ritchie closely follows Green in distinguishing between legal and moral rights.[36] Rights require social recognition, without which they are something less than rights. In other words, recognition is itself part of the concept of a right. Ritchie loosely defines a legal right as

> the claim of an individual upon others, recognised by the State. A legal right need not necessarily have been created by the State (e.g. by statute); but it must be such that the law courts will recognise it, in all orderly communities, the force of the State is at the back of all legal decisions. (*NR*, 78)

A moral right, in Ritchie's view, is 'the claim of an individual upon others recognised by society, irrespective of its recognition by the State'. Moral rights are less precisely formulated than legal rights, and much more difficult to determine because of changing public opinion, and the diversity of opinion among communities within the state. It is in these circumstances that an appeal to the law of nature, from which natural rights are said to derive, is often made.

Bosanquet goes much further than Ritchie in wanting to make a logical connection between moral and legal rights. Rights, properly understood, are morally imperative claims which ought to be and are recognised by the state.

The state has a moral end which is the rational life of its members, understood in terms of the collective or social, rather than individual, perfection of human personality. Rights constitute a system, and are the conditions for achieving the goal of perfection. For Bosanquet, a right implies a moral end and is therefore necessarily a moral right and moral imperative.[37] In contemporary political philosophy, Rex Martin takes the route followed by Green and Ritchie, and draws out more systematically the importance and implications of recognition. For him, moral claims, in themselves, are not rights. Martin argues that it is essential to take into account the practices of recognition, promotion and maintenance of such rights. Human rights, he argues, depend upon being more than valid moral claims. Valid moral claims have two distinct elements: a justifiable claim *to* something, and, in so far as it is attached to specifiable people, it is a claim *against* someone. What, in addition to being a morally valid claim, do human rights require in order to qualify as rights? Martin argues that justificatory arguments for human rights must connect up with the actual moral beliefs and practices of a community. This is not to suggest that people only have duties they believe themselves to have, but, any duties assignable to them have in some way to fit into or be derivable from the critical moral principles attached to the overall system of moral beliefs in existence in a society. People cannot have duties of which they could not become reflectively aware. In other words, a human right cannot be a human right unless, in addition to being a valid moral claim, it is also reflectively available, that is, unless it is also recognised as such. Such recognition, without the will to promote and protect it, is merely a nominal right and provides no normative direction for persons. A nominal right may have a paper existence, but it does not function as a right. A right is fully-fledged, not merely because it is a valid moral claim, but also because embodied in the very notion of right are the procedures and practices of recognition and maintenance. It must be stressed, however, that human rights do have the appropriate moral backing, but they have something else in addition:

> A human right is defective, not as a morally valid claim but as a right, in the absence of appropriate practices of recognition and maintenance. The absolute difference between morally valid claims and human rights, then, is that rights do, and claims do not, include such practices within their concept.[38]

In fact, all the above theories are closely related, because, for all of them, recognition is implied *in* the definition of right. For both Martin and Bosanquet, recognition has to take the form of legal recognition. Thus, natural or human rights which are not civil or legal rights, are no rights at all. Bosanquet's position is complicated by the fact that implicit recognition of rights may be embedded in the structure of law and institutions without individuals being fully conscious of them.[39] For Ritchie and Green, however, recognition by society, apart from the state, is enough to establish a moral right. In other words, even though rights need to be recognised, they need not be recognised *in* law. This position needs to be distinguished from the position associated with fundamental or natural rights, which asserts that a right is a right even though no one thinks it is so. Hobhouse, for instance, who was critical of the Idealists in general, and of Bosanquet in particular, thought that if anyone could demonstrate, or prove, that a certain condition is necessary for fulfilling the good life, it is therefore a right, irrespective of the fact that no one has ever recognised it.[40] In his early writings, Ronald Dworkin seemed to hold some such position with respect to the fundamental moral rights of the person to equal concern and respect.[41] His subsequent constructivism is more equivocal on this point, but recently he has again argued that there may be rights or legal principles of which the state is ignorant.[42]

To make natural rights claims, Ritchie argues, is to assert something fundamental, from which other rights may be derived. However, the question of exactly what rights every society *ought* to guarantee its citizens has been answered from different perspectives. This, then, is a distinct question from the definitional one and moves us on to the issue of justification. Authority has often been posited as external to the minds of individuals, for example, 'nature' in the sense of an 'inner voice', or 'utility', which derives from experience and reason. When premised on an external authority, natural rights can appear to rest on a contradiction. If the end of government is to preserve our natural rights, then we cannot allow governments to determine what natural rights are, because the very legitimacy of government is supposed to be judged by reference to them. Ritchie maintains, however, that those rights which people think that they ought to have, are exactly those rights which they have been accustomed to have, and are claimed because they have been sanctioned by the 'authority of social recognition'. When such traditional custom or constituted authority proves to be unsatisfactory and a disjunction appears between law and conscience in the minds of reformers, appeal may be made, not to external authority, but to the feelings that 'nature' has implanted in our breasts. The difficulty is that conscience differs from individual to individual, and when scrutinised more closely, the individual's conscience tends to mirror the society in which he or she has grown up, even to the extent that a revolt against its institutions betrays its unavoidable influence (*NR*, 85). In the conflicting impulses, desires and interest of individuals it is impossible to discern a settled standard of conduct; we must therefore go to something more fundamental and look at nature in its essentials. What is being appealed to, however, is human society and the mutual claims that it is necessary to recognise if that society is to avoid disintegration. Nature, in this respect, is not an appeal to feelings, but to reason, and, in principle, the competing claims can be adjudicated impartially with reference to the criterion of the general welfare. The result is that 'the details of a professedly Intuitionalist ethical code are filled up on Utilitarian principles' (NR, 87). In this respect, 'nature' may just as well be dispensed with and utilitarian considerations be brought in from the outset.

The difficulty is that people are just as inclined to disagree on what is useful, as they are to disagree on what is right or just, with reference to the natural law. What is useful is as ambiguous as the just, but, it is capable of further specification, because what is useful has always to be in relation to something. Although Benthamism rejects the rhetoric of natural rights it retains the abstract individualism that is an important part of that doctrine. Traditional utilitarianism treats individuals as more or less homogeneous moral atoms, with similar feelings which can be quantified, and among whom a quantity of pleasures can be distributed. It demands of institutions that they justify themselves in terms of their conduciveness to the general happiness. Ritchie maintains that Benthamite utilitarianism is itself open to many of the same criticisms of the theory of natural rights. The appeal to nature tries to reconcile the abstract individualism of the multiplicity of isolated instincts with the abstract universalism of the consent of humanity. Like the appeal to nature, utilitarianism assumes a uniformity of human nature over time and place. It combines the abstract individualism of treating every person as a discrete unit, with the abstract universalism of its view of happiness, which is taken to have an existence divorced from the concrete individuals who are singularly capable of experiencing it.

Utilitarianism is not without its merits, but, for Ritchie, it took the doctrine of evolution, particularly natural selection, to correct its errors and vindicate its truth. While Bentham and Austin did much to divorce jurisprudence and ethics from vague appeals to natural law, on the constructive side their ethical theories were too closely allied to hedonism and therefore needed to be separated from it by being reinterpreted in the light of evolutionary theory. Further, their jurisprudence needed to be permeated with an evolutionary and historical spirit (MW, 'Is Human Law the Basis of Morality, or Morality of Human Law', 127). Societies are engaged in a struggle for existence in relation to nature and other societies, and that which helps them in the struggle is good, that which hinders is bad. The development of reason, and the broadening of horizons from primitive virtues, lead to good qualities being recognised in wider spheres. A society, whose welfare determines what is right, may expand and change its character. In Ritchie's view, the good of a community provides us with the only criterion of what an individual ought to do, and is itself identical with the good of the individual. There is a mutual dependence or inclusiveness. This good is not static and constant because what the community is changes over time, and hence the standard of our moral judgement progresses. As the range of persons we take into account when we think of the common good broadens, changes are effected in our moral judgements. There are variations in moral judgements because societies are variable in character, and conflicts of duties and moral judgements are possible in complex societies because each individual belongs to many overlapping communities. Natural selection becomes transformed into rational selection among self-reflective and intelligent human beings. It is therefore feasible and desirable that some social organisms may cease to serve a useful purpose and become superseded by others of a higher type into which individuals become absorbed. Natural selection, or the struggle for existence, occurs at an altogether higher level among humans than among other gregarious animals. The struggle between social groups altogether complicates and mitigates the struggle between individuals within a particular group. Animals tend to belong only to one social organism or group, a herd, school or flock, whereas humans belong to multiple social organisms, many of them overlapping – an observation that is often ignored among writers on social evolution who equate the nation, class or humanity with the social organism. Many of the organisms may be in competition with each other for membership, and give rise to competing obligations and loyalties. We must therefore be extremely cautious in applying biological analogies such as natural selection to social organisms. It is most typically manifest not in the odd war between states, but in economic competition among individuals in the same line of business, and between commercially trading nations. There is, for Ritchie, however, a very important respect in which the ideas of the social organism and natural selection are invaluable in ethical and political thinking. They put utilitarianism on a scientific footing, rescuing it from the more obvious objections of intuitionism, while at the same time protecting ethics and politics from the arbitrary and subjective standards of intuitionists.[43] He is, for instance, directly critical of Alfred Russel Wallace because he posits a spiritual force independent of nature in order to counter utilitarian ethics. From an intuitionist standpoint, Wallace claims that there is an innate sense of right and wrong quite distinct from experiences of utility (*DP*, 104). The advantage of utilitarianism, Ritchie insists, is that it emphasises the importance of taking consequences into consideration, before pronouncing something right or wrong. It recognises that rules need to be revised, but not in the moment of their application – 'the battlefield is not the place for examining bayonets, though it certainly does test them' (*PSI*,

171). Ritchie does not believe that natural selection can serve to explain the ultimate nature of right and wrong, but it can explain the content of our ethical judgements.

This is what Ritchie calls a transition from Individualist Utilitarianism to Evolutionist Utilitarianism, by which he means a Copernican change of perspective from the eighteenth-century view that society was instituted to secure the protection of pre-existing human rights, to the modern view, influenced by advances in scientific thinking, that natural rights are those fundamental rights that *ought* to be recognised by a society, and judged wholly from the point of view of society. Social cohesiveness requires any society to adhere to certain ground rules or conditions which inform the actions of their individual members: 'In order to hold together, every society formally or informally agrees to observe, or let us say, finds itself compelled to observe these conditions of common life, and thereby creates rights and duties for its members' (*PSI*, 39). Ritchie has in mind the evolutionary theories of W. K. Clifford and Leslie Stephen who modified utilitarian principles by moving from an individualistic to a collectivist conception of the good. They moved away from the Benthamist individualistic utilitarianism of a balance of pleasures and pain, in which the common good was conceived as an aggregate of individual pleasures, to the idea of the well-being of society as a worthy ethical end (*DP*, 106). Idealism, while rejecting hedonism, could acknowledge that a modified utilitarianism was not incompatible with the idea of self-realisation, that is, the realisation of a social self in contributing to the common good (*PSI*, 116). Ritchie takes Sidgwick's broad-based utilitarianism, for example, to be compatible with Green's ethics which equates self-realisation with the common good. Sidgwick argues, however, that he cannot conceive of an argument that could succeed in proving that the good of an individual had to be sacrificed for the good of a group or community without at the same time conceding that a similar obligation is owed to the whole of humanity. Here, Ritchie suggests, Sidgwick seems to be accepting as indisputable Bentham's claim that every individual constitutes an equal unit in our moral judgements, but that such a philosophical dogma has never been manifest as the practical maxim of any considerable number of human beings. Such a criterion could only be feasible in the context of some ideal of a world state, federation or truly universal church, which Sidgwick expressly rejects (*MW*, review of Sidgwick, *Practical Ethics*, 538). The principle to be applied to human actions is to what extent they contribute to the greater well-being of that portion of mankind that we can feasibly encompass in our considerations? In other words, the question we have to ask is will society be healthier as a result of a particular act? (*PSI*, 107). Sidgwick's utilitarianism was, in Ritchie's view, a sleeker and tamer version than

Benthamism, and not only contained elements of the common good compatible with Green, but also sought in an almost Hegelian fashion to discern the rational in the real, to the extent that he claimed that the practical conclusions of utilitarian ethics will differ little from the actual code of morality that prevails (*MW*, review of Sidgwick, *Elements of Politics*, 225).[44]

Nature made human beings animals, but it is society that made them intelligent thinking beings with a capacity for moral action. Intuitionists, in arguing that morality is based on personality, denied the hedonist utilitarian contention that morality is based on the summation of individual feelings, as if they existed *per se*. The Intuitionalist, however, takes personality to be the solution to the problem of the basis of morality instead of a restatement of the problem. We must recognise, Ritchie argues, that 'personality is a conception meaningless apart from society' (*NR*, 102).

Ritchie, then, is not denying natural rights as such, but natural rights as traditionally conceived. Natural rights, understood as those rights which are socially recognised and necessary for the continuance and flourishing of society, are perfectly intelligible. In other words, as long as so-called natural rights have as part of their definition social recognition, and part of their justification the idea of the common good, they are a socially useful concept. He argues that: 'We can only allow natural rights to be talked about in the sense in which natural rights mean those legal or customary rights which we have come to think or may come to think it most advantageous to recognise' (*NR*, 270). They are an appeal to what is socially useful, not merely for the present generation, but also for future generations and as far as possible for humanity as a whole (*NR*, 103). Contrary to received opinion, none of the British Idealists saw the ethical community necessarily terminating at states' borders. Associations beyond the state were both advantageous and desirable, but not yet fully realised. For Ritchie, anything that promoted the establishment of a political federation and held out the possibility of a durable peace must be welcomed (*MW*, 'Moral Problems of the War', 495).

In the form of seeing natural rights as that which is socially useful or advantageous, it is not an appeal to the abstract conceptions of intuitionism, but one which can be tested with reference to experience, and with reference to the evolution of institutions, not an absolute immutable and imprescriptable criterion, but one which develops over time. Here Ritchie sees himself in conformity with Green, whom he contends had much more in common with Bentham and J. S. Mill than with intuitionism in using the common good, which was closely tied to self-realisation, as the criterion of natural rights, or what rights a society ought to afford its citizens (*MW*, 'Bonar's "Philosophy and Political Economy"', 549). In Ritchie's view, the common good which acts as the criterion of appropriate conduct changes from age to age and depends upon what actions and virtues contribute to the realisation of the well-being of society. Following Hegel, Ritchie maintains that historically slavery as an institution may be justified because it contributed to the amelioration of the brutality of war by making it more profitable to take prisoners than to slaughter them, and to the development of the conception of freedom (*MW*, 'Rationality of History', 142). In giving the free population the leisure to develop political liberty and a self-awareness of the worth of freedom, slavery gave rise to the ideas that eventually made slavery appear wrong. In other words, slavery was once useful and did not appear contrary to what would then be considered 'natural', but when it ceased to be an institution of progressive societies it became a violation of what people regarded as natural rights. Genuine appeals to the injustice of such an institution were not appeals to abstract principles incompatible with the continuance of organised society, but appeals to higher conceptions of society that should replace the lower. In this respect 'evolutionary ethics' teach us 'to face the problems of human society without exaggerated expectations'.[45] In other words, for New Radicals such as Ritchie, some elements of Benthamism could be retained, particularly its critical spirit of questioning existing institutions and proposing radical reconstructions (*PSI*, 80).

Not all theories of social evolution are utilitarian in form. Benjamin Kidd, for example, explicitly attacked utilitarianism for equating individual good with the good of all. In other words he denied Ritchie's justification for natural rights, that is, the common good of existing individuals and for future generations in the social organism. Kidd forcefully argues that there is an inevitable and inherent disjunction between the good of the individual centred upon personal gain and the good of the social organism largely concerned with the welfare of future generations. The error of utilitarianism, with which he associates Herbert Spencer, is in trying to establish a criterion of right conduct based on self-interest.[46] In Kidd's view, the pivot upon which history turns is constituted by two conflicting tendencies. On the one hand we have a social creature subject to the laws of retrogression, who holds his place or progresses only by subjecting himself to an onerous evolutionary process, the benefits of which are not immediately or remotely apparent to him, nor the success of which is of much interest to him as an individual. The world to the individual is one of cause and effect in which rational self-interest tells him to avoid or suspend the effects of the evolutionary process, and reason can never supply the motive for submitting to it. In essence, Kidd is arguing that the benefits of the evolutionary process are remote and of no immediate gain to the individual who cannot therefore on the grounds of rational self-interest submit to its sanctions. The motivation to act morally must be based upon something above rationality and reason, something that is 'ultra-rational'. It is in religion, he argues, that we find it. Religion both provides the ultimate motive force behind evolution and the cosmic progress of society, and also supplies the ultra rational sanction for conduct.[47] Rational self-interest unmitigated by a system of ultra-rational belief leads to disintegration and evolutionary stagnation. Only when the rational is subordinated to the ultra-rational can evolutionary progress proceed.

Ritchie had a sharp critical mind and pulled no punches when he detected a lack of intellectual rigour. He could be devastating in his comments, and Kidd made an easy target. In a review of Robert Mackintosh's *From Comte to Benjamin Kidd*, Ritchie scathingly comments: 'For persons likely to fall victims to the dogmatic exaggerations of Benjamin Kidd or the facile metaphors of the late Henry Drummond the book may be thoroughly recommended' (*MW*, 252). Elsewhere Ritchie takes Kidd to task for assuming that reason is always selfish in its precepts. While old-fashioned utilitarians gave the impression that ethical and political problems had to be resolved with reference to the pleasures and pains of those individuals now existing, Ritchie explicitly rejected this criterion and incorporated future generations into the utilitarian calculus. Ritchie argues that he cannot see the point of talking about the social organism at all if it is placed in complete antithesis to the individuals who comprise it. Furthermore, he accuses Kidd of historical naiveté in his characterisation of religions. It is only in so far as religions have become rational, not beyond rationality, that they have contributed to the long-run furtherance of society. Against Kidd, Ritchie argues that there is a social instinct independent of religions, but to which some religions lend support. Rationality may support and nurture this instinct, and it is only those religions that develop a high level of rationality that aid the social instincts of mankind (*MW*, review of Kidd, *Social Evolution*, 115–16).

– IMPLICATIONS –

What, then, are the implications of Ritchie's theory for substantive political issues, such as animal rights, the limits of state action, civil disobedience and humanitarian intervention? With the proliferation of rights in the post-1945 world, the rights of animals have been championed by many philosophers, the most prominent of whom is Peter Singer. Singer argues, for example, that just as blacks argued vigorously for an end to discrimination and the elimination of second-class status, animals too should be regarded as equal in certain morally relevant respects. Singer, however, does not really defend animal rights as such. What he actually argues for is a different kind of equality, the equal consideration of interests rather than the equal respect of rights.[48] As

Carl Wellman has argued, to talk of animal interests is to acknowledge that our mistreatment of animals is morally wrong, not because we have violated their rights, but because of the harm perpetrated against them. It is not, then, an issue of egalitarian justice, as it was in the civil rights movement, but of unnecessary and unjustifiable cruelty to animals.[49] In Ritchie's view a utilitarian argument for the rights of animals raises more problems than it can resolve. To base human and animal rights on the capacity for sentience and the experiencing of pain requires some criterion by which different degrees of sentience can be determined and what rights may pertain to them. Once some such scale is perpetrated it is difficult on logical grounds to resist gradations being applied within human society. If animal rights are compatible with the humane treatment of the horse as a beast of burden, for example, could not the humane treatment of negro-slaves be equally as compatible with natural rights? (NR, 107). In Ritchie's view all rights depend upon membership of a community, and membership of a community entails being a moral agent. Animals may be said to have rights metaphorically, or at least those that we admit with a sort of membership into our homes and families as quasi-persons. In this respect we may admit of special claims on us to which we owe obligations. Generally, however, animals do not possess legal or moral rights.

It is true that the law protects animals from cruelty, and some are classified endangered and are endowed with additional protection. This does not mean that they have rights, anymore than ancient monuments or works of art have rights because they are protected by law. We have obligations under the law and animals are the beneficiaries, but it is a perversion of the concept of rights to suggest that animals possess rights, or to suggest that they are able to claim them. Ritchie argues that pain is an evil, not in any special moral sense, but in that it is an impediment to the development of life and which every sentient being instinctively strives to avoid. Through sympathy and imagination we empathise with human and non-human animals subjected to pain, and gradually we have come to think it a duty to prevent unnecessary and gratuitous pain. Animals, then, do not possess legal rights. In the case of moral rights, those rights that are acknowledged and enforced by society, animals may with greater justification be said to have rights. But even with moral rights Ritchie thinks it more accurate to say that *we* have duties of kindness towards animals: 'these duties being duties owed to human society and enforced, more or less, by it' (CW, VI, 'The Rights of Animals', 388). What he means by this is that cruelty to animals is uncivilised and an affront to society, not a violation of the rights of animals as such (NR, 111). Carl Wellman endorses a similar position when he argues that being a right-holder necessarily presupposes moral agency.[50] His argument is based on the contention that inherent in a right are liberties and powers. The liberty inherent in the right of free speech is exercised in speaking publicly. The power of disposing of one's property is exercised in handing it over to someone else with an appropriate sign of disposal. Wellman argues that it would be pointless ascribing a liberty or power to anything or anyone incapable of exercising either.[51] Non-human animals are not citizens, nor are they persons, and because they lack moral agency they are incapable of possessing either legal or moral rights.[52]

Ritchie, like Green and Jones, did not think that substantive universal principles of state intervention could be established. There could be no *a priori* presumption for or against state intervention (*MW*, 'Moral Function of the State', 9). Little is gained when any element of state action is proposed to ask whether it falls within its sphere or whether it encroaches on the sphere of the individual. These spheres cannot be determined in advance of experience, nor need they be mutually exclusive (*PSI*, 107). In other words, it cannot be predicted on what issues the state might profitably intervene. Each case has to be taken on its merits and comply with the evolutionary utilitarian test of whether it is expedient, that is whether it contributes to or detracts from the common good of society now and for future generations. What Ritchie is emphatic about is that evil conditions that are sources of misery must be eradicated, and we as members of a moral community have a collective responsibility to eradicate them (*MW*, 'Moral Function of the State', 5).

Rights, for the Idealist, were not sacrosanct and could not be invoked as a matter of course against society. There may be instances when the well-being of society required that other considerations trump individual rights. Nevertheless, all of the British Idealists follow Green in allowing the individual the duty to resist a bad state. Green maintains that citizenship 'does not carry with it an obligation under all conditions to conform to the law of his state, since those laws may be inconsistent with the true end of the state, as the sustainer and harmoniser of social relations'.[53] They maintain that there may be rare occasions when the duty of the citizen requires acts of rebellion or resistance for the sake of the future of society and humanity, but only on condition that there is no reasonable hope of changing bad laws and constitutions.[54] Green restricted this obligation to the majority, while Ritchie acknowledged the possibility of the tyranny of the majority over the minority. Ritchie argues that should a law be so at odds with an individual's conscience, he or she is obliged to disobey at any cost. The alternative is a loss of self-respect and the degradation of character.[55] Jones argues that it is the cause that endows something with sacredness, and in its name the most humble individual has rights above those of a state which out of self-interest fails to provide the opportunities for moral realisation.[56] In addition, MacKenzie adds 'that we can often serve our country best by attacking its faults and resisting its aims'.[57]

Ritchie, like Oakeshott, distinguishes between acknowledging the authority of laws on the one hand, that is their legitimacy, and questions of the desirability of particular laws on the other, that is asking whether they are good or bad. The same licence cannot be given to persons to decide whether they should obey particular laws, as is given to them to express their reservations about the justice or expediency of those laws. This doesn't mean that Ritchie denies a right of resistance. His argument is typically that of a right to civil disobedience. Typically, civil disobedience is distinguished from other kinds of illegal activity on a number of grounds. First, it must at once be a principled and constrained act. The perpetrators of such acts of civil disobedience as liberating animals from research laboratories, or disrupting the movement of uranium for use in nuclear weapons, do so because of deeply held convictions about animal rights and the desirability of a nuclear-free world. Secondly, it is generally regarded that acts of civil disobedience are public. Unlike ordinary criminal acts which are committed secretly in the hope that the offender will escape detection, the activities of civil disobedients are necessarily public in that they want to draw attention to themselves and to their cause. A demonstration of their sincerity is the fact that they are prepared to accept the consequences of their actions. The civil disobedient, then, openly defies the law and at the same time willingly accepts the legal consequences for such law-breaking. This is what John Rawls means when he defines civil disobedience as 'disobedience to law within the limits of fidelity to law'.[58] Martin Luther King, for example, was emphatic that the civil disobedient accept punishment for the law he or she has broken, as an expression of support for the principle of the rule of law in general.[59] This distinguishes the civil disobedient from the ordinary criminal and militant revolutionary. Both the criminal and the revolutionary attempt to evade punishment; the former from motives of personal gain and the latter because he or she does not acknowledge the legitimacy of the state's jurisdiction over him or her.

Ritchie argues that if a person is convinced that a law is wrong then he or she may have a *duty* to disobey it, but it is then also that person's duty to submit to the consequences (*NR*, 197). There cannot be a legal or constitutional right to break the law, and the right or duty to resist is moral rather than legal and brings with it the heavy burden of answering the question, are the injustices and evils suffered more injurious than the possibility of disorder and widespread bloodshed. The answer will be contingent upon the circumstances and the type of people of whom it is asked, but there are certainly circumstances in which disobedience becomes a duty. There are many circumstances, Ritchie writes to Hastings Rashdall, in which breaking a bad law is the only way of bringing attention to it. In a despotism, for example, where no means of censure exists, it may even be justifiable to assassinate as the duty of a true patriot (*MW*, selected letters, 5: Cf., *DH*, 250). Assassination, however, on most modern theories of civil disobedience goes beyond acceptable political protest, but is not totally excluded if its consequences fall short of the complete overthrow of the government and constitution because that would then be revolution rather than civil disobedience.[60]

However, Ritchie argues that when people appeal to justice against society what they are really doing is claiming that a higher form of society should replace the lower, and it would be better if they were honest about it rather than appeal to abstract justice and natural rights (*NR*, 106–7). In this respect, the appeals of both Ghandi and Martin Luther King, while invoking a higher law as the criterion of the justice of current laws, were in fact appealing to a vision of a better and higher society that should replace the unjust ones they criticised.

Ritchie's argument about the social recognition of natural rights judged in relation not only to current members of society, but also for future generations and even for humanity as a whole, requires societies in which there is an advanced respect for 'human rights' to consider the consequences of their violation elsewhere. Modern international law in the post-1945 era, of course, forbids the violation of territorial integrity by interference in the internal or external affairs of a sovereign state.[61] Intervention is simply ruled out in international law. On moral grounds, however, the issue is more contentious, and is somewhat confused by the implications of the ad hoc tribunals set up to deal with humanitarian crimes perpetrated by the Germans and Japanese during the Second World War, the Serbs in the former Yugoslovia, the civil war in Rwanda, and the Serbian atrocities against Kosovan Albanians. There is recognition not only of crimes against the enemy without, but also against one's own citizens. Michael Walzer, however, endorses the strongly non-interventionist position allowing very little scope for humanitarian intervention, except in the most extreme cases of genocide. Walzer refuses to ground our ordinary notions of justice in such fundamental principles as equal treatment, desert or inalienable rights. We should, he contends, see justice as the product of particular political communities at identifiable times, and our accounts of justice should be constructed within the terms of reference dictated by these communities. Within any society, particularly liberal societies, there will be a variety of social goods whose distribution is governed by different criteria in their respective spheres of activity.[62] However, the well-known communitarian – an attribution which he renounces in his famous book on international relations – begins by positing a minimal content to human rights, the universal rights of life and liberty.[63] These rights, irrespective of how we ground them, natural or invented, are part of what we mean by being human. They are irredeemably a feature of our moral world. The authority of the state rests upon the consent of those who have authorised it to act in the interests of protecting their rights. The state is the sustainer of a common way of life which it protects against outside interference. In so far as it fulfils its purpose as a state it is worthy of moral status. This entails the state itself acquiring a persona and bearing the same rights of life and liberty against other states who might without adequate constraints attempt to impose their collective ways of life upon those of other states. States have value and worth, not because they are like individuals, but because they provide collectively for the pursuit of individuals' purposes. If states possess rights, as individuals do, then it is possible to envisage a society of states, just as there are societies comprised of individuals.[64] From the priority of rights bearing individuals who construct political communities the priority shifts to these communities themselves.[65]

Elsewhere Walzer has suggested that there is a minimal code of universal morality constituting cross-cultural requirements of justice, such as the expectation not to be deceived, treated with gross cruelty or murdered.[66] Walzer in fact posits the idea of an international society which he grounds, not on a natural or a hypothetical contract in a Rawlsian original position, but on ideals and principles that have become commonly accepted by leaders of states and their citizens. This is because he at once wants to endorse difference while subscribing to a 'thin' universalism. The universalism in Walzer is not prior to, but instead a distillation of the 'thick' morality associated with communities. This is not what he calls covering law universalism which gives priority to a way of life as uniquely right, and which can be used as the basis for imperialist arguments. Instead, his universalism is reiterative, acknowledging that subject to minimal universal constraints there are many different and valuable ways of life that have equal rights to flourish in their respective locations, and deserve equal respect to our own.[67] Walzer's fundamental point is that the international community regards infringements of territorial and political sovereignty as self-evidently wrong. Sovereign integrity is ensured by the internationally accepted right of non-intervention which is equivalent to the moral right of the individual to self-determination. Any infringements would therefore require extraordinary circumstances and special justifications. Given that the rationale of a state in his view is the protection of individual rights, particularly human rights, only gross infringements on a significant scale, for example genocide, would justify intervention if there are 'reasonable expectations of success'.[68] In such circumstances a state falls significantly below what the idea of statehood requires, and breaches the trust endowed upon it by its citizens in some form of social contract. In taking on a persona the rights of the state, although apparently derived from individuals, in Walzer's theory often come into conflict with and take priority over those of individuals. Given that states' rights are inextricably tied to individuals' rights the logic of Walzer's argument should permit humanitarian intervention well below the point when human rights are being massively violated. On practical grounds any military intervention involves a degree of coercion and ravaging. Walzer contends that it is believed that 'the citizens of a sovereign state have a right, insofar as they are to be coerced and ravaged at all, to suffer only at one another's hands'.[69] On this theory the state becomes hermetically sealed. What happens within its borders, revolution, bloody repression or tyranny should essentially be a matter of indifference to other sovereign states, irrespective of violations of individuals' rights: 'As with individuals, so with sovereign states: there are things that we cannot do to them, even for their own ostensible good'.[70] The so-called rights of the person to life and liberty constitute rather weak constraints on the activities of states, whose sovereignty only in the most extreme circumstances can be violated to redress human rights atrocities. Walzer concedes, however, that it is not always clear when a community is self-determining and thus entitled to claim the right of non-intervention.

Although it has become unfashionable to talk in terms of degrees of civilisation, when we accuse governments or peoples of systematically violating human rights, as the West has done in the cases of the Bosnian war, the Rwandan civil war and the ethnic cleansing of Kosovo by the Yugoslavs, what is being claimed is that the perpetrators have fallen below an acceptable level of civilised conduct to the extent of having reverted to barbarism. Although Ritchie's language may be unacceptable by today's standards his sentiment and argument are nevertheless ones which deny the absolute sanctity of sovereignty and acknowledge that there may be acts of gross barbarity which require humanitarian intervention. He argues that:

> In the interests of humanity we can recognise no absolute right in all governments, however bad, never to be interfered with ... All that I mean to insist on is, that a general principle of non-intervention, based on an assumed inalienable natural right of every group of human beings that may call itself an independent tribe or people, is of no use whatever for practical guidance. (NR, 235)

It would be wrong to intervene, however, if the prospects of making the situation better were not reasonable. Ritchie is not making the usual strong correlation between the state and the individual on the domestic analogy. He realises that such a correlation is merely a metaphor. He is not universally endorsing self-determination and hence avoids setting up a moral barrier around the state. Just as the contribution to the common good must be the criterion of state interference within the state, it must also be the criterion by which we judge the external actions, or consequences of the actions, of individual states. By definition the cause of intervention must be justifiable, must be a last resort, must have good prospects of success, and the means used must be proportional to achieving the end. In this respect Ritchie put forward a case for limited intervention based not on the sanctity of state sovereignty, nor on the principle of the integrity of the personality of the state or self-determination, but on a modified version of just war theory, which Gordon Graham has subsequently proposed in his *Ethics and International Relations.*[71]

Although Ritchie is similarly a constitutive theorist he takes a more humanitarian line on intervention than Walzer. He does not suggest that humanity comprises a universal society, so on what grounds could intervention be justified? He argues that the idea of a community of nations has developed which as yet is neither legal nor political, but as an idea it forms the basis for international law, albeit in the primitive sense of law, that is, usage and custom. In this respect nations have moral claims on each other. The principle of unity permeates all Idealist thought and is presupposed in the solutions to almost every problem. In this respect, the idea of humanity, the unity of the whole, is behind every sovereign state, and nothing of significance that happens in one is without its consequences on others. History, Ritchie argues, testifies to this interrelatedness, and confirms that all nations are responsible both to the future and to other nations.

An Idealist system of ethics implies equality, the recognition of others as moral agents capable of freedom of choice and rational development. The equality of human beings as such consists in their potential participation in a common society. If we are not able to think of humanity as a potential society, then we are not able to conceive of all humans as equal moral entities:

> As a matter of historical development, it is only in smaller societies that the idea of moral personality has grown up. The idea of humanity as a possible society has been of gradual growth, and therefore also the idea of every human being as a person – the idea, as it is sometimes phrased, of 'the infinite worth of every human soul'. The idea of one God, as the God of all races of mankind, is an essential element in this conception. (*NR*, 254)

Ritchie, like Bosanquet, believes, to use Walzer's terminology, that the thin universalism of an international moral community can only arise out of the thick moral particularism embedded in actual communities much closer to home. The more efficacious elements of patriotism must be built upon in order to promote close international ties, eventually leading to the attainment of a world federation. It was to be a long process with the differences between levels of civilisation presenting one of the main obstacles. Ritchie believed that we had not yet reached the stage where the citizen could be submerged in the man; citizens rights were still more tangible and historically embedded than the rights of man.

– NOTES –

The following abbreviations will be used in the text for these works by Ritchie:

BI   *The British Idealists*, ed. David Boucher (Cambridge, Cambridge University Press, 1997)

DP   *Darwinism and Politics* (London, Swan Sonnenschein, 1901: 4th edn)

MW *Miscellaneous Writings*, vol. VI of *Collected Works*, ed. Peter Nicholson (Bristol, Thoemmes, 1998)

NR   *Natural Rights* (London, Macmillan, 1894)

PS   *Philosophical Studies*, ed. with a memoir by Robert Latt (London, Macmillan, 1905)

PSI   *The Principles of State Interference* (London, Swan Sonnenschein, 1896: 2nd edn)

1. Peter Nicholson, 'Introduction', *Collected Works of David Ritchie*, vol. 1, ed. Peter Nicholson, xxiii–xxiv,
2. Sandra Den Otter, *British Idealism and Social Explanation: A Study in Late Victorian Thought* (Oxford, Clarendon Press, 1996), 114. His letter of resignation appears in *Collected Works*, vol. VI.
3. W. G. Runciman, *A Treatise on Social Theory*, vol. 2, *Substantive Social Theory* (Cambridge, Cambridge University Press, 1989). John A. Hall, *Powers and Liberties: the Causes of the Rise of the West* (Oxford, Blackwell, 1985).
4. Runciman, *Substantive Social Theory*, 295.
5. Runciman, *Substantive Social Theory*, 48.
6. Den Otter, *British Idealism and Social Explanation*, 80.
7. Wallace, *Darwinism*, 473–8.
8. In maintaining that all the races of man are descended from a common stock, for example, Darwin refers us to Huxley for substantiation. Darwin, *The Descent of Man* (London, Murray, 1888), 176.
9. T. H. Huxley, 'Natural Rights and Political Rights', *The Nineteenth Century*, 25 (1890), 179–80.
10. T. H. Huxley, 'Evolution and Ethics' in *Evolution and Ethics: T. H. Huxley's Evolution and Ethics with New Essays on its Victorian Sociobiological Context*, ed. J. Paradis and G. C. Williams (Princeton, Princeton University Press, 1989), 132.
11. Huxley, 'Evolution and Ethics', note 20. This was note 19 in the original version.
12. See also the Bosanquet essay in this volume on this point.
13. Henry Jones, 'Is the Order of Nature Opposed to the Moral Life?', An Inaugural Address (Glasgow, Maclehose, 1894), 26–30.
14. Jones, *Faith That Enquires*, 95.
15. Andrew Seth Pringle-Pattison, *Hegelianism and Personality* (Edinburgh, Blackwood, 1887), 89.
16. J. D. Y. Peel, *Herbert Spencer: The Evolution of a Sociobiologist* (London, Heinemann, 1971), 143.

17. Vitezslav Orel, *Mendel* (Oxford, Oxford University Press, 1984), 94–5.

18. Matt Ridley, *The Origin of Virtue* (Harmondsworth, Penguin, 1997), 17. Also see Richard Dawkins, *The Selfish Gene* (Oxford, Oxford University Press, 1988 edn).

19. See Ritchie, *Darwin and Hegel* (London, Swan Sonnenschein, 1893), 47.

20. Edward Caird, *The Evolution of Religion* (Glasgow, Maclehose, 1899), vol. I, 45.

21. Edward Caird, *The Critical Philosophy of Kant* (Glasgow, Maclehose, 1889), vol. I, 35.

22. Henry Jones, *Idealism as a Practical Creed* (Glasgow, Maclehose, 1909), 29. Elsewhere he argues that the power of the idea of evolution has 'transfigured the world'. Henry Jones, *The Working Faith of the Social Reformer* (London, Macmillan, 1910), 36.

23. L. T. Hobhouse, *Development and Purpose* (London, Macmillan, 1913), xx.

24. L. T. Hobhouse, 'The Diversions of a Psychologist', *Pilot*, V (1902), 12–13.

25. See, for example, B. Bosanquet, review of Hobhouse, *Development and Purpose*, *Mind*, 27 (1913), 386.

26. L. T. Hobhouse, *Mind in Evolution* (London, Allen and Unwin, 1915), 4.

27. See William Sweet, *Idealism and Rights: The Social Ontology of Human Rights in the Thought of Bernard Bosanquet* (London, University of America Press, 1997), 11–16.

28. Carl Wellman, *The Proliferation of Rights* (Oxford, Westview Press, 1999).

29. Rorty's ideas will be discussed in the Collingswood chapter.

30. Edmund Burke, *Speeches on the Impeachment of Warren Hastings* (Delhi, Discovery, 1987), vol. I, 231 and 504. He also says, 'that the laws of morality are the same everywhere', ibid., 94.

31. Jeremy Waldron (ed.), *Nonsense Upon Stilts: Bentham, Burke and Marx on the Rights of Man* (London, University Paperbacks, 1987), 93.

32. Waldron, *Nonsense Upon Stilts*, 85, 87 and 93.

33. For appeals to this circumstantial, social, or historical standard of conduct see Burke, *Works* (London, Bohn, no date), vol. III, 317 and 328–9; vol. IV, 7, 64, 65 and 67; vol. V, 19–20, and 44; vol. VI, 86, 156 and 158–9.

34. Waldron (ed.), *Nonsense Upon Stilts*.

35. M. W. Taylor, *Men Versus the State: Herbert Spencer and Late Victorian Individualism* (Oxford, Clarendon Press, 1993), 260.

36. T. H. Green, *Lectures on the Principles of Political Obligation* (London, Longmont, 1919), 9.

37. Bernard Bosanquet, *The Philosophical Theory of the State* (London, Macmillan, 1923: 4th edn), 188–9. Also see Sweet, *Idealism and Rights*, 61–3.

38. Rex Martin, *A System of Rights* (Oxford, Clarendon Press, 1993), 85.

39. Bosanquet, *Philosophical Theory of the State*, 197 and 201.

40. L. T. Hobhouse, *The Metaphysical Theory of the State* (London, Allen and Unwin, 1918), 120.

41. Ronald Dworkin, *Taking Rights Seriously* (Cambridge, MA, Harvard University Press, 1978), 182.

42. Ronald Dworkin, 'The Coming Battles Over Free Speech', *New York Review of Books*, 11 June 1992, 55–64.

43. D. G. Ritchie, 'Ethical Democracy: Evolution and Democracy', with annotations, in *The British Idealists*, ed. David Boucher (Cambridge, Cambridge University Press, 1997), 80. It is also reprinted in vol. 6 of Ritchie's *Collected Works*, ed. Nicholson.

44. Also see Taylor, *Men Versus the State*, 220. For another aspect to the relation of the Idealists with Sidgwick see the Bradley essay in this volume.

45. Ritchie, 'Ethical Democracy: Evolution and Democracy', 93.

46. Benjamin Kidd, *Social Evolution* (London, Macmillan, 1898), 295 and 341.

47. Kidd, *Social Evolution*, 344.

48. Peter Singer, 'All Animals are Equal', in *Animal Rights and Human Obligations*, ed. Tom Regain and Peter Singer (London, Prentice Hall, 1989: 2nd edn), 73.

49. Wellman, *The Proliferation of Rights* (Oxford, Westview Press, 1999), 176–7.

50. Carl Wellman, *Real Rights* (New York, Oxford University Press, 1995), 105–77.

51. Wellman, *Proliferation of Rights*, 35.

52. Wellman, *Proliferation of Rights*, 175.

53. Green, *Lectures on the Principles of Political Obligation*, 148.

54. Ritchie, 'Rights of Minorities', in D. G. Ritchie, *Darwin and Hegel* (London, Swan Sonnenschein, 1893), 141; Bosanquet, *Philosophical Theory of the State*, 199; John MacCunn, 'Cosmopolitan Duties', in *International Journal of Ethics*, 9 (1898–9), 167; Jones, 'Morality and Its Relation to War', in J. E. Carpenter (ed.), *Ethical and Religious Problems of the War* (London, Lindsey, 1916), 25.

55. Ritchie, 'Rights of Minorities', 140–1. Cf. Bosanquet, *Philosophical Theory of the State*, l.

56. Jones, 'Morality and Its Relation to War', 26–7.

57. MacKenzie, 'Use of Moral Ideas in Politics', in *International Journal of Ethics*, 12 (1901–2), 22.

58. John Rawls, *A Theory of Justice* (Oxford, Oxford University Press, 1973), 366.

59. See C. Crawford (ed.), *Civil Disobedience: A Casebook* (New York, Crowell, 1973), 235.

60. Brian Smart, 'Defining Civil Disobedience', in *Civil Disobedience in Focus*, ed. Hugo Adam Bedau (London, Routledge, 1991), 211.

61. Gordon Graham, *Ethics and International Relations* (Oxford, Blackwell, 1997), 94.

62. Michael Walzer, *Spheres of Justice* (New York, Basic Books, 1983).

63. Michael Walzer, *Just and Unjust Wars: A Moral Argument with Historical Illustrations* (New York, HarperCollins, 1992: 2nd edn), 136.

64. Walzer, *Just and Unjust Wars*, 53–60. Charles Beitz challenges similar assumptions. He argues that the state is not autonomous in the way that the principle of non-intervention requires. Modern states are heavily interdependent and unlike individuals they do not have personalities that have to be respected. The moral worth of a state cannot be attributed to its autonomy. Its value has to be assessed on the arrangements it supports for contributing to the well-being of its citizens and humanity as a whole. Beitz, *Political Theory and International Relations* (Princeton, Princeton University Press, 1979).

65. Walzer, *Just and Unjust Wars*, 254. He denies that he is a communitarian in Walzer, 1990.

66. Michael Walzer, 'Interpretation and Social Criticism', in S. M. McMurrin (ed.), *The Tanner Lectures on Human Values*, vii (Salt Lake City, University of Utah Press, 1988), 22.

67. Michael Walzer, 'The Communitarian Critique of Liberalism', *Political Theory*, 8 (1990).

68. Walzer, *Just and Unjust Wars*, 107.

69. Walzer, *Just and Unjust Wars*, 86.

70. Walzer, *Just and Unjust Wars*, 89.

71. Graham, *Ethics and International Relations*, 111.

CHAPTER 5

Henry Jones:
Beyond Socialism and Liberalism

The main issue with regards to political ideology, for Jones, relates to the endeavour to overcome all forms of dualism – whether metaphysical or political. When Jones reflects on the ideologies of both socialism and liberalism he is searching for some form of integration or higher synthesis. This higher unity would integrate the communitarian assumption of much socialist thought (and the consequent belief in the efficacy of the state in providing the groundwork for a secure and civilised life) with the best of individualistic liberalism, in ensuring that individuals had freedom, rights and responsibilities. In other words, he envisaged an integration of individual rights with social responsibilities, individual with socialised property, free markets with public action.

Jones's social and political values were religiously based, and his commitment to reform was inspired by a variant of Christian socialism, which R. H. Tawney later came to refine in the 1930s. Tawney's influence upon many figures in the British labour movement in the twentieth century is well documented, but what is little noticed is the extent to which Tawney's own Christian Socialism was also inspired by Idealist themes. Tawney was a former assistant in economics at Glasgow University, where Jones was Professor of Moral Philosophy. Tawney became friendly with the future secretary to the Cabinet, Thomas Jones, who was one of Henry Jones's ex-students and greatest advocates. Tawney also shared, in common with Jones, the teaching of Edward Caird, and a passionate belief in the power of education to eradicate many of the inequalities in society. Both Jones and Tawney were also deeply committed to the Workers' Education Association, and like Jones, Tawney rejected the Marxist explanation of history, and gave considerable emphasis to the creative force of moral ideas. Tawney's analysis of the acquisitive society and equality were underpinned by these preoccupations. For them both, the context of ideas served to explain the mode of production, rather than the reverse.

We should not lose sight of the fact that during the early years of this century mainstream intellectual debate was less compartmentalised than it is today. There was a great deal of personal and intellectual contact between people, who described themselves as belonging to different political persuasions, but who nevertheless moved in a relatively fluid social circle. Liberals and democratic socialists inhabited the same intellectual environment, belonged to the same organisations and discussion groups, and often became related to one another through marriage. R. B. Haldane was a close personal friend of the Webbs, and Jones was a friend of Sidney Ball, who implored him to join the Labour Party. It was Edward Caird who persuaded R. H. Tawney and William Beveridge to visit Toynbee Hall. Beveridge became Tawney's brother-in-law. Tawney became a member of the Fabian Society in 1906 and the Independent Labour party in 1909, but nevertheless remained close to new liberals. What united many of the Idealists, new liberals, liberal socialists and social democrats was a fundamental agreement that classical liberalism had produced social and economic conditions of such deplorable dimensions, that the deliverance of many working people from their wretched predicament was both a Christian and humanistic duty. It was thus common among progressive liberals to acknowledge the considerable debt the New Liberalism owed to Socialism in forcing liberals to think beyond the narrow confines of *laissez-faire* economics. The Italian Liberal Guido de Ruggiero is typical of this point of view when he says: 'By following the action of Socialism for the improvement of wages and the general condition of the working classes, Liberalism has had occasion to see how groundless were the arguments by which employers justified their stubborn resistance'.[1]

The first aspect of Jones's thought we want to explore in this chapter is his conceptions of metaphysics and ontology and the implications for the rights and duties of citizenship. Secondly, we will explore Jones's place within the ideological spectrum of Edwardian politics; thirdly, we will critically examine his own ideological beliefs in relation to the continuing relevance of social democratic ideas. In this respect we will compare his ideas with those of R. H. Tawney and the democratic socialism of New Labour.

– METAPHYSICS, ONTOLOGY AND CITIZENSHIP –

Philosophy was not an abstruse discipline for Jones. It was, rather, ordinary human self-consciousness and experience become reflective. Metaphysics and ontology were not therefore viewed as esoteric. For Jones, we are all, wittingly or unwittingly, metaphysicians. Metaphysical assumptions (or colligating hypotheses as Jones called them) were part of the very texture of our everyday lives. Every judgement embodied, in the final analysis, some deep-rooted metaphysical assumptions.

Jones's own philosophical position can be summed up in the term Absolute Idealism. His primary assumption was the monistic ontological unity of reality. This was not a simple monism, of the type he saw in thinkers such as Bradley and Bosanquet. Nothing short of the Absolute was acceptable; however, such an Absolute could only be appreciated through its complex differentiations. This appreciation of the differentiations was essential for grasping the nature of the Absolute. The Absolute was an 'identity of differences'. This point also led him to attack the Personal Idealists. Jones argued that they focused too intently on the differentiations at the expense of the unity. For Jones, *all* forms of dualism and fragmentation had to be overcome. There was no ultimate separation between thought and reality. There was no world of objects separate from thought. They were rather differentiations of the Absolute. This did not mean that thought was either reduced to objects or objects to thought. Both were differentiations of a deeper unity. Self-consciousness was the truth of all things and human reason was also the measure of all things. This point, for example, led Jones to oppose vigorously the discipline of epistemology. His fundamental objection was that it assumed the separation of ideas and reality before it started. For Jones, the psychical event of an idea is not knowledge of the idea, and the knowledge of an event is not the psychical event itself. Epistemology must therefore both assume and not assume reality. This was the confused and contradictory foundational premise to the whole approach. In so far as it started with this premise it was flawed.

A parallel logic characterised Jones's analysis of social and political phenomena. The individual citizen is not an isolated particular. To isolate citizens as atomistic and wholly separate is as problematic as isolating any particular in the world. As Jones put it: 'to insist on differences to the exclusion of their unity is ... futile'.[2] The particular always develops in the context of the universal. There is, in other words, an identity in difference. The particular citizen is *both* a particular person *and* a focus of a deeper unity. As Jones commented: 'It is the spirit which has built up the social world that becomes in its own members aware of what it has achieved' (IPC, 57).[3] Citizens develop through assimilating and reflecting upon the substance of their society and its traditions. Thus, as Jones liked to remark, the citizen is suckled and weaned at the breast of the universal.[4]

When Jones discussed the 'universal' in society he employed the term tradition.[5] The essence of his argument is that the tradition of a society embodies the accumulated wisdom of *Reason*. Tradition is 'continuous and cumulative'.[6] It is gradually assimilated by the growing individual through socialisation. As Jones comments:

> If man did not at first accept the beliefs and customs of his people; if he were not
> for a considerable part of his life docile, assimilating and uncritical of the rational
> habitudes of his time, receiving his nutriment prepared, simplified and made
> innocent from the larger life of the social organism … reason could not be fostered
> within him. (*IPC*, 54)

The substance of an individual nature is thus assimilated through social life. However, this is not a blind assimilation. The substance of critical reason becomes embodied in this process. Eventually, the citizen can contribute to the reform and restructuring process of society. For Jones, the 'now' of an individual or a nation 'is a very complex affair. It is the moving point in which the echoes of their past deeds are converted … into the duties and opportunities of the present. Man is always reminiscent when he acts: his past lives in him whether he knows it or not' (*OPC*, 128). Thus, Jones sees citizenship as a complex inheritance. It is a body of ideas which, when assimilated, become actions. For Jones, it must be noted, 'an idea *is* an act' (*OPC*, 144). The entailed inheritance of the idea of citizenship, assimilated from the traditions of society, modifies the perceptions and activity of individuals. For Jones, 'tradition … has its value; but only when it is taken up and made to live again in the individual's thought and will' (*IPC*, 53).

The main implication of the above argument, on the nature of the self, is that agents cannot be dissociated from tradition. This argument is also underpinned by Jones's views on the nature of individuality and his understanding of evolution as the interdependence of the agent and the environment. The self is neither an isolated abstraction or character idiosyncrasy, nor a simple psychological continuity. Rather, it is a focus of reason, bringing together the traditions of a society. As Jones put it, the self

> is the organised and living system of … past acts of willing, desiring, knowing and
> feeling … The self, in a word, is a living and operative memory: a memory which,
> so far from being the resuscitation of dead or sleeping ideas, is experience repeating
> itself, the very self iterating its operations. (*IPC*, 48)[7]

Jones claims forcefully that he has not absorbed the self into the universal of society or tradition. This, he contends, is as absurd as contending that the individual is completely independent.

Jones indicates that the above process, of the gradual and continual modification of individuals by the assimilation of tradition, is one of *evolution*. This is not a naturalistic evolution, but conversely moral and spiritual. As Jones comments: 'The application of moral principles to natural or physical circumstances injects new values into them – beauty, truth and worth. They are made working partners in the evolution of man' (*OPC*, 150). When the past develops through the individual mind – it evolves. When we reason through traditions, we evolve and experience the world in new ways. In other words, the citizen is not a static isolated entity with unchanging interests. Moral growth and development are inevitable.

Citizenship, in Jones's thought, is thus not just a political or legal category. It is a state of mind and being. Individual citizens are seen to be rational and moral agents able to advance arguments and to deliberate and judge between ends. Each individual has a colligating idea or working hypothesis (or body of key metaphysical assumptions), which 'defines the relation of his ends, determines the ranks of his needs, decides the content of his desires. It is the interpreter of his circumstances' (FE, 133). Jones occasionally calls this the 'deeper self'. The colligating idea or working hypothesis is embodied in the will, that is, the activity of citizens, and determines the character of their experience. For Jones, thought 'inevitably breaks out into practise, and ideas are deeds in the making' (PC, 31). Jones had a contiguous powerful sense of the role of ideas in reforming social reality.[8] Social and political reform denoted a change of ideas and will. Further, the breadth and character of a citizen's life will be determined by the nature of the embedded purposes or colligating ideas. Moral conduct is ultimately dependent on the nature of the purposes and ideas adopted by the agent. Thus, the 'petty life has petty and secluded interests', whereas, 'the interests of his neighbourhood, his city … thud in the arteries of the good man' (OPC, 176). The most comprehensive colligating ideas are communal in nature and thus express common values and a common sense of identity.[9]

Although in some of his discussions Jones appears to be rejecting individualism wholesale, he does make a distinction between an older and newer variant of individualism. These terms correspond, to some degree, to the notions of passive and active citizenship. The old individualism, which envisaged society as an aggregate of particulars, gave a thin reading of social life. The units of analysis were empty asocial individuals. Such individualism is potentially dangerous since, ultimately its sheer vacuity provides no limitations to conduct. It may appear innocuous, but it is not. Following Hegel, Jones saw the terror of the French Revolution, which 'rent asunder every political and social bond', as rooted in such thin individualism.[10] Thin individualism, which was both abstract and false (whether it appeared in revolutionaries or abstract liberal political economy), was the root to many expressions of passive citizenship. However, the thicker understanding of individualism recognised the social nature of humans. It was rooted in the idea of citizens having a common social identity and substance and recognising a common good. Individuality thus implied universality. For Jones, 'the least investigation will show that the tissue of the individual's soul is social in every fibre' (OPC, 178–9). The older individualism's appeal to character cut little ice with Jones. Character was not something which flourished in glorious social isolation, rather, 'The interpreter of *character* can no longer rely on the old individualism: he must study it in relation to the social life, of which it is both cause and effect, both expression and product.'[11] This doctrine undermined, to some degree, his relation with groups like the Charity Organization Society and fellow Idealists such as Bosanquet.[12]

In the light of the above argument, Jones rejected any hard distinction between the state and the citizen. For Jones, this is another false dualism presented to us by social theory. The state and citizen are compared by Jones to the concave and convex sides of a circle. They are 'ultimately nothing but different manifestations of one self-revealing, self-realizing spirit' (*OPC*, 180). Both share the same destiny. In fact, for Jones, it is the aim of the social sciences to demonstrate this fact (*OPC*, 180). The state exists to provide the conditions and means for the development of citizens. Jones was keen, in this context, to include citizenship courses within the public educational curriculum, something that has arisen once again in public debate at the close of the twentieth century. Jones even advocated university degrees in citizenship.[13] The good citizen is, therefore, not harmed by good laws which provide conditions for human development and freedom. As Jones commented: 'The good citizen does not wish to send women to work in pits, to employ little children in factories, or to sweat employees. He is not wronged by any legislation that prohibits these methods of making wealth' (*WFSR*, 253–4).

For Jones, the relationship between the individual and the state is one of both difference and mutual inclusion. Further, the state, like the individual, has a moral character, which, for Jones, necessarily means that it has a personality (*PC*, 50). If this is the case, then the state is capable of both being free and of promoting the freedom of its citizens (see *IPC*, 100). In such an organic unity, the welfare of the whole and of the individual are inseparable.[14] It is no longer possible, Jones argues, to think in terms of individual good apart from the social good, and, in this respect, the stark opposition between individualism and collectivism turns out to be false. The opposition is false because both individualists and collectivists make the same mistaken assumption. Thus individualists will often believe that an extension of the activity of states necessarily entails a curtailment or limitation of opportunities for individual enterprise. Yet, given that the individual, for Jones, is saturated with social relations, and is nothing without them, the controversy over the desirability of extending state activity is simply absurd. It was clear, to Jones, that the enhancement of individual freedom and the extension of the activities of the state had grown concurrently. He contended that there was no evidence to suggest that with the development of state intervention there had been any diminution of competition between private enterprises.

This perception of communal life actually empowers the citizen and provides more opportunities for an advanced moral and social life. The limits of state intervention could not therefore be fixed by abstract principles. Each proposed extension of the state's sphere of influence had to be assessed in terms of the criterion of whether the personality of the citizen was being presented with greater opportunities to develop, and, on the condition that no weakening of individual responsibility was involved.

It followed from the above arguments that any complete separation between the public and private realms, or private as against public rights, was false to Jones. The communal and private always grow together. As he stated:

> I should accord to individuals every *item* claimed for them, in the way of privacy, sacredness, independence ... But I would point out that all these rights that we attribute to persons exist only on a certain condition. And that condition appears to do the exact opposite of their private and individual character. They must be recognized as not less social than they are individual! – nay! that they are individual, private, personal, *because in the first place they are social*. Rights are social institutions.
>
> (*OPC*, 170–1)

Jones, like Ritchie and other Idealists, was critical of the natural rights perspective. Rights are liberties, claims and powers bestowed on individuals by society. A society 'extends to its citizens genuine rights, thereby widening the compass of their private effective wills and enlarging the significance of their personality, knits them together' (*OPC*, 171). One of the implications of Jones's views here is that he expected and argued for a high standard of public ethics. Citizenship in public office was a high calling with an immense responsibility (*WFSR*, 291).

There are a number of propositions in Jones's perspectives which admittedly rest uneasily with a more classical liberal vision of citizenship (although they resonate with aspects of the new liberalism). The public/private dichotomy is severely modified; totally private individual goods are seen as arbitrary and socially divisive; value and an objective common good are defined publicly; law is integrally involved with morality; freedom is defined via communal moral goals; human nature is seen to be social, rational, and developing in ethical awareness; and finally, the state is part of an enterprise to make humans more virtuous. This is not an exhaustive list. It indicates, however, the general ethos within which his conception of active citizenship functioned. Finally, it is worth pointing out that this particular notion of citizenship was more concerned with duties than rights and, given its concern for the public interest and common good, it stressed the common resources of moral identity and culture. For Jones, citizenship is therefore not limited in any way to extending civil, economic or social entitlements. Jones is searching for a common ethical identity amongst citizens. Citizenship is seen as an integrative experience allowing the individual to attain a higher moral ground to review his or her community and personal life.

– HENRY JONES AND EDWARDIAN IDEOLOGY –

Jones, like most British Idealists, had an ambiguous relation with contemporaneous ideologies, particularly socialism and liberalism. Despite his lifelong association and support for the Liberal Party and his own personal relations with the two main new Liberal prime ministers, Asquith and Lloyd George, Jones remarked in an article in 1910: 'If I were asked which of the political parties contains the largest proportion of able men, earnest in the pursuit of the ideal of a State ... I should say, with little hesitation, that it is the Labour Party'.[15] Jones never ceased to feel a strong affinity with the working classes, from whose ranks he had risen.[16]

Socialism in Britain, in the 1840s, was initially associated with what is now called utopian socialism, that is, the work of Saint Simon, Charles Fourier and particularly Robert Owen. This form of socialism moved into relative decline in Britain during the period 1840 to 1870. Marxian socialism, although having an impact in France and Germany over the 1870s and 1880s, had little role in British political thought and practice. It was first embodied in Britain, in an eccentric form, in the nineteenth century Social Democratic Federation, whose effect was minimal. Marxism, as such, did not really 'take off' until the 1920s, and even then tended to remain at one remove from the major focus of Labour thought. It was also rejected by the tradition of democratic socialism, beginning with the Fabians and early Independent Labour Party, in the 1890s and 1900s. British Idealists were aware of the existence of Marxian socialism from the 1880s, but understandably, took it to be relatively unimportant, qua British political thought.[17]

The perceptions of socialism in the Edwardian period depended, to some extent, on the milieu of the author and the audience addressed. The background socialist ideas in the early 1900s lay in a number of important movements and writers: the memories of Chartism; Ruskin, Carlyle and the critique of capitalism and its aesthetic destructiveness; Henry George and his idea of the single tax; Christian socialism in figures such as Charles Kingsley; the radical use of a Ricardo and neo-classical economics (this became a particular characteristic of some of the Fabians); a more radical utilitarianism with roots in the later writings of J. S. Mill, particularly his work on political economy and *Chapters on Socialism*; Chamberlain's *Radical Programme*; radicalised trade unions; and 'Lib-Labism' from the 1880s. All these, and more influences, constituted the backdrop to socialism. Thus, the grounds for the intellectual justification of socialism also varied considerably during this period, moving through Christianity, utilitarianism, evolutionary theory, natural rights theory, neo-classical economics, Comtism, Kantianism and Hegelianism. There were thus a number of, often, mutually antagonistic socialisms: Christian socialism, types of Marxism, revisionism, syndicalist, libertarian, feminist, ethical, guild, reformist state socialisms and social democracy. The socialism of the early 1900s was a hydra-headed creature.[18]

First, Jones was clearly aware of different forms of socialism, although he articulates a simpler dichotomy than that outlined above. There was some community of views here amongst British Idealists. Jones saw *two* main forms of socialist thought. The first form is instrumental and mechanistic. It maintains that material reforms, public ownership and imposition of equality, through the state, suffice. In other words, it places heavy reliance on the state doing everything for the individual. The socialism Jones has in mind here is both the administrative statism of the Fabians, Sidney and Beatrice Webb, as well as, more residually, Marxism (although Marxism is never dealt with directly by Jones). His old teacher, Edward Caird, adopts a similar view. Caird notes, like J. S. Mill in *Chapters on Socialism*, a distinction between a more 'dogmatic socialism', which he associates with Robert Owen and Charles Fourier, and a 'new socialism', which is 'ethical' in character. Caird mentions the Fabian socialist, Sidney Ball, as exemplifying this latter form. In such Fabians, Caird sees a 'truer' socialism, which provides a more effective opposition to the individualistic tendencies of liberalism. A similar distinction is drawn by Jones's colleague, J. S. Mackenzie, in his *Introduction to Social Philosophy*, where 'ethical socialism' is kept distinct from 'scientific socialism', by which Mackenzie means, quite explicitly, Marxism. However, Mackenzie does admit that 'socialism is a term of great elasticity of meaning, and it covers a variety of proposals'. Bernard Bosanquet, in a contemporaneous and well-respected article, also makes a similar distinction, although his categories are 'economic' and 'ethical' socialism.[19] Interestingly, Jones, like many contemporary Idealists, tended to think of the Fabians as a key point of reference for socialism, although this was not always a complementary reference. Bosanquet, for example, had his own long-running dispute with the Webbs over the Poor Law. Jones, also, although agreeing with Caird on the valuable ethical dimension of Sidney Ball's work, also felt that the Webbs' emphasis on 'administrative statism' was socially destructive. This more ambiguous attitude to Fabianism was due to the fact that Fabianism itself embodied such a diversity of beliefs.

Secondly, Jones saw *one* form of socialism as preferable and 'truer'. In fact, he distinguishes, on a number of occasions, 'true' and 'false' socialisms. Jones, like many of his fellow Idealists, rejected what he called authoritarian socialism, which was seen to impose external schemes that denied individuality and the expression of free will. Jones alternatively praised the socialism which was most compatible with liberalism. This was variously called 'practical, 'right' or 'true' socialism. It stressed the 'ethical' dimension over the material, economic or scientific issues. Characteristically, both types of socialism Jones associates with the growth of the state in the latter part of the nineteenth century. In other words, there are both beneficent and harmful socialist 'statisms'.

Before discussing the features of this 'true' socialism, it is important to complete the sketch of the ideological background. Jones's political commitments, as mentioned, were, on one level, to liberalism. Liberalism, however, was a movable feast. Jones's own reading of liberalism can also be divided between 'true' and 'false'. Jones saw undoubted benefits within nineteenth-century classical liberalism. It enshrined the rights to private property and individual liberty. It allowed individuals room to develop, giving maximum space to self-help and thrift. It also embodied commitments to the rule of law and constitutional government. Yet, Jones, like many Edwardian liberal contemporaries, was critical of this older version of classical liberalism, not so much as to abandon it, but rather to reinterpret it. This implied neither a seismic shift of thought, nor a simple amalgamation, rather a fluid development of interpretation around formal themes.

Classical liberal commitments to a more atomised individualism, a negative conception of liberty, the *laissez-faire* conception of the economy, and minimal state theory, became targets for reinterpretation. The older individualism found its logical outcome in anarchism. Such individualism foolishly identified the 'good' with something purely private, whereas, for Jones, the individual's true good is tied to the traditions and purposes of the community. Further, Jones held a more positive conception of liberty linked to notions like self-development. Classical liberalism, when dealing with freedom, too often identified freedom with, what Jones called, 'the pseudo-freedom of irrational caprice' (*WFSR*, 107–9). Freedom is a fundamentally important value. Yet, developed freedom, for Jones, equates with moral activity, not civil privatism. Further, for Jones, preventing humans from performing immoral or harmful actions is, in itself, no restraint on the individual. We should not, he argues, be able to 'make any bargains we please … the liberty to do wrong is not a right, but the perversion of a right' (*WFSR*, 107–8).

Finally, Jones advocated a modified conception of a market economy and a more responsive, sensitive and ethical conception of the state.[20] He was not, however, optimistic about the moral capacity of leaders in industry to recognise and accept their social responsibilities. Indeed, he often despaired at their insensitivity to the human resources they exploited. In 1916, for example, while serving on Lord Haldane's Royal Commission on University Education in Wales, Jones was clearly appalled by the evidence of the South Wales Coal owners.[21] He wrote despondently to a number of friends about the experience. In a letter to Thomas Jones, he confessed that: 'The Philistinism of it all made me sick.'[22] The upshot of the increasing stress, which some liberals at the time placed on the commercial mentality, was, for Jones, socially and politically damaging. In an article commenting upon his work in the Reconstruction Committee, Jones remarked that 'he was sometimes startled by the distortion of the purely economic mind; how the Capitalist can see nothing except through the medium in which he is soaked'.[23] The exclusive focus of the commercial mind in education policy, social policy and the like, can be deeply erroneous and destructive for both cultural and industrial development. For Jones, if once you encourage the separation of ethics from the economy then enormous social tensions arise, philistinism and greed rule the day.[24]

In summary, Jones envisaged a richer moralised individualism and a developed view of liberty evolving out of a critical reinterpretation of an asocial, amoral, atomic individualism and negative conception of liberty. For Jones, 'it is the unmoralised community and the unsocialised individual which follow methods of resistance and social exclusion' (*WFSR*, 110). In reality, the individual and the state interpenetrate. For Jones, individualism must either drift off into the absurdities of anarchy or develop and evolve through a new richer and deeper grasp of its relation to the state. For Jones, there is consequently, no *a priori* limit to state action. The limits, he says, 'are not to be fixed by any conception of the abstract antagonism of society and the individual: for each of these is true to itself precisely in the degree to which it is faithful to its opposite' (*WFSR*, 113–14). Character, a popular term in the classical liberal vocabulary, is not something that, for Jones, can be separated from society. It cannot automatically be undermined by state action. Good character rather presupposes a good enabling state. The good state and good citizen go hand in hand (*WFSR*, 177–8).

The reference point for Jones's response to classical liberalism is quite clearly the Edwardian new liberalism, and after more than a hundred years it is probably best known for laying the foundations of the post-1945 polity. The term 'new liberal' appeared in public discussion, initially, in Britain in the 1890s. Other terms were employed to denote the purported change of liberal perspective. 'Radical', 'progressive' or 'social liberal' denoted roughly the same idea. Up to 1914, it is important to realise that even the term socialism (that is liberal socialism), often implied 'new liberal'. As indicated above, none of these terms was meant to indicate a total revolutionary change of view, rather an evolution of policy and ideas. There is still, though, like the 'new right' in the 1980s, some ambiguity as to who should be associated with the new liberalism. Some historians, in tracing it back to the 1890s, have noted that its early legislative achievements were negligible. Furthermore, the matter is complicated by the fact that some who propounded it in the 1890s, such as R. B. Haldane, Herbert Asquith and Herbert Samuel, were also liberal imperialists. The better-known new liberal writers of the early 1900s, like J. A. Hobson and L. T. Hobhouse, often drew a sharp distinction between what they regarded as genuine social reformers, as against imperialists (both Liberal and Social Imperialists). The catalyst for this distinction was the Boer War. This view cast a slur on the reputation of the 1890s generation of new liberals. This is not the place to debate this issue; however, it is clear that the espousal of imperialist ideas in no way undermined the concern for change in liberal thought, particularly on domestic reform. Many other groups, like the British Idealists, were also fiercely divided over imperialism, but remained united on social reform.[25]

On one level, it is notoriously difficult to explain the activity of any political movements in the context of ideas. Thus, the development of unemployment and health insurance, under the new liberals, has been viewed as a pragmatic *ad hoc* culmination of a series of local and voluntary experiments to deal with the problem of unemployment over the latter part of the nineteenth century. It was not, therefore, part of an ideological perspective at all. In point of fact, the bulk of the historical literature on the new liberalism, up to the late 1970s, virtually ignored the ideological component. It was only in the late 1970s that the theoretical side of the new liberalism was really given serious attention. A further question, though, relates to the ideological coherence of new liberal theory. Positivism, biological and evolutionary theory, eugenics, underconsumptionist economics, utilitarianism and philosophical Idealism, all had some role to play in new liberal theory. Some commentators on the new liberalism have been happy to play upon this rich ambiguity and incoherence. Others have been keen to stress one theoretical aspect.[26] Jones's own reading of the new liberalism was premised upon philosophical Idealism. He clearly regarded the new liberalism in terms of an evolution of ideas and British society towards a more civilised condition.

– A SOCIAL LIBERAL SYNTHESIS? –

Jones was arguing that the 'true' socialism, which is committed to the ethical development of its citizens and uses the state for this end, is coterminous with a public-spirited new liberalism. This ideological fusion might be equally termed 'liberal socialism', as much as 'new liberalism' or 'ethical socialism'.

Jones also referred to it as the 'higher socialism'. However, two points are crucial for assessing this synthesis. First, it never seriously took off in practise. Essentially, the synthesis which did arise between liberalism and socialism from the 1920s up to the 1970s was of a different character, more akin to the Webbs' vision, and thus a 'false socialism' for Jones. Second, the 'higher socialism' advocated by Jones was premised upon certain deep-rooted issues, which still haunt social and political theory and practice at the turn of the twenty-first century.

On the first point: the socialism which developed in Britain might be called 'reformist state socialism'.[27] The characteristic features of this form of socialism are, first, that, it advocated democratic gradualism and constitutional reform. It did not want to dispense with parliaments, adversarial parties or representative democracy. Second, it accepted some role for the free market (either in a mixed economy, social market or market socialist format). However, the reach of the market has always been a contentious issue. Many maintained that areas of the economy give rise to natural monopolies and thus public ownership. From the 1918 Labour electoral manifesto, *Labour and the New Social Order*, reformist state socialism was associated with a *principled* commitment to public ownership of industries like coal, steel, railways and the like. In Labour theory, the Morrisonian model became dominant, with boards of public officials replacing private directors. In the 1945–51 period, particularly, many 'natural monopolies' were taken over.

Jones would undoubtedly have found much of this development unacceptable – particularly the 'principled' commitment to public ownership. In the late 1950s, some reformist state socialists, such as Hugh Gaitskell and Anthony Crosland, also felt some unease with the public ownership model as overly bureaucratic. Crosland once memorably described this Webbite administrative model of socialism as the 'politics of the filing cabinet'. Public ownership, for Crosland, as for Henry Jones, was always viewed more as a means to an end of greater equality and classlessness. Fiscal and educational policies, and industrial democracy, were seen as more effective ways of achieving this end. Doubt about public ownership was also reflected during the Wilson administrations of the 1960s, although interest returned again in the 1970s in the writings of Stuart Holland. Its presence in Labour Party debates was guaranteed by the retention of Clause Four up to the 1990s. A third aspect of reformist state socialism concerns its critique of capitalism. This critique was conducted in instrumentalist, rather than ethical, terms. The central motif, from the Webbs, was the critique of capitalism as inefficient and wasteful. The Keynesian, amoral and technocratic perspective on the economy reinforced this approach up to the 1970s. Again, for Jones, this neglect of the ethical dimension was a fundamental error in socialist thought.

Reformist state socialism formed an important aspect of the political consensus in Britain during the 1945–70 period. The spirit of this consensus lay in a political agenda, often flaky at the edges and contested in detail, but, none the less, something which held sway. The political agenda was focused on the desirability of full employment; the extension of the social rights of citizenship, in the form of a welfare state; the need for social minimums as part of any civilised society; the inevitability of a mixed form of economy, embodying a mutually beneficial mixture of public and private economic enterprises. State intervention and planning were seen as an inevitable concomitant of this agenda. For one recent commentator, new liberal reformers such as William Beveridge and J. M. Keynes had a 'crucial place in defining the terms of the civic bargain that prevailed [in Britain] from 1945 to the 1970s'.[28] David Marquand, in fact, has summed up this consensus as 'Keynesian social democracy'.[29] This civic bargain entailed guaranteed rights of protection against illness, in old age and against unemployment, as well as direct or indirect opportunities in education and employment. Social rights, financed out of general taxation, provided for social citizenship.[30] Progressive taxation was essentially used to foster civic solidarity, connecting the private and public realms in one communal enterprise. Civic (ethical) duties became largely institutionalised into the willingness to pay marginally higher levels of direct taxation for redistribution.

What is the relation of liberalism to this consensus? The pre-1914 new liberalism began to lay the foundations of the above consensus. In fact, one can push this point further to show the impact of new liberal sentiments on certain fundamentals of that consensus. Thus, many of the major policy initiatives of the immediate British post-1945 Labour governments, for example, Keynesian fiscal demand management, employment policy, public ownership and Beveridge's social security scheme, derive from new liberal modes of thinking. The new liberal Yellow book, *Britain's Industrial Future* (1928), formed the prototype of this approach; it is also important to remember here that Beveridge and Keynes remained progressive new liberals throughout their working lives, although, admittedly, of a different stripe to those of the pre-1914 period. Furthermore, many of the influential figures of the late 1920s and 1930s' Labour grouping, including R. B. Haldane, J. A. Hobson, H. W. Massingham and Charles Trevelyan, had been new liberals and had moved to Labour after the effective political demise of the Liberal Party in the 1920s. They viewed the Labour party as a more effective vehicle for the new liberalism. As Charles Trevelyan remarked, at the time of his moving to Labour, 'The Labour Party is, indeed, the safest custodian of ... cherished Liberal principles'.[31] This point had already been intimated by Jones, Hobhouse and others before 1914. In addition, purportedly socialist theorists, like R. H. Tawney, employed theoretical frameworks which were remarkably close to those of some of the new liberals.[32] As one commentator has remarked, paradoxically, the disintegration of liberalism in the 1920s was, in part, the 'triumph of liberalism'.[33] From the 1930s, particularly, reformist state socialism became the home for the new liberalism – although this was a variant of the new liberalism which showed a marked preference for a more statist and technocratic policy. As Keynes remarked in 1926, 'Possibly the Liberal Party cannot serve the State in any better way than by supplying Conservative Governments with Cabinets, and Labour Governments with ideas'.[34] The legacy of Jones's type of social liberalism was revived in the 1980s when R. H. Tawney was identified as the intellectual foundation upon which the Social Democratic Party was built by Roy Jenkins, David Owen, William Rogers and Shirley Williams. None of these politicians, nor Henry Jones, agreed with his firm line on rejecting the honours system in Britain. Like Jones, Tawney was vehemently against the class system in Britain, and detested the extent to which economic values undermined social virtues. Tawney's arguments for a better society are neatly encapsulated in one of his most famous books, *Equality*. In it he argues, like Jones, that democracy is an unstable system of government for as long as it is a mere political system insensitive to inequalities, and reflecting the deeply entrenched class divisions in society. To convert democracy from a system of government to a way of life it is necessary to eliminate all forms of special privilege, and to convert all forms of economic power which so often control society like an irresponsible tyrant, into the servant of society constrained by and accountable for its actions to a public authority. Like Jones, Tawney did not think that absolute equality could be achieved, nor did he think it desirable. A belief in equality, for both Jones and Tawney, entailed the recognition that individuals differ profoundly in their natural abilities, and constituted one of the main sources of social energy. It is the inequalities of economic wealth and social status which prevent the full flourishing of such natural abilities. The elimination of class privilege would, Tawney thought, foster progress because 'class tends to determine occupation rather than occupation class'.[35] Tawney argued that in England there were only two sets of pernicious class relations: one originating in the last century with the rapid increase in economic development, and the other of more ancient lineage, although modified by the economic, which was aristocratic in nature and strictly hierarchical. The combination of the two made the class system in Britain particularly resilient to erosion. As Tawney puts it: 'It is at once as businesslike as Manchester and as gentlemanly as Eton; if its hands can be as rough as those of Essau, its voice is as mellifluous as that of Jacob.'[36]

Two fundamental perversions result from this class system. First, there is the insistence by certain groups that they have the right to enjoy certain privileges which are advantageous to themselves, but inconvenient or injurious to others. This assertion of privilege is reinforced by the second feature of the system. The same people who seek privilege exercise power, not for the good of all, but in order to preserve and consolidate their special advantages.

The fact that one man earns more than another is not repulsive in itself as long as education and habits of life lead to a common tradition of respect and consideration for one another. If human fellowship were allowed to flourish, trivial and superficial economic contrast would become obscured. What Tawney was arguing , then, was that there should be equality of opportunity. Nature has deemed it such that everyone needs health, warmth, light, rest, food and fresh air. However, not everyone has equal access to them. The state should provide the conditions for equal enjoyment of these rights. Equal health care provisions should be open to all in order to stop the injustice of disease affecting certain groups more than others. This involves an improvement of the environment in which those diseases reside. Of equal importance, education should be equally available to all in order to make equitable the opportunities for personal attainment or self-development.

In Tawney we find many of the themes, and many of the same principles being employed, as we find in the British Idealists. Like all the Idealists Tawney rejected the idea of natural rights, and like them he argues that rights could only be sustained and justified if they fulfilled a useful common purpose. All rights are conditional on promoting the end of society, and are themselves derived from that end. The state was not absolute because its rights depended on its remaining faithful to its purpose as a state, and similarly the individual's rights were not absolute, but instead relative to the station he occupied or function he performed in society.[37]

In addition there is an emphasis upon an increased role for the state, but not at the expense of stifling individuality, equality of opportunity, nor at the expense of diminishing initiative; an attack on the inequalities of class privilege, while encouraging inequalities of talent; an emphasis upon a democratic society, and a rejection of a democratic system imbued with and driven by economic values; and an emphasis upon the keystone to it all, equal access to education in which natural talents can flourish to their capacity. In attaining this vision of society Tawney went further than Jones in envisaging a much more interventionist state. Tawney wanted to bring about greater equality by raising taxes in order to control investment in industry. He contended that a prudent community could not trust to chance that, by cutting down on the provision of social services, the money retained by individuals and industries would be used for more important objectives. This emphasis, however, is one of degree, and even the Social Democratic Party conveniently suppressed much of Tawney's radical social prescriptions.

What, however, of the new socialism of the late 1990s? It appears to view itself as a form of 'middle way' (we hesitate to say a 'third way') between the new right and the older socialist concerns of 'reformist state socialism'. This new socialism claims to accommodate both social justice and markets. It also blends elements from the liberal tradition and might indeed be described as another attempt at a new form of liberal socialist synthesis. It also has some formal resonance with the 'higher socialism' synthesis that Jones was articulating in the early 1900s.

What are the elements of this new socialism? First, there is a distinct view of market activity. The hackneyed charge made against socialism is that it is attached to a command economy, public ownership and a principled opposition to markets. This is, of course, a parody. However, the central new socialist theme is that markets can be partially decoupled from capitalism. Some public ownership of the means of production can be combined with extensive use of market mechanisms. Thus, the distributive and democratic aims of socialism can be linked with the efficiency-inducing properties of markets. Whereas capitalism may be impossible without markets, socialist markets can function without full-blooded capitalism. The market can then be retained as a useful (and *efficient*) allocator of goods and services.[38] Further, it can maximise choices (therefore *freedom*) to work, buy, sell, borrow or invest. It also helps to dissolve power by dispersing it amongst consumers. Dispersed power in a market also increases participation of ordinary people. When citizens own some property and can make decisions about their own lives, they can act responsibly. This would seem to be what is implied in the notion of 'stakeholding'. Socialist markets could thus be said to be *democratic* and *egalitarian*. Thus, in sum, markets can be used to further socialist aims, bringing together a concern for freedom, equality, welfare, democracy and ethics with economic efficiency. This point articulates a view that is central to Jones's whole position, namely, that the free markets are crucial but are premised on a background of ethical and social relations. Neither full-blooded capitalism nor principled statism are acceptable.

Second, the above issue signals another difference of emphasis from reformist state socialism, namely, misgivings about the state. This unease is premised on the point that the state tends towards bureaucracy and economic inertia. Thus, more favour is shown towards decentralised economic decision-making, premised on markets. Maximising citizens' access to production is preferred to the state becoming involved in redistributing resources. This does not mean that public goods are abandoned, but they had to be balanced with freedom of individuals and markets in many spheres. Jones was also insistent on the same theme, namely, that to achieve socialism, it is not enough to develop a more powerful state. The simple fact of the implementation of a welfare state and distributive justice is not enough. This was his central objection to the Webbs' vision. For Jones, reformist state socialism was a prime example of a more mechanistic statist socialism, in which individual moral character was neglected. Welfare rights are delivered formally in the form of pensions, health care and national insurance and yet the active moral duties or correlative responsibilities of citizens are neglected. This neglect, in Jones's view, also led to a disregard for the real benefits of individual freedom. The freedom for character development is a painful necessity of human existence. Reformist state socialism, however, will often tend, for Jones, 'to desire the profits of individualism without its pain' (*WFSR*, 271). He therefore argues that 'organic civic or state methods can be employed advantageously only where the individual character is highly developed', which also parallels his view on democracy.[39] Jones contended that favouring public action on principle (vis-à-vis reformist state socialism) is as foolish and destructive as rejecting it on principle (vis-à-vis classical liberalism). Principled commitment to state ownership is both commercially inefficient and ethically suspect.

Thirdly, there is a moral agenda within the 1990s new socialism, which links up with an older element of the socialist tradition this century, namely, Jones's, Caird's and Tawney's favoured idea of ethical socialism. Unlike the more 'mechanistic' and 'instrumental' policies of reformist state socialism this century, the new socialism has tried explicitly to develop a moral stance. It is contended that there must be moral (not just efficient) boundaries to markets – boundaries which have become increasingly blurred. They have also taken up the issue that rights imply obligations – whatever this might imply, although a form of workfare, at the moment, looks like one option. Again this is a theme which was continually stressed by Jones. Any community premised exclusively on market individualism and free-riding cannot last long without engendering social instability. There is, therefore, an assumption of the importance of non-market communal values like honesty, keeping one's contracts, respecting other persons, being a good neighbour and fulfilment of the social duties of active citizenship. Jones thought, for example, that it was Hegel's (and Bernard Bosanquet's) great blunder to give complete 'independence to the economic world'.[40] He was outraged at the idea of the implicit total 'otherness' of the economic world to ethics. What was fundamentally wrong here, for Jones, was simply that 'economic relations imply mutual trust … and a stability of will and purpose' (*FE*, 183). Economics, and the world of claims and counter-claims (Bosanquet's terminology), are premised upon a mutuality of accepted values, like trust, honesty and keeping promises. Thus, economic life is, at one level, different to ethics, yet, it is, at the same time, *premised* on ethics. It is an identity in difference. If, Jones contended, this underlying value consensus did not exist then even the free economy would falter. It would be a world of anarchy. As Jones commented, 'Mr Bosanquet ought therefore to have nothing to do with a world of exclusive wills … It should be left to Herbert Spencer.'[41]

The area where the above arguments impact most forcefully is in social policy, namely, where the social rights of citizenship will be expected to correlate with individual duties. The new socialist claim is that the state has an enabling task, both to encourage a productive economy and also to provide conditional opportunities for citizens. Thus, rights not only correlate with obligations, but, in addition, obligations relate to opportunities. The equality implied here is a 'starting-gate' equality, rather than an 'end-state' equality. Starting-gate equality provides an enriched reading of equality of opportunity, establishing 'thickened' equal conditions for citizens to compete. The problem remains, though, concerning the grounding of these moral beliefs. In a society now premised on far more obvious value pluralism, it is difficult to see how such a strongly moralistic stance (no matter how super-ficially attractive) can be communally grounded.

In the above context, Jones's stress on the ethical dimension of politics can make his views appear anachronistic. His moralism and religiosity do make some contemporary readers understandably uncomfortable. However, the problems of ethics, communal values and citizenship are not without relevance to some contemporary political issues – particularly for the new socialism. A decade of market-orientated individualism gave rise in Britain in the 1990s, once again, to a call (whether correct or not) for active civic virtue and the yearning for *some* form of communal consensus. The comparatively recent communitarian critique of liberalism, and espousal by some of civic republican beliefs, partakes of the same general intellectual ethos as Jones. Jones's stress on the intrinsic ideological compatibility of certain types of liberalism and socialism and the ethical dimension of politics, is, to say the least, mildly prescient and resonates with some of the developments in late twentieth-century ideological thought. For Jones, although socialists will often stress the importance of issues like democracy, welfare and justice, such things clearly only function, for him, if virtuous citizens participate.[42] Civic virtue or active ethical citizenship is the premise to successful democratic and just form of socialism. Moral reform and moral education must therefore precede economic or franchise reform. This theme lay behind Jones's intense interest in 'citizenship education'.

Fourthly, the new socialism has laid some stress on the theme of 'classlessness'. Socialism can no longer be exclusively for the working class.

It appeals to the commonality of citizens. This contemporary stress meets one of Jones's greatest anxieties about all forms of socialism (at the time). He argued that the major danger of socialism is working-class cupidity and the very concept of 'class' itself as a social category. The Labour Party and the socialist movement, he commented, 'are by aim and profession the representative of the interests of one class of citizens'. Any class (working or aristocratic) which monopolises the state 'taints the very spirit of citizenship'.[43] He was clearly not keen on organised labour representation and advocated, at times, that it would be in the interests of the working class if there were *no* Labour candidates and *no* Labour party. Jones did not even like the title 'Labour Party', as such, since it immediately conjured up a vision of sectarianism. A party, for Jones, should not represent one class alone, it must represent the common good. Apart from publishing critical articles on this theme of 'the corruption of the citizenship of the working man' – answered in one case very testily by Ramsay MacDonald – Jones mentions the above point as the key reason why he does not join the Labour Party. In a letter to Sidney Webb, who had tried to persuade him to join the Labour Party, Jones writes:

> if I believed that by joining the Labour Party I could strengthen its power for good in the State, I should join it today and wear its label as a badge of honour. I want a working man … to be a good citizen … But, my dear Mr. Webb, just here is what you will regard as my stone of stumbling. The Labour Party, as I understand it, is in the contradictory position of suspending and obscuring the well-being of the State as a whole, instead of placing it first and making the particular ends of labour the means of its attainment … Were I to join the Labour Party, the first and last service I should like to perform for it would be that of asking it forget itself, cease to speak of 'class', especially the class interpreted in terms of economics … I love the working man too well to ask him to be legislate primarily for himself.[44]

However, the above more critical points should not mislead us. For Jones, there were fundamental truths embodied in socialism. The first and most important idea grasped by socialists is the basic communitarian assumption that the community and tradition are prior to the individual. Jones takes this as axiomatic, and thinks the converse individualistic premise a deep error. Second, socialists have no difficulty in relating freedom, justice and rights to communal life. Socialists intuitively divine 'that the State itself may be free, and the means of the freedom of its members' (*IPC*, 100). In consequence, socialists, unlike classical liberals, were not made uneasy by Jones's beloved theme of 'citizen education'. Socialists easily grasped the idea that the state broadens and extends the powers of individuals by increasing its activities. Jones contends, for example, that

> the Post Office managed by the State enlarges the capacities of the individual. I can

use its utilities ... You can't send a private messenger from John of Groats to Land's End for 1d ... The State does not dispossess the individual of his property. It takes his money and returns it in increased utilities.[45]

Well-financed state education, pensions for the aged, school meals, medical inspection in schools, and the large viable public utilities, are, for Jones, examples of how the state can enhance the freedom of the individual. It is this form of socialism which carries letters, provides health care, educates children, and so forth. This does not undermine property rights, rather 'it is defending them by defining them a little more justly, which is their surest defence'.[46] Individuals are not undermined by public ownership, *per se*, but rather each becomes a mutual shareholder in the vast enterprise for the common good. Jones contended, long before the Thatcherite classical liberal enthusiasm for privatisation in the 1980s, that 'it is a significant fact that there is hardly any desire in England to take back enterprise which has once been committed to the State'.[47] To some extent, it is also worth noting here that Jones was probably (ironically) far more sympathetic to some uses of the state, than certain new socialists in the 1990s.

– Conclusion –

One should not push the comparison between Jones's 'higher socialism' and recent events in socialist thought and practice too far. It can look deeply anachronistic. Jones clearly worked under a different set of social, political and economic circumstances. His thought was also embedded in a body of cultural suppositions which no longer so clearly demand our allegiance or interest. However, many of the broad issues he deals with, for example, the relation of ethics and politics or economics and ethics, the link between public and private rights and the state and the individual, and so forth, are still very much *our* problems. The particular terms in which we still discuss these issues are also not so different from Jones. Jones's attempt to mediate between the ideologies of liberalism and socialism, to provide some kind of acceptable political and economic synthesis, has been a prevalent theme of British politics for the whole of the twentieth century.

However, another reason to be slightly uneasy with any overly detailed comparison, is that Jones's own particular resolution to the diversity of political doctrine (socialism and liberalism) was to use the idiosyncratic Hegelian device of 'identity in difference' and the 'overcoming of dualism'. The 'overcoming dualism' theme pervaded Jones' thought from metaphysics through to economics and politics. Although it might be a useful, *ex post facto*, intellectual device to resist hard distinctions being drawn between ideas, it is difficult to see how Jones envisaged that it could be widely socially accepted.

Possibly, on one level, he did not expect it to be; as long as the basic idea of liberalism and socialism, being some form of actual unity in difference, was accepted in practice, it did not matter how this was theoretically explained. Jones's analysis of the relation of the individual and society is a classic example of an identity in difference logic. He comments, for example, that 'we know that the public good will not be obtained by separating man from man, securing each unit in a charmed circle of personal rights ... We must find a place for the individual within the social organism.'[48] The reality of the situation is that the individual cannot do without society. The very *nature* of individuality implies society. This does not entail that individuality is lost, rather, both are preserved in a deeper and richer unity (which thus also embodies difference). States and individuals, for Jones, 'are ultimately nothing but different manifestations of one self-revealing spirit, – the spirit of *man*' (*OPC*, 180).

The concept of property provides another example which illustrates, more precisely, the application of the 'identity in difference' logic. Private property is valued by most citizens and it appears, *prima facie*, to be deeply exclusive to classical liberals. Communal property apparently negates this value. Physical property simply cannot be shared. It necessarily resists commonality. For many, this is the great stumbling block to socialism. Public ownership and nationalisation are seen in this negative light by many classical liberals. Jones, however, reflects upon this issue via Philosophical Idealism which resists all hard materiality and rigid separations of objects and overcomes dualisms. Private property is seen to be premised upon a crude dualist assumption of self and not-self, subject and object. For Jones, property is more than mere possession. It is a right. Possession *per se* does not entail owning. Property requires more than just a private will to possess. Something becomes mine, but, more precisely, mine by right and right implies recognition. A right is something, in fact, that '*ought* to be recognised' and other wills in the organ- ised setting of a society recognise and respect my appropriation. Thus, my exclusive private property is not something gained or acquired *through* my privacy, rather my possession and private use are granted by society (or more precisely the organised will of society – the state). Private property is a reality which must be respected, but we must realise its point of origin and justification.[49] Both socialists and individualist liberals, in their different ways, therefore embody an aspect of the truth of property. Private property is an ethical fact, but its essence 'is that it is the result of an act whereby society endows its individual members with rights against itself' (*WFSR*, 98). On the other hand, individualists are right to insist that private property is unconditionally necessary to the individual and state. Unless its privacy and necessity were recognised by the state it would not function as a liberating force. Jones deploys a similar argument on a number of disputed issues. Freedom is often seen as a negative principle of opposition to public authority and order. However, for Jones, in reality there is no opposition, 'the State itself is free, and the means of the freedom of its members' (*IPC*, 100). As argued earlier, the opposition between character and environment is another false distinction. The substance of character, as unique and private, is formed out of the social environment. Further, the state 'can provide the means for the development of a character ... [in fact] the prime and paramount business of the State *is* to provide the means'.[50]

The above attempts to overcome dualisms inform his analysis of both socialism and liberalism. He was not alone in this judgement. L. T. Hobhouse had also pointed out in his book, *Democracy and Reaction*, that the older liberalism had done considerable service. The newer social liberalism 'appears not as an infringement of the two distinctive ideals of the older Liberalism "Liberty and Equality". It appears rather as a necessary means to their fulfilment. It comes not to destroy but to fulfil.'[51] Jones uses virtually the same argument. His view is that liberalism is neither superseded by socialism, nor that liberalism has two distinct faces, but rather that the dualism and separation between the two is misleading. He attempts, therefore, to show the inner evolving unity of the two ideologies.[52] True socialism and true liberal individualism are therefore not opposed. Private and public enterprise grow together.[53] The truth for Jones is that 'The individual gains by that which strengthens the State, and the State by that which increases the efficiency of the individual.'[54]

It is important to realise that Jones was perturbed by the lack of moral integrity and virtue in contemporary British political life. He viewed the cultural and political level of the British people as depressingly philistine and commercially orientated. Politicians, the general public, employers and employees (whom Jones regularly encountered on a number of committees of inquiry and Royal commissions on which he sat over a long period), tended towards consistent cupidity and total self-interest. Jones, however, still looked with some small hope toward a future where the fundamental truths of both socialism and liberalism could be mutually realised. In this respect he was ever the optimist and looked forward to the day when every factory and workshop would become a school of virtue. The dualism of collectivism and individualism had to be overcome. Individualism needed to develop or evolve within the richer framework of an ethical state. Such an overcoming would be an 'identity in difference'. Individuality was not lost but preserved and sanctified in the higher unity of the state. In fact, both state and individual were viewed as different manifestations of the one self-revealing spirit. As Jones liked to assert, the coming of socialism was also the coming of individualism. Although, at one level, we might view many of his cultural assumptions as somewhat anachronistic, at another level, he was not totally askew in his readings of political developments.

– NOTES –

The following abbreviations will be used in this chapter for these works by Jones:

IP   *Idealism as a Practical Creed* (Glasgow, Maclehose, 1909)

OPC   'The Obligations and Privileges of Citizenship: A Plea for the Study of Social Science', *Rice Institute Studies*, VI (1919)

WFSR   *The Working Faith of the Social Reformer and other Essays* (London, Macmillan, 1910)

PC   *The Principles of Citizenship* (London, Macmillan, 1919)

FE   *A Faith That Enquires*, The Gifford Lectures, 1920–1 (London, Macmillan, 1922)

1. Guido de Ruggiero, *The History of European Liberalism*, translated by R. G. Collingwood (Oxford, Clarendon Press, 1927), 394.
2. Jones, 'Idealism and Epistemology', *Mind*, n.s., II (1893), in two parts. Part 1, 292.
3. Jones contends that 'Society lends to [the individual] her wisdom, imparts to him the rational elements of her own life, in order that by means of them he may scrutinise her opinions, challenge her faith, and reform her ways. Otherwise, her customs would become stale and her faith a lifeless creed', *IPC*, 56.
4. See Jones, 'Idealism and Epistemology', I, 292. Jones is thinking here of the universal premised in the state; however, the universal as such transcended the state. Religion, for example, and philosophy moved beyond the confines of the state.
5. He is in fact far closer here to Burke and the conservative position than to liberalism, to which he was overtly politically committed. The main difference from Burke, and Oakeshott for that matter, is the way he deploys the concept tradition in the argument. Tradition certainly does not denote unreason or practical knowledge. Jones was conscious of his relation to Burke; see *IPC*, 61ff. Tradition is viewed by Jones as 'wiser' than any particular individual, *IPC*, 50.
6. Henry Jones, 'Modern Science and Philosophical Thought', in J. B. Paton, P. W. Bunting and A. E. Garvie (eds), *Christ and Civilisation* (London, 1910), 493.
7. It followed for Jones that given that the self was characterised by reason and purposes, derived from tradition, the greater and more comprehensive the purposes the greater and more comprehensive the self. Thus, for Jones, 'It is the morally great man who takes upon himself the burdens of the world', *FE*, 167.
8. As he commented: 'There is no practice which is not the carrying out of some conception, and no theory which is otiose and inert. Ideas have hands and feet. We live to carry them out. A wrong theory of the State and of its relations to its citizens … is bound in the long run to tell upon its practice', Jones, *PC*, 35.
9. Morality is a social practice, but not thereby simply relative to social forms. Underlying the changing practices of social and historical existence Jones detects a static universal substance which makes teleological and universal sense of moral conduct. For Jones my own good is at the same time a universal good. This argument again parallels those in his metaphysics. As Jones commented: 'Moral good is like truth in this respect', *OPC*, 165. However the unchanging character of truth and moral good are fairly clearly upheld – 'The "good" maintains its character of being ultimate and necessary … for it is the object

of every desire', he continues that, 'The whole of the activities of mankind which together make up "history" is the self-evolution and gradual manifestation of the good.' See Henry Jones, 'Morality as Freedom', *Time*, n.s. 7 (1888), 317. He refers to the *good* on the next page as an 'eternal law'. There is a problem here in Jones's argument between his insistence on a changing historical process, evolving over time, and an underlying unchanging unity of substance. It is something he never quite resolved in his whole metaphysical enterprise.

10. Jones, 'The Social Organism', in A. Seth and R. B. Haldane (eds), *Essays in Philosophical Criticism* (London, Longmans, 1888), 192.

11. Henry Jones, 'The Present Attitude of Reflective Thought Towards Religion', *Hibbert Journal*, I and II (1902–3 and 1903–4), I, 229.

12. This particular difficulty can be clearly seen in his address 'Corporate and Individual Charity' given to the Sixth Annual Conference of the Charity Organization and Relief Societies of the United Kingdom in May 1897. The gist of Jones's paper is that there is no hard and fast distinction to be made between individual and corporate charity. Corporate power 'is nothing more nor less than an expression, more or less inadequate, of the wills of the individuals who have created it', 35. Corporate methods are 'instruments for the realisation of individual, or private ends, and nothing more', 36. Each municipal and state function, for Jones, is ultimately traceable back to private desires and will. The public/private distinction or corporate and individual distinction is another phantom of false dualism. Such an idea did not go down well with the COS president, C. S. Loch, who complained in his reply that private charity was needed and could never be adequately performed by a corporate body like the state, 43. For Jones, however, 'the municipality, or the State, or … the Charity Organisations, were only an instrument to carry out the desires of individuals', 46.

13. See 'The Education of the Citizen', in Henry Jones, *Essays in Literature and Education* (London, Hodder and Stoughton, 1924).

14. Jones, 'Social Organism', 190–1.

15. Henry Jones, 'The Ethical Demand of the Present Political Situation', *The Hibbert Journal* (1909–10), 539. In a letter to Sidney Webb he wrote: 'I should find it difficult to name any better way of spending what remnant of my life that may stand over me than that of working for the working class: I belong to it', Jones to Webb, 29 March 1918, Thomas Jones Papers, Class U, vol. iii, National Library of Wales. See also *IPC*, 218.

16. Jones came from a very poor background in North Wales. His father was a shoe maker, see David Boucher and Andrew Vincent, *A Radical Hegelian: The Political and Social Philosophy of Henry Jones* (Cardiff and New York, University of Wales Press and St Martins Press, 1993 and 1994), ch. 1.

17. Even on the self-conscious left of the Labour theory in the 1970s, Tony Benn could still remark on socialism's roots being 'nourished by the Bible … the Peasants Revolt, the Levellers, Tom Paine, the Chartists, Robert Owen, the Webbs and Bernard Shaw … and occasionally by Marxists', see A. W. Benn *Arguments for Socialism* (London, Cape, 1979), 146.

18. See Willard Wolfe, *From Radicalism to Socialism: Men and Ideas in the Formation of Fabian Socialist Doctrines 1881–1889* (New Haven, CT, Yale University Press, 1975).

19. See J. S. Mackenzie, *An Introduction to Social Philosophy* (Glasgow, Maclehose, 1985), 323. Bernard Bosanquet, 'The Antithesis between Individualism and Socialism Philosophically Considered', in Bernard Bosanquet, *The Civilization of Christendom* (London, Swann Sonnenschein, 1899), 304–57.

20. For a full outline of new liberal ideas set against the classical liberalism, see Andrew

Vincent and Raymond Plant, *Philosophy Politics and Citizenship* (Oxford, Blackwell, 1984), ch. 5; Andrew Vincent, *Modern Political Ideologies* (Oxford, Blackwell, 1995: 2nd edn), ch. 2.

21. Appointed in April 1916, reported in February 1918.

22. Letter dated 15 December 1916, Thomas Jones Papers, Class U, vol. I, fol. 18. National Library of Wales.

23. Jones, 'A League of Peace Now' (London, League of Nations Union, 1918), 10.

24. Jones, *Essays in Literature and Education*, 179.

25. On the British Idealist divisions see Vincent and Plant, *Philosophy Politics and Citizenship*, 87–90; Boucher and Vincent, *A Radical Hegelian*, 140ff.

26. On the rich texture of new liberal thought, see Peter Clarke, *Liberals and Social Democrats* (Cambridge, Cambridge University Press 1978), and Stefan Collini, *Liberalism and Sociology: L. T. Hobhouse and Political Argument in Britain 1880–1915* (Cambridge, Cambridge University Press, 1979). On the question of intellectual coherence: Michael Freeden stressed the role of evolutionary theory in *The New Liberalism: An Ideology of Social Reform* (Oxford, Clarendon Press, 1978); John Allett stressed the role of Hobson's underconsumptionist economic theory in *New Liberalism: The Political Economy of J. A. Hobson* (Toronto, Toronto University Press, 1981); Vincent and Plant stressed the role of philosophical Idealism in *Philosophy Politics and Citizenship*, chs 4 and 5.

27. Which admittedly was at odds with the pluralist decentralist strand. Some, like G. D. H. Cole, seemed to move back and forth between the pluralist and statist positions. For a discussion of this and other issues on the state, see Andrew Vincent, 'Socialism, Law and the State Tradition', in *Socialism and Law: Proceedings of the 17th Annual Conference of the Association for Legal and Social Philosophy, Archiv Für Rechts-und SozialPhilosophie,* Beiheft no. 49, Franz Steiner Verlag, Wiesbaden, Stuttgart, 1992, 45–64.

28. Michael Ignatieff, 'The Myth of Citizenship', in R. Beiner (ed.), *Theorizing Citizenship* (New York, State University of New York Press, 1995), 67.

29. David Marquand, *The Unprincipled Society* (London, Collins Fontana, 1988), ch. 1.

30. Social citizenship, for Marshall, was the phase which developed after the civil and political citizenship, see T. H. Marshall, *Citizenship and Social Class* (Cambridge, Cambridge University Press, 1950).

31. C. P. Trevelyan, introduction to H. Langshaw, *Liberalism and the Historic Basis of Socialism* (1925), pp. vii–viii, quoted in Michael Freeden, *Liberalism Divided: A Study in British Political Thought 1914–1939* (Oxford, Clarendon Press, 1986), 210, n. 123.

32. As Michael Freeden remarks 'some of the major British socialist thinkers Laski, Tawney and, to a lesser extent, Cole were at times within the left-liberal tradition in all senses save that of self-awareness'. Freeden, *Liberalism Divided*, 14; also Andrew Vincent, 'Divided Liberalisms?', *History of Political Thought*, IX (1988), 161–6.

33. Robert Eccleshall, *British Liberalism: Liberal Thought from the 1640s to 1980s* (London, Longman, 1986), 56.

34. J. M. Keynes, 'Liberalism and Labour', *Nation*, 20 February 1926. The question remains, though, what was the character of this new liberalism? The picture becomes more cloudy from the 1920s. There were formal new liberal concerns, as outlined earlier, namely, a more socialised understanding of the individual, a more positive conception of liberty, a modified conception of a market economy, and a more collectivised conception of the state. Yet, whereas there was more unanimity in the pre-1914 period, the 1914–18 war experience, the collapse of the parliamentary Liberal party in the 1920s and the rise of the Labour party, did modify the new liberalism. The new liberalism basically fractured –

although some of the potential fracture lines were present in the pre-1914 setting. Although formally united by the above concerns, differing *emphases* were given to the formal themes. The new liberalism fractured into three major strands, with considerable overlaps. On one side, were the more left-leaning liberals like H. W. Massingham and J. A. Hobson – many who subsequently moved into the Labour party. On the other side, were, what might be called, the 'rightward' leaning new liberals, like W. H. Beveridge and J. M. Keynes, some would even deny the title liberal to them. Finally, there were the more centrist social liberals, like Ramsay Muir, L. T. Hobhouse, C. F. G. Masterman and Herbert Samuel; see Andrew Vincent, 'New Ideology for Old?', *Political Quarterly*, vol. 69, no. 1 (1998), pp. 48–58

35. R. H. Tawney, *Equality* (London, George Allen and Unwin, 1952: 4th edn; first published 1931), 61.
36. Tawney, *Equality*, 64.
37. R. H. Tawney, *The Acquisitive Society* (London, G. Bell, 1921), 53–4. Also see Matthew Carter, *The Impact of British Idealism on Ethical Socialism*, unpublished PhD thesis, University of York, 1999, p. 260.
38. One central point here would be that types of markets should be distinguished. 'Product' markets particularly are more acceptable than markets in 'labour'. It is the former which would be encouraged by socialism, not the latter.
39. Henry Jones, 'Corporate and Individual Charity' (Glasgow, Glasgow Charity Organisation Society, 1897), 35.
40. Jones, in Hetherington, *The Life and Letters of Sir Henry Jones* (London, Hodder and Stoughton, 1924), 251.
41. Jones, 'The Huge Machinery of Sin and Sorrow', *The Free Catholic*, I (1916), 186–7.
42. 'Democracy was a most dangerous form of government in the hands of people who were not fit for it', Jones, Report on Lecture in Australia, 'True and False Socialism', *Newcastle Morning Herald*; see also Jones, *IPC*, 219.
43. Jones, 'The Ethical Demand of the Present Political Situation' *Hibbert Journal* (1909–10), 539–40. Jones also attacked Keir Hardie on the same ground: 'I don't like the banner under which Labour fights. Some members of it, and especially Mr Keir Hardie, are bitter and harmful, and they are corrupting the working men', letter to Lloyd Thomas, 9 April 1910, Thomas Jones Papers, Class U, vol. ii, National Library of Wales.
44. Jones to Sidney Webb, 29 March 1918, Thomas Jones Papers, Class U, vol. iii. National Library of Wales.
45. Jones to Fisher 1916, Fisher Papers MS, Bodleian Library Oxford, fol. 259–60, 7. In another work Jones writes, 'It is quite true that common ownership and common enterprise turns us into limited proprietors; but they make us limited proprietors of indefinitely large utilities', *WFSR*, 110.
46. As Jones notes, 'if we endeavour to forget "names" and substitute the observation of actual facts for prophetic utterances regarding tendencies, we shall see, I believe, nothing worse nor better than an attempt to employ the organisation of the State and of the municipalities so as to place at the disposal of their members means for meeting their individual wants. These social means have been adopted little by little in the face of the most searching criticism.' Jones, 'Ethical Demand', 537.
47. Jones to Fisher, 16 December 1918, Fisher Papers MS, Bodleian Library, Oxford, fol. 62, 6–7; see also 'Ethical Demand', 538, although this comment looks slightly strange in the late 1990s.
48. Jones, *Browning as a Philosophical and Religious Thinker* (Glasgow, Maclehose, 1891), 62.

49. As Jones says: 'whenever it becomes a right, [it] is due not alone nor primarily to his having said *Mine*, but to the State having said *Thine*', *WFSR*, 97.

50. Jones, 'The Function of the University in the State', Inaugural Lecture delivered at the University College of Wales, Aberystwyth (1905), 14.

51. L. T. Hobhouse, *Democracy and Reaction* (London, T. Fischer Unwin, 1904), 217. Hobhouse later comments: 'I venture to conclude that the differences between a true, consistent, public-spirited Liberalism and a rational Collectivism ought, with genuine effort at mutual understanding to disappear', 237. Interestingly, Hobhouse quotes extensively from the German SPD programme and argues that it is very close to liberal beliefs, 234ff.

52. For Jones, true political awareness is 'content neither with public order nor private freedom; it will neither make the State subordinate to the individual, nor the individual to the State; it is neither Socialism nor Individualism. Yet it will curtail none of the *rights* of either. It will even make the evolution of the one depend upon the evolution of the other', 'Idealism and Politics', II, *Contemporary Review*, 42 (1907), 742 (reprinted in *WFSR*).

53. Jones says that 'the State while limiting caprice has enlarged freedom; that in appropriating industrial enterprises it has liberated the economic power of its citizens', *WFSR*, 105. Jones is obviously reading socialism as collectivism or state socialism. It is a shame, in this context, that we do not have any detailed response to guild socialism. For similar views to Jones see also Caird, 'Individualism and Socialism', 3–4; J. S. Mackenzie, *A Manual of Ethics* (London, W. B. Clive, 1897), 308; L. T. Hobhouse, *Democracy and Reaction*, 237; Ruggiero, *The History of European Liberalism*, 393.

54. Jones, 'Function of the University', 14.

CHAPTER 6

R. G. Collingwood:
The Enemy Within and the Crisis of Civilisation

Collingwood was a product of an Oxford still very much imbued with the legacy of T. H. Green, and at the same time of a generation of teachers reacting against this legacy. He was taught by the Realists John Cook Wilson and E. F. Carritt, but nevertheless found himself more philosophically inclined towards J. A. Smith, H. H. Joachim and F. H. Bradley. He had an unusual upbringing in a household in which John Ruskin's teachings loomed large – a strong attachment to the natural beauty of the countryside, and a fear that the ever encroaching values of capitalism would destroy traditional values which were the foundation of social relations – and in which his natural inquisitiveness was allowed to develop into a passion for languages, art, religion, natural science, history and philosophy. When fused with his formal academic concerns, this produced an unusual variant of Idealist thinking, owing more to Hegel, Croce, Gentile, de Ruggierro and John Ruskin, than to English and Scottish Idealism. It is Ruskin who inspires the Englishness in Collingwood's very continental brand of Idealism. The very close family connection with Ruskin makes it unsurprising that Collingwood should not only be familiar with, but would also mirror some of Ruskin's concerns. W. G. Collingwood, Robin George's father, was part-time assistant and later secretary to Ruskin for many years. In 1882, for instance, the elder Collingwood spent four months in Italy with Ruskin, and in 1893 published Ruskin's biography, *The Life and Work of John Ruskin*. He also designed the Ruskin memorial in Coniston churchyard. W. G. Collingwood was a graduate of Oxford and saw himself as a follower of the school of Green. In fact, Bernard Bosanquet was his tutor.[1] R. G. Collingwood was always very close to his father and described him in the dedication to *Speculum Mentis* as his 'first and best teacher of art, religion, science, history and philosophy'.

Through his father Collingwood was inspired by Ruskin's thought, and was more generally introduced to the ideas of Green and Bosanquet. Collingwood himself delivered a lecture on Ruskin in 1919 in which he extolled the virtues of Ruskin's synthetic style, and admired the intensity with which he cared for modern civilisation. Ruskin was not a philosopher, but he had a philosophy which resembled that of Hegel in its imaginative and sensitive historical appreciation of the past without adoration or desire for re-creation.[2] Collingwood interpreted Ruskin as primarily a lover of mountains whose multifarious interests were all connected with this central passion manifesting itself in a sensitivity to town and country relations, and the duties of a tourist both to the landscape and inhabitants of a foreign land.[3] It could be argued that Ruskin's historical imagination, concern that a corrupt society and degrading working conditions were inimical to the production of art and anything else of value in society, and his fear that the culture of the town was encroaching upon and dominating the countryside, were themes that pervaded the whole of Collingwood's work. Civilisation, for him, was constantly under threat, and since civilisation is a thing of the mind, self-understanding of that mind, in all its aspects, was both therapeutic and necessary to combat the dangers.

The published books towards the end of his life all reflect his lifelong preoccupation with identifying and combating the enemies of civilisation, by coming to a better self-understanding. In *The Principles of Art* he is concerned that we get in touch with our emotions and learn to express, rather than repress them. To deny one's emotions results in a corruption of consciousness which corrodes and destroys social relations. In *An Essay on Metaphysics* Collingwood is similarly at pains to demonstrate the healthy working of the mind and the corruptions which lead to its perversion. The processes of human thought, he argues, rest upon constellations of unquestioned assumptions, or absolute presuppositions, something like T. S. Kuhn's paradigms. The absolute presuppositions are the bedrock upon which the whole edifice of the thought of an age is built. The business of metaphysics is to identify what absolute presuppositions are being absolutely presupposed at a particular time, and not to ask whether they are true or false, questions which are inappropriate and admit of no answer. The business of logic is to give an account of the criteria of self criticism and account for their role in processes of thought. In this respect thought is criteriological in that we set our selves purposes and are able to ask with reference to criteria whether we have succeeded or failed in achieving them.

Psychology differentiates itself from logic in that it ignores the self-critical aspects of thought. In failing to address questions of criteria for self-criticism psychology does not succeed in being what it purports to be, namely, a science of thought because it avoids all questions of truth and falsity in human thought and therefore implicitly teaches that there is no difference between scientific, meaning rigorous and systematic, thinking and sophistry, the promulgations of truth and the inoculations of error. This form of irrationalism constitutes a threat to European civilisation because it undermines its very principles of individual responsibility, rational thought and freedom of choice, by eliminating the criteria of success and failure, right and wrong, from human thought.

History, in Collingwood's view, rather than psychology, is the genuine science of the mind. It is criteriological in that it identifies human purposes and intentions and is able to judge success and failure in their execution. Moreover, history is self-knowledge of the mind. It opens up to us the whole realm of human possibility, makes intelligible for us our present and assists us in making choices about the future. This is a position with which both Hannah Arendt, and Alasdair MacIntyre would agree. Even though Arendt rejects the possibility of returning to traditional concepts and values in the light of the Holocaust, she nevertheless believes that the past must be retrieved in order to repair the fractured consciousness of time in modern society. Only by retrieving the past can we redeem and restore meaning to our contemporary world, and better orient ourselves towards the future. She believes that in the light of the breakdown of tradition it is no longer possible to retrieve the past as a whole, but we are able to rescue fragments which reaffirm the link between past and present. Arendt thus maintains that in this selective reappropriation 'the cultural treasures of the past, believed to be dead, are being made to speak, in the course of which it turns out that they propose things altogether different from the familiar, worn-out trivialities they had been presumed to say'.[4] Whereas Collingwood is cognisant of the difficulties of retrieving the past, and is aware, like Croce before him and MacIntyre after, that there will always be contemporary problems resonating in our souls which have a bearing upon such retrieval, as well as the fact that there is also a history of historiography relating to the problems of the past, Arendt thinks that the past can be accessed undistorted by tradition, and authors read as if for the first time.

– THE SOCIAL CONTRACT AND FREEDOM OF CHOICE –

Collingwood's concern with the larger questions in social and political theory allies him much more closely with modern theorists, such as Hannah Arendt, Charles Taylor, Alasdair MacIntyre, and Richard Rorty, who have sought to uncover the fundamental forces serving to corrupt contemporary civilisation, than with those who explore issues of social justice and economic redistribution. Even though Collingwood is a social contract theorist of sorts he does not use the device for the same purposes as modern contractarians. Like them, freedom of will and choice are crucial to his conception of what it is to be human. Positively to exercise free will is to choose, and negatively it is to be free from desires in the sense of not being at their mercy (*NL*, 13.25). Given this emphasis upon choice it is not surprising that civil association, or society, for him is best characterised as the result of freedom of choice. It is interesting that for him the capacity for free choice is not itself freely chosen, it is an achievement but not consciously willed.[5] It is attained by an act of self-liberation at a crucial stage in the development of mind. It is liberation from one's desires, and liberation to make decisions, to choose between alternatives rather than merely to express preferences. To prefer one thing rather than another is simply to suffer desire for one thing among alternatives. Self-liberation from desire is achieved by naming the desire, it is an act of speech, using the language of the community to which the person belongs. He is not therefore talking about an isolated individual, historical or hypothetical, in a state of nature. It is an individual who belongs to a community, but who is not yet social. A body politic, for Collingwood, is a community comprised of non-social and social elements, people capable of exercising free will, or choice, and those who are not. The former are self-governing and have freely agreed to associate, the latter are incapable of such choice and are therefore governed by those who comprise the social element. Because the relationship is unequal, the one ruling over the other without their consent, an element of force is invariably involved and which cannot be totally eradicated because a body politic can never completely eliminate the non-social element, that is, those who have not yet reached mental maturity. What Collingwood means by force is moral or mental strength exercised by one person on another in order to make him or her perform an act which the mentally stronger wants. Force is relative in that anyone occupying a place at a higher level of consciousness than another is able to make that weaker person comply with his or her will by the exercise of mental strength or superiority (*NL*, 20.49–53).

The contemporary equivalent of such suppression of consciousness is the emergence of the technocratic society in which people have greater and greater recourse to the expert for the resolution of problems. The non-executive epistemic authority which technical knowledge commands in a specialised area of expertise is claimed to be transferable into the political realm of executive authority. In other words, to use de George's terminology, non-executive epistemic authority is being confused with executive political authority.[6] In Beiner's view, this is to the detriment of the citizen's capacity to deliberate and choose between desirable and wished-for lifestyles for the community. The capacity for political judgement in the ordinary citizen has been usurped.[7] Hans-Georg Gadamer, for example, argues that our ability to comprehend and participate in modern politics has become dangerously eroded by the ideal of a technocratic society in which 'one has recourse to the expert and looks to him for the discharging of the practical, political, and economic decisions one needs to make'.[8]

To liberate oneself from desire and to be free to make choices is not to be conscious of that freedom. The act of self-liberation, then, may be pre-conscious, and the way to make the individual conscious of his or her capacity to choose is to arouse self-respect. This, Collingwood maintains, is particularly important to the work of governments and education. Just as some societies foster this capacity for choice, others retard it by undermining the self-respect of the individual. The point at which an individual becomes capable and conscious of making decisions is not necessarily the point at which members of the ruling class, or the self-governing society, accept them into its ranks. There is always a tension in any society between the principles of aristocracy and democracy, those who wish to expand membership to the greatest number possible, and those who wish to restrict it to a minimum. This is the point at which Collingwood is best understood as a theorist of the politics of recognition. It is a concept which in modern political theory shoulders an immense burden and has become central to discussions of indi-vidual, sexual, cultural and state authenticity. Francis Fukayama, for instance, sees the need for recognition as the driving force, parallel with scientific and economic development, but more important than both, behind the ascendancy of liberal democracy and the end of history. Liberal democracy best satisfies what Plato had identified as the *thymotic*, or spirited element, in the human *psyche*.[9] Recognition is about having a voice, one's own voice, an authentic voice which expresses a genuine and self-reflective identity rather than an imposed and alien identity. Misrecognition, as Charles Taylor argues, is a form of oppression.[10] Collingwood makes the move from the politics of distribution to the politics of recognition, but without losing sight of econ-omic oppression and inequalities, fifty years before it has become fashionable to focus upon such issues. Charles Taylor's important discussion has served to make issues of recognition central to questions of multiculturalism. Taylor talks of two types of recognition. That of equal dignity in which other per-sons are recognised as equal to oneself as citizens, human beings, or creatures of God. The second, and the one that Taylor tends to favour, is recognition of a person's distinctness, difference, or situated identity. Here he tends to associate recognition of a person as a member of a cultural group, or the dis-tinctiveness of the cultural group itself, with the assessment of its forms of cultural expression as having equal worth. Nancy Fraser criticises theorists of Taylor's ilk for supplanting concerns of economic injustice with concerns of injustices of recognition.[11] Like Nancy Fraser, Collingwood thinks that problems of redistribution and recognition are usually inseparable in practice.

Those who are economically oppressed often lack self-esteem and are also psychologically oppressed by the unequal power relation in which they stand to employers, and the state. Collingwood's theory needs to be distinguished into two forms of recognition. First there is recognition of others within one's own community, and it is recognition of their capacity to choose freely, that is their possession of rational consciousness. Secondly, there is recognition of others outside of one's community, and the necessity of desisting from imposing our own criteria of value upon them.

The criterion of rule-worthiness, in Collingwood, is the measure by which recognition is achieved within a community. It is not, however, a fixed measure. Not only does it depend upon the interplay of the principles of aristocracy and democracy, but also upon the complexity of the tasks performed within the body politic. The age of reason, or consent, differs according to the level of sophistication a society has achieved. Free will is not an absolute. It is a matter of degree. Collingwood argues that: 'a given society, being formed for the prosecution of a given joint enterprise, is possible only between agents having the strength of will which that enterprise demands' (*NL*, 20.62). The mere capacity for choice must be developed into higher levels of rational consciousness, and this is only possible as a member of a community in which education, in the broadest sense of the term, is directed towards the development of the rational capacities of its members, enhancing their powers of practical reason, both those who comprise the non-social element, and those who constitute the social. The point at which conversion from the non-social to the social takes effect is determined by those who comprise the ruling class or social community. They decide at what level to set the criteria and at what point they wish to induct individuals into the social class. There is always a danger that the challenges of society may be greater than the strength of will possessed to face them. In such circumstances a society may degenerate into a non-social community. To guard against this those who constitute a society may assign the responsibility of giving orders to those among them who they think most capable of withstanding the strains likely to face them all. In addition, they may institute a mechanism which forcibly restrains anyone whose will has cracked from impeding the political work of the rest of the associates. This, of course, is the criminal law (*NL*, 21.81–4).

Collingwood contends that persons who join a society must be free before joining it in the sense that they are equal with others who possess the degree of freedom that joining that society demands (*NL*, 21.6) It could be argued that the situation Collingwood describes is not essentially a relationship among equals – the ruling class deciding upon at what point the ruled class may pass the permeable barrier – and therefore can by no stretch of the imagination be described as a contract.[12] To be conscious of one's freedom, Collingwood argues, is also to be conscious of the freedom of others, and of the social relations which hold between them. To deem another person capable of entering into society is in itself a recognition of that person's attainment of freedom and the capacity to choose: it is acknowledging that person as an equal, possessing 'that degree of freedom which the decision to join that society demands' (*NL*, 21.6). Each person is conscious of his or her freedom, and this consciousness amounts to possessing self-respect (*NL*, 13.18 and 37.11). The politics of recognition is, of course, all about attributing equal value and affording equal respect to others, while at the same time acknowledging their differences. On joining individuals are equal in the 'further sense that they now equally posses the status of membership' (*NL*, 21.61). This, of course, does not preclude other forms of inequality from arising or existing.

The social contract, then, is not a once and for all agreement, but a continuous process of converting the non-social element of the community into the social. It is the responsibility of the rulers to facilitate this process by providing the social and educational opportunities that promote the development of consciously free individuals capable of participating in the political life of their society.

Thus, Collingwood's theory is neither like that of David Gauthier, designed to arrive at the principles of morality that every rational person could agree upon, nor to arrive at the procedural rules by which to achieve a just distribution of resources such as that of John Rawls. Even though ideas of social justice are not central to the theory, they are not excluded in the way that Arendt excludes them from her discussion about the public sphere. For her the social realm is the sphere of labour – physical and biological necessity – whose dominance has emerged from the end of the eighteenth century with the growth of the economy. In identifying the household with the economy she maintains that questions of economics are pre-political, and thus excludes from her discussion of politics questions of economic power and exploitation. Questions of justice do not arise in the public realm because for her they belong to the social private sphere of the economy and household. She argues that the ancient dividing line in political thought between the public and the private, the sphere of the polis and that of the household and family, has become hazy 'because we see the body of peoples and political communities in the image of a family whose everyday affairs have to be taken care of by a gigantic, nation-wide administration of housekeeping'.[13] This is an aspect of her thought that even sympathetic critics such as Sheldon Wolin, Hannah Pitkin, Jean Bethke Elshtain and Nancy Fraser, have found least satisfactory.[14] In general they take the separation of the economic and political to be too restrictive and exclusive, relegating major social issues to the realm of the non-political. Even though Collingwood distinguishes between capricious action, for which we can give no reason for our act, and utility, right and duty – the economic, political and moral – they are not mutually exclusive. They are related to each other as different specifications of human action comprising a linked hierarchy of forms in which the succeeding specifications take up the prior, and transform them into more adequate characterisations. Although Collingwood is extremely critical of Marx in *The New Leviathan* for presenting a dialectical materialism which denied freedom of the will (*NL*, 33.99), he does elsewhere acknowledge the importance of Marx's emphasis upon the economic realm in history even if, like Hegel, Marx narrowly equates rationality with a selective aspect of the whole. In Hegel's case it was logic, and for Marx economics (*IH*, 122–6, and *AA*, 152–4). Collingwood was well aware, as we will see, that inequalities in wealth give rise to relations of power and force.

– A JUST SOCIETY –

Collingwood's emphasis upon freedom and the correlative capacity to choose has implications for morality and social justice. A civilised society is one where force is gradually being eliminated from social relations, never totally because of the existence of the non-social community, but in the sense that social relations are conducted dialectically rather than eristically, and force gives way to rational discussion and agreement. There are three aspects to this civilising process, all derivable from what Collingwood regards as the essence of this process – civility. Collingwood calls them constituents (*NL*, 35.38); the elimination of force in our relations with each other within the body politic (*NL*, 35.44); the elimination of unintelligent exploitation in our relations with nature; and, the elimination of force in relations between bodies politic. What, then, are the practical implications of this civilising process? The civilising process is in fact based upon a theory of recognition, one which relates not only to other persons, but also to nature.

The first constituent in the process is one of promoting members of the same community to behave more civilly in their relations with each other. This means that we should not act in such a way towards another person as to diminish his or her self-respect and thus threaten his or her consciousness of freedom by undermining the power of choice. To treat someone in this way is to exercise force over a person and puts him or her at risk of desire or passion taking charge. Collingwood's use of the term force to encompass both mental and physical coercion in relation to mental consciousness, while at first sight appearing unnecessarily to collapse the distinction between force and coercion, nevertheless highlights the fact that violence may be perpetrated by the state, community or individual upon other persons without physical force. It puts psychological and physical damage on a par. Those who wish to sever the relation between sovereignty and the state by adhering to a distinction between coercion and force underestimate the dangers of psychological coercion. Hinsley, for example, suggests that in stateless societies authority rests not on force, but on 'psychological and moral coercion'.[15] In John Hoffman's view maintaining the distinction is crucial to demonstrate how order may be sustained in a community without a state. He argues that 'coercion is simply a "pressure" which causes individuals to act in ways which they would otherwise have avoided'.[16] For him, force prevents people from acting, while coercion allows choice. What Collingwood is arguing is that within the body politic – a term he uses to encompass the non-social and social communities, and the council or state which rules – there are always people incapable of choice, and that essentially choices are made for them. His theory also acknowledges that the capacity to choose is variable according to the complexity of the choices required to be made in a body politic. Hoffman's theory assumes the elimination of force, but maintains that the state although able to be the agent of change cannot be the end result because force is inherent in its nature. In wishing to relate sovereignty to individuals in relation to a variety of local, national and regional institutions the state can assist the process from statism to government or governance. This it can do by 'promoting policies which make the use of force increasingly redundant'.[17] What Hoffman is arguing is that the transformation is one in kind. In Collingwood's view, the civilising process, that, is the gradual elimination of force, is a question of both degree and kind. The realisation that the instrument set up to eliminate the nightmare of the brutality of an uncivilised existence is itself the agent of such brutalities does not necessarily lead to the conclusion that the state must be abolished (*NL*, 12.93). A social community is self-governing, and may decide to confer authority on institutions to act on its behalf, but there are always those who are outside the social community, such as minors or criminals (who have placed themselves outside), who are not self-governing. Will and not force is the basis of the relationship among members of the social community, but not among them and members of the non-social community. In this respect a theory of rewards and punishments is applicable only to the non-social community. The degree of force exercised by the social community on the non-social community is relative to the degree of civilisation attained. Collingwood's theory is developmental in that it is relational rather than relative. This distinction is more forcefully made by Stephen Toulmin, ironically in criticism of Collingwood. In Toulmin's view Collingwood posed one of the most important questions with regard to conceptual changes. In formulating his theory of absolute presuppositions in *An Essay on Metaphysics* Collingwood asked why and upon what occasions do conceptual changes occur? In answering that they are the result of 'unconscious thought' Collingwood, Toulmin claims, denies rational choices and lapses into relativism, thus depriving us of the possibility of giving rational descriptions of conceptual change.[18] Toulmin claims that Collingwood fails to acknowledge the difference between historical relativity, that is the need to accommodate different contexts in making rational comparisons, and historical relativism, which restricts judgements to the relations which hold within the contexts. Whatever the merits of this criticism in relation to Collingwood's metaphysics,[19] it is clear from what I have argued that Collingwood's political philosophy is an instance of historical relativity and not historical relativism.

Collingwood's conception of rights is unsurprisingly Idealist in its formulation. Like all of the British Idealists, Collingwood identified rights with membership of a society. The idea of natural rights standing independent of society implied some form of intuitivism, and could be invoked as an impediment upon the legitimate expansion of government activity. British Idealists were opposed to the idea of an abstract individual possessing rights, the protection of which they secured through a social contract on entering into society.[20] Rights are the creature of society and develop according to the needs of individuals in society. Rights belong to individuals as members of a community. They are justifiable claims recognised as rational and necessary for the common good of society.

Collingwood develops this perspective. The political rulers in a body politic, comprising a social and non-social element, determine the citizenship, according to the level of competency required, who are to hold rights. The Athenians in Ancient Greece excluded women, children, slaves and foreigners who were dependent upon the citizen right holders. Collingwood contends that the city was the focus of Ancient political life and theory, whereas for medieval times it was the state – where a person's status legally defined his rights and duties dependent upon to which estate he belonged. In the later Middle Ages, the body politic began to be conceived differently. Sovereigns and subjects dominate the theory, but they are terms which relate to many different relationships including that between man and wife. Liberties were conferred by the sovereign upon individuals and corporations

Hannah Arendt is similarly disposed to view the public and the political as humanly instituted, divorced from any idea of a universal human nature or endemic natural needs. Human beings are not naturally equal, until such equality is endowed upon individuals on entering the public sphere. The right to civil equality, for example, is secured not by some fictitious natural right, but in being recognised and maintained by democratic political institutions. The political experience of the twentieth century, with an exponential increase in stateless people, more perniciously renamed displaced persons, has exposed the weakness of the idea of the rights of man standing somehow independent of state or governmental authority. To fall back on humanity for the maintenance of basic rights, those of being human, when stripped of political and civil rights – the rights of a citizen – is to have a status worse than a criminal who at least remains under the law and is protected by it. To be outside the law, excluded from civil rights, is to be deprived of community and culture, one's personal identity, 'a distinct place in the world'.[21] Those whose rights were violated in Germany found that it was futile to appeal to human rights in their defence because the Nazi regime excluded them from having a 'right to have rights'.[22] The Nazis completely deprived Jews of rights (even as second-class citizens), satisfied themselves that no other nation would claim the people they displaced, withdrew the Jews from the world by placing them in labour and concentration camps, and then finally challenged their right to live.[23] Arendt contends that:

> Because only savages have nothing more to fall back upon than the minimum fact of their human origin, people cling to their nationality all the more desperately when they have lost their rights and protection that such nationality once gave them. Only their past with its 'entailed inheritance' seems to attest to the fact that they still belong to the civilised world.[24]

Given the occasion which impelled Collingwood to write, it is curious that he did not focus more closely upon how German barbarism, the revolt against civilisation, manifested itself in relation to the Jews. Jews were not only denied the rights of full German citizenship – they were second-class citizens – but were eventually denied a place in the non-social community over which the social ruled. In other words they were excluded from the body politic in being completely deprived of rights.

It is certainly the case that Collingwood makes no special provision, as Will Kymlicka does, for special rights for national and ethnic minorities within the body politic which itself reflects the dominant culture. His theory does, nevertheless, afford opportunities for preserving and developing cultural diversity. His main concern is that the state education system does not homogenise us all, and eradicate traditional customs and practices in the name of progress. His particular fear was the imposition of town values upon the countryside, but the provision he makes for the preservation of the values of the rural community would equally serve to preserve and allow to flourish ethnic communities.

The concern for education is evident throughout Collingwood's work. In *Speculum Mentis*, for example, he argues that its purpose is 'helping a mind to create itself, to grow into an active and vigorous contributor to the life of the world' (*SM*, 316). The onus is upon those who exercise authority to institute a wide-ranging educational programme, social and political, which facilitates the development of self-respect and the attainment of freedom of choice. Socially, the purpose is to facilitate the attainment of self-respect which enables the person to exercise free choice. Politically its purpose must be to induct mentally mature persons into the self-governing class, ensuring that the barrier is permeable in an upward direction. The equation of education with freedom is a familiar theme in Idealist political philosophy. They all thought, along with Green, that education is the great social leveller. In fact they reiterate the point of Plato, Aristotle and Hegel that the best education a person can have is that of being a citizen in a good state. The British Idealists were concerned not with equality of outcomes, but with equality of opportunities. No child should be disadvantaged by accidents of birth and impeded by social or political obstacles to self-realisation. Education was seen as the key to removing the obstacles. This entailed greater state provision of education.

Where Collingwood differs is in seeing such education as homogeneous and potentially stifling. He advocated that parents should take a much greater responsibility for the education of their children, reflecting in fact his own experience of being taught at home until the age of twelve in the Lake District. For Green, the 1870 Education Act which was introduced to combat illiteracy, tackle juvenile crime and ensure a standard curriculum did not go far enough, whereas for Collingwood it went much too far (*PA*, 102). The details of his argument may appear eccentric and even quaint, but the point he is making was important. He believed that through the state provision of education, the values of the town were being imposed upon the countryside, and much of what was valued in civilisation might in consequence die out.[25] Here he meant the traditional skills and knowledge, including the deeply rooted fairy tales, imparted by one generation to another.[26]

After the elimination of force in our relations with fellow members of one's own body politic, Collingwood identifies the second constituent of the civilising process as the elimination of force in relation to the natural world, which is closely related to the third, that is, the elimination of force in relations between members of other bodies politic. Civility, in a person's relations with nature, means securing the means of sustenance not as a gift, but as the reward of human effort. It is not the exercise of mere labour, but the intelligent use of labour informed by scientific knowledge in the broadest sense. The third constituent has historically been an extremely difficult one for a community to effect. It involves asking the question whether civility entails treating members of other communities civilly? The answer depends upon how that community responds to the prior question, are foreigners human? In Collingwood's view if we do not regard the foreigner as human, he or she becomes part of the natural world and is considered prime material for being exploited as scientifically as possible. Even those who enjoy a relatively high degree of civilisation treat strangers with the utmost incivility, often maiming and murdering them with impunity, despite having a conviction that fellow human beings deserve to be treated civilly: 'all that is lacking is a conviction that strangers are human beings' (*NL*, 35.67).

The question 'are foreigners human' may appear to be an odd or eccentric question, but it is precisely the question which Richard Rorty identifies as the key to understanding the uncivil attitude of Nazis towards Jews, white racists towards blacks, men towards women and Serbs towards Muslims in Bosnia. It is in regarding others as sub-human that we are able to act inhumanely towards them. Rorty's denial of anything like human essences, human nature, or foundations of any kind makes it impossible to invoke any notion of transhistorical principles at times when human institutions and traditional notions of decency and humane behaviour are collapsing, as in the case of Auschwitz and more recently the conflict between Serbs and Muslims in Bosnia. At such times, we want to appeal to some notion of human solidarity and declare that because these people, the Muslims and Jews, are like us it is inhuman to be committing such crimes against them. In his Amnesty lecture, Rorty argues that inhuman treatment, or the refusal to treat people equally, is justified by the perpetrators in regarding the victims as non-human or pseudo-human. Firstly, the victim can be portrayed as an animal as opposed to human. This is how the Nazis portrayed Jews. Secondly, humans can be portrayed as children as opposed to adults and therefore have no claim to equal treatment – blacks, for instance, when referred to as 'boy'. A third form of exclusion is to use man as the generic term for men and women. Rorty wants to argue in the final chapter of *Contingency, Irony, and Solidarity* that the notion of we or us is crucial in understanding the idea of moral obligation.[27] The idea of a fellow comrade, a co-national, a fellow Catholic all invoke strong senses of being one of us. Rorty says quite emphatically: 'that the force of "us" is, typically, contrastive in the sense that it contrasts with "they" which is also made up of human beings – the wrong sort of human beings'.[28]

Philosophers have tried to find some essential ingredient that defines human nature in order to avoid arbitrary exclusions, but, Rorty argues, 'We have come to see that the only lesson of either history or anthropology is our extraordinary malleability. We are coming to think of ourselves as the flexible, protean, self-shaping, animal rather than as the rational animal or the cruel animal.' Our human rights culture is one such recent shape that human nature has taken. What Rorty wants to argue is that 'nothing relevant to moral choice separates human beings from animals except historically contingent facts of the world, cultural facts'.[29]

Both Collingwood and Rorty emphasise the contingency of the human condition, and of the human capacity to create its own future. The interesting difference between Collingwood and Rorty is that Rorty disparages the power of rational thinking to overcome the barrier of regarding the other as one of us, that is, someone who like us possesses a will and exercises freedom of choice. To include others in the moral community we regard as our own is possible only by broadening our emotional experience and by playing upon our sympathies through great literary works which tell us sad and sentimental stories. He states quite clearly in *Contingency, Irony, and Solidarity* 'that detailed descriptions of particular varieties of pain and humiliation (in e.g. novels or ethnographies), rather than philosophical or religious treatises, were the modern intellectual's principal contributions to moral progress'.[30] The aim of focusing on sentiment in this way is to extend the boundaries of who we are prepared to regard as one of us. Rational argument did not persuade the Serbs that the Muslims deserve equal respect as humans, nor many men that women, or Nazis that Jews, deserve equal status as humans. Feelings of solidarity with others arise in the context of which similarities and dissimilarities strike us as important at any historical time. Which are important is a matter of contingency. He claims that his position is not incompatible with extending the terms of reference of 'we' to those whom we have historically regarded as 'they'. In Collingwood's view civility demands that recognition of a civil demeanour in another requires acting civilly towards that person. In acknowledging that foreigners are human, civility demands that we treat them civilly. To the extent that we ourselves are civilised our own rules and moral standards give people from outside our community a right to be treated civilly by us (*NL*, 35.63).

Collingwood, like Rorty, emphasises the importance of emotion; a society that prides itself upon its rationality is a utilitarian civilisation deluding itself that it has overcome superstition and irrational sentiments (*EPP*, 197–200). Self-knowledge of one's emotions is a crucial aspect of sociality. To suppress or deny one's emotions, that is, preventing them from being expressed, results in a corruption of consciousness, a form of delusion which undermines social relations (*PA*, 282–5).[31] An emotional attachment to, or sympathy for, strangers is not in itself enough to regard them as human or to treat them civilly. After all we can have sympathy for and feel sentimental about the suffering of animals, but this in itself is not an invitation to include them in our moral community. Collingwood argues that:

> The social consciousness on my part towards a foreigner, which brings him from
> my point of view within the circle of human beings and converts him from

something I exploit or even, if so disposed, murder with a clear conscience into something which in proportion as I am a civilised man I have to treat civilly, and see to it that others shall treat civilly, is an entirely different thing from an affectionate or expansive emotion, what is called 'liking' him or 'being fond of' him. (NL, 35.73)

Indeed, liking someone who is not regarded as one of us, as not fully human, is perfectly compatible with treating that person uncivilly, whereas disliking someone who is a fellow human being is completely incompatible with treating him or her uncivilly. Collingwood does not think, however, that human co-operation rests on a foundation of human reason (NL, 36.73). His description of our nascent propensity to associate is similar to Kant's characterisation of the unsocial sociability of man in the state of nature.[32] Our propensity to need others while being hostile towards them; our desire to co-operate and at the same time as wanting to dominate, to comply and to compete, to be confrontational and conciliatory, are all part of the 'tangled skein' of what we carry with us at the level of will. Our confused, contradictory and ambivalent feelings, appetites, passions and desires need not, however, alarm us because within limits we can choose between these contradictory tendencies: 'We can now use our wills instead of being blown about by the veering winds of emotion. We can think which we will do, live eristically or live dialectically' (NL, 36.83). It is by means of some form of common action that we develop our social consciousness and recognise foreigners not as other, but as one of us. Frequently this common action which facilitates our becoming accustomed to treat strangers with civility is commercial activity, that is, trading relations.

Collingwood's ideas are close to those of Michael Walzer who suggests that the thin morality we claim to be universally valid among human beings by the very fact that they are human, and among different states as the instruments through which they act on the world stage, is a projection of the thick morality that pertains in civilised communities. Walzer argues that the type of morality embedded in our societies and social practices, what he calls maximal morality, precedes universal minimal morality, which is in fact abstracted from the former.[33] This is because he wants to maintain an emphasis upon difference while at the same time give credence to a 'thin' universalism. Walzer has suggested that there is a minimal code of universal morality constituting cross-cultural requirements of justice, such as the expectation not to be deceived, treated with gross cruelty or murdered.[34] He suggests that there is an international society which is grounded, not on a natural or hypothetical contract in a Rawlsian original position, but on norms that have become commonly acknowledged by leaders of states and their citizens.[35]

Collingwood's version of a social contract theory in its practical implications has far-reaching consequences. These implications are evident in what Collingwood terms the properties of civilisation. The context in which civility operates is that of respect for the rule of law. That European civilisation has attached such a premium to this principle as a mark of civilisation is a matter of contingency. It is a principle to which the European mind has become accustomed under the influence of Rome. In so far as civilisation is the process of converting occasions of non-agreement into occasions of agreement (*NL*, 40.42), abjuring eristic and embracing dialectical methods, the rule of law in all cases to which it is applicable, substitutes dialectical for eristic methods (*NL*, 39.52).

His theory is designed to include the socially excluded, not only those who are too young to exercise freedom of choice, but also those whose wills have been broken, whose self-respect is diminished because of the demeaning conditions in which they find themselves, or because they have been psychologically damaged by the exercise of an overbearing force (*NL*, 13.63). In this respect, he differs considerably from Gauthier whose reliance upon rational choice includes only those with something to bargain with in the process of agreeing principles of morality. His contractees, unlike those of Rawls, are fully aware of their talents, and what they agree to distribute among themselves is not the whole product of co-operation, but the co-operative surplus – the additional product produced as a result of co-operation. The individual naturally inclined to straight maximisation, follows a course of constrained maximisation, in the expectation of an equitable share of the surplus. Justice is therefore a matter of distribution commensurate with one's talents and effort. Those with nothing to offer are excluded from the very idea of just distribution.[36]

The corollary of strengthening one's will through education is that no one should be so economically disadvantaged as to be at the mercy of someone who is in a position to coerce him or her to accept employment under unacceptable conditions. This is the exercise of force which militates against the freedom of the will. In other words, diminishing the gap between the rich and poor, in order to eliminate the exercise of force which crushes self-respect, necessitates a programme of social justice. Wealth, Collingwood argues, primarily relates to the community and only incidentally to the individual as a member of that community. It is a comparative term which means that it is a concept which relates to a standard. The needs of a community grow in conjunction with the civilising process. A civilised community is able to satisfy these needs by the intelligent use of its resources, which necessarily entails in Collingwood's mind the conservation of traditional skills which enable a community to exploit nature intelligently.

The more civilised a community the more wealthy it becomes. Wealth is something that the community shares and is dispersed throughout that community.

Riches, on the other hand, is a term that pertains to individuals and is a relative term, 'one which involves *contrast with its own correlative*, no reference to a standard being necessarily implied' (*NL*, 38.41). Someone is rich relative to someone who is poor. A rich person stands in a relation of power relative to the poor person, and the exercise of that power is force. An economic transaction, uncomplicated by force, is one in which two individuals of their own free will agree upon an exchange because they both think that they will be better off. The just price is what each party to the transaction is willing to pay. A just price is logically premised on free will. Where there is a contrast between rich and poor force is exercised and an element of barbarity exists within that community. It may be that some contrast is tolerated because it is deemed that the rich contribute generally to the generation of wealth in society. However, in proportion to the extent to which a civilisation is civil-ised it becomes wealthy in the sense that the increase in its needs are matched by its ability to satisfy them by means of the intelligent use of resources. The diffusion of such wealth entails the abolition of poverty which in turn means the abolition of riches (*NL*, 39.19).

Modern liberalism has failed, Collingwood argues, to affect this dispersal adequately. In clinging to the sacrosanct distinction between public and private, concerning itself with eliciting political views as guides to its policies, in private matters it preferred not to intrude if nothing illegal was being done. What this meant in practice was that individuals pursuing their business interests were of little concern to government. Just as there was anarchy in international relations among liberal polities, anarchy was also the principle by which the economy operated internal to the state. Collingwood argues that:

> This was tolerable in theory only because of the extraordinary doctrine, learnt from Adam Smith, that free pursuit of individual interest best subserved the interest of all; in practice it was soon found wholly intolerable, and the misery of the weaker, to which it gave rise, was the source of modern socialism.[37]

– SUPPRESSION OF EMOTIONS –

Collingwood has often been accused of having too intellectualist a view of history, that is, of excluding emotions and the irrational from his theory of history. His discussion of re-enactment in *The Idea of History*, posthumously compiled by T. M. Knox, certainly gives the impression that only rational purposive thought, that is, deliberative criteriological thought, qualifies as the subject of historical knowledge, and hence contributes to self-knowledge of the mind. It is clear, however, that in the manuscript he called *The Principles of History* and authorised for publication, but which was discarded in substance by Knox, Collingwood did not wish to disregard the irrational or the emotional, and in the 'Folk Tales' manuscripts, for example, he talks of re-experiencing the emotional life of the savage in order to understand the savage within ourselves.[38] However, it is perfectly clear from *The Principles of Art* the importance that Collingwood attached to emotions in the healthy functioning of civilisation. Emotion, he claims, is the dynamo that drives practical life (*PA*, 68–9), and therefore its faithful expression is imperative. To express an emotion is to become conscious of it, and to acknowledge its existence to ourselves. Failure to express emotions is to disown or repress them. It is a failure of consciousness to convert psychical emotions into imaginative expressions and leads to what Collingwood calls 'corruption of consciousness' (*PA*, 217–20, 251, 282–5, 336). Elsewhere, Collingwood argues that there are two types of emotion essential to a healthy civilisation. Those that are at the heart of emotional life relating to our bodies, personalities and relations with parents, mate, children and other human beings, and those that are fundamental to a particular civilisation, such as love of God and love of nature.[39]

In our own civilisation we have persistently and systematically gradually eradicated its emotional basis. In Collingwood's view the role of magic in society has been misunderstood as primitive bad science. As a result its importance is undervalued and its influence has been suppressed. The ritualised and conventionally accepted ways of discharging emotions into practical activities have been undermined. Magic, which is the organised and systematic arousal of emotion discharged through socially practical activities, is not bad science, but the necessary expression of emotion through such activities as fertility dances, war dances and harvest rituals. Our utilitarian civilisation prides itself on eradicating superstition and 'irrational' emotions and does not realise that the denial of such emotions amounts to a corruption of consciousness. Collingwood argues that: 'To live within the scheme of modern European-American civilisation involves doing a certain violence to one's emotional nature, treating emotion as something that must be repressed, a hostile force within us whose outbreaks are feared as destructive of civilised life' ('The Utilitarian Civilisation', *EPP*, 198).

In addition, throughout his writings Collingwood emphasised the importance of religion, not only to the life of the mind, but also to the healthy flourishing of communities and civilisations. Collingwood describes religion as an inward flame making us conscious of our relation to 'the infinite mystery of the universe'.[40] Religion is the vital energy of our civilisation whose flame must be kept burning. Religion is the passion which impels a society to hold on to a certain way of life, to regard its values as absolute by being faithful to the rules which define it at all costs. Without this conviction the rules become hollow and meaningless. Our civilisation, however, has systematically stripped religion of its emotional element by philosophers and scientists who claimed to have distilled the rational element and discarded the superstitious ideas and magical rituals embodied in it.

The importance of Christianity to civilisation is, of course, a theme that has occupied Alasdair MacIntyre for over forty years, and the point he makes is essentially the same as that of Collingwood. In his first book, MacIntyre argues that it comes naturally to Western civilisation to divide human life into the sacred and the secular, but this very division, having its origins in Christianity, augurs the demise of a truly religious culture. In separating the religious and the secular, religion becomes yet another discrete aspect of life, one activity among many. Only a religion, practised as a way of life, permeating every sphere and through which the secular is viewed as sacred, can endure and ensure that rituals do not become ends in themselves divorced from 'hallowing the world'.[41] In a society where religion has become irrelevant to politics, the political becomes a sphere outside of the reign of God whose actions therefore become confined to the narrowest limits. In *After Virtue* this nascent theme becomes fully developed, and it is interesting how the fragmentation of experience is a theme in both Collingwood and MacIntyre. They are both, of course, concerned to discern the differences between social and positivist explanations of human action, emphasising the importance of identifying intentions in any adequate characterisation. As MacIntyre suggests: 'There is no such thing as "behaviour", to be identified prior to and independently of intentions, beliefs and settings.'[42] They both see the crisis of civilisation resulting from the breaking-up of the unity of experience, although they differ in their specifications of the nature of the fragmentation and its causes. In *Speculum Mentis* Collingwood identifies the fragmentation and compartmentalisation of thought as the main source of the crisis of modern civilisation. Philosophy, religion and art fail to connect with a modern audience, hence they are isolated from each other, and from the world eager for all, but which fails to hear their voices (*SP*, 16–17). The Renaissance represents the point at which the contentment of the Middle Ages in embodying religion, art, philosophy and other aspects of life in the same individual, or at least in the same social organism, reaches a new level of consciousness no longer satisfied with the compromise that living together entailed, realising that vocational choice had become necessary. Philosophers, priests, and artists no longer lived together in harmony instead they became antagonistic, refused to serve two masters and devoted themselves wholeheartedly to their chosen vocation. Each isolated from the others led their followers into more and more esoteric avenues of specialism, speaking only to specialists, and being useless both to the rest of humanity and to the specialist themselves when they questioned their reasons for pursuing it (*SM*, 34). The mistake was in believing that they could live without each other. In the case of religion it must have churches, and hence architects and artists to design and adorn them, and theology, and hence philosophers to produce it: 'But now that art and philosophy have parted from religion and gone their own irreligious way, she can no longer employ them' (*SP*, 33). The result is that religion can only look backwards to the days before the fragmentation, and instead of incorporating modern art and religion into its organism it invented neo-Gothic and neo-Scholasticism. Collingwood argues that it is both 'strange and pathethic' to see the various sects building chapels and churches in the style of the original date of their foundation. The failure is the responsibility of both art and religion and constitutes the reason for their inability to connect with the modern individuals who, as a consequence of the detachment of the forms of experience from each other, have become 'wrecks and fragments of men' (*SM*, 35). The answer, if we are to be redeemed, is the reunion of the forms in 'a completed and undivided life' (*SM*, 36). Collingwood argues that there is nothing novel or original in this answer. It is in fact the fundamental principle of Christianity that only the holistic life is a life worth pursuing.

In MacIntyre's view there are two types of obstacle which make it difficult to envisage each person as a unified character providing the virtues with a *telos*. The first is social. Contemporary society divides the life of the individual into segments, work is separate from leisure, public from private, corporate from personal. The second is philosophical and has two components, both of which contribute to the invisibility of the unity of human experience. Analytic philosophy views individuals atomistically and breaks down complex actions into simple components. In addition, the separation between the individual and the roles and quasi-roles played makes the life of an individual appear as if it is a series of unconnected episodes. MacIntyre contends that it is not from analytic philosophy, nor from phenomenology that the vocabulary for conceptualising the unity will come, but instead from the philosophies of history of Hegel and Collingwood.[43] The unity of an individual's life, for MacIntyre, 'is the unity of a narrative embodied in a single life'.[44]

Having isolated itself, Collingwood argues, the process of marginalising religion continued apace. The purging of religion of superstition and emotion gathered strength over the last two centuries under the influence of 'Illuminism'. Illuminism both attempted to formulate the rational principles which could be distilled from Christianity, and to declare itself an enemy to all superstition and magic, especially those associated with Christianity. Our liberal and democratic principles, he claims, derive from a religious love of God who loves us and sent his son to die for us. God places an absolute value on every individual and sanctified human life. Collingwood argues that:

> The doctrines concerning human nature on which liberal or democratic practice was based were not empirically derived from research into anthropological and psychological data; they were a matter of faith; and these Christian doctrines were a source from which they were derived.　　　('Fascism and Nazism', *EPP*, 190)

Fascism and Nazism, Collingwood maintains, owe their success to the fact that they have tapped an emotional source – a revival of pagan beliefs and superstitions – capable of arousing emotions in their followers. Fascism and Nazism have a power far more effective and dynamic than liberalism which has lost its emotional energy. Simultaneously, however, incorporating the argument of *The New Leviathan* into our account, they have suppressed aspects of rational consciousness and developed a herd mentality, that is, individuals incapable of thinking and acting for themselves, dependent upon a leader to make the decisions for them. In other words, what would be a healthy sign in other communities, that is, the cultivation of the emotional life of the people, in bodies politic where emotion is aroused at the expense of rational consciousness, the barbarity – the revolt against civilisation – is far more intense and dramatic than the barbarism exhibited in suppressing emotions and cultivating rational consciousness, even if that consciousness is somewhat perverse because of its denial of emotions.

The purpose of discussing art as magic and art as amusement is not merely to categorise different human endeavours commonly missidentified as art, but also to warn of the dangers of allowing art proper to be displaced by them. While both magic and amusement have essential roles to play in society, the eradication of each, or the dominance of either, has serious consequences for the future of our civilisation. Similarly, the role of amusement is misunderstood, and instead of being seen as an aspect of a healthy society, a way in which emotions are discharged in the amusement itself, it has come to be seen as the dominant purpose of life, the end to which all one's activities should be directed.

All historical knowledge, Collingwood argues, involves the re-creation in the historian's own mind of the lived experiences of the people he or she studies. If magic, which is the common element found in fairy tales, were peculiar to primitive peoples and absolutely alien to modern civilised people, and on that count deemed irrational, the historian would not be able to understand it. The types of behaviour which fall under the general description of magic must be comprehended as rational purposive activity. In other words it must be understood as criteriological. He is not here then talking of the involuntary, but, instead, the controlled and intentional expression of emotions. This puts them into the category of the criterio-logical human sciences, that is, thought as a self-critical and self-referential activity, setting itself purposes and devising ways to enact them.

Collingwood is making quite a different claim about magic from Malinowski. For Malinowski magic is resorted to in acknowledgement of a society's impotence in the rational control of nature. In other words, magic begins where technology ends. Collingwood, on the other hand, sees magic, not as a result of failure, but as an essential way of expressing and thus acknowledging emotions. 'Magical activity', he says, 'is a kind of dynamo supplying the mechanism of practical life with the emotional current that drives it. Hence magic is a necessity for every sort of condition of man, and is actually found in every healthy society' (PA, 69). It should not, however, be judged as art. The role of the art critic, Collingwood contends, is not only to distinguish good and bad art, but also to identify what is and what is not art. Because much of what passes as art these days is a combination of magical and amusement art the job of the critic is both difficult and ambivalent: 'to condemn magic for being bad art is just as foolish as to praise art for being good magic' (PA, 94). The artist, in Collingwood's view, provides the medicine for the worst disease that a community can suffer, corruption of consciousness. The artist reveals to the community the secrets of the hearts of it members (PA, 336).

– CONCLUSION –

Collingwood, then, is a political philosopher in the grand theory tradition. His concerns are not those of the narrow analytic philosopher, but those of the Hegelian tradition which look to history for the unfolding of human experience. Like Arendt and MacIntyre he is concerned with the dis-continuity between the past and the present, and the fragmentation of human experience. He does, however, offer a version of social contract theory which offers the prospect of including the socially excluded. His theory, while entailing principles of social justice, also entails a politics of recognition. A continuing process of education, conceived in the broadest terms, inducts the individual into the civilising process which excludes, as far as possible, force from our relations with our fellow citizens, the natural world and citizens of foreign countries. Here his concern is similar to that of Rorty in exploring the way that 'they' can be conceived as one of 'us'. Here Collingwood places much more emphasise upon rational processes, without diminishing the importance of the role of emotions in human activity.

– NOTES –

The following abbreviations will be used throughout this chapter for these works by Collingwood:

RP   *Religion and Philosophy* (London, Macmillan, 1916)

SP   *Speculum Mentis* (Oxford, Clarendon Press, 1924)

EPM   *Essay on Philosophical Method* (Oxford, Clarendon Press, 1933)

PA   *Principles of Art* (Oxford, Clarendon Press, 1938)

AA   *An Autobiography* (Oxford, Clarendon Press, 1939)

EM   *An Essay on Metaphysics* (Oxford, Clarendon Press, 1938; revised edition, ed. Rex Martin 1998)

NL   *The New Leviathan* (Oxford, Clarendon Press, 1941; revised edition 1992, ed. David Boucher)

IH   *The Idea of History* (Oxford, Clarendon Press, 1946; revised edition 1993, ed. Jan van der Dussen)

EPP   *Essays in Political Philosophy*, ed. David Boucher (Oxford, Clarendon Press, 1989)

1. Douglas H. Johnson, 'W. G. Collingwood and the Beginnings of the Idea of History', *Collingwood Studies*, I (1994), 3.
2. R. G. Collingwood, *Ruskin's Philosophy: an address delivered at the Ruskin Centenary Conference 1919* (Kendal, Titus Wilson, 1922).
3. R. G. Collingwood, 'Ruskin and the Mountains', introduced by James Connelly, *Collingwood Studies*, II (1995), 185–9.
4. Hannah Arendt, 'Martin Heidegger at Eighty' in *Heidegger and Modern Philosophy*, ed. M. Murray (New Haven, Yale University Press, 1978), 295. Also see Maurizio Passerin d'Entrèves, *The Political Philosophy of Hannah Arendt* (London, Routledge, 1994), 28–34.
5. See Peter Nicholson, 'Collingwood's *New Leviathan* Then and Now', *Collingwood Studies*, I (1994), 164.
6. The distinction between epistemic and political authority is made by Richard de George, *The Nature and Limits of Authority* (Lawrence, Kansas University Press, 1985).
7. Ronald Beiner, *Political Judgment* (London, Methuen, 1983), 3.
8. Hans-Georg Gadamer, *Reason in the Age of Science*, trans. Frederick G. Lawrence (Cambridge, MA, MIT Press, 1981), 72.
9. Francis Fukayama, *The End of History and the Last Man* (Harmondsworth, Penguin, 1993).
10. Charles Taylor, *Multiculturalism and the 'Politics of Recognition'* (Princeton New Jersey, Princeton University Press, 1992).
11. Nancy Fraser, 'From Redistribution to Recognition? Dilemmas of Justice in a "Post-Socialist" Age', in *Theorizing Multiculturalism*, ed. Cynthia Willet (London, Blackwell, 1998). For a discussion and criticism of both Taylor's and Fraser's views see the chapter by Lawrence Blum in the same volume: 'Recognition, Value and Equality: A Critique of Charles Taylor's and Nancy Fraser's Accounts of Multiculturalism'.
12. As, for example, K. B. McIntyre argues in 'Collingwood, Oakeshott and the Social Contract', *Collingwood Studies*, III (1996).
13. Hannah Arendt, *The Human Condition* (Chicago, University of Chicago Press, 1958), 28.
14. See d'Entrèves, *Hannah Arendt*, 58–63.
15. F. H. Hinsley, *Sovereignty* (Cambridge, Cambridge University Press, 1986), 16.
16. John Hoffman, *Sovereignty* (Buckingham, Open University Press, 1998), 52.
17. Hoffman, *Sovereignty*, 106.

18. Stephen Toulmin, 'Conceptual Change and the Problem of Relativity' in *Critical Essays on the Philosophy of R. G. Collingwood*, ed. Michael Krausz (Oxford, Clarendon Press, 1972), 201–21; and, *Human Understanding* (Oxford, Clarendon Press, 1972), 66–85.

19. It is beyond the scope of this chapter to enter into this debate, but both Rex Martin and Adrian Oldfield, for example, deny that Collingwood's *An Essay On Metaphysics* is relativist. See their contributions to D. Boucher, J. Connelly and T. Modood (eds), *Philosophy, History and Civilization: Interdisciplinary Perspectives on R. G. Collingwood* (Cardiff, University of Wales Press, 1995).

20. See the Ritchie essay on this issue.

21. Hannah Arendt, *The Origins of Totalitarianism*, new edition (New York, Harcourt Brace and World Inc., 1966), 293.

22. Arendt, *Origins of Totalitarianism*, 298.

23. Arendt, *Origins of Totalitarianism*, 296.

24. Arendt, *Origins of Totalitarianism*, 300.

25. See David Boucher, 'The Place of Education in Civilisation' in David Boucher, James Connelly and Tariq Modood (eds), *Philosophy, History and Civilization: Interdisciplinary Perspectives on R. G. Collingwood* (Cardiff, Wales University Press, 1995).

26. See R. G. Collingwood, Folk Tale Manuscripts, 'F: The Concluding Chapter', 9.

27. Richard Rorty, *Contingency, Irony, and Solidarity* (Cambridge, Cambridge University Press, 1989).

28. Rorty, *Contingency, Irony, and Solidarity*, 190.

29. Rorty, 'Human Rights, Rationality and Sentimentality', in Stephen Shute and Susan Hurley (eds), *On Human Rights* (New York, Basic Books, 1993), 115, 116.

30. Rorty, *Contingency, Irony, and Solidarity*, 192.

31. The corruption of consciousness occurs when feelings or emotions fail to be converted by imagination into ideas: 'first we direct our attention towards a certain feeling, or become conscious of it. Then we take fright at what we have recognised: not because the idea into which we are converting it proves an alarming impression, but because the idea into which we are converting it proves an alarming idea. We cannot see our way to dominate it, and shrink from persevering in the attempt. We therefore give it up, and turn our attention to something less intimidating' (*PA*, 217).

32. See Howard Williams, *Kant's Political Philosophy* (Oxford, Blackwell, 1983), 8.

33. Walzer, *Thick and Thin*, 13.

34. Michael Walzer, 'Interpretation and Social Criticism', *The Tanner Lectures on Human Values*, vii, ed. S. M. McMurrin (Salt Lake City, University of Utah Press, 1988), 22.

35. This is not what he calls covering law universalism which holds up a way of life as superior and uniquely right, and which explicitly or implicitly implies a form of cultural or political imperialism. Instead, his universalism is reiterative, acknowledging that subject to minimal universal constraints there are many different and valuable ways of life that have equal rights to flourish in their respective locations, and deserve equal respect to our own; see Michael Walzer, 'Nation and Universe', *The Tanner Lectures on Human Values*, xi, ed. G. B. Peterson (Salt Lake City, University of Utah Press, 1990).

36. David Gauthier, *Morals By Agreement* (Oxford, Oxford University Press, 1986).

37. R. G. Collingwood, 'Modern Politics', extract from 'Man Goes Mad', printed in *Essays in Political Philosophy*, ed. D. Boucher.

38. For discussions of these matters see D. Boucher, '*The Principles of History* and the Cosmology conclusion to the *Idea of Nature*', *Collingwood Studies*, II (1995); and, 'The Significance of Collingwood's *Principles of History*', *Journal of the History of Ideas* (1996).

39. R. G. Collingwood, 'Man Goes Mad', unpublished manuscript, pp. 31–2. Bodleian Library, Oxford.
40. R. G. Collingwood, 'Science, Religion and Civilisation', unpublished manuscript, p. 15. Bodleian Library, Oxford.
41. Alasdair MacIntyre, *Marxism: An Interpretation* (London, SMC Press, 1953), 9–10.
42. Alasdair MacIntyre, *After Virtue*, second edition (London, Duckworth, 1985), 208.
43. MacIntyre, *After Virtue*, 3, 4 and 265.
44. MacIntyre, *After Virtue*, 216.

CHAPTER 7

Michael Oakeshott:
The Non-Economic Character
of Civil Association

In this chapter, Oakeshott's general philosophical position will first be out-lined. The discussion will then focus upon his political theory, particularly his distinction between civil association and enterprise association, the relation of this distinction to jurisprudence and the type of relationship between individuals that civil association postulates. This latter account entails a conception of law which has some parallels with H. L. A. Hart's theory of law. Thirdly, Oakeshott's theory will be related to the preoccupation of modern political theorists with social justice. Finally, some criticisms of the type of enquiry in which Oakeshott purports to be engaged will be considered.[1]

– OAKESHOTT AND PHILOSOPHY –

Philosophy, for Oakeshott, is a personal endeavour. The philosopher seeks neither practical influence nor devoted followers. Philosophy is not a search for new knowledge, intelligibility out of ignorance, but instead the attempt to understand differently something that is to some extent already understood. Experience is differentiated by thought into modally distinct co-ordinate worlds. All experience, for Oakeshott, is a world of ideas, or imaginings. Each world is conditional, in that it rests on unquestioned postulates, yet each is defective in terms of its self-understanding and in the understanding it generates of experience. Philosophy is distinguished from the modes by the fact that it is unconditional insofar as it takes each unquestioned assumption as an invitation to explore that assumption's conditionality.

There is no limit to the number of possible modes, but some become more defined and coherent than others. They rest on unquestioned postulates capable of generating conclusions appropriate to themselves. Each mode is a world of ideas or imaginings which creates its own objects (*OHC*, 17 and *OH*, 2). In this respect, nature is created by scientists, and is not an independently existing object of inquiry. To put it in Bradley's words, nature is a convenient fiction which scientists have every right to employ. Truth depends upon the coherence of the world of ideas in which a statement is uttered and not upon its correspondence to an external object. The modes are completely autonomous, and cannot intrude upon each other without irrelevance. They are all inadequate and conditional modifications of experience as a whole, each incapable of recognising, in terms of its postulates, its own limitations. Each time we interpret or understand we invoke the principles and procedures prescribed by the different worlds of ideas or imaginings. The conclusions we reach are conditionally intelligible only because they are sustained by the postulates in terms of which they are reached. They have no independent validity; cannot be confirmed by appeal to an external reality; and cannot be introduced into any other world of ideas without irrelevance. It is because of their exclusiveness and because each is true for itself that none can confirm or deny the conclusions of the other worlds, nor act as the foundation upon which the others are built (*EM*, 5). Oakeshott, with the possible exception of Bradley, is more radical and sceptical in his philosophical Idealism than any of the thinkers discussed in this book, denying any reality outside of the modes. There can be nothing outside of experience and experience is the creature of a world of ideas. There is no 'prior and fixed "something" upon which the interpreter works', for Oakeshott, 'text and interpretation are one and inseparable' (*EM*, 196 and 113).[2] He rejects the notion of any pre-existing *it* or text independent of interpretation conceived in modally or idiomatically distinct terms (*EM*, 31–2).

Each of the worlds of ideas is in fact a language in which we do not merely recite ready-made literatures, but instead use the language to create our own. The conclusions are not themselves prescribed. Only the postulates or conditions are given. They are invoked in order to reach the conclusions and which make utterances in a particular idiom intelligible. Oakeshott initially distinguished between practical and participatory languages, like politics and morality, whose utterances were purposively persuasive and injunctive, and explanatory languages characterised by reflective theorising, both of which he differentiated from the contemplative language of poetry (*RP*, 63, 65–6, 509–10, 191–2, 193–4, 205-6 and 211–12). Explanatory languages, like history and science, differ from practical languages in the clarity of their criteria of relevance; the appropriateness of these criteria to their conclusions; and the capacity of explanatory languages to identify errors and pronounce certain utterances out of character. Furthermore, unlike practical languages, 'they do not pretend to have injunctive force' (*RP*, 212).

The distinction formulated in these terms was untenable because it excluded explanation from practical languages like politics and morality. In *On*

Human Conduct, Oakeshott revised his position and acknowledged that both persuasion and explanation are appropriate activities of agents who diagnose and respond to practical situations. As a response to a persuasive act, which may be unintelligible, the performer may be asked for the supplementary act of explanation, which is not itself an act designed to bring about a wished for response, but one which is meant to clarify the original act (*OHC*, 49). Similarly, the element of 'doing' intrinsic to practical languages could not be entirely excluded from what he had called the explanatory languages. The latter category of languages he came to refer to as idioms or platforms of theorising, whereas philosophy is characterised by its determination to remain unconditional. To engage or invoke these idioms of theorising involves an element of 'doing', in that knowledge is required of how to participate, but, whereas in conduct, the 'doing' 'is intrinsic to the engagement', in theorising it is 'incidental' (*OHC*, 34 and 35).

Initially, Oakeshott identified three modes, practice, science and history, to which he later added poetry, at which time he came to talk of worlds of imaginings in order to accommodate the non-propositional discourse of the voice of poetry and to avoid the passive connotation which the term experience implied.[3] In *Rationalism in Politics* (1962 and 1991) Oakeshott suggests that the appropriate image of the relations between the various worlds of imaginings is that of a conversation in which each voice has a say, but none is dominant nor takes priority over the rest. Oakeshott's philosophy is certainly anti-foundationalist and abjures the very idea of the Enlightenment's search for a unified philosophy to which all knowledge can be related or reduced. Philosophy is itself a voice which reflects upon the other voices and their relations, but has no specific contribution of its own to make to the conversation. The idea of a conversation is not meant to specify the exact terms by which each voice tolerates the others. It is presented as an 'appropriate image' to facilitate comprehension of the 'manifold' which constitutes 'the meeting place' of the various idioms which comprise the variety of human utterance (*RP*, 198–9). This is an image which Rorty has found conducive in distinguishing between 'systematic' philosophers, who search for epistemological foundations, and 'edifying' philosophers, who destroy for the sake of their own generation, denying absolutism and keeping the path of enquiry open. Edifying philosophers are related conversationally rather than adversarially. Like Oakeshott, it is an elevated sense of the term conversation which Rorty invokes, it is a useful abbreviation that stands for the whole human endeavour, namely culture.[4] It is a metaphor meant to evoke the proper image of human endeavour as polite, respectful, civilised, congenial and good-humoured, as opposed to eristic and confrontational.[5]

In *On Human Conduct* (1975), Oakeshott extends his theory. The voices now become idioms of discourse, or platforms of conditional understanding, belonging to one of two categorially distinct orders of enquiry. Something which is not yet understood has first to be identified in categorially unambiguous terms as belonging either to a process devoid of intelligence, or, to a practice subscribed to and learned by those who participate in it, and which exhibits human intelligence. Each logically exclusive order prescribes an idiom in terms of which a more precise understanding can be achieved. For example, the identification of a process may further prescribe biological, chemical or mechanical idioms. Understanding is achieved by means of ideal characters composed of characteristics. They are the instruments of identification. They may be crude and unsophisticated or refined and relatively complex. Something which is identified in terms of an ideal character composed of relatively few characteristics may subsequently be redefined in terms of an ideal character far more complex. What is identified, Oakeshott argues, 'is always as intelligible as the terms in which it is being understood allow it to be' (*OHC*, 6). The task of theorising or philosophising is that it identifies the postulates and characteristics of the ideal characters in terms of which we understand the world.

Here Oakeshott appears to be subscribing to a distinction which Onora O'Neill later elaborates. O'Neill distinguishes between abstraction and idealisation. Often when modern philosophers level the charge of abstraction against a philosophy what they are actually objecting to is idealisation, that is, they are not objecting to the fact that too much of human agency is left out in the process of abstraction, but that something else is being accentuated to a point where it is no longer faithful to what we may know of agency. They are not then objecting to abstraction from known conditions, but to the introduction of ungrounded idealised premises.[6] For example, the post-Enlightenment rational man is almost unrecognisable in his cognitive powers and volitional capacities. In addition, models of man take on a second sense of idealisation. They are held up as ideals to be emulated:

> Rational economic men, ideal moral spectators, utilitarian legislators, and legions of rational choosers are taken as *standards* for human economic or political action. We are to think of idealized agents and their flawless compliance with rational norms as admirable and super-human rather than as irrelevant to human choosing, let alone sub-human.[7]

What O'Neill calls idealisation Oakeshott calls abridgement. Rationalists typically abridge a tradition to the point of caricature. The very features that O'Neill identifies in the post-Enlightenment as characteristic of idealisation are the features that Oakeshott identifies as characteristic of rationalism in politics. Oakeshott's ideal characters of civil and enterprise association are not idealisations in O'Neill's sense of the word. They are what she would call abstractions. Oakeshott argues that they are ideal, not because they present us with the perfect condition of things to which we must aspire, but because they are 'abstracted from the contingencies and ambiguities of actual goings-on in the world' (*OHC*, 109).

In marked contrast with other Idealists in this book, with the exception of Bradley, and probably more faithful to the spirit of Hegel, Oakeshott declares philosophy, or any theoretical mode such as history or science, *incapable* of offering injunctions for practical conduct. The world of practice to which politics, religion and the moral life belong is modally distinct, and generates its own prescriptive conclusions for action. Oakeshott is opposed to the philosopher who wants to have a practical impact upon the world, pejoratively calling him or her a *theoretician* or *philosophe*. Such a theorist is seriously mistaken about the nature of his or her undertaking and fails to see that there is a categorial distinction between theory and practice which is insurmountable. Oakeshott argues that: 'This deplorable character has no respectable occupation. In virtue of being a theorist he purports to be concerned with the postulates of conduct, but he mistakes these postulates for principles from which "correct" performances may be deduced or somehow elicited' (*OHC*, 26).

Oakeshott is often allied, by his friends and critics, with the ideology of conservatism. In so far as the least an ideology purports to do is offer some practical prescriptions for political conduct, Oakeshott's professed separation of theory and practice, his disdainful hostility to politicians, and his refusal publicly to express a view on current political controversies would seem to distance him somewhat from such a style of politics. The ideologue is a rationalist who Oakeshott continuously criticises for trying to conduct a style of politics which is radically flawed in that it cannot succeed in what it claims to be doing. To accuse Oakeshott of having ulterior practical motives or of being an ideologue is to place him in the company of the theoreticians he deplored. This is a charge that will need to be addressed as the different aspects of his thought are explored.

Oakeshott himself acknowledges that the intensely practical nature of politics has a potentially corrupting influence on the philosopher. The philosopher does not always succeed in sustaining the level of disinterestedness intrinsic to his or her calling, and from time to time may succumb to the allure of public moralising in moments of distraction and on highly emotive issues. He claims that such outbursts and interventions are not themselves the conclusions of philosophical reasoning, but a disengagement from theorising and a temporary relapse into a different mode of thinking. Although philosophers do not always suppress the preacher in themselves, 'we must learn not to follow the philosophers upon these holiday excursions' (*EM*, 1).

For Oakeshott, human conduct is best understood in terms of the idiomatically distinct theoretical language of history. Throughout his life he formulated his views on history, culminating in *On History* (1983), and has been justifiably acknowledged as one of the foremost defenders of the integrity of history against the prevailing slavish reverence for science. Historians create history in so far as they infer a past from present evidence. The past of the participant is irrecoverable and dead all we have left are the vestiges from which the historical past is constructed. Historical events are not in themselves contingent, but their relation to each other is one of contingency. They are not related organically, chemically or causally (except in a non-scientific, non-technical sense of the word), nor are they instances of covering laws. Instead each event 'touches' another and serves to illuminate it as its significant antecedent, coincident, or consequent.[8] History assumes an order of enquiry which is categorially unambiguous. It assumes the identification of something going on as an exhibition of intelligence, where individuals subscribe to practices, but whose actions are not determined by them. The sciences, however, predicate a different order of enquiry which identify something going on as a process which things undergo, and which do not exhibit intelligence. Both human conduct or practical life and history are idiomatically distinct languages within the categorially distinct order of enquiry which identifies something that is going on as an exhibition of intelligence related to practices which must be learnt by those who subscribe to them. Contrary to the commonplace view, history does not derive its 'facts' from, nor does it have its foundations in, practical life; and similarly the latter has nothing to learn from the idiomatically irrelevant mode of history.

Preston King has criticised Oakeshott for severely compromising the autonomy of the modes by allowing that each has its own notion of a past. King assumes that to talk of a past necessarily entails talking historically. In this respect, King has seriously misunderstood Oakeshott. Each of the modes evokes its own conception of the past, but not all conceptions of the past are historical. For Oakeshott each of the pasts related to the different modes or idioms is distinct and autonomous. Each mode does not merely offer a different perspective on the past: each creates its own past in terms of its procedures and postulates. They do not even create their own pasts out of the same evidence, because there is no distinction between evidence and its interpretation. Evidence, insofar as it is recognised as evidence, is the creature of the interpretative idiom. The point which Oakeshott insists upon is that the other idioms do not have histories unless they are endowed with them by historians (*OH*, 5). The idioms or modes all have their own idiomatically relevant pasts which they may wish to call histories and which they use in some way to further their idiomatic understandings, but history in its strict sense is an autonomous manner of theorising with no relevance to the engagements of the other distinct idioms. To write a history of science, for example, is not to engage in the activity of being a scientist: it is not an attempt to quantify, measure or generalise, but instead the attempt to construct in accordance with the postulates of history a contingently related account of what scientists have done.

In practical life, which encompasses the language of politics, there are idiomatically distinct procedures for evoking a past, and in which the categories of past, present and future stand in a special relation. The past is a useful past comprised of examples, evoked in the present with a view to affecting future conduct. The past and future are seen in terms relative to our present selves. Practical activity is a present–future relation in which the past it evokes is understood in terms of its worth to us in bringing about a future condition. It is a past inseparable from the injunctive force which the participants invested in it (*OH*, 14). In practical life, our present encapsulates our past: in other words, we are, to some extent, the outcome or residue of all that may have happened to us, irrespective of it being remembered or recollected. The remembered past is, in fact, our consciousness of our own continuity, which is to be distinguished from the recollected past which we periodically consult for guidance to further our current practical concerns. It is a past of heroic deeds, cautionary parables, moral lessons, exemplars and images to be emulated. For Oakeshott, 'this is a "living" past which may be said to "teach by example", or more generally to afford us a current vocabulary of self-understanding and self-expression' (*OH*, 19, 37 and 39). It is a past which has nothing to do with history. It is invoked by practical activity and remains in the idiom of practicalities: it is imbued with moral judgements, and the individual's purposes and intentions which are idiomatically excluded from history. The past in history 'is without the moral, the political or the social structure which the practical man transfers from *his* present to *his* past' (*RP*, 169).

Oakeshott's many essays on politics, although not comprising a system, betray a certain unity in that they persistently explore and develop common themes, even though the vocabulary in terms of which these themes are discussed is constantly modified. He identifies and articulates what he calls 'ideal characters', exposes the postulates which determine their conditionality and subjects them to interrogation.

– POLITICAL AND LEGAL PHILOSOPHY –

What, then, are the ideal characters in terms of which political activity may be understood? Oakeshott's contribution to political philosophy has been the exploration of two notionally distinct and categorially opposed understandings of the mode of association which characterise the state, the style of politics and the understanding of law associated with them, and the conception of the individual that each entails. Neither of the ideal characters in terms of which the state has been understood is found in pure form, and each is always found qualified by the other, although neither is inherently in need of the other. They are found together as characteristics of the modern European state, not by logical implication, but contingently as the outcome of human choices. Even though the one in recent times gained the favour of many theorists, they are related to each other 'as dominant and recessive dispositions' (*OHC*, 323). While it is clear which one Oakeshott favours as appropriate to the understanding of a state, it is equally clear that he acknowledges the importance of the other and is not recommending its expulsion from the activity of the modern state. In fact, it is the polarisation of the two conceptions of the state, related to each other as 'sweet enemies' (*OHC*, 326), which in Oakeshott's view enables us to understand the fundamentally ambivalent character of the modern state better than any of the almost useless labels like right and left, or conservative and liberal, current in the modern political vocabulary (*RP*, 438–61).

The first of the ideal characters in terms of which the modern European state has been understood is 'civil association', '*Societas*', 'nomocracy' or 'libertarianism'. It is associated with the emergence of the 'individual' in early modern Europe, and the flourishing of personal freedom, and typically exhibits a politics of scepticism.

The development of the character of the individual is seen by Oakeshott as a reaction against an earlier morality which he calls '*the morality of communal ties*' (*MPME*, 19), in which membership of the community is not a matter of choice and whose model is the family in which property is the family's property and one's station, rights and duties are dictated by custom. In this form of association loyalties are not to principles but to persons. The self-knowledge of the person is not as an individual, but as a member of the community, where these communities are understood to be small and localised and in which governing is strictly hierarchical and conceived as the administration of laws and customs through the courts. The ruler is the custodian of such laws and customs.

The modern individual, or the '*morality of individuality*' (*MPME*, 20) arrives on the scene most notably in Italy with the demise of medieval communal life, and is characterised not by subservience to a master or lord but by being accustomed to making choices for oneself (*RP*, 364). For this new individual: 'Every practical undertaking and every intellectual pursuit revealed itself as an assemblage of opportunities for self-enactment' (*OHC*, 240). The rise of this individualism was the most significant event in modern European history (philosophically conceived!). Oakeshott's fascination with Hobbes is explicable by the fact that it was he who was the first 'to take candid account of the current experience of individuality' (*RP*, 367).

The manner of political discourse which becomes this individual is persuasive, as all political discourse must be, but not demonstrative. Its currency is probabilities and conjectures, rather than proofs and disproofs of political propositions. It is persuasion by argument, rather than demonstration (*RP*, 80). This individual who speaks a non-demonstrative political language is related to other individuals, not by an agreement or contract to pursue common aims and goals, but by a common acknowledgement of the authority of *respublica*, where this acknowledgement does not preclude the possibility of questioning the desirability of the laws which emanate from that authority. This morality of individualism gives rise to a distinctive conception of the office of government which excludes the imposition of ideals and programmes upon citizens, and does not attempt to educate them or make them happier in ways that they have not chosen for themselves. Government is conceived in terms of ruling where the 'image of the ruler is not that of the manager but that of the umpire whose business it is to administer the rules of the game in which he does not himself participate' (*MPME*, 49).

The relationship to which each individual stands to others in civil association is that of subscribing to 'the conditions of a practice' (*OHC*, 119). The conditions, such as customs, maxims, regulations, or laws, all of which are 'considerations' constitutive of the practice, qualify but do not determine human performances. It is a relationship not in terms of common beliefs and the pursuit of common substantive goals, but instead the acknowledgement of the conditions and considerations which compose the practice and which one uses like a language, not to reiterate a common stock of phrases, or recite predetermined lines, but to compose one's own utterances. This is what Oakeshott calls moral conduct, 'the acknowledgement of the authority of a practice composed of conditions ...' (*OHC*, 60).

The individuals, or *cives*, in civil association subscribe to a practice composed of rules, or *lex*, which are non-instrumental insofar as they are not directed to the attainment of a substantive goal or end. In Oakeshott's view, the most troublesome feature to identify, characterise and adequately place in the ideal character of civil association is law. This is because so many theorists of law have misidentified it and associated it with commands, or with instrumental rules for achieving substantive purposes, and have been more concerned with its sources and contingent opinions about its authority and purpose than with what law actually is (*OHC*, 181). Like H. L. A. Hart, Oakeshott rejects Austin's command theory of law. A rule, Oakeshott argues, is a not a command because a command is directed towards an identifiable agent and is a response to a particular situation, and is exhausted by that situation. Unlike rules, commands are injunctions to perform substantive actions and require obedience. Oakeshott maintains that:

> a command, properly speaking, is an authoritative condition of things (the action performed and perhaps the wished-for and expected more distant outcome), and its validity lies neither in the character or quality of what is commanded, nor in any power to penalise disobedience which may be annexed to it, but solely in its authority or authenticity. And this authenticity may be determined only by reference to a rule. Commands are not themselves rules, but they postulate association in terms of rules. Competence to command belongs to an office, a *persona* identified in terms of obligations to obey may be the subject of a command. (*OH*, 129–30)

Furthermore, John Austin, like many before him, including Bentham, failed to distinguish between the authority of law and its truth or desirability.[9] This was because Austin understood the state not as a civil association but instead as an enterprise association whose purpose was to maximise the general happiness. His theory suggests that the authority of rules of law rests upon their relation to accurate information about their capacity to conduce to the general happiness. Acknowledgement of their authority rests upon due deference to the legislator's supposedly superior knowledge of the result of the inductive science of legislation, which in fact, due to its relative newness, was only marginally better than that of the subject (*OHC*, 171).

Civil association is a practice differing from most others in that it is composed entirely of rules, and the associates are related purely in their 'recognition of the rules which constitute a practice of civility'. They are constitutive rather than instrumental rules (*OHC*, 128). They are not rules commanding substantive actions of assignable agents, they do not tell us what to do and what not to do, but instead set the conditions which have to be acknowledged and taken into account in formulating our own purposes and performing our own substantive actions (*OHC*, 108–84, 203 and 254: Cf. *OH*, 130). Mere recognition is not sufficient in itself. The manner of recognition is crucial for the relationship of civil associates. It is the recognition of a rule as a rule for which the question of approval or disapproval does not arise. It makes no difference to the authority of a law and our duty to obey it whether we approve or disapprove of it, nor does recognition entail liking or disliking its consequences. The recognition of a rule is purely in terms of its authority, which entails the acknowledgement that compliance with it is a civil obligation. Such recognition does not exclude attending to rules in terms of their desirability. Deliberation over the desirability of the rules, or conditions, of civil association, is to be engaged in 'politics'.

This common acknowledgement of the authority of *respublica* and the subscription to a practice composed of non-instrumental rules is what Oakeshott calls the rule of law, because what is important 'is the kind of law: "moral" or instrumental' (*OHC*, 318). For Oakeshott the rule of law is a moral practice in which citizens or *cives* are related in their common acknowledgement of the authority, and in which the laws articulate and impose obligations without assigning the performance of specified actions to designated persons in order to achieve a desired substantive result. The rule of law, then, is a mode of moral association which specifies the 'procedural conditions' subscribed to in the performance of substantive actions. Both Hart and Oakeshott contend that moral rules are not identical with legal rules, although the obligation to obey legal rules is a moral one. Hart's position is less clear on this issue. He is emphatic about the point that legal and moral rights cannot be viewed as identical, but that nevertheless there is an intimate connection between the two. The concept of a moral right entails addressing such questions as what limitations on another person's freedom are appropriate for incorporation into a system of coercive legal rules. Invoking Hobbes, Oakeshott contends that the rule of law does not determine actions, but is 'the measure of the good and evil of actions' (*OH*, 150). The maintenance of freedom through the diversity of relations with others can only be sustained in the context of the rule of law, which is the same law for the lion and for the fox, where both have transparent and adequate reasons for complying with it (*RP*, 344).

Oakeshott contends that the state has everywhere been a form of compulsory association and that therefore the language of consenting and promising appropriate to other types of obligation, or what Hart calls 'right creating transactions',[10] is misplaced in the context of political obligation. Political society for Hart, however, is not a unique form of association, but merely the most complex of a particular type. Whenever a group of people engaged in a joint enterprise submit themselves to rules which restrict their liberty each person has a right to expect of the beneficiaries of his or her submission reciprocity. The rules may empower and authorise officials to enforce them and even to create new ones which constitute a system of legal rights and duties, 'but the moral obligation to obey the rules in such circumstances is *due* to the co-operating members of society, and they have a correlative moral right to obedience'.[11] In associations such as these the obligation to obey the rules is distinct from whatever other moral reasons there may be for obedience in terms of good consequences. Hart's point is that while social contract theorists are right to identify the obligation to obey the law as something arising out of the mutual relations in which members of a society stand to one another, they were wrong to equate the adoption of mutual restrictions with promising. In Oakeshott's view it is only when the state is understood as a civil association that we are adequately able to see *cives* related to each other in terms of the rule of law, where the law is moral and not instrumental, and that the individual's moral autonomy is preserved in that he or she chooses his or her own purposes in performing substantive actions which are not imposed by the state. This would be consistent with Hart's contention that if there are any moral rights at all it follows that there is one natural right, 'the equal right of all men to be free'.[12] The language of natural right would, however, be anathema to Oakeshott's way of thinking. It is Oakeshott's identification of civil society as a mode of association comprised of non-instrumental laws, as little substantive and as much procedural as possible, which has led John Gray to credit Oakeshott with isolating and articulating the heart of liberalism.[13]

Both Oakeshott and Hart maintain that there is never a complete correlation between what a society regards as morally wrong and conduct designated unlawful. One of the achievements of modern European societies is that they have distinguished sin from crime. They are at one in maintaining that moral rules are very different from legal rules, although the obligation to obey legal rules is a moral obligation. They argue that rules which exhibit the norms of a moral community, while not formal, may nevertheless spontaneously or otherwise change over time and may be subject to scrutiny and debate, but no procedure or institution exists to change, repeal or replace them deliberately. Hart argues, for example, that: 'The fact that morals and traditions cannot be directly changed, as laws may be, by legislative enactment must not be mistaken for immunity from other forms of change.'[14] Oakeshott argues that recognition of the moral rule is almost indistinguishable from approval of it. He maintains that the force of a moral rule depends solely upon the subject's conviction of its rightness (*OHC*, 160–1). The force of a moral rule ceases if it loses approval. The authority of a legal rule, however, is not dependent upon its approval by civil associates or *cives*. Like Hart, Oakeshott wants to maintain that considerations about the legitimacy or authority of law are conceptually different from those about its moral worth.

This does not mean that there is no relation between morality and law. Even though they both deny that traditional natural law doctrines can provide criteria for the validity of law, they do not think that law can have any arbitrary content as long as it fulfils the formal requirements of law. In Hart's case, there are certain minimum considerations about the human condition which although they may be logically contingent nevertheless need to be satisfied if law is genuinely to be legitimate. This is what he calls the minimum content of natural law. This content is derived from the simple fact of the desire for human survival. For Oakeshott both the constitutions of governments and the activities that governments undertake are constantly the subject of moral approval and disapproval. Recognition and acknowledgement of the authority of law is, however, distinct from the question of its desirability, or to put it in Hart's terms, quite separate from whatever other moral reasons there may be for obedience in terms of good consequences. In the philosophy of Hobbes acknowledging the authority of a government to make law, the question of the justice or injustice of the law does not arise. Even unjust laws are laws. Oakeshott, like Hobbes, denies natural law doctrines which prescribe abstract criteria of validity, failure to comply with which renders law illegitimate. Even Hart's minimum conception of natural law would be unacceptable to Oakeshott who does not believe that anything about the content of law or its justness can be inferred from so called facts about human nature. Oakeshott does nevertheless think that there are certain moral considerations intrinsic to law which allies him to one of Hart's severest critics, Lon Fuller. There are, both Fuller and Oakeshott argue, standards intrinsic to a legal order, without which that order could not persist. These principles intrinsic to law would include its general character as indifferent to particular persons and interests, equality before the law, the exclusion of privilege and the prohibition of secret and retroactive laws.[15] A law that is not known, for example, can only be complied with by chance, and a law that is not generally observed undermines the terms of civil association which is solely in terms of the acknowledgement of the authority of non-instrumental laws where this acknowledgement implies obligation. Going beyond Hobbes Oakeshott believes that laws may certainly be unjust if they fail to comply with the general character of law, but they may also be unjust on the basis of wider considerations: 'considerations in terms of which a law may be recognised, not merely as properly enacted, but as proper or not improper to be or to have been enacted ...' (OH, 141). They are considerations, not in relation to an abstract and absolute natural law, but in relation to the developed historical moral sensibilities of its citizens:

> the prescriptions of the law should not conflict with a prevailing educated moral sensibility capable of distinguishing between the conditions of 'virtue', the conditions of moral association ('good conduct'), and those which are of such a kind that they should be imposed by law ('justice'). (OH, 160)

The mere proclamation and enforcement of law do not, however, satisfy the conditions of a law being known and on the whole observed. To be aware of the general considerations which the law promulgates when choosing to act leaves undetermined 'what will count as an adequate or acceptable subscription in a contingent situation' (*OHC*, 130). There must be not only sanctions but a way of settling disputes about whether contingent compliances are faithful to the law. This is the office of adjudication related to a court of law. It is not merely a matter of applying laws to situations because all law is underdetermined in the sense that it does not specify 'how a prescribed norm of conduct stands in relation to a contingent situation' (*OHC*, 133). Like Hart and Dworkin, Oakeshott does not subscribe to 'rule scepticism' or legal pragmatism, which, in summary form, maintain that 'there is no law'[16] and that talk about rules is superfluous and disguises the fact that law is what arises from the decisions of the courts.[17] Oakeshott agrees that the conclusions reached in a court of law are not inherent in the law itself. But this does not mean that there is no law. Adjudications are amplifications of law, specifying what was unspecific in the general conditions which do not try to anticipate their relation to every contingent situation. Such amplifications are not merely the judges' subjective musings. They must necessarily make reference to the law, not as a deduction from or exemplification of it, but almost always as a novel illustration of it. The purpose of adjudication is to amplify the meaning of law as it relates to the specific contingent circumstances where it is invoked.

The amplification of the law by a judge makes the conclusions available for subsequent adjudications where they may be employed analogically to further contingent circumstances, and where these conclusions are deemed authoritative not only by subsequent adjudicators, but also by citizens who subscribe to the amplified considerations in choosing future conduct. It follows, for Oakeshott, that 'civil association is necessarily relationship in terms of the accumulated meanings of *lex* which emerge in the adjudication of disputes' (*OHC*, 137).

Recognition of the authority of rules and the deliberations concerning their desirability are, then, two distinct activities. Politics, understood as the deliberation of the desirability of the conditions of what Oakeshott calls *respublica*, must for him exclude certain types of consideration. Whereas proposals may arise from the substantive interests and desires of a group they must lose this self-interested character before acquiring the demeanour of a serious political proposal. The rules or amendments proposed have to be general and non-instrumental in nature, imposing no desired substantive purposes on the associates. Politics, to use his famous phrase, is a 'boundless and bottomless sea' with no ultimate end or final destination, whose purpose is to keep the ship afloat rather than steer it towards an imagined utopia (*RP*, 60). Politics is characterised by deliberation and argument, the purpose of which is to persuade others, especially those who have authority to make and alter law, of their merits. This is not to say that much else beside its ideal character as politics may grace itself with the title, and substantive ends may be proposed as a result of considering the desirability of the conditions of civil association. Such considerations extrinsic to political activity should not, however, be confused with it.

Civil association is an ideal character in terms of which we can understand the state, but it was never presented by Oakeshott as a comprehensive or complete account of the state. It is an attempt to legitimise the use of force by a state in morally justifiable terms appropriate to associates who have made no decision to join civil association. Nowhere in the practices of modern European states is civil association found undiluted by an alternative conception of their character.

– Enterprise Association –

Correlative with the emergence of the moral agent, or the individual accustomed to the responsibility of making moral choices, arose the anti-individual whose experience had ill-equipped him for the responsibility of moral action, and who longed for the life of the community in which decisions were made for him. In Oakeshott's view 'the "anti-individual" had feelings rather than thoughts, impulses rather than opinions, inabilities rather than passions, and was only dimly aware of his power' (*RP*, 370–1). Individuality and moral choice were revolted against in favour of conceptions of the common or public good. In this respect 'the morality of collectivism' was just as much a reaction to the disintegration of the morality of communal ties as was the morality of individualism (*MPME*, 24). In addition, however, the morality of collectivism is itself in part a reaction against the morality of individualism. The anti-individual is a person who generates an understanding of morality, rule and association commensurate with himself. Association understood as a framework of procedural and non-instrumental rules is completely inappropriate for the anti-individual incapable of sustaining an individual life for himself, and who requires his substantive goals and purposes to be chosen for him. Such a person can be accommodated only in a state understood on the analogy of *universitas* (*OHC*, 274).

The state on this understanding is a compulsory enterprise association whose associates are joined not in a moral but transactional or prudential relationship in the pursuit of common substantive goals, and in which the rules which govern the associates are instrumental to achieving the goals. On this understanding governing is a managerial activity. It is important at this point to draw out the political and moral implications because what is being contended is that such a form of association is a denial and perversion of the freedom and autonomy of the individual upon which human agency depends. This criticism is the implication of a distinction made in the first essay of *On Human Conduct*, and reiterated in his essay 'The Rule of Law' (*OH*, 119–64), in which Oakeshott distinguishes between transactional and practical relationships. In the former individuals pursue substantive benefits from the responses of those agents with whom they associate. Two or more people are related in terms of the pursuit of satisfying their current wants, and assembling power for the most efficient course of action instrumental to the desired end (*OH*, 121–3). Enterprise association is a transactional relationship in that it has a common substantive purpose and seeks to promote substantive goals and benefits through actions and language instrumental to achieving them. Such a relationship, Oakeshott contends, presupposes that it is chosen by the agent, and that should he or she no longer identify with the substantive goals pursued dissociate his or her own by a choice. Compulsion, then, is anathema to the very idea of a transactional relationship. Oakeshott argues that:

> enterprise association is necessarily constituted by the continuous choice of each associate to be related to others in terms of a common purpose, a choice from which he must be able to extricate himself. There is no such thing as collective choice. (*OHC*, 119)

A state which is necessarily a compulsory association conceived in terms of enterprise association therefore undermines the moral autonomy of its agents.[18] Enterprise association is, of course, constrained by moral considerations external to its purpose. Such rules are observed but they are not constitutive of the practice they govern. The instrumental rules of an enterprise association are constitutive of it and designed to better achieve its purpose. Unlike moral rules they can be changed at will and are readily adapted if they are deemed in any way to impede the joint purpose without altering its character as an enterprise association for mutual benefit.

Collectivism, the synonym for the state conceived as an enterprise association, may impose different goals upon society depending upon what preoccupations that society may have. It first appeared in early modern Europe in a religious version because it was believed that the purpose of human beings was to do the will of God and devote one's life to his glory. This was not new in itself. It was the belief that the proper function of government was to impose this exclusively upon its subjects and that it had the capacity and authority to do so which was new. This conception of the activity of government in collectivist terms, whether it be religious or secular Oakeshott calls the politics of faith. One version of this, the productivist, privileges productivity and the exploitation of resources. Oakeshott suggests that this might even be called the Baconian or technological version (*MPME*, 101 and

OH, 153) because he is essentially the 'chief architect of the politics of faith', particularly in this form (*PFPS*, 52 and 62). Bacon's understanding of the purpose of government was both redemptive and perfectionist (*PFPS*, 52–3). Bacon believed that, first, the proper preoccupation of human beings was the unlimited exploitation of natural resources. Secondly, he believed that perfection consisted in pursuing this goal to the limits of current knowledge. And third, he maintained that such an endeavour must be co-operative and was to be appropriately managed by government (*MPME*, 101–3). Marx, Oakeshott contends, offers us an extremely influential variant of the pro-ductivist version of collectivism in that: 'The fault of "capitalism" (or one of its faults) is recognised to be its inefficiency as a method of production; and the fault of *bourgeois* government is identified as its inability to organise the productive enterprise of mankind' (*MPME*, 106). Alternatively there is the welfare or distributivist version in which perfection is not seen to be the subordination of all human activity to production, but instead the equal share of each member of society of the products of human endeavour. Oakeshott is not suggesting that any of these versions with their central goals excluded other human activities, only that all other activities were subordinate to the central purpose which governments pursued. Nor was the emergence of each ever completely able to eradicate individualism.

The anti-individual who may be referred to collectively as the masses, not because of their numbers but because of their rejection of individuality and longing for the security of the community, required leaders who could direct him (*RP*, 370–4; *OHC*, 275–6). It is a conception of government driven by a desire to save mankind. It is the politics of redemption and salvation, which appears in various circumstantially related conditions. It is what Oakeshott earlier called the politics of faith as opposed to the politics of scepticism, and like rationalism, which is its more familiar name in Oakeshott's writings, it believes in the certainty of its conclusions and the possibility of perfection (*PFPS*, 26–7).

Leading or managing the masses requires a different mode of political dis-course from that appropriate to ruling *cives*. The masses as an audience for political discourse are ill-suited to the non-demonstrative kind of discourse. Here persuasion adopts the guise of purported demonstration, which in the modern era has frequently taken the form of 'scientific proof' (*RP*, 82). The leader purports to prove the correctness of political proposals with reference to 'indisputable' axioms from which they can be deduced, or scientific laws of which the proposals are said to be instances.

It is Oakeshott's famous Rationalist who epitomises the leader of the masses. The Rationalist mistakenly believes that all practical knowledge can be abjured in favour of the technical knowledge acquired by the exercise of pure practical reason. Politics for the Rationalist is a problem-solving activity, the solutions to which are capable of demonstrative certainty. Politics is capable of perfection in that right answers are attainable, and diversity is discouraged on the ground that there can be only one right answer to a problem. The Rationalist is preoccupied with certainty and believes in the sovereignty of 'reason', which means for him the sovereignty of technique. The Rationalist equates politics with social engineering and devises plans or rules instrumental to achieving the substantive goals he has set.

Oakeshott contends, however, that the rationalist is under a fundamental misapprehension about the nature of human knowledge and its relation to political activity. What the rationalist purports to do is impossible. All concrete activity entails a combination of technical and practical knowledge. Technical knowledge is the distillation of an activity into a body of technical rules. Practical knowledge, unlike rules, cannot be taught and instead has to be imparted. Politics cannot simply be the application of technical knowledge to political problems, but must by necessity be combined with the practical knowledge inherent in the social practices of a society.

The state understood as an enterprise association whose laws are instrumental in achieving the substantive goals for which the associates are joined together in a common purpose, embodies a fundamental contradiction which undermines and compromises the moral freedom of the individual. Oakeshott contends that enterprise association is not by its very nature particularly 'free'. An element of choice regarding responses to contingent situations is certainly allowed, but is severely restricted by the purpose to be pursued: 'conduct here is either correct or incorrect' (*OHC*, 248). It is the choice to associate with or dissociate oneself from the common enterprise which constitutes the freedom in this mode of activity, and therefore 'to make enterprise association compulsory would be to deprive an agent of that "freedom" or "autonomy" which is the condition of agency' (*OHC*, 181). The alternative to understanding the state as a civil association is to see it as a compulsory enterprise association and thus to divest the associates of their 'freedom': 'the member of such a state enjoys the composure of the conscript assured of his dinner. His "freedom" is warm, compensated servility' (*OHC*, 317).

Enterprise association Oakeshott clearly regards as a mischaracterisation of the state because it is a denial of the essential moral basis of the civil association and offers a prudential rather than a moral justification for political obligation. To understand the state purely in terms of enterprise association is to miss the fundamental ambivalence at once representing the two voices of enterprise and civil association, however faint a whisper the latter might be.

What Oakeshott has attempted to do is to purge our understanding of the state in terms of civil association of any substantive economic considerations which have from time to time been invoked to recommend the degree and scope of state activity, whether it is invoked on the side of the interventionist, or minimalist. Understanding civil association is not a matter of equating it, as Nozick does, with the minimalist state, this is merely to confuse the degree of state activity with the kind. It is the mode, not the degree of state activity which concerns Oakeshott. Civil association is a distinct mode of understanding the modern European state from which nothing can be deduced about the amount of state activity permissible: it specifies only the type of activity permissible. Here he is at variance with Hayek who justifies minimal state activity on substantive economic grounds. Hayek is concerned to explore, as Marx did, the economic constituents of what it is to be human, whereas Oakeshott is always concerned to identify the specifically moral character of being human. Prosperity may be a contingent consequence of civil association but it cannot be the ground for recommending it, because such recommendation would actually prescribe a different form of association (RP, 457).

– SOCIAL JUSTICE –

In the above respect there can be no place in the understanding of a state as civil association for a theory of distributive justice. Distributive justice requires a substantive end to be posited and imposed, with rules which are instrumental to its attainment, and these are features alien to civil association and more at home with enterprise association (OHC, 153, f.n. 1). Oakeshott's political philosophy in emphasising the formal, non-instrumental character of the laws of civil association is considerably at variance with much modern political philosophy which focuses on distributive justice, or multiculturalism and the role of the state in rectifying inequalities resulting from multi-national and ethnic relations. Both Rawls and Ackerman, for example, on the surface look as if they avoid characterising the state as an enterprise association in emphasising the procedural nature of their theories of justice. For Rawls the assumption is that rules or principles which result from a fair procedure in which the right has priority over the good must be just. In place of fairness, and building upon Rawls, Ackerman contends that laws or principles must be neutral in relation to competing notions of the good. Proposals for public policies based on the superiority of the idea of the good subscribed to by the proposer are ruled out by Ackerman's principle of neutrality. Neutrality is justified on the liberal assumption of the intrinsic value of human autonomy. This means not having a conception of the good imposed upon oneself, but choosing it freely even if that choice proves to be personally disastrous. People should be free to make their own mistakes.[19] Both Rawls and Ackerman, however, equate the authority or legitimacy of laws with the justice of their consequences or outcomes. In other words they fail to distinguish between the questions of authority and desirability. A law is both authoritative and desirable if it has complied with a fair procedure or is neutral between conceptions of the good and is therefore just in relation to the distribution of scarce resources. Rawls's difference principle, for example, requiring that social and economic inequalities are designed to conduce to the greatest benefit of the least advantaged, posits a substantive outcome as the measure of the justness of laws instrumental to achieving it.[20] Oakeshott refuses, save in a footnote, to consider contemporary theories of justice such as those of Rawls and Ackerman because:

> They identify *jus* as a consideration of 'fairness' in the distribution of scarce resources, and 'fairness' as what rational competitors, in certain ideal circumstances, must agree is an equitable distribution. Here, *lex*, if it exists at all, is composed of regulations understood in terms of the consequences of their operation and as guides to the achievement of a substantive state of affairs.   (*OHC*, 156, f.n. 13)

Besides employing the contractarian mode of analysis which is the language of enterprise association and anathema to the idea of a civil association, Rawls characterises his project in *A Theory of Justice* in terms which although procedural posit a substantive purpose towards the achievement of which laws and principles are instrumental. Society for him 'is a cooperative venture for mutual advantage'.[21] Individuals thus associated are not indifferent to the distribution of the greater benefits which are the product of their cooperation. Rawls argues that principles are required which discriminate between differing institutional and social arrangements which determine the distribution of advantages, and which more or less guarantee the pattern agreed by the associates. These are the principles of social justice. Rawls is not, however, typically a theorist of justice as mutual advantage in that his individuals are not solely motivated by rational self-interest. Brian Barry claims Rawls as a theorist of justice as impartiality where the principle of fairness is translated into a motivating desire for formulating the rules and principles which provide the basis for reasonable agreements. This is what Barry calls second order impartiality, which needs to be distinguished from the requirement to behave impartially that is incorporated into injunctive rules or precepts, and may be termed first order impartiality. At the first order level behaving impartially means motivation free of 'private considerations'.[22] Barry suggests that rules and principles of impartiality capable of attracting reasonable agreement at the first order level do not necessarily require universal precepts of impartial behaviour at the second. Some areas require universal impartiality, some allow differing levels of discretion and some are completely discretionary. Because there cannot be certainty in the ultimate value of any conception of the good, justice as impartiality has to be capable of mediating between them while not privileging any one, while at the same time providing the grounds for mutually acceptable accommodation of competing conceptions of the good. In other words, a theory of justice must provide the basis for exercising restraint in the pursuit of one's conception of the good. An adequate theory of justice, Barry contends, has to answer the questions, what are the motives for behaving justly? What are the criteria for a just set of rules? And, demonstrate how the answers to these two questions are related. Finding both justice as mutual advantage, and justice as reciprocity, which is ultimately reduced to the first, internally contradictory and incapable of giving consistent answers to the questions, the answers given by justice as impartiality are that the motive to act is a desire to behave fairly, and the 'criterion of just rules and institutions is that they should be fair … The answer to the third question is that the two fit together perfectly.'[23]

On Oakeshott's postulates of civil association, even this characterisation of justice as impartiality would fail to meet the qualifying criteria. First it is couched in the language of social contract in which the contractees reach reasonable agreement about second order principles of justice. What drives Barry's project is a commitment to liberal egalitarianism and a just distribution of wealth from which, on the basis of the principles reasonably agreed, no one could reasonably dissent. In other words, like Rawls and Ackerman, Barry posits a substantive outcome, based on the principle of fairness, as the criterion of the justness of the first order precepts, having complied with the procedures of the second order principles of impartiality. The precepts or laws are instrumental in the redistribution of wealth according to what has reasonably been agreed by the associates. Ultimately the authority of the laws rests on their desirability, the criterion of which is their effectiveness as instruments in a just redistribution of wealth.

Oakeshott's refusal to address modern theories of social justice may be better illustrated with reference to David Gauthier, not because he sees the state as enterprise association but because he fails to see it as anything else. Gauthier contends that if the state, or society, is to be rationally supported by its members it must be characterised as 'a cooperative venture for mutual advantage … based on principles of expected–utility maximisation'.[24] Individuals in Rawls's state of nature are ignorant of their abilities and the benefits they may be capable of commanding. The agreements reached cannot genuinely be said to be a result of bargaining because technically they have nothing to bargain with. Furthermore what they are deciding upon are principles which determine the just distribution of the cooperative product.

In Gauthier's state of nature, on the other hand, individuals are aware of their talents, their individual productive capacities, and the increase that may occur as a result of cooperation. Each person is entitled to what he or she could produce individually. No one would agree to constraints on their behaviour if they were to be worse off as a result of cooperation. The assumption is that each person will attempt to maximise his or her utility as a result of social cooperation. It is not a utilitarian theory, because utilitarianism could justify some individuals being worse off as a result of cooperation as long as the total utility and greatest happiness is maximised. Justice as mutual advantage assumes there is equal rationality in that each person will have a consistent set of preferences, and that no one will be worse off by cooperating with others. They have no pre-social sense of justice or morality. Having knowledge of their attributes and talents individuals are able to bargain over a 'just' share of the social product commensurate with what they contribute. What is being bargained for, then, is the cooperative surplus. The bargaining outcome will be one in which the grounds for complaint are minimised, these grounds being the relative concessions each individual makes. Each individual will be seeking to make the minimum–maximum relative concession in accepting constraints on the pursuit of his or her conception of the good in order to maximise utility. The aim is to convert one's capacity or strength into personal advantage. Gauthier is arguing that it is rational to desist from being a straight utility maximiser and to become a constrained maximiser by accepting constraints on one's behaviour. It is an instrumental theory of rationality in which the distinction between prudential and moral reasoning is denied. The question of what it is in my interest to do and what I ought to do are one and the same. Apart from the fact that this is a theory of social justice which excludes the very people, such as the handicapped and dis-advantaged, from a claim on the social surplus because they have nothing to bargain with, and which would convert most of social welfare into charity supererogatory to moral obligations, it is essentially a theory that conceives justice in economic terms. The principle of minimax relative concession appears appropriate only to a theory of distributive justice, and the morality of which he speaks is instrumental purely in terms of the distribution of goods. In Oakeshottian terms, then, Gauthier is a theorist of enterprise association. It is a voluntary association whose laws and morality are instrumental in achieving the substantive goal of maximising individual utility; the justice of the laws or constraints is therefore measured against their capacity to deliver the desired end. Under the guise of morality it is effectively an exploration of the economic character of human beings, blind to the broader considerations of both justice understood as just procedures and just treatment, and to morality which is a consideration in conduct but not a determinant of it. It is a conception of morality that cannot account for human actions which cannot be reduced to utility maximisation.

– CONCLUSION –

The historical efficacy of Oakeshott's ideal characters may leave a lot to be desired. Indeed, his accounts of the rise of the individual are caricatures of the transformations which Michelet and Burckhardt tried to capture in their accounts of the flourishing of the renaissance man freed from the stultifying constraints of the 'dark ages', and such fanciful poetic imagery in character-ising the past has long commanded the disapproval of historians, and certainly falls far short of subscription to the postulates of history as Oakeshott himself identified them. Such licence may be permissible in philosophical history, but we are nowhere told, except by exemplification, what this entails.

Because philosophy is not itself a substantive voice in the conversation of mankind in that it does not make, recommend or circumscribe its subject, Oakeshott is compelled to demonstrate the authenticity of his ideal characters by tracing their emergence and development in European history. This is the point in Oakeshott's order of enquiry which is the most ambiguous. In his accounts of the emergence of the famous 'rationalist', of 'mass man', and of demonstrative political discourse, for example, we get highly selective, severely foreshortened and over-schematic accounts of identities which are deemed to have come into existence and changed over time. It is apparent, however, that these accounts do not by any stretch of the imagination satisfy the criteria, nor subscribe to the practices, which Oakeshott has identified as the differentiae of the historical mode of enquiry.

Even though Oakeshott frequently refers to 'European history' and declares that he proposes 'to engage in a piece of historical description' (*RP*, 365. Cf. *OHC*, 185), what he offers is something quite different. In *The Politics of Faith and the Politics of Scepticism* he declares that the type of exercise in which he engages, a manner of enquiry persistently invoked in his subsequent writings, is not strictly speaking historical because while it is a study of change it does not concern itself with the mediation of change in which the historian is primarily interested (*PFPS*, 19). He wrote this in 1952 and it was posthumously published. One may therefore legitimately say that such a denial on Oakeshott's part may only have been tentative and even mistaken. He does, however, make a similar confession in his characterisation of the rationalist:

> The ambition of the historian is to escape that gross abridgement of the process which gives the new shape a too early or too late and a too precise definition,

and to avoid the false emphasis which springs from being over-impressed by the moment of unmistakable emergence. Yet that moment must have a dominating interest for those whose ambitions are not pitched so high.   (*RP*, 18)

One may say that what he actually offers us is a philosophical past, or philosophical history. The problem is that Oakeshott's view of philosophy, or unconditional theorising, does not easily accommodate this philosophical past. Oakeshott has extensively discussed the practical and historical pasts, how they are evoked, and how they differ from each other. The past does not itself exist. It is a postulate or presupposition of the activities to which it is related, and in this respect it is conditional. Philosophy or theorising is distinguished by its determination to pursue unconditional knowledge, and to remain dissatisfied with all that is conditional. Strictly speaking there cannot be a philosophical past without renouncing the commitment to unconditionality. This is not to say that there cannot be a history of philosophy, just as there can be a history of science, but the point is that such histories cannot be philosophy or science. What I am suggesting is this: the past which Oakeshott invokes in his philosophical enquiries cannot itself be intrinsic to the activity of philosophising, and either belongs to a determinate mode of conditional understanding or it is nothing. Because philosophy cannot begin *de novo* there must be some conception of what philosophers have done before, and because philosophical enquiry must begin with everyday conceptions, not to extend but to transform their meanings, it is obvious that philosophy cannot be related to the practical or historical pasts because philosophical conclusions must stand on their own feet and cannot be authenticated with reference to non-philosophical criteria.

The philosophical past, one can infer from the little that Oakeshott says about it, is one whose pastness is of little consequence. The present–past relation indicative of historical enquiry, and the present–future relation integral to practical life are absent from philosophy. The past in philosophy is 'philosophically conceived, seen as a living, extemporary whole in which past and present are comparatively insignificant'.[25] We should not be deluded into thinking, then, that the ideal characters which Oakeshott distils from European history have anything to do with history at all: they are philosophical constructions, philosophically conceived and presented 'on the analogy of human history' (*HCA*, 7). In this respect Paul Franco is quite wrong to suggest that Oakeshott's critique of rationalism owes 'as much to historical experience as to anything else'.[26] If it is the case that Oakeshott uses history as a critique, then he stands convicted of the most insidious of logical infelicities, namely irrelevance. History is a disinterested activity seeking to know the past for its own sake, and is incapable of confirming or denying the conclusions reached in any other mode (*OH*, 2).

Notwithstanding their ambivalent theoretical character, Oakeshott's two modes of association, related to each other as polar opposites and sweet enemies, whose mutual implication is circumstantial rather than logical, must stand as the most fruitful candidates in terms of which to explore the relation between the citizen and political society. Oakeshott's political philosophy, grounded in a sophisticated and fully articulated theory of interpretation, stands at the forefront of the modern revival of interest in citizenship and civil society, and points the way to liberating ourselves from the ossified contemporary political vocabulary whose well-worn clichés serve to obscure rather than illuminate the obligations of the citizen in the modern world. The force of his argument, however, is considerably detracted from by his refusal to acknowledge, except parenthetically, or address directly the current preoccupations of modern political philosophers. In this respect he is very different from most of his British Idealist predecessors who felt it necessary to dispel any misapprehensions perpetrated by so-called *philosophes* or theoreticians upon the unsuspecting masses. They had little regard, for example, for Herbert Spencer either as a scientist or philosopher, but they nevertheless recognised that his ideas about the state, which they thought a gross mischaracterisation, were both insidious and socially divisive.

– NOTES –

The following abbreviations will be used in parentheses in the text for these works by Oakeshott:

EM   *Experience and Its Modes* (Cambridge, Cambridge University Press, 1933)

RP   *Rationalism in Politics*, new and expanded edition (Indianapolis, Liberty Press, 1991: first edn, 1963)

OHC   *On Human Conduct* (Oxford, Clarendon Press, 1975)

HCA   *Hobbes on Civil Association* (Oxford, Blackwell, 1975)

OH   *On History and Other Essays* (Oxford, Blackwell, 1983)

MPME   *Morality and Politics in Modern Europe* (New Haven, Yale University Press, 1993: Harvard lectures delivered in 1958)

PFPS   *The Politics of Faith and the Politics of Scepticism* (New Haven, Yale University Press, 1996: probably completed in about 1953)

1. This chapter draws freely upon, modifies with reference to posthumously published works and greatly extends some aspects of David Boucher, 'Politics in a Different Mode: An Appreciation of Michael Oakeshott 1901–1990', *History of Political Thought*, XII (1991), 717–28.
2. Also see Michael Oakeshott, 'The Concept of a Philosophical Jurisprudence', *Politica*, 3 (1938), 204.
3. For discussions of the relations among the modes and between the modes and the whole see David Boucher, 'Overlap and Autonomy: the Different Worlds of Collingwood and Oakeshott', *Storia*, 4 (1979) and 'Human Conduct, History and Social Science in the Writings of Collingwood and Oakeshott', *New Literary History*, 24 (1993).

4. See Richard Rorty's contribution to the discussion in *Review of Metaphysics*, 34 (1980), 52.

5. Richard Rorty, *Philosophy and the Mirror of Nature* (Oxford, Blackwell, 1980), 12. Cf. 163.

6. Onora O'Neill, *Towards Justice and Virtue: A Constructive Account of Practical Reasoning* (Cambridge, Cambridge University Press, 1996), 40.

7. Onora O'Neill, 'Abstraction, Idealization and Ideology in Ethics', *Moral Philosophy and Contemporary Problems*, ed. J. D. G. Evans (Cambridge, Cambridge University Press, 1987), 56.

8. For Oakeshott's theory of history see David Boucher, 'The Creation of the Past: British Idealism and Michael Oakeshott's Philosophy of History', *History and Theory*, 23 (1984).

9. Oakeshott's view is at variance with that of H. L. A. Hart on this point. In his important 1958 article on the separation of law and morals Hart reads both Austin and Bentham as subscribing to a distinction between legality and desirability. H. L. A. Hart, 'Positivism and the Separation of Law and Morals', *Harvard Law Review*, 71 (1958).

10. H. L. A. Hart, 'Are There Any Natural Rights?' in *Human Rights*, ed. A. I. Melden (Belmont, CA, Wadsworth Publishing, 1970), 70.

11. Hart, 'Are There Any Natural Rights?', 70.

12. Hart, 'Are There Any Natural Rights?', 61.

13. John Gray, 'Oakeshott on Law, Liberty and Civil Association', in *Liberalisms: Essays in Political Philosophy* (London, Routledge, 1989), 199.

14. H. L. A. Hart, *The Concept of Law* (Oxford, Clarendon Press, 1994: 2nd edn).

15. Lon Fuller, *The Morality of Law* (New Haven, CT, Yale University Press, 1972: rev. edn), 176.

16. Ronald Dworkin, *Law's Empire* (London, Fontana, 1986), 430n. See especially Chapter 5, 'Pragmatism and Personification'. Also see Hart, *The Concept of Law*, 136.

17. In an oblique allusion to Dworkin, Oakeshott seems to associate him with something close to rule scepticism. In insisting upon the categorical distinction between deliberation in the adjudication of law and deliberation in making it he refers to the 'Dworkinesque judge [who] usurps the office of the legislator' (*OH*, 145, f.n. 6).

18. This point is well made by Paul Franco, *The Political Philosophy of Michael Oakeshott* (New Haven, CT, Yale University Press, 1980), 180–1. This is also an emphasis to be found in Bruce Haddock, 'Michael Oakeshott: *Rationalism in Politics*' in *The Political Classics: Green to Dworkin*, ed. M. Forsyth and M. Keens-Soper (Oxford, Oxford University Press, 1996).

19. Bruce Ackerman, *Social Justice and the Liberal State* (New Haven, CT, Yale University Press, 1980), 370.

20. John Rawls, *A Theory of Justice* (Oxford, Oxford University Press, 1970), 302.

21. Rawls, *Theory of Justice*, 4.

22. Brian Barry, *Justice as Impartiality* (Oxford, Clarendon Press, 1995), 11. It should be noted that Barry concentrates almost wholly on Rawls's *Theory of Justice* because he does not subscribe to the principle that what comes later must be better. He thinks Rawls' *Political Liberalism* (New York, Columbia University Press, 1993) far inferior to *Theory of Justice*.

23. Barry, *Justice as Impartiality*, 51.

24. David Gauthier, 'Justice as Social Choice', in *Social Contract Theory*, ed. Michael Lessnoff (Oxford, Blackwell, 1990), 211. Cf. 201. Also see David Gauthier, *Morals by Agreement* (Oxford, Clarendon Press, 1986), 10–13. Gauthier gives a slightly different emphasis in 'The Social Contract As Ideology', *Philosophy and Public Affairs*, 6 (1977), 130–64.

25. Oakeshott, 'Concept of a Philosophical Jurisprudence', 359.

26. Franco, *Political Philosophy of Michael Oakeshott*, 125.

Biographical Materials

– T. H. Green –

T. H. Green was born at Birkin, the West Riding of Yorkshire on 7 April 1836. His father Valentine Green was an evangelical rector, the son of a squire from Leicestershire. Green's mother, who died when he was one year old, was the daughter of Edward Thomas Vaughan, a vicar in Leicester. Green was distantly related to Cromwell and held a great admiration for his place in English constitutional history. In 1850 he went to Rugby school where he was undistinguished in his educational attainment. He went up to Balliol College in 1855 where he gained a second class in classical moderations. Spurred on by a sense of failure and the stimulus of Benjamin Jowett and Charles Parker he gained a first class in *literae humaniores*. He became a Fellow of Balliol in 1860, and was re-elected in 1872, shortly after marrying Charlotte Symonds in 1871. In 1864 he was unsuccessful in his application for the chair of Moral Philosophy at St Andrews. He received a LL.D. from Glasgow University in 1875, and was appointed Whyte's Professor of Moral Philosophy at Oxford in 1878.

For parts of 1865 and 1866 Green discharged his duties as an assistant commissioner appointed under the terms of reference of the royal commission of 1864 to enquire into educational provision for the middle class in England. Green was a radical on most of the important issues of his day. He was a champion of the North against slavery in the American Civil War and actively supported educational, parliamentary and social reform (including liquor legislation). He was a personal inspiration to many leading reformers including Asquith, Alfred Milner, Charles Gore and Scott Holland. In 1876 he was elected to Oxford Town Council. On 15 March 1882 he was taken seriously ill with blood poisoning. He died on 26 March and is buried in St Sepulchre's cemetery, North Oxford.

Biographical: R. L. Nettleship, 'Memoir' in *Works of Thomas Hill Green* (London, Longmans Green, 1888); J. H. Muirhead, 'Thomas Hill Green 1832–1882', in *Great Democrats*, ed. A. Barrat Brown (London, 1934); Alan P. F. Sell, *Philosophical Idealism and Christian Belief* (Cardiff, University of Wales Press, 1995).

Principal writings: *Prolegomena to Ethics* (Oxford, Clarendon Press, 1883); *The Works of Thomas Hill Green*, ed. R. L. Nettleship, 3 vols (London, Longmans Green, 1885–8). A new reprint of *The Works of T. H. Green* has been published by Thoemmes Press (1997), edited by Peter Nicholson. A fifth volume of materials has been added.

– F. H. BRADLEY –

Francis Herbert Bradley was born in Clapham, London, on 30 January 1846 to Emma Linton, the second wife of a clergyman Charles Bradley, the father of twenty-two children in two marriages. The family moved to Cheltenham in 1854 and Bradley went to Cheltenham College, Marlborough School and University College, Oxford, where in 1867 he was awarded first class in classical moderations, and in 1869 second class in *literae humaniores*. In 1870 he became a life Fellow of Merton College, on condition, with which he complied, that he remained a bachelor. He took little part in the intellectual life of Oxford after 1871 because of severe ill health. He became more and more reclusive as he grew older, but he played his part in College administration. In the winters he travelled on the continent for the benefit of his health and became a close friend of Miss E. Radcliff, to whom he wrote nearly every day. He dedicated *Appearance and Reality*, *Essays in Truth and Reality*, and the second edition of *The Principles of Logic* to her. He was also a friend of the famous novelist Elinor Glynn whose novel *Halcyone* includes a character, Cheiron, based on Bradley. He was the recipient of many awards, including an honorary doctorate from Glasgow University in 1883, membership of the Royal Danish Academy in 1922, an honorary fellowship of the British Academy in 1923, and the Order of Merit in 1924. He died of blood poisoning in 1924.

Biographical: A. E. Taylor, 'Francis Herbert Bradley, 1846–1924', *Proceedings of the British Academy*, xi (1924–5); G. R. G. Mure, 'F. H. Bradley: Towards a Portrait', *Encounter*, xvi (1961); A. E. Taylor, 'Bradley, Francis Herbert', *Dictionary of National Biography 1922–1930*.

Principal writings: included *Ethical Studies* (London, King, 1876); *The Principles of Logic* (London, Oxford University Press, 1833: 2nd edn 1922); *Appearance and Reality* (London, Oxford University Press, 1893: 2nd edn 1897); *Essays on Truth and Reality* (Oxford, Clarendon Press, 1914); *Collected Essays* (Oxford, Clarendon Press, 1935). Thoemmes has also published Bradley's collected works in twelve volumes (1999), edited by W. J. Mander and C. A. Keene.

– BERNARD BOSANQUET –

Bernard Bosanquet was born on 14 June 1848 at Rock Hall, the family estate, near Alnwick, Northumberland, the youngest of the five sons of Rev. Robert William Bosanquet, four of whom were to his second wife Caroline Macdowall. He was educated at Harrow and Balliol College, Oxford where he gained firsts in classical moderations (1868) and *literae humaniores* (1870). As an undergraduate he was greatly influenced by Jowett and Green. Green thought him one of the ablest men of his generation. From 1870 to 1881 he was a fellow of University College. He did not find Oxford much to his liking and went instead to live in London where he became a prominent figure in the activities of The London Ethical Society and the Charity Organization Society (COS), of which he became chairman of the Council in 1916. He married Helen Dendy in 1895, a fellow worker at the COS, and later to serve on the Poor Law Commission of 1906. Bosanquet was President of the Aristotelian Society from 1894–8. In 1903 he succeeded D. G. Ritchie in the chair of Logic, Rhetoric, and Metaphysics at the University of St Andrews where he stayed until 1908, when he returned to Oxshott (where he had bought a house in 1899) in order to devote his energies to writing. He delivered the Gifford Lectures at Edinburgh in 1911 and 1912. The Bosanquets remained at Oxshott until moving to Hampstead shortly before his death in 1923. With Green and Bradley, Bosanquet was one of the three leading figures in the school of Idealism. He was, with Henry Jones, one of the most Hegelian thinkers among the British Idealists, and a prolific writer on all aspects of philosophy and politics.

Biographical: A. D. Lindsay, *Dictionary of National Biography 1922–30*; A. C. Bradley and R. B. Haldane, 'Bernard Bosanquet (1848–1923)', *Proceedings and the British Academy*, x (1921–3); J. H. Muirhead, 'Bernard Bosanquet', *Mind*, xxxii (1923); Helen Bosanquet, *Bernard Bosanquet: A Short Account of His Life* (London, Macmillan, 1924); J. H. Muirhead (ed.), *Bernard Bosanquet and his Friends* (London, Allen and Unwin, 1935).

Principal writings: included (ed.), *Aspects of the Social Problem* (1895); *The Philosophical Theory of the State* (1899); *The Civilisation of Christendom* (London, Swan Sonnenschein, 1899); *The Principle of Individuality and Value* (1912); *The Value and Destiny of the Individual* (1913); *Social and International Ideals: Being Studies in Patriotism* (1917); *Some Suggestions in Ethics* (1918). All published by Macmillan London. The *Collected Works of Bernard Bosanquet* have been published by Thoemmes Press in twenty volumes, edited by William Sweet (1999).

– DAVID G. RITCHIE –

David George Ritchie was born in Jedburgh, Scotland, on 26 October 1853, into a cultured family which included among its number academics and clergymen. He was the only son of three children born to George Ritchie and Elizabeth Bradfute Dudgeon. His father was the parish minister, elected as Moderator to the general assembly of the Church of Scotland in 1870. There were family connections with the Carlyles and in 1889 Ritchie edited the *Early Letters of Jane Welsh Carlyle*. He was educated at Jedburgh Academy, and entered Edinburgh University in 1869 where he was introduced to philosophy by Campbell Fraser and Henry Calderwood. While at Edinburgh he attended a botany class which stimulated a lifelong interest that was to find expression in his ethical and political writings. His main subject was classics in which he graduated with first class honours in 1875. He then went to Balliol College, Oxford, where he gained a first in classical moderations (1875) and in the 1878 final Greats examinations. In the same year he became a Fellow of Jesus College, and in 1881 was made a lecturer in classics, a position which he also held at Balliol from 1882–6. While at Oxford he was influenced by both T. H. Green and Arnold Toynbee. Ritchie was unsuccessful in his application for the chair of Logic, Rhetoric and Metaphysics at St Andrews in 1891 against Henry Jones and W. R. Sorley. Sorley lost out by one vote to Jones and went on to chairs at Cardiff, Aberdeen and Cambridge (where he influenced the young Michael Oakeshott). When Jones left St Andrew's in 1894 Ritchie was appointed to that chair. He was awarded an honorary LL.D. by Edinburgh University in 1898, and in 1898–9 he was president of the Aristotelian Society.

Ritchie married twice, the first time to Flora Lindsay Macdonnell in 1881, who gave birth to a daughter. She was a politically minded activist who was Secretary of the Oxford Women's Liberal Association. In 1889, the year after Flora died, he married Ellen S. Haycraft with whom he had a son. Ellen was a Fabian socialist and successful novelist. She was also the sister of John Berry Haycraft, a physiologist who wrote on evolution and questions of race. Ritchie died after a short illness on 3 February 1903 at St Andrews, where he is buried.

Biographical: E. S. Haldane, 'Ritchie, David George (1853–1903)', *Dictionary of National Biography 1901–1911*; Robert Latter, 'Memoir' in *Philosophical Studies* by David D. Ritchie (London, Macmillan, 1905).

Principal writings: *Darwinism and Politics* (1889); *The Principles of State Interference* (1891);

Darwin and Hegel with other philosophical studies (1893); *Natural Rights* (1894); *Studies in Political and Social Ethics* (1902). All published by Sonnenschein in London. Ritchie's *Collected Works* have been recently published by Thoemmes Press (1998), edited by Peter Nicholson.

– HENRY JONES –

Henry Jones was born on 30 November 1852 at Llangernyw, Denbighshire, the third son of Elias Jones, a shoemaker, and Elizabeth Williams, who were Calvinistic Methodists, the denomination in which Henry Jones later became a registered minister. He left school at twelve years of age to follow his father's trade. He continued his education by working through the night and sleeping for only four hours. He succeeded in winning a scholarship to Bangor Normal teacher training college in 1870, and became the headmaster of the Ironworks School at Brynammam, South Wales, in 1873. He then won a scholarship to study at Glasgow University in 1875 where he came under the influence of Edward Caird and John Nicol. They persuaded him to give up his religious aspirations and to concentrate upon philosophy, a subject for which Jones had a natural aptitude. Although he followed their advice, he nevertheless transposed the style of the Welsh preacher onto Idealism. He saw no useful distinction to be made between philosophy, religion and poetry, and like Caird, seasons his philosophical essays with poetic quotations. On graduating with first class honours Jones won the Clark fellowship which enabled him to study for four more years, the bulk of which were spent in Glasgow. In 1882 he married Annie Walker and was appointed to a lectureship at University College, Aberystwyth, which he lost after crossing swords with the Principal. In 1884 he became Professor of Philosophy and Political Economy in the newly established University College of North Wales, Bangor. He was treated rather badly in Wales, mainly because of his unorthodox religious views. Intellectually he felt much more at home in Scotland, where he returned in 1891 to take up the chair of Logic, Rhetoric and Metaphysics at St Andrews. In 1894 he succeeded to Caird's chair of Moral Philosophy at Glasgow, beating John Watson and David George Ritchie in the competition.

In 1904 he was elected a Fellow of the British Academy and was honoured with doctorates from the University of St Andrews and the University of Wales. He was knighted in 1912 and became a Companion of Honour a few weeks before his death in 1922. He was also Hibbert lecturer at Manchester College, Oxford, for many years, and in 1908 delivered a series of lectures at Sydney University which was published as *Idealism as a Practical Creed*. He was the Gifford Lecturer at Glasgow University in 1920 and 1921.

Jones believed passionately in the responsibility of university professors to give moral guidance to the general community. He took a lead in establishing and supporting the University Settlement in Glasgow, and the Civic Society devoted to promoting the better understanding of widely opposing views. He was also committed to forging links between the University and business, and of getting businessmen to acknowledge their responsibilities to the broader community. He campaigned vigorously in Wales and Scotland for educational reform, including university education for women. He served on Haldane's Royal Commission of 1916–17 into the University of Wales. He was a strong supporter of the federal structure of the University of Wales and was instrumental in preventing moves to establish the autonomy of the constituent colleges. He was a member of the Universities Mission to America in 1918. During the war he campaigned on behalf of the Parliamentary Recruitment Committee throughout Wales in an attempt to quell syndicalist opposition from miners in Merthyr and North Wales slate quarrymen.

Jones endured a great deal of personal tragedy, but his optimism and faith in God were never shaken. Two of his six children died young, and a third was taken prisoner of war in Turkey. A fourth was killed in France during the First World War. After a prolonged and painful battle against mouth cancer he died on 4 February 1922. He is buried in the churchyard at Kilbride, the Isle of Bute.

Biographical: Henry Jones, *Old Memories*, ed. Thomas Jones (London, Hodder and Stoughton, 1922); J. H. Muirhead, 'Sir Henry Jones', *Proceeding of the British Academy*, x (1921–3); H. J. W. Hetherington, *The Life and Letters of Sir Henry Jones* (London, Hodder and Stoughton, 1924); H. J. W. Hetherington, 'Jones, Henry 1852–1922', *Dictionary of National Biography 1921–1931*; *The Times*, 6 February 1922; *John O'London's Weekly*, 11 March 1922; *Western Mail*, 6 February 1922; Leonard Russell, 'Sir Henry Jones', *Mind*, xxxi (1922); David Boucher and Andrew Vincent, *A Radical Hegelian: the Political and Social Philosophy of Henry Jones* (Cardiff, University of Wales Press, 1993), ch. 1.

Principal writings: *Browning as a Philosophical and Religions Teacher* (Glasgow, Maclehose, 1891); *The Philosophy of Lotze* (Glasgow, Maclehose, 1895); *Idealism as a Practical Creed* (Glasgow, Maclehose, 1909); *The Working Faith of the Social Reformer* (London, Macmillan, 1910); *The Principles of Citizenship* (London, Macmillan, 1919); *A Faith That Enquires* (London, Macmillan, 1922).

– ROBIN G. COLLINGWOOD –

R. G. Collingwood was born on 22 February 1889 at Cartmel Fell, Lancashire. He was educated up to the age of thirteen by his father, W. G. Collingwood, and his mother Dorothy. W. G. was an accomplished author, painter and archaeologist in his own right, and Dorothy was a talented artist, as were Collingwood's sisters. Robin Collingwood was then sent to Rugby public school where he was obviously ill at ease. In 1908 he followed his father in becoming a student at University College, Oxford, where he showed great academic aptitude. Upon obtaining his first class honours in *literae humaniores* 1912 he was elected to a fellowship at Pembroke College. He became a university lecturer in philosophy and Roman history, between 1927 and 1935, and remained on the university faculty until 1935, with the exception of 1914–18 when he served with his father in the intelligence department of the Admiralty, specialising in Luxemburg and Belgium. Collingwood had a considerable reputation as a brilliant lecturer. He was elected as a fellow of the British Academy in 1934. In 1935 he was appointed to the Waynflete professorship of Metaphysical Philosophy at Magdalen College, on the retirement of one of the lesser Idealists, J. A. Smith, who was influential in introducing the ideas of the Italian Idealists into Great Britain. Collingwood resigned his chair in 1941 on grounds of ill health. He began to suffer from high blood pressure in 1931 and went on to suffer a series of strokes that was eventually to incapacitate him. Despite the seriousness of his condition he managed to complete most of his life's work, with the exception of a work on the philosophy of history. The *Idea of History* is a compilation of material conceived and compiled by T. M. Knox. Collingwood had, however, completed four chapters of *The Principles of History* which have recently been rediscovered and were published for the first time in 1999. He died of pneumonia on 9 January 1943 at Lanehead, Conniston, at the age of 53.

Politically, Collingwood described himself as a liberal of the continental type, by which he meant that he rejected the principles of classical liberalism and *laissez-faire* economics. He was in favour of state intervention in order to narrow the gap between the rich and poor on the grounds that such an unequal relationship was an affront to civility in that it was based upon force, the poor being deprived of the capacity for freedom of choice. He was so critical of the

Attlee Government, strongly anti-Fascist and anti-Nazi, and so vehemently against the policy of appeasement that even his friends mistakenly suspected that he may have become a communist.

Collingwood was one of the last renaissance men, refusing to restrict his interests within disciplinary boundaries. As well as being a philosopher, he was the world's leading authority on the Roman inscriptions in Britain, and wrote a number of seminal textbooks on the Romans in Britain, including *Roman Britain and the English Settlements*, with A. L. Myers, for the *Oxford History of Britain*. From 1924 to 1933 he was joint editor with his father of the *Transactions of the Cumberland and Westmoreland Antiquarian and Archaeological Society*. He retained keen and extensive archaeological interests throughout his career.

Biographical: R. G. Collingwood, *An Autobiography* (1939); T. M. Knox 'R. G. Collingwood', *Dictionary of National Biography*; T. M. Knox, I. A. Richmond and R. B. MacCallum, 'Robin George Collingwood', *Proceedings of the British Academy*, xxix (1943); C. H. L. Bouch, 'In Memoriam', *Transactions of the Cumberland and Westmoreland Antiquarian and Archaeological Society*, 43 (1943), 212. David Boucher, *The Social and Political Philosophy of R. G. Collingwood* (Cambridge, Cambridge University Press, 1989). Oxford University Press Archives.

Principal writings: *Religion and Philosophy* (1916); Speculum *Mentis* (1924); *Essay on Philosophical Method* (1933); *The Principles of Art* (1938); *An Autobiography* (1939); *Essay on Metaphysics* (1940 and 1998); *The New Leviathan* (1942 and 1992); *The Idea of Nature* (1945); *The Idea of History* (1946 and 1993); *Essays in Political Philosophy* (1989); *The Principles of History* (1999). All published by the Clarendon Press, Oxford, except *Religion and Philosophy*, London, Macmillan.

– Michael Joseph Oakeshott –

Born in 1901, the second of three sons, to a Fabian socialist middle-class civil servant father, who was a friend of George Bernard Shaw, and to a mother who was a qualified nurse, Oakeshott went to school from the age of eleven at the Quaker sponsored co-educational St George's School, Harpenden. His university education was at Cambridge, where he studied history, Tübingen and Marburg. As was once famously said about him, he was not un-accustomed to the matrimonial condition, having been married four times. For the latter years of his life he lived with his artist wife in a small Spartan cottage in Dorset. He taught English at Lytham St Anne's Grammar School before being appointed a Fellow of Gonville and Caius College, Cambridge, in 1927. He spent a brief spell at Nuffield College, Oxford, after serving as a commander of a squadron in the Second World War. His appointment to the chair of Political Science at the London School of Economics and Political Science in 1950, at the age of 49, succeeding Harold Laski, caused a considerable stir. His barely disguised disdain for the Labour government and well-known Conservative sympathies made him a controversial choice for the School, which had such strong roots in Fabian socialism. He remained at the LSE until well over a decade after his formal retirement in 1968. Oakeshott was an English Idealist philosopher, taught by McTaggart, and greatly influenced by Aristotle, Hegel, Dilthey and Bradley, but also by the optimism of Montaigne and Burke's reverence for tradition. All of his books, published during his lifetime, with the exception of the first, *Experience and Its Modes* (1933), are collections of essays in which he professes to say too little for fear of saying too much. His reputation as a philosopher has largely come to rest upon his political writings, despite the fact of his professed conservatism, unfashionable rejection of the idea of a social contract, and rejection of redistributive or social justice as intrinsic to the conception of the work of the state. He is the most famous political philosopher of the twentieth century to have been associated with British Conservatism. He was claimed in the Joseph and Thatcher era as one of the leading intellectual lights of the Party, but this simply betrayed an ignorance of his abhorrence, not only of practising politicians, but also of the style of politics that had come to characterise all British parties, including the Conservative. He always claimed that philosophy had nothing to contribute to practical activities such as politics, and although privately he held strong political views he refused to express them publicly. He claimed, for example, that he found it unnecessary to have an opinion on whether Britain should stay in the Common Market. Despite his own disavowals, his disciples were not averse to drawing the political implications of his philosophy. He died at the age of 89 on 21 December 1990.

Biographical: Obituaries: 22 December 1990, *The Times, Daily Telegraph, The Guardian, The Independent.* Jesse Norman (ed.), *The Achievement of Michael Oakeshott* (London, Duckworth, 1993); Robert Grant, *Thinkers of Our Time: Oakeshott* (London, Claridge, 1990).

Principal writings: *Experience and Its Modes* (Cambridge, Cambridge University Press, 1933); *Rationalism in Politics*, new and expanded edition (Indianapolis, Liberty Press, 1991: first edn 1963); *On Human Conduct* (Oxford, Clarendon Press, 1975); *Hobbes on Civil Association* (Oxford, Blackwell, 1975); *On History and Other Essays* (Oxford, Blackwell, 1983); *Morality and Politics in Modern Europe* (New Haven, Yale University Press, 1993: Harvard lectures delivered in 1958); *The Politics of Faith and the Politics of Scepticism* (New Haven, Yale University Press, 1996: probably completed in about 1953).

Index

Abrams, Philip, 88, 122n, 123n
absolute assumptions *see* absolute presuppositions
absolute presuppositions, 45, 133, 186, 193–4
Ackerman, Bruce, 228–9, 230, 235n
Ackland, Arthur, 28
acquisitive society, 157
action, 70, 75, 79, 81, 99–100, 101, 106, 117–18, 157,
    160, 192, 203, 212, 215, 219, 220, 232
Adorno, Theodore, 95, 123n
aesthetics, 3, 112, 116, 131
Alexander, Samuel, 17
Allett, John, 182n
Althusser, L., 118
ancient Greece, 31, 35, 50, 62, 68, 93, 103, 194
Anderson, Francis, 14, 15, 17, 20, 21, 25n, 26n
Anderson, John, 14, 17, 20
Anderson, William, 14
anthropology, 7, 88, 99, 109, 197, 205
anti-foundational, 212
Appleman, Philip, 23n
Aquinas, Thomas, 43
Arendt, H., 1, 187, 191, 194, 206, 207n, 208n
Aristocracy, 189, 190
Aristotle, 8, 43, 62, 68, 91, 95, 103, 134, 196, 241
Arnold, Matthew, 7
Asquith, H., 12, 28, 164, 168
assassination, 150
association, 219, 220
    civil, 210, 217–19, 221–4, 234
    enterprise, 210, 219n, 224–8, 229, 230, 231, 234
Attlee, Clement, 28, 241
Augustine, St, 43
Austin, John, 141, 219, 234n
Australian Association of Psychology and Philosophy,
    17
Australian Idealists, 14–22
authority, 140, 149, 179, 188–9, 193, 218–19, 220,
    221–2, 229
Aves, Ernest, 28

Baconian, 94–5, 225–6
Bagehot, Walter, 7
Bain, A., 86n
Ball, Sidney, 158, 165
Barry, Brian, 229–30, 235n
Baur, Friedrich Christian, 36, 38, 39
Beiner, R., 188, 207n
Beitz, Charles, 156n
Benn, A. W. (Tony), 181n
Bentham, Jeremy, 61, 64, 135, 141, 144, 219, 235n

Benthamism, 61, 64, 69, 128, 141, 143
Berlin, Isaiah, 74
Bernard, L. L., 105
Beveridge, W. H., 28, 158, 170, 183n
biology, 3, 7, 11, 60, 87, 89, 90, 98–101, 104, 109,
    110, 111, 112, 120, 130, 133, 134, 142, 168, 191
Blanchard, Brand, 15, 23n
Boer, War, 168
Booth, William, 88
Bosanquet, (Dendy) Helen, 122n, 237
Bosanquet, B., vii, 1, 2, 5, 6, 11, 12, 13–14, 15, 18, 20,
    21, 24n, 26n, 28, 39, 84n, 88–126, 130, 132, 135,
    138, 140, 153, 154n, 155n, 156n, 159, 162, 165,
    174–5, 181n, 185, 237
Bosanquet, Rev. Robert William, 237
Bouch, C. H. L., 241
Boucher, D., vii, 22n, 23n, 24n, 124n, 181n, 182n,
    208n, 234n, 235n, 240n, 241
Bourdieu, Pierre, 118
Bradley, A. C., 28, 83n, 238
Bradley, C., 237
Bradley, F. H., vii, 1, 2, 5, 6, 9, 10, 11, 15, 23n, 24n,
    26n, 39, 55–86, 155n, 159, 185, 211, 214, 237,
    241
Braithwaite, W. J., 28
Brennan, Christopher, 17
Bright, John, 29
Broad, C. D., 60, 83n, 84n
Brookes, Herbert, 19
Brown, Jethro, 16, 18–19, 25n
Browning, Robert, 7, 19
Buckle, William, 102
Burckhardt, J., 232
Burke, Edmund, 61, 72, 129–35, 136–7, 155, 180n,
    241
Burrows, J. W., 23n, 83n
Butler, Bishop, 75, 76

Caird, Edward, 2, 4, 5, 6, 8, 10, 13, 15, 16, 17, 20, 22n,
    23n, 24n, 97, 134, 155n, 157, 158, 165, 174,
    184n, 239
Caird, John, 5
Calderwell, Henry, 238
Calvinist Methodists, 239
Campbell, Craig, 21, 26n
Carlyle, Thomas, 164, 238
Carnap, Rudolph, 114
Carpenter, J. E., 156n
Carritt, E. F., 185
Carter, M., 183n

casuistry, 67, 82
Chamberlain, Neville, 164
character, 161–2, 167, 179
Charcot, J. M., 104
Charity Organization Society, 88, 89, 90, 96, 101,
    106, 107, 108, 124n, 162, 181n, 237
Charles, Algernon, 7
Chartism, 164, 181n
citizenship, 1, 10, 12, 27–54, 127, 154, 158–64,
    170–80, 194, 206, 234
civic republicanism, 175
civil disobedience, 128, 146, 148–9
civil society, 101, 221
civilisation, 1, 154, 185–209
civilised, 152, 157, 170, 192, 195, 197, 200–1
civility, 192, 196–7, 198, 200, 219, 240
Clark, Alex, 26n
Clarke, Peter, 182n
class, 175–7, 181n, 189, 190
Clifford, W. K., 143
Cobden, Richard, 29
coherence theory of truth, 3, 211
Cole, G. D. H., 182n
collectivism, 5, 13, 21, 99, 105, 143, 162, 179, 184n,
    184, 224, 226
Colley, Linda, 54
Collingwood, R. G., vii, 1, 2, 3, 4, 6, 9, 14, 20, 23n,
    26n, 28, 45, 52n, 117, 185–209, 240
Collingwood, W. G., 185, 240
Collini, Stefan, 61, 83n, 84n, 121n, 182n
common good, 9, 11, 12, 29, 47, 128, 141, 142, 143,
    144, 152, 156n, 161, 162, 163, 172, 177, 194, 224
communitarianism, 3, 11, 13, 27, 28, 45, 56, 69, 73,
    81, 82, 104, 114, 150, 157, 175, 176
Comte, Auguste, 87, 88, 92–8, 116, 120, 122n
Comtean, 72, 87, 89, 165
concrete universal, 120
Connelly, James, 208n
Connelly, W. E., 52
consequentialism, 64, 123n, 142, 220
conservative, 60, 61, 129, 171, 180n, 214, 241, 242
contingency, 215
contract, 29, 72, 151, 187–92, 199–200, 206, 220,
    228–30, 241
contradiction, 70–1
corruption of consciousness, 186, 198, 202, 206, 208n
Crawford, C., 156n
crime, 21, 111–13, 149, 190, 196, 192, 221
criteriological, 186–7, 201, 206
critical theory, 91, 95
Croce, B., 185, 187
Cromwell, Oliver, 38, 236
Crosland, Anthony, 169

D'Entrève, Maurizio Passerin, 207n
Darwin, Charles, 7, 8, 23n, 98, 104, 124n, 129, 130,
    131, 132, 134
Dawkins, Richard, 7, 133, 155
Deakin, Alfred, 19, 25n, 26n
democracy, 7, 30, 171–4, 175, 183n, 189, 190, 205
Derrida, J., 118
Dewey, John, 15, 118
dialectic, 61, 62, 68, 69, 71, 73, 82, 95, 192, 199, 200
dialectic materialism, 192
Dilthey, W., 96, 122n, 241

Donagan, Alan, 20
Drummond, Henry, 146
dualisms, 5
Dudgeon, Elizabeth Bradfute, 238
Dunlap, Knight, 105
Durkheim, Émile, 1m, 88, 94, 97, 109–21, 125n,
    126n
duty, 75, 77, 115, 147, 149, 158, 163, 192, 194, 219
Dworkin, Ronald, 43, 140, 155n, 223, 235n

Easton, David, 46, 53n
Eccleshall, Robert, 182n
economics, 3, 10, 12, 21, 98, 102, 111, 112, 120, 129,
    163, 164, 165, 166, 167, 168, 170, 172, 173,
    174–5, 176–7, 182n, 187, 189, 191, 192, 200,
    201, 212, 228, 231, 240
education, 7, 10, 21, 28, 29, 124n, 157, 162, 167, 169,
    170, 172, 175, 177, 189, 190, 195–6, 200, 206,
    236, 239
Elshtain, Jean Bethke, 191
emanation, 9, 99–100, 132–3, 134
English civil war, 32–3, 35
enterprise, 190, 191, 200
eternal consciousness, 42–3
Eucken, Rudolph, 6, 20, 22n
eugenics, 89, 91, 98, 168
evolution, 1, 2, 6–9, 10, 19, 22, 23n, 60, 89, 91,
    98–101, 102, 110, 112, 124n, 125n, 127, 128–35,
    138, 141, 142, 145–6, 160, 168, 184n, 238
evolutionary ethics, 128, 138
experience, 3, 4, 6, 10, 65, 66, 97, 103, 107, 130, 140,
    144, 158, 204, 206, 210–11

Fabianism, 98, 127, 158, 164, 165, 238
facts and values, 113–19
Fascism, 3, 205, 241
federation, 144, 153
Fichte, J. G., 62
First World War, 90
Fisher, H. A. L., 12, 28, 183n
Fitzgerald, Edward, 7
Foucault, Michel, 118
Fourier, Charles, 164, 165
Franco, Paul, 233, 235n
Frankfurt School, 95
Fraser, Campbell, 2, 18, 238
Fraser, Nancy, 189, 191, 207n
free trade, 20
Freeden, Michael, 182n, 196
freedom, 12, 14, 22, 29, 30–1, 34, 47, 49, 134, 145,
    153, 157, 162, 163, 166, 172–3, 176, 179, 184n,
    187–92, 198, 200, 201, 216, 217, 220, 224–7,
    229, 240
French Revolution, 161
Freud, Sigmund, 105, 125n
Fukayama, Francis, 189, 207n
Fuller, Lon, 222, 235n

Gadamer, Hans-Georg, 96, 117, 123n, 188, 207n
Gaitskell, Hugh, 169
Galton, Francis, 98
Gauthier, David, 191, 200, 208n, 230–2, 235n
Geddes, Patrick, 89
general welfare see common good
general will, 11, 12, 24n, 106, 107–8

Gentile, G., 185
geology, 7, 23n
George, David Lloyd, 164
George, Henry, 164
George, Richard de, 188, 207n
Ghandi, M., 150
Gibson, Alexander Boyce, 20
Gibson, W. R. Boyce, 6, 10, 14, 15, 16, 19–20, 23n, 24n, 25n, 26n
Gibson-Carmichael, Thomas, 19
Gidding, Franklin H., 98
Gifford Lectures, 17, 133, 237, 239
Gladstone, David, 25n
Gladstone, W. E., 61, 127
Glynn, Elinor, 237
good, 30, 32, 38, 41, 43, 130, 143, 166, 180–1, 228–9, 230, 231
Goodin, Robert E., 55, 83n
Gore, Charles, 28, 236
Graham, Gordon, 156
Gramsci, A., 67, 69
Grant, Robert, 242
Grave, S. A., 25n
Gray, John, 221, 235n
greatest happiness, 63, 64, 72, 73, 79, 80, 81, 219, 231
Green, T. H., vii, 1, 2, 3, 5, 6, 9, 10, 11, 12, 13, 14, 15, 16, 17, 19, 21, 22n, 24, 27–54, 55, 56, 57, 81, 83n, 84, 85, 94, 104, 105, 127, 138, 139–40, 143, 148, 155n, 156, 185, 196, 236, 237, 238
Green, Valentine, 236
Greenleaf, W. H., vii
Griffin, Nicholas, 83n

Habermas, J., 95
Haddock, Bruce, 234n
Haering, Theodor, 39
Haldane, E. S., 238
Haldane, R. B., 13, 28, 123n, 125n, 158, 167, 168, 170, 238, 239
Hall, John A., 128, 154n
Hamilton, William, 6, 15, 133
Hardie, Keir, 183n
Hare, R. M., 67, 69, 85n, 86n
Harnack, Adolf von, 39
Harris, Jose, 24n
Harsanyi, J. C., 85n
Hart, H. L. A., 210, 216, 220–1, 234n, 235n
Hartley, D., 104
Haycraft, Ellen S., 238
Haycraft, John Berry, 238
hedonism, 56, 58, 59, 61, 62, 72, 78, 82, 85n, 143, 144
Hegel, G. W. F., 4, 5, 8, 9, 10, 16, 19, 24n, 32, 34, 37, 48, 49–50, 53n, 54n, 55, 62, 64, 69, 74, 84n, 87, 101, 109, 125n, 130, 133, 138, 145, 161, 174, 185, 186, 192, 196, 204, 214, 241
Hegelianism, 1, 8, 16, 36, 38, 39, 51, 56, 57, 60, 61, 62, 64, 69, 81, 85n, 104, 116, 125n, 165, 206, 238
heredity, 130, 133
    inherited characters, 7, 8, 133
hermeneutics, 95–7, 104, 117, 119, 123n
Herrman, Wilhelm, 39
Hetherington, H. J. W., 25n, 124n, 126n, 183n, 240
Hinsley, F. H., 193, 207n
history, 7, 9, 32, 88, 120, 130, 134, 157, 181, 185, 186, 192, 193, 197, 201–2, 204, 205, 211, 212, 214,
215–16, 222, 232
Hobbes, Thomas, 4, 91, 104, 220, 222
Hobhouse, L. T., 12, 88–9, 91, 92, 109, 123n, 134, 140, 155n, 168, 179, 183n, 184n
Hobson, J. A., 12, 109, 168, 170, 182n, 183n
Hoernlé, R. F. A., 15
Hoffman, John, 193, 207n
Holland, Henry Scott, 28, 34, 53n, 236
Holland, Stuart, 169
Homans, George, 113, 126n
Home Rule, 127
Homer, 103
Hopkins, Gerard Manley, 34
Horkheimer, Max, 95, 123n
Hughes, H. Stuart, 125n
human conduct, 95, 140, 161, 210–35
humanitarian intervention, 128, 146, 150–2, 156n
Hume, David, 4, 58, 104, 106
Husserl, E., 20
Hutcheson, Francis, 91
Huxley, T. H., 7, 8, 89, 100, 101, 130, 131–3, 134, 154n

ideal character, 213–14, 216, 232, 233
identity in difference, 108, 110, 159, 175, 177, 178, 179
ideology, 1, 3, 118, 129, 157, 158, 164, 175, 214
Ignatieff, Michael, 184n
imperialism, 7, 168
Independent Labour Party, 158, 164
individualism, 5, 11, 13, 20, 21, 48, 59, 69, 72, 73, 78, 105, 134, 137, 141, 143, 157, 161–2, 165, 166, 167, 174, 175, 176, 179–80, 184, 217–19, 224, 226, 230–2
    methodological, 105
industrialisation, 21
instrumental, 97
intuitionism, 72, 73, 78, 138, 142, 144, 194

James, D. G., 84n
James, William, 15, 19, 118
Jenkins, Roy, 171
Jews, 195, 197, 198
Joachim, H. H., 185
Joad, C. E. M., 12
Johnson, Douglas H., 207n
Jones, Elias, 239
Jones, Henry, vii, 1, 2, 4, 5, 6, 9, 10, 12, 13, 14, 15, 16, 17, 18, 19, 20, 21, 22n, 23n, 24n, 25n, 26n, 129–30, 132, 133, 134, 148, 154n, 155n, 157–84, 237, 238, 239–40
Jones, Thomas, 157, 167, 182n, 183n, 240
Joseph, Keith, 242
Jowett, Benjamin, 236, 237
Jung, Carl, 105
jurisprudence, 112–13, 141, 210
justice, 27, 30–47, 147, 149, 150, 175, 176, 191, 192, 199–200, 222
    social, 1, 174, 187, 189–90, 191–2, 200, 206, 210, 228–32, 241

Kamenka, Eugene, 14
Kant, I., 39, 40, 53n, 75, 77, 85n, 115
Kantianism, 1, 38–9, 42, 45, 47, 51, 56, 62, 76, 97, 104, 113, 116, 118, 122n, 126n, 165

Keene, Carol A., 83n
Keynes, J. M., 170, 171, 183n
Keynesianism, 169, 170
Kidd, Benjamin, 7, 98, 145, 155n
King, Martin Luther, 149
King, Preston, 215
Kingsley, Charles, 164
Knox, T. M., 201, 241
Kuhn, Thomas, 96
Kymlicka, Will, 195

Labour
  New, 158, 169
  Party, 158, 164, 169, 170, 176, 183n, 241
Lamarck, Jean-Baptiste, 7, 124n, 133
Larmore, Charles, 52–3n
Laski, Harold, 12, 182n, 241
Latter, Robert, 238
Laud, Archbishop, 33, 35
Laurie, Henry, 14, 16, 18, 19, 20, 25n
law, 1, 18–19, 71, 88, 112–13, 135, 140, 147, 148,
    149, 150, 162, 163, 190, 194, 210, 218–24, 229,
    231
  international, 150, 153
  rule of, 149, 200, 220–2, 225
Le Bon, Gustav, 104, 106, 108, 109, 110, 125n
Le Play, F., 102
Levellers, 181n
Lévy-Bruhl, Claude, 105, 109
Liberal
  New, 12, 24n, 158, 163, 167, 170, 181–2n
  Party, 164, 170, 171
liberalism, 1, 3, 13, 14, 21, 27–31, 35, 43, 44, 45, 48,
    49, 51, 52n, 61, 89, 91, 125n, 150, 157, 158, 161,
    163, 164, 165–71, 174, 175, 176, 177, 179, 180n,
    181–2n, 201, 205, 221, 228, 238, 240
liberty, 137–8, 166, 167, 179, 188, 194
  negative and positive, 135–6, 166, 167
Lindsay, A. D., 238
Linton, Emma, 237
Loch, C. S., 181n
Locke, John, 6, 104
London Ethical Movement, 89
London Ethical Society, 89, 237
Lotze, H., 22n, 39
Lukes, Steven, 119–20, 125n, 126n
Luther, Martin, 33, 38

McBriar, A. M., 123n
MacCallum, Mungo, 16, 25n, 26n
MacCallum, R. B., 241
MacCunn, J., 156n
MacDonald, Ramsey, 176
McDougall, William, 104, 105, 109, 125n
Macdowall, Caroline, 237
MacIntyre, A., 1, 59, 64, 81, 84n, 85n, 187, 203–4,
    206, 209n
McIntyre, K. B., 207n
Mackenzie, J. S., 2, 10, 22n, 122n, 149–50, 156n, 165,
    181n, 184n
Mackintosh, Robert, 146
Maclaren, Sir Norman, 25n
McTaggart, J. M. E., 2, 10, 23n, 24n, 241
Maine, Sir Henry, 134
Maitland, F. W., 59

Malinowski, B., 206
Malthus, T. R., 7, 101
Mansel, Henry, 6
Marcuse, H., 95
Marquand, David, 170, 182n
Marshall, T. H., 88, 182n
Martin, Rex, vii, 139, 155n, 208n
Marxism, 20, 67, 90, 95, 102, 135, 157, 164, 165,
    181n, 192, 226
masses, 226–7
Massingham, H. W., 12, 170, 183n
Mendel, Gregor, 133
metaphysics, 1, 3, 4, 27, 35–6, 38–9, 40, 41–8, 50,
    53–4n, 55, 56, 62, 70, 78, 79, 85n, 97, 110, 116,
    125, 130, 131, 157, 158–64, 180–1n, 186
Michelet, Jules, 232
Midgley, Mary, 124n
Mill, J. S., 43, 56, 62, 64, 66, 69, 70, 72, 83n, 85n, 96,
    135, 137, 144, 164, 165
Miller, E. Morris, 25n, 26n
Miller, F. D., 86n
Milner, Alfred, 28, 236
mind, 4, 5, 10, 42, 92, 96, 101, 102, 103, 104, 105,
    107–8, 109, 110, 113, 116, 124n, 126n, 131, 132,
    134, 186, 188, 202
Mitchell, William, 15, 16, 17–18, 20, 21, 25n, 26n
modernisation, 21
modes, 65, 66
  of experience, 210–16
Modood, Tariq, 208n
Montaigne, Michel Eyquem de, 241
Moore, G. E., 2, 60
morality, 3, 5, 9, 10–14, 22, 29, 30–1, 35, 37, 38, 40,
    42–4, 49–50, 55–86, 112, 115, 116, 120, 123,
    132, 145, 151, 153, 155n, 157, 160, 163, 174,
    180n, 192, 212, 218, 220, 221, 222, 224–5, 231
  universalism versus particularism, 55, 63, 69, 71,
    73, 75, 76, 151, 153, 199–200
Morant, R. B., 28
Muir, Ramsey, 182n
Muirhead, J. H., 10, 13, 14, 24n, 25n, 28, 37, 53n, 89,
    98, 122n, 124n, 125n, 126n, 236, 238, 240
Mulhall, S., 86n
multiculturalism, 41, 48, 51, 189, 195, 199–200, 228
Murdoch, Iris, 84n
Murdoch, Walter, 19, 25n, 26n
Mure, G. R. G., 237
Murray, John Clark, 15

natural selection, 7, 8, 98, 100, 101, 124n, 128, 129,
    130, 131, 132, 141, 142–3
naturalism, 6, 22, 92–8, 122n, 130, 131, 132, 133, 134
nature, 5, 7, 8, 9, 22, 40, 42–3, 93, 101, 109, 125n,
    130, 131–3, 134, 138, 140–1, 142, 144, 172, 188,
    192, 196–7, 200–1, 206, 210–11
  human, 6, 47, 135, 163, 194, 197, 205, 222
Nazis, 195, 197, 198, 205, 241
Nazism, 3
Nettleship, R. L., 28, 236
Nicholson, Peter, vii, 52n, 53n, 58, 84n, 154, 207n
Nicol, John, 16, 239
Nietzsche, F., 95, 123n
Norman, Jesse, 242
Norman, Richard, 22n
normative, 65, 130

Nozick, Robert, 228

O'Neill, Onora, 86n, 213–14, 235n
Oakeshott, M., vii, 1, 2, 3, 4, 5, 6, 10, 14, 23n, 24n, 26n, 65, 81, 84n, 117, 149, 180n, 238
Oldfield, A., 208n
ontology, 5, 6, 40, 69, 72, 73, 78, 96, 106, 111, 115, 118, 158–64
Orel, Vitezslav, 154n
Otter, Sandra den, 121n, 125n, 126n, 154
Owen, David, 171
Owen, Robert, 164, 165, 181n

Paget, S., 53n
Paine, Tom, 181n
palaeontology, 7, 23n
Paley, William, 77
paranormal, 63–4
Parker, Charles, 236
Parsons, Talcott, 97, 118, 128
Passmore Edwards Settlement, 28
Passmore, John, 14, 17, 25n
Paul, E. F., 86n
Paul, J., 86n
Pearson, Karl, 98
peasants revolt, 181n
Peel, J. D. Y., 154
Personal Idealism, 6, 10, 15, 19, 22n, 23n, 42, 159
phenomenalist, 6
Plant, Raymond, vii, 24n, 52n, 121n, 182n
Plato, 5, 43, 103, 189, 196
pluralism, 1, 30, 31–2, 40, 41, 52n, 182n
    value, 113
poetry, 7, 16, 18, 19, 128, 130, 211, 212, 139
political economy, 87, 88, 90, 91, 101–3, 109, 120
political obligation, 12, 220, 222
poll tax, 127
Poor Law see poverty relief
positivist, 87, 89, 91, 92–8, 113–21, 122n, 123n, 126n, 168, 203
poverty, 7, 21, 88, 122n, 201
    relief, 13, 24n, 90, 122n, 165, 237
power, 128–9, 188, 191, 192, 200, 201, 206, 240
Primrose League, 137
privilege, 172
property, 29, 157, 166, 177, 178
protectionism, 20
psychology, 87, 99, 103–9, 120–1, 186–7, 190, 193, 205

Quine, W. V. O., 114, 126n

Rabinow, Paul, 123n
Radcliff, Miss E., 237
Radicals, New, 145
Rashdall, Hastings, 4, 22, 23n, 149
rational choice, 46, 194, 212
rationalism, 4, 81, 101, 118, 125n, 212–13, 214, 226–7, 232, 233
rationality, 6, 75, 76, 112, 125n, 132, 146, 153, 161–2, 163, 180n, 187, 190, 197, 198, 201–2, 206, 212, 228–30, 231
Rawls, John, 1, 27, 30–4, 40, 41–7, 48, 51, 52n, 53n, 55, 149, 151, 156n, 191, 199, 228–9, 230, 235n
Raz, Joseph, 43

realism, 14, 17, 20, 96, 185
reason, 30, 33, 35, 37, 38, 39, 40, 41, 47, 75, 77, 95, 109, 129, 137, 140, 141, 145, 146, 159–60, 180n, 190, 227
recognition, 1, 138, 139, 140, 141, 178, 189, 190–1, 192, 198–9, 206, 219, 221, 222
Regan, Tom, 156n
relativism, 114, 118, 194
religion, 3, 5, 7, 9–10, 11, 16, 18, 24n, 26n, 27, 30, 31–2, 40, 46, 60, 68, 75, 77, 112, 116, 145–6, 180n, 198, 202–6, 239
    Bible, 181n
    Catholic, 33, 34, 35, 49
    Christ, 9, 36–7, 38, 40
    Christian, 23n, 31–2, 36, 40, 50, 158, 165, 203, 205
    Church of England, 34
    God, 4, 9–10, 22, 34, 38, 39, 42, 49–50, 53n, 115, 153, 189, 202, 205, 240
    Jesuits, 33, 34
    Protestant, 34, 35, 47–50, 135
    Puritan, 33
    Reformation, 31–3, 35, 36, 38, 41, 48, 53n
    St Paul, 36, 37–8, 53n
Renouvier, M., 116, 126n
Reyburn, Hugh, 15
Ricardo, David, 101, 164
Richmond, A. I., 241
Ridley, Matt, 133, 155n
rights, 12, 29, 135, 138, 141, 151, 157, 158, 163, 166, 170, 176–7, 194, 195
    animal, 128, 146–8, 149, 198–9
    human, 139, 143, 147, 150, 152, 195, 197–8
    legal, 138, 144, 147, 148, 149, 216
    moral, 138, 139, 140, 147, 148, 149, 216
    natural, 1, 127–8, 131, 135–53, 165, 172, 194, 221
Ritchie, David George, vii, 1, 2, 8, 9, 11, 12, 20, 21, 23n, 24n, 26n, 84n, 127–56, 208n, 237, 238–9
Ritchie, George, 238
Ritschl, Albrecht, 39, 40
Roe, Michael, 25n
Rogers, William, 171
Rome, 50
Rorty, Richard, 1, 31, 86n, 135, 187, 197–8, 206, 208n, 212, 235n
Rousseau, J. J., 91
Rowntree, Joseph, 88
Royal Statistical Society, 88, 89
Royce, Josiah, 6, 15
Ruggiero, Guido de, 158, 180n, 184n, 185
Runciman, W. G., 7, 127–8, 154n
Ruskin, John, 56, 164, 185–6
Russell, Bertrand, 2, 57, 109

Saint Simon, Henri de, 164
Samuel, Herbert, 168n, 183n
Sandel, Michael, 64, 73, 86n
Schäffle, Albert, 98
Schiller, F. C. S., 20
Schneewind, J. B., 56, 57, 59, 64, 80, 81, 84n, 85n, 86n
School of Ethics and Social Philosophy, 89, 103
Schopenhauer, A., 73
Scott, Walter, 17
secularisation, 21, 50
self-interest, 75, 77, 108, 145, 229

self-realisation, 9, 11, 13, 22, 29, 42, 58, 69, 70, 73, 74, 130, 143, 144, 148, 196
Sell, Alan P. F., 236
Sen, A. K., 85n
Seth Pringle Pattison, Andrew, 2, 4, 6, 19, 22n, 23n, 42, 53n, 124n, 132, 133, 154
Shaw, George Bernard, 181n, 241
Shklar, Judith, 31, 32, 53n
Sidgwick, Henry, 1, 55, 56–86, 89, 143, 155n
Simmel, Georg, 98
Simon, Herbert, 46, 53n
Singer, Peter, 146, 156n
slavery, 145
Smith, Adam, 201
Smith, J. A., 185, 240
Smith, Llewellyn, 28
Social Democratic Federation, 164
Social Democratic party, 171, 173
social organism, 11, 69–75, 98, 99, 100, 125n, 130, 134, 142, 145, 146, 160, 178
social science, 3, 7, 88–126, 123n, 128, 162
socialism, 1, 5, 13, 21, 24n, 99, 127, 157, 158, 164–77, 178, 184n
    Christian, 13, 157, 164, 165
sociobiology, 7, 100, 124n
Sociological Society, 89, 109
sociology, 10, 21, 60, 64, 71, 73, 87, 88–126, 128
Sorel, George, 105
Sorley, W. R., 2, 238
sovereignty, 11, 150, 152–3, 193, 194, 227
Spencer, Herbert, 6, 7, 8, 11, 17, 20–1, 23n, 72, 98–100, 104, 105, 124n, 130, 133, 135, 145, 175, 234
Spender, J. A., 28
Spirit, 4, 7, 8, 9, 10, 11, 16, 17, 22, 130, 131–3, 134
State, 11, 87, 138–9, 140, 144, 148, 151, 157, 164, 166, 170, 171, 173–4, 176, 178, 179, 180, 180n
    intervention, 13–14, 19, 20–1, 22, 27, 28–53, 146, 148, 152, 156n, 162–3, 165, 167, 168, 170, 171, 172–3, 176–7, 179, 181n, 184n, 210, 219, 224–8
    as a moral agent, 12, 151–2, 153, 156n, 162
Stephen, Leslie, 7, 10, 24n, 89, 143
Stephen, Sir James Fitzjames, 86n
Stevenson, Lionel, 23n
Stewart, J. McKellar, 19
Stirner, Max, 79
Stout, Alan Ker, 20, 26n
Strawson, P. F., 46, 53n
Strong, Tracy B., 52
Sturt, Henry, 6, 20, 23n, 26n
Sullivan, William M., 123n
survival of the fittest see natural selection
Sweet, William, 155n
Swift, Adam, 86n
Swinburne, A. C., 7
Symonds, Charlotte, 236

Tarde, G., 98, 103, 104–5, 106, 109, 110, 119, 125n
Tawney, R. H., 13, 28, 157, 158, 171, 174, 182n, 183n
Taylor, A. E., 237
Taylor, Charles, 1, 97, 123n, 187, 189, 207n
Taylor, M. W., 155n
technocratic society, 188–9

teleology, 32–3, 43, 48, 51, 117, 180n, 204
Tennyson, Alfred Lord, 7
Thatcherism, 177, 242
theoretician, 214, 234
Thoreau, Henry David, 120
Titmus, R. M., 88
Tönnies, Ferdinand, 89, 109
Torrens, R., 101
Toulmin, Stephen, 193–4, 208n
Toynbee Hall,, 28, 90, 158
Toynbee, A., 28, 52n, 238
Trevelyan, C. P., 182n
Trotter, Wilfred, 105

unity, 4, 5, 6, 8, 10, 16, 42, 58, 92, 109, 120, 130, 132, 153, 157, 159, 179, 202–4
university expansion, 14
Urwick, E. J., 89, 90, 122n
utilitarianism, 1, 2, 3, 4, 11, 20, 55, 86, 128, 135, 140, 141, 142–3, 145, 146, 164, 165, 168, 198, 212, 230–2

Vane, Thomas, 35, 38
Vaughan, Edward Thomas, 236
Vico, Giambattista, 18, 93
Vincent, Andrew, vii, 22n, 23n, 24n, 52n, 121n, 124n, 181–2n, 240
virtue, 22, 81, 164, 171, 175, 179, 204, 222
volition, 85–6n
Vries, Hugo de, 133

Waldron, Jeremy, 135, 136, 155n
Walker, Annie, 239
Wallace, Alfred R., 7, 130–1, 142, 154n
Wallace, Graham, 104, 105
Wallace, William, 2, 53n, 55, 122n
Walsh, W. H., 54n
Walzer, Michael, 64, 150–2, 153, 156n, 199–200, 208n
Ward, Mrs Humphrey, 28, 52n
Warnock, G. J., 46, 53n
Watson, John, 2, 10, 15, 23n, 239
Webb, Sidney and Beatrice, 88, 92, 94, 96, 122n, 123n, 124n, 127, 158, 165, 169, 174, 176, 181n, 183
Weber, Max, 95, 123n
Weissmann, Auguste, 133
Wellman, Carl, 146–8, 155n, 156n
Westermarck, E., 89
Wiggins, David, 126n
Williams, Bernard, 60, 81, 84n, 85n, 86n, 126n
Williams, George, 133
Williams, Howard, 208n
Williams, Shirley, 171
Wilson, Harold, 169
Wilson, John Cook, 2, 185
Wilson, T. J., 16–17
Winch, Donald, 83n
Winch, Peter, 96, 117, 118–19, 126n
Wittgenstein, Ludwig, 20, 46, 54n, 60, 96, 117
Wolfe, Willard, 181n
Wolin, Sheldon, 191
Workers Education Association, 157